# THE
# KAZAKHS

STUDIES OF NATIONALITIES IN THE USSR
Wayne S. Vucinich, Editor

# THE KAZAKHS

## Martha Brill Olcott

HOOVER INSTITUTION PRESS
Stanford University
Stanford, California

The Hoover Institution on War, Revolution and Peace, founded at Stanford University in 1919 by the late President Herbert Hoover, is an interdisciplinary research center for advanced study on domestic and international affairs in the twentieth century. The views expressed in its publications are entirely those of the authors and do not necessarily reflect the views of the staff, officers, or Board of Overseers of the Hoover Institution.

Hoover Press Publication 338

First printing, 1987

Manufactured in the United States of America

91  90  89  88  87      9  8  7  6  5  4  3  2  1

Library of Congress Cataloging in Publication Data

Olcott, Martha Brill, 1949–
  The Kazakhs.

  (Studies of nationalities in the USSR)
  Bibliography: p.
  Includes index.
  1. Kazakh S.S.R.—History.  I. Title.  II. Series.
DK908.043  1987      958′.45      86-21376
ISBN 0-8179-8381-3 (alk. paper)
ISBN 0-8179-8382-1 (pbk. : alk. paper)

*Design by P. Kelley Baker*

*To Tony*

# Contents

# List of Appendixes

# Foreword

The author of this book, the third in the Hoover Institution's series on Soviet nationalities, is a highly regarded professor of political science at Colgate University. Her work demonstrates an intimate knowledge of Kazakh history and the contemporary scene. There are other books on the Kazakhs and Kazakhstan, but none of the same magnitude and scholarly quality as Professor Olcott's. The controversial questions have been treated objectively and adequately, and, in so doing, the author has demonstrated a solid grasp of Russian and Kazakh history. Professor Olcott comments on all of the major events in Kazakh history, explains the ethnogenesis and early history of the Kazakhs, discusses the Kazakh traditional society and the Kazakhs under Russian imperial and Soviet rules, and assesses the impact of these rules on the traditional Kazakh society. In addition, she alludes to the heated historiographic controversy in the Soviet Union over the interpretation of the historical significance of Russian rule over the Kazakhs and the Kazakh anti-Russian activities.

Until recently the systematic investigation of most Soviet nationalities has been neglected by U.S. scholars. When investigating the historical and contemporary Soviet scene, the tendency has been to concentrate on the dominant Russians and to slight the other Soviet nationalities. Scholars have simply shied away from the unknown and complex, and the Kazakhs have been among those who have not received the attention they deserve. It is for this reason also that Professor Olcott's study of the Kazakhs is most welcome. The comprehensive character of the book, the extensive bibliography of works in Russian and other languages, the critical and exacting use of data, and the modern research methods are particular attributes of this work. Moreover, the scope of the book and the diversity of topics treated in it will make Professor Olcott's study an enduring reference work that every library will wish to have on its shelves.

Most of the Soviet socialist republics are small in territory and population. The Kazakh Soviet Socialist Republic, however, encompasses an area of more than one million square miles (and a long border with China), is larger than Western Europe, and has a population that is the fourth largest in the Soviet Union. The physical size of Kazakhstan might not be so significant if the republic were not at the same time of great economic and strategic significance. By putting its so-called Virgin Lands under cultivation, Kazakhstan in recent years has become a major Soviet producer of grain. The long border with China has given Kazakhstan special strategic importance. Large Soviet forces are stationed there, from whence they can be deployed against Afghanistan and China. This strategic importance has been enhanced by the fact that Kazakhstan has become the major Soviet space center.

The Soviet republics usually bear the name of the dominant ethnic group inhabiting them, but in Kazakhstan there are more Russians than Kazakhs. The Russians constitute the largest percentage (42 percent) of the population of Kazakhstan, and the Kazakhs follow in size (32 percent). The Ukrainians and Byelo-Russians make up 9 percent of the population. The combined Slavic population is thus in excess of 50 percent of the total.

The Kazakh ancestors were a mixture of Turkish tribes, who lived on the territory of today's Kazakhstan in the eighth century, and the Mongols who moved into the region in the thirteenth century. Today the Kazakhs speak a Turkic language but have Mongol physical features. Like most Turkic peoples, they profess Islam as their religion and appear to have been converted late because of a number of shamanistic practices that survive in their religious practices. Islam has shown strong resilience to modernization, which in our time has been a source of some concern to the Soviet government because the "religious survivals" impede Sovietization and modernization. Professor Olcott examines the question and ventures her own views on it.

In focusing on contemporary Kazakh history, Professor Olcott does not neglect the earlier history of the Kazakhs. She shows how they are a "nationality" and discusses their tribal organization and culture. She vividly portrays the plight of the Kazakhs and shows how one branch of the Kazakhs succumbed to the Russians in 1731 but continued to resist their rule, especially in the second half of the eighteenth century. Nonetheless, the Russians gradually consolidated their hold over the Kazakhs, and in the 1830s they began to colonize the Kazakh lands and to build a system of fortresses on it. In that decade, however, under Kenisary Qasimov, the Kazakhs rebelled against the Russians. After a bitter struggle Qasimov was killed in 1847, but his work won a lasting place in Kazakh history. The Kazakh resistance to Russian rule, like that of some other Soviet nationalities, constitutes a controversial question in Soviet historiography. The crux of it is whether the native resistance to Russian rule should be interpreted as a progressive or a retrogressive historical phenomenon. Soviet historians have vacillated between one position and the other, and Professor Olcott discusses the question in some detail. She notes that the Russian oppression and exploitation of the Kazakhs was accompanied by a slow transformation of Kazakh society from nomadic to sedentary life and from pastoral activity to agriculture. The Russians became the transmitters of their own and European civilization to the Kazakhs, and this challenged Kazakh institutions and their way of life.

A new generation of Kazakhs began to collect the rich Kazakh oral poetry. The native men of learning, such as Abai Kunanbaev, undertook to modernize the Kazakh language and literature. All of this invariably led to a conflict between the Muslim traditionalists and the Muslim modernists; while continuing to produce literary works in the traditional Islamic mold, the Kazakhs began to publish works in the modern literary style that were modeled on the works of the great nineteenth-century Russian authors and poets. The modern Kazakh intellectuals, modeling themselves on Russian writers and thinkers, became the leaders of the Kazakh nationalist movement, the purpose of which was to unite the Kazakhs and to reform Kazakh society. A young generation of Kazakhs, fed on western philosophical and political thought and influenced by Russian revolutionary currents, began to espouse Kazakh nationalism. Against Slavophilism, Westernism, Populism, and Pan-Slavism, the Kazakhs responded with Pan-Turkism, Pan-Islamism, Turkism, and various other nationalistic and Islamic ideas and movements.

To varying degrees the Kazakhs experienced the major crises and vicissitudes of Imperial Russia. They could not escape the effects of the Russo-Japanese War (1904–1905) and the Russian Revolution of 1905, nor remain unaffected by the revolutionary movements that swept Russia at the time. By the outbreak of World War I, the Kazakhs had their own political leaders, their own newspapers, and a small industrial proletariat. Since they were exempt from military conscription, they were initially spared from participating in that war. This suited the Kazakhs, who, as a Turkic people and as Muslims, sympathized with the Ottoman empire and its powerful German ally. When the Russian government decided to recruit the Kazakhs in 1916 into an auxiliary armed force, Amangeldy Imanov led the Kazakhs into a rebellion. It was suppressed, but the revolutionary momentum that it generated was not.

Professor Olcott has allocated substantial space in her book to the two Russian revolutions in 1917. With the news of the February Revolution and the collapse of Imperial Russia, the Kazakhs rose under the leadership of Ali Khan Bukeikhanov, proclaimed a state of their own, gave it the name of Alash Orda, and demanded autonomy. Joined by the Kirgiz, the Kazakhs attacked the

Russians and other Slavs who had settled among them. Professor Olcott explains how, after the October Revolution, the Bolsheviks began founding revolutionary committees—and later also armed units—in Kazakhstan. The Kazakhs and other Turkic peoples fought both the Russian Whites and the Reds. For a time the Bolshevik Red Army units were no match for the stronger forces of the Russian Whites and the Alash Orda. The Civil War between the Whites and the Reds, fought in a state of chaos, was won by the Reds. Unable to continue their own struggle for independence, most of the Alash Orda accepted Soviet rule, and some of its leaders became Communists. On August 26, 1920, the Autonomous Kirgiz (Kazakh) Soviet Socialist Republic was created, and in 1936 it was raised to a full republican status, the Kazakh Soviet Socialist Republic. Yet for a time leaders of this republic were mostly foreigners, and Kazakhstan was greatly underrepresented in the government of the Kazakh republic.

In the years of civil strife between 1916 and 1923, the Kazakhs suffered heavy human and material losses. A large number of Kazakhs fled to China and Afghanistan, taking their livestock with them. It is estimated that almost a million Kazakhs died from hunger during the famine of 1921–1922.

In this volume, Professor Olcott also discusses the successes and failures of Sovietization in Kazakhstan. In some detail she explains how the Kazakhs were integrated into the Soviet state system. By the late 1920s the Soviet government had stabilized its control over Kazakhstan, and in 1929 it launched the drive to collectivize the peasantry, which was finally accomplished by 1937 at heavy costs, including further Kazakh emigration to China and Afghanistan. The settlement of the nomads, the Five-Year Plan of industrialization, and a cultural revolution resulted in a profound change of Kazakh traditional life. Those who resisted the Soviet policies were vigorously prosecuted, usually labeled "bourgeois nationalists," and given harsh sentences. During the notorious Stalinist purges of 1937–1938, no less than eighteen Kazakh Communist leaders were executed.

As industry expanded in Kazakhstan, it was natural that a certain amount of immigration to Kazakhstan from other parts of the Soviet Union would take place. The industrial establishments required skilled labor from other parts of the Soviet Union. Many Russians and Ukrainians moved in, and the influx of Russians gradually reduced the Kazakhs to a minority in their own land. The immigration continued during and after World War II. For punitive reasons the Soviet authorities settled various peoples in Kazakhstan—including Volga Germans, Crimean Tatars, Poles, and Ukrainians—who were either distrusted or had collaborated with Germany during the war. The mosaic of ethnic elements was further enriched by the immigration of various Muslim peoples from neighboring Muslim republics and from Azerbaijan, and by more than 100,000 Uighurs who fled from China. Moreover, an influx of Russians and

Ukrainians accompanied the 1954 campaign to put the Virgin Lands under plow and thereby markedly increase Soviet grain production. The Russian occupation of the Kazakh lands disrupted the Kazakh culture, and Kazakh society splintered into those who still live in extended families, those who live on large collective farms (mostly settled by non-Kazakhs) especially on the Virgin Lands to the north and east, and those who live in urban communities (largely non-Kazakh).

The fact that the Soviet government selected Kazakhstan for space launchings has also attracted immigrants. The space center (cosmodrome) was established at Baykonur, and many technical personnel were stationed there. In 1959 the Soviet Space Program was established in Kazakhstan.

The influx of immigrants caused a crisis in the republic that led to the removal of several Kazakh leaders from government and other important positions. This setback notwithstanding, the Kazakh position in the government and party leadership has improved. One Kazakh, D. Kunaev, was made a member of the Politburo of the Communist Party of the Soviet Union. Although the Kazakhs remain a minority in the Communist Party organization in Kazakhstan, their number is larger than the size of their population merits.

What has been accomplished in the economy and technology of Kazakhstan has been matched by progress in the fields of learning, arts, and sciences. Since the end of World War II the Kazakhs acquired an Academy of Sciences (1946), a National Theater (1954), and an Academy of Agricultural Sciences (1957). Kazakhstan has its own university. Nonetheless, the percentage of the Kazakh population in that republic has been steadily declining. Moreover, the Slavic population—Russians and Ukrainians—has been moving out of the rural areas, and this has made the Kazakhs a predominantly rural population. However, the natural increase of population among Kazakhs is higher than among the Russians.

The Kazakhs are one of several Soviet peoples who speak a Turkic language. Until the 1930s they wrote their language in Arabic script, which they acquired when they accepted Islam as their religion. In 1930 the Soviet authorities replaced the Arabic with the Latin script and then, on the eve of World War II, replaced Latin with a Cyrillic script. Nevertheless, resistance to the introduction of alien alphabets was strong, especially in traditionalist and religious circles.

The introduction of the Cyrillic alphabet, incorporation into the Kazakh vocabulary of many Russian and Russified terms, Russification of place names, and Russian radio and television transmissions pose to the Kazakhs and their language a growing threat. Today as many as two-fifths of all Kazakhs speak Russian as their second language. An occasional voice of protest can still be heard against Russification and Sovietization; yet, as Professor Olcott writes, the fact that Russians predominate in Kazakhstan and that the Kazakhs are a minority in their own state, and that the Kazakh intelligentsia is small, may explain lesser nationalist manifestations in Kazakhstan than elsewhere among Muslim populations. Nevertheless, the existence of a certain amount of national discontent can be deduced from periodic declarations against nationalist manifestations and from criticism of political works that were allegedly flavored by nationalist and ethnic sentiment.

Yet the Kazakh ethnic and cultural separateness persists. This does not mean that the Kazakhs would want to be fully independent from the Soviet federal system. Their intellectuals are not of one mind; most of them wish merely for a more autonomous Kazakh republic within the Soviet system, a kind of republic in which they might enjoy broader powers than those they now have.

The interpretation of major historical events and prominent figures has been a particular source of controversy in Soviet historiography. The most important questions in this connection are interpretations of historical significance of the Kazakh submission to Russian rule and the significance of the Kazakh anti-Russian movements. Kenisary Qasimov, for example, was at first viewed as a leader of a "progressive" native endeavor to win liberation from Tsarist oppression, but later the same movement was rejected and assessed as a reactionary undertaking. A definite formula on how to interpret anti-Russian movements has not yet been supplied. The essence of the problem is whether the Kazakh entry into Russia was a Russian "conquest" or a "lesser evil"—that is, a release from feudal oppression, hence a "lesser evil." There have been many other similar controversies over the historical interpretation of events and people in Kazakh history. One prominent native historian, E. Bekmakhanov, who disregarded the official interpretation in writing about his country's past, was severely criticized.

To be sure, each Soviet nationality has its own historical specifics, but it also has historical experiences common to most Soviet nationalities. The study of the history of the Kazakhs under Russian and Soviet rule provides a picture that resembles, in many respects, the experiences of other Soviet nationalities. Consequently, Professor Olcott's book has wider implications than its title suggests.

August 1986                                    WAYNE S. VUCINICH

# Note on Transliteration

I have used the system of transliteration of Russian employed by the Library of Congress, modified to omit diacritical marks. I have tried to use a minimum of foreign words in the text, only transliterating those terms for which there is no accurate English equivalent and those proper names for which common English usage does not exist. Thus Petr Velikii appears as Peter the Great, and the city of Kazan' is spelled Kazan. Since there is no uniformly accepted standard for the spelling of Kazakh names in English for either the modern or prerevolutionary period, I have transliterated from the commonly used Russian spellings of Kazakh names. For better or worse, that is common usage in present-day Kazakhstan, and virtually all the secondary literature on the Kazakhs published in the USSR is in Russian. For those who predated Soviet rule, I have used transliterations of Kazakh as it would be written in Arabic script. I am not a linguist, however, and have not used prerevolutionary Kazakh archives; my spellings may be imprecise, but they will be consistent. I beg the reader's indulgence, as my intentions were better than my sources.

# Preface

Of all the Soviet peoples, the Kazakhs are the ones of whom most Westerners think they have heard. In fact, however, this Turkic people of Muslim origin bear no ethnic relationship to the soldiers of fortune—the cossacks—who guarded Catherine's frontiers. This book provides an introduction to the history of the Kazakh people: it describes their formation; the rise and fall of the Kazakh khanate; the annexation, conquest, and colonization by the Russians; and, finally, the fate of the Kazakhs under Soviet rule. The Kazakhs have been pastoral nomads for most of their existence, engaged in a constant struggle to preserve their traditional, self-sufficient, livestock-based economy. Finding sufficient pasture to serve the needs of the entire community posed a challenge in the steppe and semidesert lands that they controlled, and maintaining domination of their territory put the Kazakhs ever at odds with more powerful neighbors, first the Uzbeks, then the Kalmyks, and finally the Russians.

Despite all challenges to their survival, the Kazakhs exist today as a distinct ethnic group of nearly 7 million people, clearly shaped by the experience of nearly 70 years of Soviet rule, yet retaining strong cultural ties with their past and taking pride in their heritage. The Kazakhs have demonstrated their national resilience by transforming their economy and adapting their culture. Their traditional nomadic society has been exposed to more complex civilizations but has not been absorbed by them. Although the Kazakhs have borrowed much from other cultures, coloring contemporary life with Islamic, Russian, and Soviet influences, the Kazakhs remain unique—similar but not identical to other Central Asian nationalities.

The formation of the Kazakh people began in the mid-fifteenth century, when two princes of the Mongol White Horde successfully laid claim to the frozen lands between the Chu and Talas rivers. Over the next century their descendants were joined by indigenous Turkic clans and Turko-Mongol pastoral nomads who moved to the area to find pasture on the ever-increasing lands under Kazakh control. By the mid-sixteenth century these people, who were calling themselves Kazakhs, had divided into three tribal groupings (the Small, Middle, and Great hordes) ruled by a single khan. Thus members of the Kazakh khanates were ethnically undistinguishable from their near neighbors, the Uzbeks, Kirgiz, and Karakalpaks. All were Sunni Muslims (Kazakhs and Kirgiz more nominal than practicing); all were of predominantly Turkic stock with greater (the Kirgiz) or lesser (the Karakalpak) infusions of Mongol stock; and all spoke Turkic languages. The three Kazakh dialects, two Kirgiz dialects, and two Karakalpak dialects were from the same Nogai subdivision of the Qipchak group of Turkic languages (the Uzbeks all spoke Karluk dialects). These people were divided, however, by their political allegiances; the Uzbeks fled to the Uzbek khanate, the Kirgiz to Mughulistan, and the Karakalpaks, who farmed the lands along the Syr Darya River, struggled to preserve their autonomy from the grass-hungry livestock breeders to the north and east. The drive for land and the subsequent need to protect it led to the emergence of four separate political formations in northern Central Asia. Consanguinity remained an important bond, and marriages between Kipchaks and Naimans of the various peoples continued to be common. Nevertheless, ethnic groups became more distinct as the political divisions became self-perpetuating, economies developed separately, handicrafts and national dress became distinctive, and most customary practices became locally specific in the way in which they fused Islamic and pre-Islamic ritual.

The term Kazakh first came into use in the seventeenth and eighteenth centuries, but early Russian travelers confused the Kazakhs with the Kirgiz and dubbed them the Kirgiz-Kaisak; they referred to the Kirgiz as the Kara-Kirgiz (Black Kirgiz) or Gorno-Kirgiz (Mountain Kirgiz). By the late 1820s the Kazakhs were simply known as the Kirgiz, and this misnomer was used until the mid-1920s.

As the northernmost of these peoples, the Kazakhs have always been a frontier population living on the boundaries of more powerful states. This has made them more susceptible to conquest but may also have insured their survival. Their conquerors often sought to pacify them in an attempt to create secure borders; only when the Kazakhs could not be peacefully absorbed did their traditional way of life come under attack.

This dilemma of conquest or concession was certainly the Russian experience in Kazakhstan. For the modern reader, Russian interest in the Kazakhs is the most important element of their history, since the Russians have orchestrated Kazakh development from the mid-nineteenth century through today and show no sign of relinquishing their hold. The history of Kazakh-Russian relations provides an interesting perspective from which to study both colonial and Soviet history. Criteria applied by the Russians in deciding whether to expand into new territory, and how to treat the newly absorbed population, are recurrent questions with broad implications for both domestic and foreign policy.

Both the colonial Russian and modern Soviet regimes have had to grapple with the nature of the subject and the citizen in a multinational state. How are the desires of the periphery to be weighed when they conflict with the perceived needs of the center? The well-being of the center has been paramount in the organic view of the state, which makes the whole not merely the sum of its parts. Still, protection of state security has equally had to recognize that force cannot constantly be applied to fractious populations on the edges of the empire. Both the colonial officials and their Soviet successors have sought a solution that assures the dominance of the center (the Russians) over the periphery (the non-Russians). This approach, however, has assumed that at least in the long run the non-Russian nationalities would define a peaceful relationship with St. Petersburg (and then Moscow) as a matter of mutual self-interest.

The Kazakhs became a key element in securing such an accommodation not only in the steppe but for the rest of Central Asia as well. When the Russians took control of the area they hoped that the Kazakhs would function much as the Tatar intermediaries had in earlier periods—that is, as a positive model for more troublesome neighbors. The Kazakhs were not devout Muslims, so the Russians should not have seemed infidels to them. Nonetheless, the Kazakhs were nomads and heathens, and the Bolsheviks as well as the tsarists saw them as unruly people who had to be civilized before they could be expected to give meaningfully to the state. Kazakh resistance in the Civil War had been better structured and less violent than that of the Central Asians, and when the Kazakh nationalists agreed to serve the Bolshevik government, the Soviets hoped the Kazakhs would help create popular support for Bolshevik rule.

The Kazakhs have proven to be adaptable. They participated more fully in the tsarist colonial system and have been better integrated into the Soviet polity than the other Central Asian nationalities, but the course of Kazakh-Russian relations has been neither peaceful nor without costs to both parties. In the eighteenth century the Kazakh khans welcomed a defensive alliance with the Russian tsarina, but by 1860 most Kazakhs viewed the Russians with suspicion and resisted the annexation of the steppe. Resistance became rebellion in the last days of the empire; the masses revolted in 1916, and a year later the elite joined the opposition when it created the Alash Orda autonomous government. The Kazakhs did later accept Bolshevik rule, but those who served the new state quickly became frustrated; frustration became violence when the policy of forced collectivization was introduced. By the end of the 1930s the acquiescence of the Kazakhs was achieved: they were literally starved into submission. This acceptance without alternative of Stalin's economic experiment has in subsequent generations become a more positive commitment to the Soviet system.

The story of the development of the modern Kazakh people is difficult to recount, particularly for the Western analyst who is confronted with a remote nomadic culture, scarce and inaccessible sources, and, most critically, the need to interpret both Russian and Soviet historiography. During the colonial period there was both censorship and a relative lack of interest in studying the Kazakhs. Nevertheless, the problems of using Soviet sources are far more acute: materials are not only censored but history, an important means of socialization, has become teleological. Moscow demands that historians make the emergence of communism appear inevitable for all the Soviet peoples, an outgrowth of their long and happy association with the Russians.

This has created serious problems for authors attempting to write a history of the Kazakhs or of the non-Russian peoples more generally. Since the late 1940s Soviet historiography has explicitly assumed that the expansion of the Russian empire was achieved by the so-called voluntary submission of the non-Russian populations; opposition movements have either been concealed or cast in the most negative light possible. In the case of the Kazakhs this has led to particularly great distortions, because the greatest supporters of the Russian authorities were the sultans and khans, so-called feudal elements who cannot be portrayed positively. The current official histories of the conquest are filled with huge gaps, compensated for by reinterpretations designed to recast popular rebellions against both Russian and khanate rule as peasant uprisings against the feudal authorities.

The whole question of Kazakh feudalism has been another thorny issue. It seriously hampered scholarship in the 1940s and 1950s and continues to have a negative effect today, largely because of questions regarding the meaning of nomadism and the proper classification of a subsistence-based economy in the Marxist hierarchy of economic forms. For a long time Soviet scholars were forced to present their materials in a way that validated the conclusion that nomadic society was feudal. That approach has made it difficult to gauge with any accuracy the impact of colonial policies on the Kazakh economy. These difficulties, however, are inconsequential when compared to the problems of writing about the Soviet period. Recounting the history of the Russian Revolution and Civil War in Kazakhstan has led to the death of more than one Soviet historian, and the purges and the terror have created still-insurmountable problems for historians writing about the 1920s and 1930s.

Nevertheless, hundreds of previously untapped sources for studying the history of the Kazakhs exist, and when materials from the pre- and early postrevolutionary periods are combined with modern sources we are able to gain a far clearer picture of what occurred in the remote steppe region. The present volume is intended as a general introduction for the Western reader. I have attempted to highlight the critical economic and political problems that the Kazakhs have confronted and the means by which they were resolved, either by the Kazakhs or by the various external forces they encountered. The book is designed to supplement, but not supplant, earlier work done by others; where Western scholars have already made significant studies, in such areas as the history of the Civil War or the creation of the Virgin Lands, only new information relating directly to the Kazakhs is included.

This book would not have been possible without the support of a large number of people. Many have generously given their time to read and discuss all or part of the manuscript; most important have been Owen Lattimore, Mikhail Bernstam, and the late Arcadius Kahan. In the later stages of writing I relied heavily on the support of various colleagues at the Russian Research Center at Harvard University, including Donald Carlisle, David Powell, and Mark Beissinger. The book would never have been completed without the financial support of the Colgate Research Council, the Bunting Institute of Radcliffe College, and the National Council of Soviet and East European Research. Finally, last but not least, I would like to thank Professor Wayne Vucinich as well as his colleagues at Hoover Institution for their advice and patience during the long incubation period of the book.

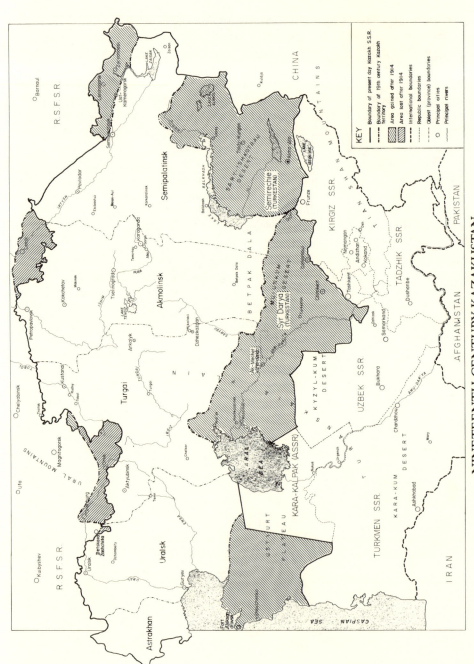

NINETEENTH-CENTURY KAZAKHSTAN

KEY

Boundary of present day Kazakh S.S.R.
Boundary of 19th century Kazakh territory
Area gained after 1914
Area lost after 1914
International boundaries
Republic boundaries
Oblast (province) boundaries
Principal cities
Principal rivers

R S F S R

Barnaul

CHINA

KIRGIZ SSR

TIEN SHAN MOUNTAINS

Semipalatinsk

Semirechie
(TURKESTAN)

Frunze

Lake
Issyk-kul

TADZHIK SSR

Ust-
Kamenogorsk

Pavlodar

LAKE ZAISAN

Kokdju

Namangan
Osh
Andizhan
Kokand

Dushanbe

PAKISTAN

Petropavlovsk

Kokchetov

Tselinograd

Akmolinsk

BETPAK DALA

SYR DARYA
(TURKESTAN) DESERT

Tashkent

UZBEK SSR

Samarkand

AFGHANISTAN

Chelyabinsk

Kustanai

Turgai

Atbasar

Karaganda

MUIUN KUM

Ak-Mechet
(Kzyl-Orda)

KYZYL-KUM
DESERT

Bukhara

Chardzhou

AMU DARYA

URAL MOUNTAINS

Magnitogorsk

Aktyubinsk

KARA-KALPAK (ASSR)

Mary

Ufa

Orsk

ARAL
SEA

KARA-KUM
DESERT

TURKMEN SSR

IRAN

Kuibyshev

Uralsk

Uralsk

Gur'yev

Fort
Aleksandrovsk

Ashkhabad

CASPIAN SEA

Astrakhan

R S F S R

USTYURT PLATEAU

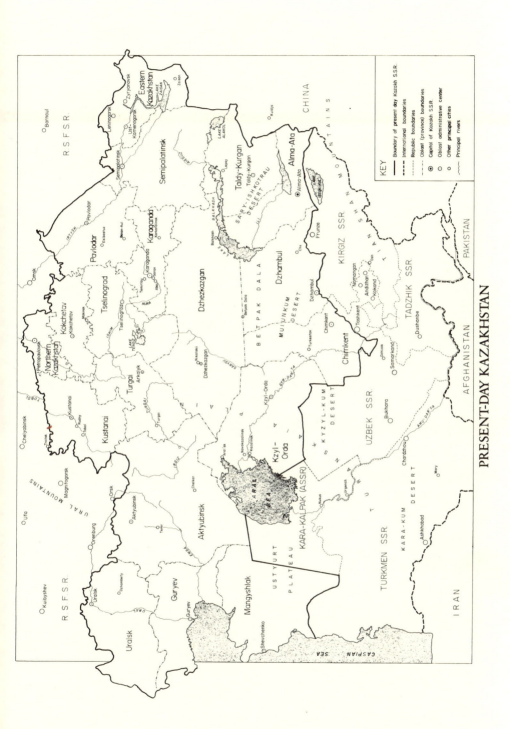

PRESENT-DAY KAZAKHSTAN

KEY

Boundary of present day Kazakh S.S.R.
International boundaries
Republic boundaries
Oblast (province) boundaries
Capital of Kazakh SSR
Oblast administrative center
Other principal cities
Principal rivers

MAP SOURCES

Allen F. Chew, *An Atlas of Russian History* (New Haven: Yale University Press, 1977), p. 77.

John Bartholomew, ed., *The Times Atlas of the World: South-West Asia and Russia, Vol. II* (Boston: Houghton Mifflin, 1959), plate 43.

Gavin Hambly, ed., *Central Asia* (New York: Delacorte Press, 1966), p. 367.

*Kazakhskaia Sovetskaia Sotsialisticheskaia Respublika: Entsiklopedicheskii Spravochnik* (Alma-Ata, 1981), pp. 40–41, 170–176.

# THE RISE AND FALL OF THE KAZAKH KHANATE

## PART ONE

# 1 Origin of the Kazakhs and the Formation of the Kazakh Khanate

## THE FORMATION OF THE KAZAKH PEOPLE

There is no agreement on how the Kazakh people were formed, largely because of the paucity of contemporary sources.[1] Almost no Europeans traveled to the area, Eastern chroniclers were far more interested in events in the oasis cities than in the lives of the nomadic steppe populations, and the nomads themselves left no legacy apart from a fragmentary, often legendary, oral history. Much of what we know about the formation of the Kazakh people comes from the observations and records of eighteenth-century Russian emissaries and officials who traveled among the Kazakhs during the period of the Russian annexation and conquest.[2]

The consensus is that the Kazakh people or Kazakh nation was formed in the mid-fifteenth century when Janibek (Dzhanibek) and Kirai (Girei), sons of Barak Khan of the White Horde of the Mongol empire, broke away from Abu'l Khayr (Abulkair), khan of the Uzbeks. Janibek and Kirai sought to capitalize on the power vacuum created by Abu'l Khayr's defeat by the Oirats (Mongols), and they moved with their supporters to western Semirech'e—the land between the Chu and Talas rivers, formerly controlled by the Uzbeks. Here their supporters increased in number, and they established a rival khanate whose center was the Betpak-Dala desert, between the Chu and Sarysu rivers. The territory of the Kazakh khanate continued to expand, so that by the middle of the sixteenth century it included most of the environs of Lake Balkhash and the lands immediately above and below the Syr Darya River, north to the Turgai River, and west to the lands just northwest of the Aral Sea. The Kazakh khanate was a political confederation composed primarily of Turkish-speaking nomadic tribes of Uzbek-Turkic stock (mostly Nogai) that had migrated to the area from the Dashti-Qipchak (the Kipchak Steppe), and Naiman, Argyn, and Chagatai tribesmen from the Uzbek khanate, as well as some indigenous population. By the time of Qasim (Kasym) Khan (reigned 1511–1523), the Kazakh nation was estimated at over one million people.[3]

The term Kazakh came into use by the residents of the area possibly as early as the end of the fifteenth century and certainly by the mid-sixteenth century.[4] Many theories have been advanced to explain the origin of the term. Some speculate that it comes from the Turkish verb *qaz* (to wander), because the Kazakhs were wandering steppemen; or that it is the combined form of two Kazakh tribal names, Kaspy and Saki; or that it traces from the Mongol word *khasaq* (a wheeled cart used by the Kazakhs to transport their *yurts* [felt tents] and belongings).[5] Another explanation advanced in the nineteenth century is that the term comes from the Turkish words *ak* (white) and *kaz* (goose), from a popular Kazakh legend of a white steppe goose that turned into a princess, who in turn gave birth to the first Kazakh.[6]

The tale of the white goose is only one of many legends of the formation of the first Kazakh tribe. The most celebrated is that of Alash (or Alach). In most of these tales, Alash is depicted as the founder of the Kazakh people, whose three sons each established one of the three Kazakh hordes. In other tales he is described merely as a great khan whose last direct "descendant," Tokhtamish, was killed at the battle of Saray Su (1395) when Timur (Tamerlane) defeated the Golden Horde. There is no historical evidence for the existence of a Kazakh nation at this time, but the legend of Alash has always played an important unifying role for the Kazakhs; the first Kazakh political party and autonomous Kazakh government (1917) were named the Alash Orda, the Horde of Alash. Despite such legends, it seems quite certain that all claims of consanguinity, of a single people inhabiting this region from antiquity to the present, are spurious.

Archaeology is still a young science in Kazakhstan. The first excavations were begun in 1940 and the retracing of early steppe life has gone on slowly but steadily since that time. The record of prehistoric life in this area is still a fragmentary one. Campsites dating from the Lower Paleolithic period have been found in caves of the Karatau mountains, and flint scrapers from the Middle Paleolithic period have been found in eastern Kazakhstan. Weapons and religious objects from the Paleolithic period have been found in most parts of Kazakhstan, and there appear to have been a large group of settlements around the Aral Sea in the Upper Paleolithic period. Crude weapons from the Upper Paleolithic and weapons and shards of pottery from the Neolithic period have been found in most parts of the steppe. Evidence suggests that some localized livestock breeding and hoe farming began in the Aeneolithic epoch (during the fourth and third millenia B.C.), but the first evidence of a widespread and organized pastoral nomadic economy are the relics of the Andronovo culture from the Bronze Age (mid-second to early first millenium B.C.), which are found throughout the steppe. Andronovo settlements of up to forty rectangular, semisubterranean dwellings have been excavated at Atasu and Karkaralinsk in Karaganda Oblast and Alekseevka in Kustanai Oblast.[7] Remains of primitive mines from this same period have been found in Dzhezkazgan and Zyryanovsk.

During the first millenium B.C., southern Kazakhstan came under the control of a group of loosely united, pastoral nomadic tribes of Iranian stock, referred to in the Achaemenid uniform texts as Sacae (Scythians).[8] Substantial information about their life-style has been gathered from the contents of *kurgans* (burial grounds) found in Begaza in central Kazakhstan and at several locations in Semirech'e and around the Aral Sea.

In the period 300–200 B.C., the Sacae were gradually overrun by the Usun, a group of allied tribes of pastoral nomads who were Turkic-speaking but of Mongol stock. Accounts of their emergence appear in Chinese sources from the second and first centuries B.C. In the year 73 B.C., the Usun, then headed by a hereditary ruler, the *kunmi*, were said to number over 600,000. They were divided into two groups, the Kangly (many of whom were sedentary farmers), who lived in the Karatau region and along the middle course of the Syr Darya, and the Alani, who migrated from the northern shores of the Aral Sea to the northern banks of the Caspian Sea. Excavations at Aktyubinsk (on the right bank of the Syr Darya) reveal that the Usun erected permanent dwellings as winter residences for tribal notables; the most elaborate of these were two-story dwellings with enclosed courtyards.[9]

The Usun union began to disintegrate in the fifth and sixth centuries A.D., after successive invasions by the Altai Turks. Much of the population remained in the area, but came first under the rule of the western Turkish kaganates (formed from Turkish-speaking tribes from southern Kazakhstan and Semirech'e) and then under their successor, the Turgesh kaganate, with its center at Shash, near present-day Tashkent. These kaganates were complex and stratified societies consisting of aristocrats, urban traders, oasis farmers, pastoral nomads, and a professional warrior class sufficiently skilled to prevent the Arab armies from crossing the Syr Darya until A.D. 739.

After the Arabs carved off the southernmost part of the kaganate, the Turgesh were attacked by the Uighurs and then were completely defeated by the Karluks (Turks from the western Altai). The Karluk kaganate was established in 766 over all the Turgesh lands except western Kazakhstan, whose tribesmen allied themselves with the Oguz state (in what is now Turkmenistan). At its origin the Karluk state went from Kashgaria to the middle course of the Syr Darya. It continued to expand, so that by the tenth century it also encompassed the area between lakes Issyk-Kul and Balkhash as well as the Ili, Chu, and Talas river valleys. Under the Karluks the first large cities were built in the steppe, including Taraz (present-day Dzhambul), Isfijab (renamed Sairam), and Farab (renamed Otrar).

In 940 the Karluks lost a dynastic struggle to the Karakhanid family, who ruled the steppe for another two hundred years. In 960 the Karakhanid ruler, called the *tamgach* khan, embraced Islam and then succeeded in extending his rule over the Muslim populations of the Amu Darya and the lower course of the Syr Darya. The steppe economy flourished under Karakhanid rule; the number of sedentary farmers increased since the system of irrigation was sufficiently advanced to allow for the cultivation of fruits and vegetables as well as grains. Taraz, the Karakhanid capital, developed into a city of more than ten thousand people, and a number of new cities developed along the Syr Darya, including Otrar (the rebuilt Farab), Sygnak, and Suan.[10]

The Seljuk conquest of Transoxiana (also known as Mawarannahr) early in the twelfth century left the Karakhanids vulnerable, and in 1130 the Karakhanids were overthrown by the Karakitae, a Mongol people who invaded from the west. The Karakitae ruled the steppe for nearly a century. In the first decade of the thirteenth century the Naimans and Kerei, Turkic tribes from the Altai, invaded the steppe and overthrew the gur (khan) of the Karakitae.[11] They in turn were quickly defeated by the armies of Chingis Khan, which conquered Semirech'e in 1218. These armies remained on Naiman land for several years, using it as a launching base for campaigns against the Khwarizm Shah, whose state included Khwarizm (now Khorezm), Mawarannahr, and much of present-day Iran and Afghanistan. Once the Khwarizm Shah was defeated, the Mongol armies withdrew, leaving only an administrative superstructure behind.

The Mongol conquest did have a disruptive economic effect upon the region, destroying what some historians have considered the preconditions of nationhood that had been present under the Karakhanids and Karakitae (that is, a single language, common economy, and shared way of life). The Mongol invasion also destroyed the Syr Darya River towns and trading posts of Sauran, Otrar, and Sygnak, and with them the sedentary culture that had provided a basis for the unity of these tribes. The Mongol rulers influenced language and culture as well as the social organization of the Turkic tribes of Central Asia. The Kazakh language took on Mongol words, and clan structure was modified to resemble the Mongol *ulu* (clan) system. Perhaps the longest-lasting innovation of Mongol rule was the application of the *Yasa*, a codified law based on a combination of customary practice and Muslim precepts, which served as precedent for a Kazakh system of customary law. When Chingis Khan's empire was distributed among his heirs, the territory of present-day Kazakhstan was divided between his sons, Jochi and Chagatai. Jochi predeceased his father, and so his inheritance (the lands west of the Irtysh River) passed to his son, Batu, who expanded his territory westward and founded the Golden Horde. Chagatai controlled the Semirech'e region as well as western Jungaria (also known as Dzhungaria and later as Kashgaria) and Mawarannahr.

During the first half of the thirteenth century Batu's territories continued to expand westward, but his headquarters remained at Sarai (in the heart of the Dashti-Qipchak), 65 miles north of Astrakhan. The vastness of his holdings made it easy for loyal but independent khanates to emerge within the territory of the Golden Horde. Over the first quarter of the fourteenth century, a semiautonomous Mongol khanate gradually emerged, known as the White Horde (*Ak Orda*) and encompassing the Syr Darya region. The khan of the White Horde, who wintered around Sygnak, controlled the steppe northwest of the Aral Sea as far as the Ishim and Sarysu rivers. The first khan of the White Horde paid tribute to the khans of the Golden Horde. Eight successive khans tried unsuccessfully to gain complete autonomy for the White Horde, but it was not until 1364 that independence from the Golden Horde was achieved. Even this was short-lived, as Tokhtamish (reigned 1381–1395), khan of the Golden Horde, succeeded in reuniting the Golden and White Hordes. This period saw the redevelopment of agriculture, the founding or reconstruction of trading centers in southern Kazakhstan, and the re-establishment of a unified and viable economic region in Kazakhstan, all necessary preconditions for the emergence of a united Kazakh people one hundred years later.

The beginning of the fourteenth century also saw the breakup of the Chagatai khanate and the establishment of rival branches of the family in Mawarannahr and newly formed Mughulistan (which included the Ili region, Semirech'e, and Eastern Turkestan). The violent rivalry among these three powers (the White Horde, Mawarannahr, and Mughulistan) made the third quarter of the fourteenth century a period of economic upheaval; trade connections were broken and the agricultural oasis cities (especially in Mawarannahr) went into a period of decline. The economic and political stagnation of the region continued; Timur made repeated forays into both the Kazakh steppe and northwestern Mughulistan in the 1370s and 1380s, and in 1395 he defeated Tokhtamish at Sarai Berke. This defeat marked the end of Mongol rule in Central Asia. The Golden Horde and White Horde quickly broke up. The first two decades of the fifteenth century saw the creation of two new confederations of nomadic Turkish tribes in Central Asia, the Nogai Horde (a union of Kipchak tribes living between the Ural and Volga rivers) and the more important Uzbek khanate (1420), which controlled the steppe land from the headwaters of the Syr Darya river basin to the Aral Sea and north to the Irtysh River. It was in this period that the term *Uzbek* came into common use to designate the Turkish tribes that migrated over present-day Kazakhstan and Uzbekistan.

Stability was short-lived, however. A rivalry quickly developed between the ruler of the new Uzbek khanate, Barak Khan, and Ulugh beg (Timur's grandson), the ruler of Mawarannahr, who retained control of the Syr Darya river basin. After Barak's death, with the connivance of Ulugh beg, the title of khan passed to Abu'l Khayr (reigned 1428–1468) of the Shayban (Sheiban) family. During Abu'l Khayr's rule the Uzbek khanate became the major power in Central Asia. Abu'l Khayr quickly unified the Turkic tribesmen, his northern holdings reaching the border of the khanate of Sibir. He then moved southward toward Mawarannahr. In 1430 Abu'l Khayr captured Khwarizm and Urgench, and by 1442, after capturing the entire Syr Darya region, he had established his capital at Sygnak, the trading center for the steppe oasis communities of Central Asia. Complete control of Mawarannahr eluded him, however. The drive of Abu'l Khayr was thwarted by the emergent Oirat (Mongol) hordes of Mughulistan in the middle of the fifteenth century, who rapidly became a superior military force. The Oirats (also known as Jungars) crossed from Mughulistan to the Dashti-Qipchak, burning the cities and destroying the economy of the area, and then returned to Mongolia. They (and their Kalmyk-Mongol successors) were to pose periodic threats to the Kazakhs until the end of the seventeenth century.

Two sons of Barak Khan, Janibek and Kirai, were quick to take advantage of Abu'l Khayr's reverses. As representatives of a rival claimant, they had been in opposition to Abu'l Khayr since he assumed power. In the mid-1460s Janibek and Kirai led the tribes of their supporters (remnants of the old White Horde) west from Mughulistan into the territory of Abu'l Khayr. With the support of the rulers of Mughulistan, they lay claim to pastureland in western Semirech'e from the lower Chu River valley across the Talas valley to the Betpak-Dala Desert. Abu'l Khayr refused to recognize Janibek's claim over this territory and led an expedition to oppose him; Abu'l Khayr and his son, Shaikh Haidar, died fighting Janibek's troops in 1468. Abu'l Khayr was succeeded by his grandson, Muhammad Shaybani (reigned 1468–1510), who occupied Samarkand and Bukhara and established the Shaybanid dynasty. Fighting between the Uzbeks and Kazakhs continued for most of the remainder of the fifteenth century. In the process, the nomadic economy of Syr Darya and Semirech'e was severely disrupted, animals were killed, and towns and trading posts were plundered.

It is hard to date the formation of a Kazakh khanate precisely, since none of the contemporary accounts of the late fifteenth century paid much attention to the steppe. The official Soviet history of Kazakhstan considers Janibek the first Kazakh khan, holding that, upon Janibek's death in 1480, Kirai's son Buyunduk (reigned 1480–1511) was elected his successor. Other sources maintain that Kirai was the first *elected* khan, ruling until his death in 1488, when he was succeeded by Buyunduk.[12] Regardless of which account is correct, clearly the Uzbek-Kazakh rivalry continued throughout the last quarter of the fifteenth century as Muhammad Shaybani and Buyunduk competed for control of the Syr Darya cities. The largest and most important city, Yasi (later called Turkestan), became the headquarters of the Kazakh khan. The rivalry ended temporarily when the two rulers signed a peace treaty in 1500. Peace allowed Shaybani to turn his attentions south, to the conquest of Bukhara and Samarkand.

The shift of Uzbek authority to Mawarannahr enabled the Kazakhs to concentrate on the establishment of a stable khanate of their own. Buyunduk's successor, Qasim Khan, is generally credited with the creation of a centralized and unified Kazakh khanate. He expanded the territory under Kazakh control to include some of the eastern pasturelands of the Dashti-Qipchak, more of the Syr Darya valley, and all of the Chu River valley. In 1513 he got as far south as Tashkent but was unable to make an all-out attack on the city; winter was approaching and the Kazakh tribes that had summered in the lower Chu valley had to migrate north to find winter grazing. Qasim strengthened the Kazakh hold over the cities of the lower Syr Darya, which was essential for the regulation of trade between the livestock breeders and the sedentary populations to the south. Control of these cities made the Kazakh territory a viable economic system, self-regulating and self-sufficient. Still, the Kazakh economy and Kazakh khanate remained in the shadow of the more powerful Shaybani khanate in Mawarannahr.

During this period the Kazakh confederation expanded as Qasim welcomed other Turkish tribes, including Kipchaks from the Nogai group and Naimans and Argyns from the eastern branch of the Chagatais. It was possible for the first time to consider the Kazakhs a people: they were approximately one million strong, spoke the same Turkish language, utilized the same type of livestock breeding, and shared a culture and a form of social organization. Under Qasim, political unity was established as well, for his authority was recognized by the sultans who lived in the Kazakh territory. The Kazakh people at this time was essentially a political union, distinguished solely by territorial and political criteria from the Uzbeks, who came from the same ethnic stock and whose language, economy, and culture were virtually identical to those of the Kazakhs. The Uzbeks, who migrated in the territory of Mawarannahr, recognized the authority of Shaybani and paid him tribute, whereas the Kazakh population, concentrated along the Syr Darya and to the north and east, not only did not recognize Shaybani's authority but instead established a distinct and sometimes rival political structure. From the reign of Qasim Khan on, Uzbeks and Kazakhs lived side by side, but they never again considered themselves one people.

## THE POLITICAL AND
## SOCIAL STRUCTURE OF THE KAZAKHS

At the end of the fifteenth century, and for most of the sixteenth century, the Kazakhs were primarily a political union. The Kazakh khanate and the Kazakh people were synonymous, a people formed by the union of previously disparate clans and tribes of Turkish descent. They converged in the steppe lands around the Chu River and Betpak-Dala Desert, where a political void had existed and where, as pastoral nomads, they found new and unused pasturelands, a rarity in the late fifteenth century. Once they occupied the land, these nomads sought to maintain control of it; the Kazakh union, founded by Janibek and Kirai, offered potential for both continued control and future expansion. Tribal unity implied increased military potential, with more warriors to mount a common defense against outside invaders.

With growing strength came growing numbers. Nogai, Uzbek, and Mongol (Altai) tribes in need of pasturage came to join the Janibek-Kirai federation. As these tribes gained pastureland, their livestock holdings increased, requiring additional pasturage. This, coupled with the constant need to shift pasturelands that the free grazing of animals demands, led the Kazakhs continually to acquire new territory, so that by the last quarter of the seventeenth century they controlled most of present-day Kazakhstan. As the allied tribes became more numerous and their holdings increased, problems of social organization and tribal unity were compounded. Apparently in the first half of the sixteenth century, following the death of Qasim and the consequent breakup of his holdings, the Kazakhs formed their distinctive three hordes, reintroducing a sense of organization and order.

Because of difficulties with source materials, it is not possible to date precisely the formation of the three Kazakh hordes. The earliest reference to the three hordes was made in 1731 by Tevkelev, the Russian ambassador to the Small Horde, and their existence was confirmed in 1734 by Kirillov, the head of an expedition to Orenburg. Both these accounts, as well as those of Rychkov and Georgii—eighteenth-century Russian travelers to the steppe—gave similar accounts of the size and location of the hordes. Vostrov and Mukanov, the most authoritative Soviet students of Kazakh tribal makeup, place the formation of the Great, Middle, and Small Hordes in the middle of the sixteenth century, during the rule of Haq Nazar (1538–1580). This view, which dominates contemporary Soviet scholarship, conflicts with the accepted nineteenth-century opinion of V. V. Veliaminsky-Zvernov, who argued that the hordes were formed in the mid-seventeenth century.[13] Since Vostrov and Mukanov have been more exhaustive, their conclusions are probably more accurate.

The nature and composition of the hordes has also been a source of contention. Although used by Western and Soviet scholars alike, the term *horde* is probably a misnomer; the Kazakhs referred to these three groups as the *Ulu Zhuz*, *Orta Zhuz*, and *Kichi Zhuz*, literally the Great Hundred, Middle Hundred, and Small Hundred. This distinction between horde and hundred is important, since the former implies consanguinity and common ancestry, whereas the latter does not. The Kazakh hordes were, in fact, federations or unions of tribes that typically did not share a common ancestry. They were instead simply an extension of the temporary military unions formed by both Turkish and Mongol tribes. Such unions were often called *Zhuz*; there are references to the existence of various (short-lived) *Zhuz* in Kazakh territory prior to the sixteenth century.[14] It is thus probable that the Kazakh hordes formed largely for military purposes—to make the Kazakh lands more secure in the absence of any stronger central authority.

Even given the explanation that the Kazakh hordes were created for military-political purposes, the question remains why three such hordes were formed. The legend of Alash and his three sons may be dismissed as fiction, as may the tale repeated by Aristov of a legendary Kazakh, Kosanin, who had three sons, Aktol (Middle Horde), Alchin (Small Horde), and Usun (Great Horde). Such stories seem clearly to have been invented to strengthen the legitimacy of the three hordes by the creation of a legendary common ancestor.[15] The most convincing explanation is the commonly accepted one: that the tripartite division of the Kazakh people was in response to the unique geography of the steppe. Within the Kazakh-held territories of the sixteenth century there were three natural geographic regions, each containing both summer and winter pasturage. One such area was the Semirech'e region, where the Great Horde migrated along the river basins of the Chu, Talas, and Ili rivers, with summer pasturage in the mountains of the Ala Tau, an area that had its own internal trade network based on pre-existing agricultural oasis settlements. The second region encompassed central Kazakhstan, where the Middle Horde wintered around the lower course of the Syr Darya and in summer migrated to the tributaries of the Sarysu, Tobol, and Ishim rivers in the central steppe region, trading with the cities of Central Asia by water transport on the Syr Darya. The third territory was western Kazakhstan, where the Small Horde wintered along the lower course of the Syr Darya and Ural rivers and in the region between the Irgiz River and Turgai mountains, summering along the tributaries of the Ural River, the headwaters of the Tobol, and in the Irgiz and Mugodzhan hills.

Despite the division into three hordes, the Kazakhs were one people, with a common language, culture, and economy. Initially, in the sixteenth century, the divisions were ephemeral, depending as much on land usage as any voluntary allegiance to the constituent tribes and clans that formed each horde. As Kazakh control of the steppe expanded during the seventeenth century, the hordes gradually evolved into three stable unions with reasonably well defined and stable territories under their control. When the Kazakh khanate began to break up at the beginning of the eighteenth century (after Khan Tauke's death), the khan of each horde assumed the powers of sovereign ruler in his own territory, including the right to negotiate treaties with foreign powers. Although the Russians dealt with the Kazakhs as separate hordes, the Kazakhs continued to view themselves as one people, as is shown by the number of Kazakh legends and tales of a common ancestor that date from this period.

There are several conflicting accounts of the composition of the three hordes during the sixteenth century. Here too the most authoritative treatment is that of Vostrov and Mukanov. They maintain that the Great Horde was dominated by the Usun tribal confederation but was also composed of ten distinct tribes; since most of these tribes were age-old inhabitants of the Semi-rech'e region, the Great Horde is often assumed to have been formed first. Although tribal confederation existed in the area before the hordes, there is no evidence that the Great Horde was formed significantly earlier than the other two hordes. In addition to the Usun, who came to the steppe after the Mongol invasion, the Great Horde included the Kangly, a people who inhabited the lower and middle course of the Syr Darya from the third or second centuries B.C.; the Dulat, who occupied Semirech'e from the sixth or seventh century and reportedly lived in Mughulistan as early as the second century B.C.; and the Alban and Suan tribes, often considered to have evolved from the same ancestor as the more numerous Dulat, with whom they united on the territory of Semirech'e as early as the sixth century. Several other tribal groups joined later: the Jalair and the Usty, first traced to Central Asia in the thirteenth century; the Srgeli, first mentioned in the late fifteenth century; and the Chanyshkly and the Choprashti, who are not mentioned in source materials until the seventeenth century.

The Middle Horde by the seventeenth century had expanded to include all territory from the Aral Sea in the west, to Omsk in the north, the Irtysh River and the Altai in the east, and the Syr Darya and Sarysu rivers in the south. According to Vostrov and Mukanov, it included six tribes, the Kerei, Naiman, Argyn, Kipchak, Konrat, and Uak.[16] The oldest constituent people were the Kerei, descendants of the ancient Keraits, themselves of unclear origin (either Turkish or Mongol), who had dominated central Kazakhstan before the Mongol conquest. The Naiman, who, although Turkish-speaking, are gener-ally considered to be of Mongol origin, became a major population group in the region in the thirteenth century but may have been present in smaller numbers as early as the eighth or ninth centuries A.D. The Argyn, the most numerous tribe, were mentioned by Rashid al Din and are thought to be Mongols descended from the Chagatai Horde. The Kipchak formed a tribal union in the tenth century and began moving east from the Dashti-Qipchak in the thirteenth century, in increasing numbers after the formation of the Kazakh khanate.[17] The Middle Horde also consisted of Uak tribes, first mentioned in the thirteenth century, about whom virtually nothing is known. The Konrat tribes, who separated from the Middle Horde in the early nineteenth century, later joined with Uzbek farmers in the Kokand khanate.

The ethnogenesis of the Small Horde is particularly difficult to trace. As best as can be determined, this horde seems to have been a clanic rather than a tribal confederation. It was sometimes known as the Alchin clanic union, since eighteen clans of the Small Horde claimed common descent from the Alchins, and the remaining clans were known as the Jedgira (in Kazakh, seven clans), who were said to have attached themselves to the Alchins later on. However, it is doubtful that even the majority of the Small Horde, the so-called Alchin, shared a common ancestor. The three most numerous clans of the Small Horde were the Kerder, found around the Aral Sea in the tenth century; the Adai, believed by Vostrov and Mukhanov to be descendants of the Dakhi peoples, reported in the Mangyshlak region in the sixth and seventh centuries; and the Kereit (possibly a clan of the Kerei), who seem first to appear in the thirteenth century.

ʳ Each horde was ruled in roughly the same manner. A khan was elected at a meeting of sultans, *bii*s (lesser nobles), and clan or family elders, who met annually to affirm the khan's leadership, to advise him, and to receive his instructions. At these annual meetings the year's migration was planned and each clan and *aul* (the Kazakh migratory unit) was allocated winter pastureland. The power of the khan was vested in the person, not the office, so the power a particular Kazakh khan enjoyed was a reflection of his perceived particular fitness to rule. Periods of Kazakh unity, such as the reigns of Qasim, Haq Nazar, and Khan Tauke (reigned 1680–1718), occurred because the khans of the other hordes recognized the military superiority of these individuals and were willing to defer to their authority. After the deaths of Haq Nazar and Tauke, the three hordes again became separate entities.

The Kazakhs had a dual authority structure; an aristocracy of khans and sultans was superimposed upon a clan-based authority system. The Kazakhs had several great families, and each of these (either a clan or, more typically, a branch of a clan) was divided among several auls that migrated together and generally grazed their animals on adjoining pastureland. An aul, which in winter might have numbered as many as thirty to forty yurts (round felt tents), consisted of a few related, extended families. Each aul had an elder, usually referred to as an *aksakal* (white beard), who was charged with the protection of his pasturelands and people. The elders met to choose a bii to represent the family in negotiations with other families and to mediate internal disputes, regulate the migration, and allocate pastureland. Although the title of *bii* often went from father to son, the office was not hereditary and could be shifted if the elders so chose.

The biis met to choose the sultans, who typically functioned as sub-khans ruling over particular territory and governing relations between clans, as well as to choose the khan, who governed the entire horde. Sometimes semi-autonomous territories existed within a horde, ruled by lesser khans who had sworn loyalty to the khan of the horde. The khan generally served for life and, in keeping with the local tradition, was succeeded first by his brother and then by his son; nonetheless, since to become khan an individual had to prove his own competence, ruling families were often eclipsed by new claimants.

The Kazakhs adopted their system of princely rule from the Mongols. Therefore, membership in the Kazakh aristocracy (the white bone—*ak suiuk*) was restricted to individuals who at least in theory could trace their descent to Chingis Khan. By the end of the eighteenth century the White Bone had expanded to include *hojas* (the Turkish term for individuals who had made the pilgrimage to Mecca) and descendants of the caliph. Still, Kazakh aristocracy remained primarily linked to Mongol heritage, and important clanic leaders often went to some trouble to invent fictitious pedigrees. The general population of Kazakhs was known as black bone (*kara suiuk*), from which group the majority of Kazakh biis and aul leaders were chosen; they were eligible as well to serve as khans or sultans.

Many Soviet sources, particularly those written in the 1950s and 1960s, maintain that the Kazakh khanate was a feudal state.[18] More recent examinations of early Kazakh society, particularly those by professors Tolybekov and Markov, provide a more detailed and apparently more accurate view of the role played by the aristocracy.[19] These writers consider the early Kazakh state to be not a feudal society but rather a military democracy; they argue that the political authority of the khan was an extension of his military prowess. In general, Kazakh society rewarded military skills. *Batirs* (heroic warriors) were invited to migrate with the retinues of sultans and khans, and they were often elected themselves to be khans. Demonstrated military skills were required for selection as khan, since the khan led his horde in military campaigns and routine plundering.

Although the khans functioned primarily as military leaders, the Kazakhs did not maintain standing armies. Instead, they depended on the lesser khans, sultans, and biis, all of whom raised and commanded their own armies from the populations that they governed. Each family accepted the obligation to provide one warrior to its particular bii or elder. These elders, however, were under no compulsion to lend these warriors to the khan, who thus was compelled to win the support of lesser authorities for any campaigns in which he might wish to engage. It appears that the khan attempted to tax his allied clans only in times of war, when the livestock and food collected was used to provision troops. Evidence for this is found in *Jhety Jharga* (Khan Tauke's code), which records the levying of an extraordinary tax of $\frac{1}{20}$th of an individual's wealth to pay for the provisioning of men to bear arms.[20] This is further supported by Tevkelev's observation in the 1730s: "and from the nomadic Kirgiz-Kaisaks to the khans no tribute is gathered nor is required, but only that which pleases them [is collected] as there are few who would give and none who could take it from those who were unwilling."[21]

Since the Kazakh khans did not exact regular tribute from their subject populations, it is difficult to consider them feudal rulers. Furthermore, while livestock holdings of the sultans and khans were greater than those of the average Kazakh, the rulers' life-style was not distinct. The khan or sultan lived in an aul, which, like all others, migrated in a seasonal pattern. Although that aul might have been slightly larger than the norm, the only major distinction was that sultans and khans lived in ornate, white felt yurts rather than in simple, black felt ones. Each sultan maintained a retinue that included his immediate family, his aides and their families, and possibly a holy man, a batir, and a few *tulengut*s or slaves. Tulenguts were a hereditary class of slave warriors who were descendants of captives from raids on non-Kazakh populations, generally of Turkmen, Khivan, or Kokand stock. A vestige of the warrior culture that had dominated the area before the Kazakh khanate, the tulenguts declined in number throughout the period of the khanate, because the organizational structure of the khanate eased the problem of raising troops and eventually made the tulenguts obsolete. Although the Kazakhs continued to take captives, their raids were more often to capture animals than humans.

The khan controlled the relations between clans and auls. He also made the principal decisions about wars as well as preparing defensive arrangements for the horde. The khan allocated pasturelands for the clans and decided when and where the horde would migrate. This choice was closely connected to the military position of the horde, since it depended upon which lands were safely under the khan's control.

Within the larger Kazakh community, the clan leaders and elders had far more influence than the khan. They allocated lands to the auls and families, they had control of the warriors, and, unlike the khan, they had an unquestioned right of taxation—as their right to part of each family's herd (the number of animals to be surrendered varied annually, according to local custom). The Kazakhs did not distinguish between civil and criminal law; until the seventeenth century, Kazakh customary law, the *adat*, was uncodified and administered locally. Khan Tauke made the first attempt to regularize Kazakh customary practice by formalizing some Mongol, Russian, and Muslim legal practices that were already in popular use. His code, the *Jhety Jharga*, was not written down until the 1820s, when M. M. Speransky incorporated it in his legal reforms. Until then each khan modified the code slightly in oral transmission, to mirror his own preferences.

Tauke's customary law encouraged formalization of the legal process. Since the biis were charged with adjudicating disputes, by the end of the eighteenth century the term *bii* had come to mean judge. Each bii had his own court (generally a tent and a scribe), which he supported by collecting 10 percent of all fines levied. Kazakh justice was harsh, and the principle that blood demands blood was firmly entrenched; crimes of theft and plunder were punishable by loss of limb or by death. In cases of raids or attacks on an aul, the offending individual or community was forced to pay a *kun* (blood price); in the eighteenth century this was based on a standard of one thousand rams for a man's life, five hundred rams for a woman's, one hundred for the loss of a thumb, and twenty for the severance of a small finger. Furthermore, a scale of livestock equivalents was derived, by which one hundred camels equaled three hundred horses equaled one thousand sheep. The biis also adjudicated disputes involving inheritance and contractual agreements involving employment, marriage, and divorce. Peaceful adjudication of disputes was not universally acknowledged, as is attested to by the great number of *barymta*s (punitive raids in which livestock was captured).

Tauke's law also included an enumeration of social duties and obligations of the individual to his family and clan. The most important of these were *jilu*, the right of an individual to appeal to relatives for assistance after the loss of livestock due to natural disasters, and *ume* (also known as *asar*), the right to request unpaid labor of one's relatives in order to complete seasonal work such as shearing or well-digging. If these rights were refused, the offending individuals could be brought before a bii or elder and forced to comply. In general, Kazakh customary law was designed to maximize the stability and economic self-sufficiency of the community, which was constantly threatened both by external dangers and by the harshness and unpredictability of natural conditions.

## THE KAZAKH ECONOMY

The Kazakhs were a pastoral nomadic people whose life-style was defined by their migratory, livestock-breeding economy. They had an established pattern of annual migration between their summer and winter campsites. The principal campsite was the *kstau* (the winter site), at which the Kazakhs spent four or five months a year. This site was in a sheltered, wooded place, with water and grazing accessible. For the whole of this winter period the Kazakhs remained relatively immobile, grazing the animals nearby or feeding them with the limited grass and grain that they may have gathered or obtained through barter. Here, too, they erected their yurts and, in some communities, made *shoshala*s, mound-like residences of dirt, sticks, and stone. The long winter stopover allowed the Kazakhs to make the utensils, clothes, and personal possessions that they would need when the long trek resumed. Once the snows melted and the new grass had begun to grow, the Kazakhs began the spring migration (the *kokteu*) to their summer pastures. Slowed by the still-sparse grazing, they would travel for a few days and then camp where they found water, continuing this pattern until they reached the site chosen for summer pasture, usually in May or June. When these pastures were reached, an aul would generally divide into smaller units for more efficient grazing. The Kazakhs remained at the summer campsite (the *jailu*) until August or September. The campsite might be shifted within the same general area several times during the summer as grazing or water supply was exhausted. At the end of the summer the sub-auls reassembled and began the rapid autumn migration (*kuzeu*) to the winter site.

The distances involved in the annual migration varied by region, from 200 or 300 kilometers in southern Kazakhstan and Semirech'e to as many as 1,000 kilometers in western and central Kazakhstan, where the annual cycle was rarely less than 700 kilometers. Although at this time fixed migratory paths were unknown, each tribe, which might consist of 100 auls or more, migrated within an established geographic zone. The auls remained in contact through a runner system known as the *uyun uzak* (long ear), which enabled them to orchestrate the migration as well as to warn one another of impending danger.

Each Kazakh household maintained its own herd, which grazed in common with the other herds of the aul. The Kazakhs bred mixed herds, primarily of sheep interspersed with goats, since they were relatively easy to maintain and were a source of both food and clothing. Next in importance were horses, necessary as beasts of burden and to carry the Kazakh cavalry. The Kazakhs of central and southern Kazakhstan used camels in place of horses. Cattle were relatively unknown in the steppe until the beginning of the eighteenth century; even then cattle were found almost exclusively in the north. The number of animals per family varied considerably within a community. Markov claims that in the first part of the eighteenth century an average family in the Middle Horde owned about one hundred sheep, thirty to fifty horses, twenty to twenty-five goats, fifteen to twenty-five heads of cattle, and a few camels, whereas a wealthy family might own ten to twenty times that number.[22] Such wealthy households were, however, extremely rare.

The greatest weakness of the Kazakh economic system was that of pastoral nomadism in general: dependence upon natural conditions. The very makeup of the Kazakh herd was determined by conditions; sheep are relatively easy to maintain and eat most kinds of grass. In contrast, cattle require much greater quantities of grass and of more specific types, making it difficult to provide for a large free-ranging herd. The biggest problem that the Kazakhs faced was the starvation of livestock, usually from winter and its *jut*, ice storms that covered the grass with impenetrable ice. In bad years, a quarter to a half of a herd might perish. Drought was also a problem. The Kazakhs dug shallow wells along their migratory paths; during drought years these might dry up completely, while the water level in deeper wells that the Kazakhs dug at their winter and summer campsites dropped too low to support the entire herd. The water problem was magnified by the salinity of many steppe lakes and rivers.

Despite these problems the Kazakhs were committed to a pastoral, nomadic life-style. To be a Kazakh was to be a nomad, as the Kazakh language suggests. Kazakh has terms for those who do not migrate, such as *balykshi* (fisherman), *eginshi* (grain-grower), and the derogatory term *jatak* (literally, lie-about), used to describe individuals who had lost their animals. In summer jataks planted grain (wheat, barley, and millet) on communal land that they ate and sold for feed; the rest of the year they worked as hired hands, hoping to purchase or obtain livestock from their relatives. For the nomad and nomadism itself, Kazakh has no term.

To the Kazakhs land had no intrinsic value; Kazakhs owned their livestock but grazed these animals on common pasturelands over which tribes had usage rights but did not own. The primary impetus of Kazakh expansion was to secure grazing land, which the Kazakhs viewed as a depletable resource under temporary control. The basis of a man's wealth was his herd, not his land.

The Kazakhs viewed farmers as their natural enemy, since agricultural settlements inhibited migration by otherwise employing potential pasturelands and claimed ownership to wells and water sources. Such settlements were raided when the Kazakhs needed grain, but the marauders were careful not to destroy them, since the oasis settlements of southern Kazakhstan were necessary as a place to barter and trade. The cities of the Syr Darya declined under Kazakh rule, because after the collapse of the Silk Road few traders from outside the steppe were willing to risk a trip across Kazakh-dominated territory. The trading needs of the Kazakhs themselves were quite minimal, and only Yasi had a sizable bazaar.

## KAZAKH CULTURE AND RELIGION

Kazakh culture and religion were heavily influenced by the nomadic economy. Their society was self-contained, without regard to the cities, and they sought to link customary practices to conditions of day-to-day life. The Kazakhs maintained cultural continuity with the practices of the Turkish tribes who had inhabited the area for the past millenia, and although regional and tribal differences existed, basic cultural homogeneity continued throughout the steppe as new tribes took up the dominant cultural practices. Even the Mongol tribes who remained in the area assimilated most of the local Turkic culture, while, it is true, imprinting it with Mongol political culture and systems of law.[23]

Possibly the best proof of the stability of this Kazakh-Turkish culture was that popular religious practices were not deeply changed by Islam until the late eighteenth or nineteenth century, in spite of the fact that Islam was introduced to the cities of southern Kazakhstan in the eighth century, at the time of the Arab conquest, and that the Turkish nomads of the Kazakh steppe nominally embraced Islam in 1043. The Jochid princes who established the Kazakh state considered themselves Muslims and were accepted as such by the Muslim world.[24] Those few Kazakhs who lived in the cities (mostly traders) did become practicing Muslims, but the pastoral nomads (the Kazakh masses and most of the Kazakh nobility) had only the sketchiest knowledge of Muslim tenets and practices.

One reason for this stability was the relative self-sufficiency of Kazakh society. The Kazakh tribes were not closely tied to the cities, in whose seminaries and mosques Islam flourished. Sultans and khans were somewhat more religious, even including mullahs or seminary students in their entourages; still, these Muslims served primarily as scribes and were generally unsuccessful in spreading the teachings of Islam. The Kazakh princes respected Muslim institutions, and as they advanced southward into the cities of Syr Darya they openly courted the Muslim clergy. Such contact increased their knowledge of Islam; by the end of the seventeenth century, Kazakh oral literature included poems venerating Allah and Muhammad.[25]

The code of Tauke also shows that the Kazakhs had accepted some of the principles of *Shari'a* law by the end of the seventeenth century. The Kazakhs appear to have been introduced through the Uzbek example; there is no evidence that they actually understood the moral precepts on which the laws were based. It seems unlikely that there was any sort of formal Muslim religious establishment in the steppe at this time; the proof most often cited is that before the Russian conquest the Kazakhs did not collect the Muslim tithes on livestock (*zaakat*) or on grain (*ushur*). The only real contact that most Kazakhs had with Islam seems to have been through the Sufi holy men who traveled the steppe.[26]

The Islam of most of the Kazakh sultans and princes appears to have been little more than a basic acceptance of the ascendance of one god, Allah, over all others. Eighteenth-century observers note the complete absence of mosques and madrasahs in the steppe, while those in Semirech'e and southern Kazakhstan do not seem to have been rebuilt after the Mongol devastation of the cities. The Kazakhs appear not to have understood Arabic and to have had no direct knowledge of the teachings of the Koran. Although Islam was deeply entrenched in the cities south of the steppe, there was little proselytizing in this period, in large part because of the eclipse of the cities in south and southeastern Kazakhstan and the decline of the Kazakh steppe as a trade route. The self-sufficient nomads did not have much contact with the Muslim centers of the Tatars to the northwest or the Chagatai to the south.

Because of this isolation, Kazakh religious practice retained elements of earlier shamanism, animism, and ancestor worship. In the 1850s the great Kazakh ethnographer Chokan Valikhanov (Chokan Vali Khan uli) wrote that Kazakh folk religion was largely unchanged from the time of Timur. The Kazakhs believed that the spirits of the dead inhabited the sun, moon, earth, and various animals, and that such spirits could be contacted and urged to mediate against the forces of evil. The Kazakhs believed that there was a struggle between good (*kei*) and evil (*kesir*), and when Islam was ultimately adopted it was set upon this framework, with Muhammad and his teachings assuming the identity of *kei*. The spirits of one's ancestors would mediate for one, but only if the spirits of the departed were kept well-situated and happy; to serve the dead was a more sacred duty than to serve the living.[27] For this propitiation, animals were sacrificed during funeral rites and on festive occasions to show gratitude to the spirits. Communication with the spirits was believed to occur when the oil or rendered fat of a sacrificed animal was poured on a fire, aided by the services of shamans.

The Kazakhs believed that separate spirits inhabited the earth (*jher-ana*), water (*su-ana*), fire (*ot-ana*), and each of the animals that they tended, sheep (*shopan-ana*), cows (*zengi-baba*), horses (*kambar-ata*), and camels (*oisal kara*). In some accounts such spirits are represented as a patron saint or holy father who was prayed to when the occasion demanded; for example, prayers to jher-ana were offered in times of ice storms, to su-ana when there was drought, and to the various animal spirits when the herds were ill or needed replenishment.[28]

Livestock breeding was the Kazakh's livelihood and his life. His fortune depended upon the vagaries of nature: if a Kazakh had healthy animals, adequate pasturage, and sweet water, he considered himself blessed indeed. Hence, it is not surprising that animal worship, or more precisely the belief that the spirit of one's ancestors came somehow to rest within the bodies of animals, was widespread. As Abai Kunanbaev, the nineteenth-century poet, wrote: "Honor, reason, science, all for them [the Kazakhs] is less than livestock. They think that by the gift of livestock they may receive the good opinion even of god. For them religion is livestock, the people is livestock, knowledge is livestock, and influence is livestock."[29]

The Kazakh's preoccupation with their animals permeated their language and speech. In nineteenth-century spoken Kazakh there were still 112 terms associated with camel breeding and more than 40 terms for a camel. The traditional Kazakh greeting, still used in parts of the countryside, was "Are your livestock and your soul still healthy?", while almost all traditional Kazakh expressions of good and evil were linked to animals. A Kazakh wishing someone well said "May god give you one thousand sheep with lambs, eighty camels, and eight married sons." Kazakh curses involved calamities to livestock, such as "May you never have your own livestock and be unable to migrate with your own people," and "May you have neither horse nor camel, and always go by foot." Most Kazakh folk wisdom compared man with his animals, in such sayings as "A hornless goat, wishing to gain horns, loses his ears." Praise came through comparisons to animals as well; a fearless man was a wolf, a pretty woman a dromedary. Many places in the steppe are named for animals and animal themes dominated Kazakh crafts.[30]

Their economy also strongly influenced the development of the Kazakh literary tradition. Like the tales of other nomadic peoples, the Kazakh epic tales, poems, and songs describe migratory life and the perils of nature and man that Kazakhs faced. The hero of most Kazakh tales is the batir, or warrior, and his unfailing steed, who serve the elder and protect the lives and herd of the clan. The Kazakh oral epics are anonymous sagas combining poetry with prose. These tales were repeated from generation to generation throughout the steppe, surviving to form a part of the Kazakh literary tradition. These include the heroic epics *Koblandy-Batir* (fifteenth-sixteenth century), *Er Sain* (sixteenth century), and *Er Targyn* (sixteenth century), all of which deal with fighting between Kazakhs and Kalmyks, and the lyric epics *Kozy Korpesh* and *Bain Sulu* (possibly from the fourteenth century), *Aiman and Sholpan*, and the most famous Kazkah love story, *Kiz-Jhibek*. Except for the brief period at the end of Stalin's life, these epic tales have enjoyed continuous Soviet approval, since they predate Islam influence and so contain far fewer un-Soviet elements than later Kazakh literature.

Poems and poetic songs by known Kazakh poets of the khanate period have also survived. These compositions, as well as accounts of their authors, were preserved orally until the 1870s, when they were recorded by Kazakh intellectuals; these records, however, were suppressed by the Soviets until the 1960s.[31] These poets, who set the style of Kazakh poetic tradition, were closely associated with Kazakh aristocracy and migrated with the princely retinues. Their poetry reflects a closer association with Islamic, and particularly Sufi, thought than do the anonymous pieces. Such poets were called *jhyrau* in Kazakh, to distinguish them from *akyn*s, the itinerant poets who went from aul to aul reciting the oral epics. The jyrau lived as honored members of their tribes, often serving as tribal elders and advisers to the sultans. One recent Soviet source claims that these poets fulfilled a spiritual function as well, probably as followers of Sufi thought. Unlike the akyns, these jyraus had some contact with the world beyond the Kazakh steppe; at least one poet, Dosbambet-Jhyrau (c. 1490–1523), is known to have traveled to Istanbul. The poets had some awareness of other Muslim literatures at that time, as is shown by the following excerpt of a poem by Jhalkiz Jhyrau (1465–1560), which shows a merging of Muslim (Sufi) spirituality with the more traditional glorification of the Kazakh warrior:

> If the beautiful Argamak [warrior] were a coward,
> He wouldn't go so much as a step away from the white yurts,
> If we want to migrate only in dreams,

> Why then put on our silver belt?
> So until Allah takes our soul,
> And while you have broken a path through the mountain,
> And while you the hunter with bow in your hands,
> Have not ridden over the entire steppe and have not beat all strengths,
> From the horse who was recalcitrant and frisky,
> You've not brought glory to yourself, where there is no one
> And, overtaking the others, have not [yet] become a bii
> [And] you only in dreams and empty hopes
> Become a *batir*, the heir of your forefathers.[32]

The lives and works of these poets give a vivid picture of Kazakh life in the period of the khanate, a time for which there are few other contemporary accounts. For example, Asan Kangi, or Asan the Sad (1361 or 1370–1465)—who was perhaps the most talented of these early poets and whom Chokan Valikhanov called the "nomadic philosopher" of the Kazakhs—left the court of the former khan of the Golden Horde, Ulugh Muhammad, to aid Kirai and Janibek in their attempt to create a unified Turkic state in the Kazakh steppe. In his poem, "Greetings to Khan Janibek," Asan uses images of happiness and good fortune that are clearly specific to pastoral nomads:

> Valleys where livestock are not grazed
> And grass perishes for no reason is misfortune.
> Lakes in the steppe where there live no geese and ducks is misfortune.[33]

Much of our knowledge of Kazakh customary practices in the khanate period is gleaned from its literature, for which oral epics are a richer source than the poetry. The legend of *Kiz-Jhibek* is the story of an already betrothed young girl, Kiz-Jhibek, who is wooed by a young chief of the Small Horde, Tulegan. Tulegan is slain by the rejected fiancé, who is in turn slain by Kiz-Jhibek's brother. Eight years later, Sansizbai, a warrior, returns from fighting, hears of his older brother Tulegan's death, and goes to Kiz-Jhibek to marry her; he arrives to find her about to be married to a Kalmyk khan. He escapes with her; in the ensuing fight the Kalmyk is killed. Sansizbai and Kiz-Jhibek marry and so honor Tulegan's memory. The epic describes Kazakh betrothal and marriage ceremonies, showing too that the Kazakhs observed levirate.

Marriage was the central event in the life of a Kazakh. Kazakh women were generally married by age thirteen or fourteen, men by fifteen or sixteen. Marriages were arranged by the parents, sometimes as much as ten years before the event. Betrothal was achieved with the payment of a *kalym* (bride-price), set to reflect the status of the bride's family. A princely family received several hundred or even a thousand animals, but a typical kalym was fewer than one hundred animals, mostly sheep. Most Kazakhs were monogamous and only the rare exception had more than two wives. Since, according to Kazakh law, each wife was entitled to her own yurt, only a wealthy man could afford polygamy.

The wedding festivities (the *toi*) resembled the celebrations marking birth and death (the *as*). Such occasions allowed a clan or extended family to gather, and they were marked by animal sacrifices, songs, and games, including horse races and team sports such as toss the goat's head. After the wedding party, the bride, with her dowry of household goods, moved in a ceremonial procession to the yurt of her husband, generally established in the same aul as that of the groom's father. At the time of marriage a young man usually received his inheritance of a yurt and a part of his father's herd. Every son was entitled to a part of his father's herd. The youngest son generally remained in his father's yurt, which he inherited with his share of the herd, upon the father's death; it was also the youngest son who traditionally cared for his widowed mother. Women generally had no rights of inheritance, although an unmarried daughter was entitled to a share of the herd, and a widow whose sons had not yet reached majority retained control of the herd until her sons married. If a man died without issue, his animals were returned to his father, who was also charged with responsibility for the widow; in such instances levirate was common. The Kazakhs were a patrilineal society; if a widow remarried, her children had to remain in their father's aul, as was also true in the case of divorce.[34]

The customary practices of the Kazakhs were closely interwoven with the demands of pastoral nomadism. Both the kalym and the patterns of inheritance were designed to make the family an economically viable unit. The primary goal of the Kazakhs was to maintain stability within their society and within the steppe territory they controlled. In the first century and a half that the Kazakhs were emerging as a distinct people, most of their customary practices were indistinguishable from those of the Muslim Uzbeks to the south and the Mongol Kalmyks to the east. During these years the survival of a culturally distinct Kazakh people was always in doubt. Both the Uzbeks and the Kalmyks were stronger than the Kazakhs militarily, and conquest by either would have meant the absorption of the Kazakhs and their pasturelands. The menace posed by these powerful neighbors continued to grow, so that, although the Kazakhs were able to remain a distinct people, the history of the seventeenth and early eighteenth centuries records the defeat and destruction of the Kazakh khanate.

## THE DECLINE OF THE KAZAKH KHANATE

At the time of Qasim's death in 1523, the Kazakh state spread from the Ural River to the lands of Semirech'e and north to the Irtysh River. In the sixteenth century the Kazakhs focused their expansion on the Syr Darya region (the Talas and Zeravshan River valley), where they sought to inherit Uzbek domination. The territory of Kazakh control was not precisely fixed, reflecting instead the ability of the various khans to combine military success with personal persuasiveness. Qasim's successors were unable to maintain the unity that he had achieved, partly because they were less forceful rulers and partly because Kazakh territory had increased greatly during the last 25 years of Qasim's lifetime. Consequently, immediately after Qasim's death, the three Kazakh hordes were important as political entities; a single, unified Kazakh state as such did not then exist. However, one of the khans generally functioned as the pre-eminent authority or military commander for the whole Kazakh nation.

Qasim was succeeded briefly by his son, Mamush, who was killed while trying to consolidate his authority. His successor, Qasim's nephew, Tahir (reigned 1523–1533) attempted unsuccessfully to gain control of Tashkent. After Tahir's death, Buidashe (reigned 1533–1538) came to power but ruled in alliance with two other powerful khans of the day, Ahmed Khan (western Kazakhstan) and Tugun Khan (Semirech'e). During the second quarter of the sixteenth century, the Kazakhs received additional immigrants from the Dashti-Qipchak. The steppe economy flourished as the political stability of the steppe allowed the reintroduction of trade through the area, providing incentive to rebuild the cities Sygnak, Sairam, and Yasi.[35] By the end of the sixteenth century they had become walled towns with some brick structures and served as centers of exchange for the Kazakhs and traders from Kashgaria and Mawarannahr. The growth of these cities provided expanded markets for the Kazakhs, which in turn encouraged an increase in the size of the average herd and the general improvement of the Kazakh economic position.

In 1538 Haq Nazar (a son of Qasim) came to power, and in the 1550s he expanded the borders of the Kazakh state by absorbing the eastern section of the Nogai territory.[36] In the late 1560s, unsuccessful in his attempt to conquer Mughulistan, Haq Nazar turned his attention toward the trading centers in the Syr Darya region, which had been thriving in the peaceful and lucrative 1560s and 1570s. He and a group of Kazakh sultans swore loyalty to the emir of Bukhara, Abdul II, the pre-eminent political figure in the area, and they supported Abdul's claims against Baba-Sultan of Tashkent. In 1580, after receiving some cities from Baba-Sultan, the Kazakhs briefly switched sides, but once their control of the new territory was consolidated they again took up the Bukharan cause. Haq Nazar was killed in battle in 1580. He was succeeded by Tahir's nephew, Shigai (reigned 1580–1582), but it was Shigai's son, Taulkel (reigned 1586–1598), who was the effective leader of the Kazakhs. Taulkel defeated Baba-Sultan in 1582, whose head he exchanged with Abdul for the Zeravshan River valley. Shortly after this he broke with Abdul. In 1586 he was elected khan by the Kazakhs and led them in their struggle for control of the cities of the Syr Darya River basin. By the end of the century the Kazakhs controlled the cities of Turkestan, Tashkent, and Samarkand, and they had even managed to capture Bukhara for a brief period of time. Taulkel died in 1598, after taking Tashkent, and was succeeded by Esim (reigned 1598–1628). In his first year of rule Esim concluded peace with the emir of Bukhara, Abdullah, who recognized Kazakh control of the Syr Darya region.

The peace achieved was short-lived. Abdullah died in 1598, and Boqi Muhammad (reigned 1599–1605), the first of the *Ashtarkhanid* dynasty, chose not to recognize Kazakh hegemony. A far graver threat to the Kazakhs was the rise of the Kalmyk state in the east, which by 1630 contained western Mongolia, the Ili River region, and part of eastern and southeastern Kazakhstan (the eastern portion of Semirech'e). In the early part of the seventeenth century, the Kalmyks, pastoral nomads of Mongol stock, began migrating in sizeable numbers into the lands just east of the Kazakhs.[37] Attracted by the goods traded in the Syr Darya cities, they began periodically to attack the cities as well as the Kazakh population whose herds grazed on the periphery. The economic balance of the steppe was quickly upset; the number of caravans crossing the Kazakh steppe was sharply reduced. The decline of trade in the Syr Darya cities led the Kazakhs to the cities of Mawarannahr for their goods, which they raided when their attempts at conquest failed. Florio Beneveni, the Russian ambassador to Bukhara during the first decades of the seventeenth century, reported that the whole area was a turmoil of periodic fighting between Afghans, Russians, Khivans, Bukharans, Karakalpaks, Kazakhs, Kirgiz, and Kalmyks.[38] The major east-west trade routes had moved; the relative isolation of Central Asia forced all the constituent states and peoples to vie for the limited economic resources available.

The Kalmyks, fattened by the Kazakh animals they had seized, continued to grow in strength until, by the last quarter of the sixteenth century, they were the dominant military force in Central Asia. With over 100,000 armed fighters, they turned their strength against the Kazakh state and seized Kazakh pasturelands. By the late 1620s the Kalmyks were established along the Omi, Tobol, Ishim, and Irtysh rivers, which placed them in direct contact with Russian settlements in Siberia. The Russians were determined to maintain peaceful relations with the Kalmyks, since the Russian forces were thinly strung from the Baltic Sea to Siberia and the Kalmyks were not considered a serious or direct threat to Russian plans.[39] In fact, a group of Kalmyks in Nogai territory actually came under Russian rule during this period. Russia's primary interest was to have a pacified steppe, so the Russians watched, anxiously but quietly, as the Kalmyks began a systematic conquest of the Kazakh steppe in the last quarter of the seventeenth century.

The Kalmyk leader (*khungtaji*), Batur, attacked southern Kazakhstan in

1643; his forces were held there by the Kazakh khan Jangir (Esim's successor), but not before Batur had briefly controlled Semirech'e and the lands of the Great Horde. Before the Kalmyks could attack again, however, the Manchu dynasty came to power in Peking, which supported Khalka Mongol claims over the Western Mongols (including the Kalmyks of Jungaria). The Kalmyks became involved in fighting in the east, and so it wasn't until 1681, having in the interim been forced to recognize Manchu suzerainty, that they renewed their attempt to gain control of southern Kazakhstan. The Kazakhs, led by Jangir's son, Khan Tauke (reigned 1680–1718), were unable to protect their lands. From 1681 through 1685 Khungtaji Galdan (reigned 1671–1699) gradually took possession of almost all of southern Kazakhstan; he razed the cities (Sairam was completely destroyed) and controlled the caravan routes, effectively ending all trade through the area. Tsewang Rabtan (reigned 1699–1729) crossed the Sarysu River and with his troops simultaneously invaded the northeast region of the Middle Horde and surrounded Khan Tauke's headquarters near Turkestan. Representatives of all the Kazakh clans and tribes gathered in the Kara Kum Desert, so managing to hold out against the further expansion of the Jungar state until 1716, when Kazakh resistance faltered before a renewed Kalmyk offensive. The Kalmyks crossed the Ili River in that same year and reached the Ayaguz and Anysi rivers in 1718.

In 1716–1718 the Russians introduced a string of forts on the edge of the steppe, in southern Siberia. The construction of the so-called Orenburg fortified line was an expression of Russian concern with developments in the steppe, a concern which was heightened in 1723, when the Kalmyks crossed the Karatau to take control of the Talas valley. The Kazakhs were caught by surprise as they prepared to leave their winter campsites and fled, leaving most of their possessions and livestock. This attack began the *Aqtaban Shubirindi*, the Great Retreat.

During their subsequent campaign, 1723–1725, the Kalmyks quickly captured the Syr Darya River basin from Yasi to Tashkent, forcing the Kazakhs to flee from their ancestral pasturelands. The clans and tribes of the Great Horde migrated south into the disputed territory between Khiva and Bukhara. Most of the Middle and Small hordes, led by Khan Abu'l Khayr (reigned 1718–1749), migrated west and northwest toward the Russian-held lands along the Emba, Ural, Ilek, Or, and Ui rivers. The Kalmyks continued to absorb territory; in 1728 they took over the land around Lake Tengiz, so posing a direct threat to Chimkent in the south. They also took control over Lake Balkhash and the lands of the Small and Middle hordes in central Kazakhstan. It was now evident to the Russians that without some form of outside assitance the Kazakh steppe would be entirely overrun by the aggressive Kalmyks, thus threatening not only Russian expansion but Russia's position in southern Siberia as well. Therefore, where in 1716 and 1718 Peter I had declined to assist the Kazakhs, in 1730 Anna Ioannovna granted a request for assistance from Khan Abu'l Khayr. She sent a delegation to the steppe, where in 1731 Abu'l Khayr, with his sons and deputies, swore their loyalty to the Russian empress. This action marked the end of an independent Kazakh state.

The Kazakh khanate was a relatively short-lived and generally unsuccessful political institution. The Kazakh state was unable and ill-equipped to maintain a strong military presence in the steppe. The Kazakhs, though descendants of an indigenous warrior culture, were primarily pastoralists, more concerned with grazing than fighting; their military organization, predicated on temporary periods of service, was no match for the Kalmyk forces.

The Kazakhs did, however, hold their own against the rival Uzbeks—the Shaybanids and their Ashtarkhanid successors. The Kazakhs gained control of the Syr Darya cities and established a trading network that connected these cities with the steppe. Although they ruled the cities, they were not absorbed by them, and the Kazakhs emerged during the khanate as a distinct ethnic group. The end of the Kazakh khanate did not mark the end of the Kazakh people, however; instead, it introduced them to a life of conquest and colonial rule.

# 2 The Russian Conquest

## THE FIRST CONTACTS

The Russian conquest of the Kazakh Steppe occurred in two distinct phases. First, under Peter I and Anna Ioannovna, was the relatively bloodless acquisition of the northern part of the steppe, which was the territory of the Small and Middle hordes. This was followed by the military conquest of the Syr Darya region (the territory of the Great Horde) in the second quarter of the nineteenth century. The first phase of the conquest was the logical extension of Russia's interest in Siberia; that is, the pacification of the Kazakh Steppe helped secure the borders of southern Siberia and permitted the expansion of Russian trade with Central Asia. The second phase was directly related to Russian goals for conquest of Central Asia and the establishment of full-fledged colonial rule throughout the steppe and Turkestan regions.

The Russians traditionally sought to maintain trade with the East. This interest was part of what prompted Ivan IV's southeastward expansion in the sixteenth century. Following the Russian conquest of Kazan (1552) and Astrakhan (1554), even farther eastward expansion became tempting. The Stroganov family was given the right to exclusive control of trade with Kazakhstan, Central Asia, and points east; during the sixteenth and seventeenth centuries, however, they were preoccupied with the Siberian fur trade, and so the Kazakh Steppe was of relatively little importance. Still, the Russians gained some knowledge of the Kazakhs through the steppe travels of Herberstein (1517 and 1526), Danil Gubin (1534), Anthony Jenkinson (1557–1571), and Semen Moltsev (1569). A 1533 *ukase* (decree) records Kazakh traders at two posts established by Stroganov merchants,[1] and the sixteenth-century *Kniga Bol'shago*

*Chertazha* makes reference to the Kazakh hordes (Kazachei Ordy).[2] Russia's interest in the Kazakhs was briefly stirred in the last quarter of the sixteenth century, during Russia's campaign against Kuchum, Khan of Sibir'. Since Kuchum's enemies, the Kazakhs, seemed natural allies, in 1573 a mission headed by Tret'iak Chebutov (who was killed en route) was sent to Haq Nazar to try to enlist the Kazakhs to move openly against Kuchum. This proved unnecessary when Iermak, with a force of approximately five hundred cossacks and a few hundred men provided by Stroganov, defeated Kuchum Khan in 1580. The regular Russian forces then moved into the area and in 1587 founded the fortified town of Troitsk.

With the establishment of Troitsk, the Russians had only a minimal interest in the Kazakh Steppe to the south and were more interested in expanding east, toward the Pacific Ocean; they built several towns in western Siberia (Tyumen and Tobolsk date from this period). For their part, the Kazakhs now came to see the Russians as a possible source of assistance; in 1588 Khan Taulkel sent a deputation to Moscow, led by his relative Sultan Oraz Muhammad, who himself had been held in *amanat* (hostage) by the *voevoda* (governor) of Tobolsk from 1580 until 1588.[3] Oraz Muhammad stayed in Moscow for two years seeking arms from the Russians, but no precise terms of alliance were worked out. Another Kazakh overture came in March 1595, when Taulkel sent word to Moscow that the Kazakhs wished to recognize the authority of the Russian tsar; in May 1595 Tsar Fedor sent an emissary to the Kazakhs and Taulkel sent his son Murat to Moscow. Taulkel considered the terms of citizenship offered by the Russians too harsh, for they required that he maintain a state of enmity with both Kuchum Khan and Bukhara and that he surrender a son as hostage. Formal contact between the Kazakh and Russian authorities was then broken off. There is no record of direct relations between the Kazakh khanate and Russian tsar for nearly 100 years, until Tauke sent an ambassador to Russia in 1687. In those years Russia preferred to deal with the rival and stronger power in the steppe, the Oirat-Jungar tribal confederation.

Throughout the seventeenth century there was nonetheless some limited contact between the Russians and Kazakhs. The Russians were greatly expanding their presence in the Urals: the town of Yaitskii Gorodok (Uralsk) was founded in 1620; in 1645 Mikhail Gurev established Guryev (Gurev), also in the Yaik (later known as the Ural) River region; and the Yaik fortified line was built. Russia also conducted limited trade with Central Asia across the Kazakh Steppe. One caravan route went from Tobolsk to Central Asia across the Irtysh and lower Ishim rivers, along the Ulu Tau mountains to the Sarysu river to Turkestan, thence across the Syr Darya and across the Zeravshan river system to Bukhara. A second route went overland from Astrakhan to Ufa, across the upper Ural River (through Guryev) to the Irgiz and Talas rivers, thence along the Ala Tau mountains and on to Tashkent. Both routes were long (75 days from

Tobolsk to Bukhara) and trade was costly, since the caravans were subject to the periodic attacks of Kazakh tribesmen who would seize the goods and capture the Russians. In the last quarter of the seventeenth century these already difficult conditions of trade worsened to near impossibility when the rivalry between Kazakhs and Jungars for control of the steppe pastures intensified. Kazakh interest in Russia increased in this period as Tauke realized that Russia was his only potentially effective ally in the Kazakh fight against the Kalmyks of Jungaria; between 1680 and 1693 Tauke sent six separate emissaries to the Russians in Siberia, seeking protection for the Kazakhs.

During this same period, the late seventeenth and early eighteenth centuries, the Russian economy was expanding. The *Statistiko-finansovaia kartina v 1698–1700 godakh* shows that one result of this expansion was increased trade with both Kazakhs and Kalmyks.[4] However, pacification of the steppe was important less because of the potential of the Kazakhs as trading partners than as a necessary precondition for an expansion of Russian trade with Central Asia and with the markets of Persia and India. In 1695 a Moscow merchant, Semen Malenkii, was sent through the Kazakh Steppe to investigate how the expansion of Russian influence could best be achieved. Subsequently, in 1714–1716, the Bukholtz mission to Eastern Turkestan traveled along the Irtysh River. A second mission was led by Aleksandr Bekovich-Cherkasskii. He crossed the Caspian Sea with some 6,600 men and traveled on to Khiva. This alarmed the khan of Khiva, who, believing a mission of this size was a prelude to a Russian attack on his city, attacked Bekovich-Cherkasskii and caused the latter to retreat.

The Bukholtz mission was rather more successful and resulted in the creation of the Irtysh fortified line, begun in 1716 and completed in 1752; the line consisted of 11 fortresses, 33 redoubts, and 42 beacons. The first 3 fortresses—at Omsk (1717), Semipalatinsk (1718), and Ust-Kamenogorsk (1720)—were built by the Bukholtz expedition. The leaders of this expedition confirmed St. Petersburg's suspicion that the Kalmyks, who were rapidly increasing their control of the steppe, were less likely to support an expanded Russian military trading presence in the area than were the weaker Kazakhs, who, as they were pushed from their traditional pasturelands, were moving closer and closer to the Russian line of settlement along the Emba River.

The Kazakhs, particularly those of the Small Horde, became dependent upon Russian goodwill for the use of pasturelands along the Emba and Ural rivers. Abu'l Khayr believed that only with the support of Russia could the Kazakhs avoid losing the entire steppe to the Kalmyks. When in 1726 he failed to receive the governor of Astrakhan's permission to migrate within his territory, Abu'l Khayr sent an emissary to St. Petersburg asking permission for the Small Horde to migrate in the Ural region on territory controlled by both the Yaitskii cossacks and the Bashkirs. He offered in return to protect Russian interests in the territory of the Small Horde.

## THE SMALL HORDE AND THE
## UNIFICATION WITH RUSSIA

On September 8, 1730, Abu'l Khayr, khan of the Small Horde, sent a letter to Empress Anna Ioannovna requesting to become her subject by asking for citizenship (*poddanstvo*).[5] The letter, sent without the knowledge or support of the Kazakh people or the other leading sultans, was from one ruler to another, stating Abu'l Khayr's willingness to swear fealty to Anna Ioannovna. It was brought by messenger to Ufa, where it was presented to the voevoda, Brigadier Buturlin; he sent it on to St. Petersburg where it was debated by the College of Foreign Affairs. In early 1731, Anna Ioannovna offered Abu'l Khayr the same terms of citizenship that had previously been accepted by the Bashkir and Volga Kalmyks, who had pledged themselves to serve the empress, accepted that Russia was to specify their hunting grounds, and promised to provide safe passage for Russian caravans and merchants. This sworn offer, dated March 26, 1731, was brought to Abu'l Khayr by Aleksander Ivanovich Tevkelev (Mirza Kutlu Muhammad), a Muslim who served as Tatar translator for the College of Foreign Affairs; the accepting oath was sworn by Abu'l Khayr, his sons (Nur Ali and Er Ali) and his deputies, on October 10, 1731.

This agreement was mutually advantageous. To Abu'l Khayr it offered the possibility of improving his political position as well as of increasing economic stability, for the Kazakhs and their neighbors saw that Russia was the superior military force in the region.[6] Stability was crucial, for the economy of the Small Horde was in ruin. Abu'l Khayr, his followers, and their herds—some 100,000 households or 400,000 people (principally from the Baiulin, Jeti, and Alimulin clans)—had been driven from Turkestan, moving from the Syr Darya river region to pasturelands in the Ural and Tobol river regions. During this time many thousands of animals were killed. Abu'l Khayr also had a powerful rival for control of the Small Horde in the person of Sultan Qayip (Kaip); Anna Ioannovna was both aware of this rivalry and prepared to exploit it, for she knew that Abu'l Khayr (and his heirs) needed the stability provided by an alliance with Russia to remain in power.

For Russia's part, the treaties with Abu'l Khayr and those with the khans of the Middle Horde (Semeke in 1732, Ablai in 1740) gave added security to the fortified line along the Irtysh River. This enabled the Russians to think seriously about expanding commerce in the area; they did not, however, view these treaties as providing for the annexation of the steppe. Annexation was probably considered by Anna, and was definitely desired by Catherine, but was thought a project for a later time, when the internal situation of the hordes was more stable. The Small and Middle hordes, though considered to be under Russian protection, were not a part of the empire; all maps from the late eighteenth century show the Russian border north of the Ural and Mias rivers just south of Orsk and Troitsk over Omsk and thence along the Irtysh River to the Altai mountains. Kazakh merchants in the markets of Orenburg, Orsk, and Troitsk were charged the same tariff as other foreign merchants.

The Russians maintained a minimum of contact with the Kazakhs through the various khans, their sons, and deputies. Anna Ioannovna did not even try to collect the *yasak* (tribute) that Abu'l Khayr had agreed to pay in 1734; she was advised that the process of collection would be far more costly than the value of the tribute collected. Because the Russians did not believe that their alliance with Abu'l Khayr was stable, they used every formal meeting between representatives of the two powers as an occasion to renew the oath. In 1734 Anna Ioannovna's representative, I. K. Kirillov, told her that Abu'l Khayr's influence was not great within the Small Horde. He wrote: "[the Kazakhs] have a Khan in name only, for he has no power over them, for affirming himself in his khanic rule or for turning his subjects away from the *kungtaji* (leader) over to Russian power."[7]

In fact, Abu'l Khayr was not a particularly faithful servant of the empress; he periodically allowed himself to be courted by the Jungar rulers. There was also considerable resistance within Abu'l Khayr's own entourage to accepting Russian suzerainty. Nonetheless, Russia saw the alliance as sufficiently stable to permit expansion along the Irtysh; in 1734 Kirillov organized the Orenburg Expedition (known as the *Izvestnaia Ekspeditsiia*). This expedition received added support within the imperial circle when Abu'l Khayr's son, Sultan Er Ali, while on a mission to St. Petersburg in 1734, urged the creation of a Russian fortress and trading post at the confluence of the Or (a branch of the Tobol) and Ural rivers. Abu'l Khayr promised the safety of this town and reaffirmed his promise of safe conduct for the Russian convoys, in return for a guarantee that the dignity of the khan would be permanently settled on his family. The expedition, about 200 men, was ordered to explore the agriculture, mining, and trade opportunities of the region and to navigate the length of the Syr Darya to investigate the possibilities of an Aral Sea fleet. This latter charge, never undertaken, was based on a Russian misconception that the Syr Darya connected the Aral to the Caspian Sea.

When the mission reported favorable possibilities for an expanded Russian presence in the region, Kirillov was instructed to establish a fortified Russian trading center, Orenburg, at the mouth of the Ural River (this site later became Orsk when Orenburg was moved further west on the river). The foundation of the city was laid in August 1735, although work was not completed until 1737. While work was in progress, Kirillov, led by Kazakh guides, established a Russian caravan trade with Khiva, Bukhara, and Tashkent. Settlers moving to Orenburg were given free land, ten-year interest-free loans for the purchase of construction materials, and exemption from residence tax. Russian merchants who moved to the city were permitted three years of duty-free trade (1735–1738).

Kirillov died on April 14, 1737. On May 17, 1737, V. N. Tatishchev, a geographer who had made a reputation for himself as head of the Ural Mining Administration, was named head of what now was renamed the Orenburg Frontier Commission. Tatishchev was particularly interested in expanding trade with the Kazakhs, and he had a market and trading post built on their side of the Ural River. Although the charge to Kirillov had given the Kazakhs permission to build residences and mosques in Orenburg and to pasture their livestock in its environs, most Kazakhs, including Abu'l Khayr and his sons, were not willing to appear on such intimate terms with the Russians.[8] Tatishchev was soon forced to move his efforts from expanding trade to quelling the Bashkir revolt. Although Tatishchev attempted to play upon the traditional enmity between the two peoples to attract the Kazakhs to the Russian cause (for example, he offered Abu'l Khayr 60–100 rubles per Bashkir head in February 1738), Abu'l Khayr chose instead to side with the Bashkirs and launched an unsuccessful attack on Orenburg. The Kazakh-Bashkir alliance was difficult from the outset, however, since the two peoples were competing for the same Bashkir pastureland and Abu'l Khayr's support of the Bashkirs was strongly resisted by powerful leaders of both the Small and Middle hordes.[9] In June 1738 Abu'l Khayr, with his sons, deputies, and allied sultans of the Small and Middle hordes, met with Tatishchev in Orenburg to renew their oath of loyalty to the empress and to promise safe passage to the Russian caravans.

Improving the difficult conditions for trade was the main charge given to Tatishchev's successor, Prince V. A. Urussov, named commander of the Orenburg Expedition in June 1739. He sought to expand Russia's influence to the Middle Horde, and in 1740 he convinced Sultans Abu'l Muhammad and Ablai to swear loyalty to the empress. Urussov's most notable achievement was the expansion and strengthening of the fortified line between Orenburg and Troitsk. During his administration he was able to maintain relatively good relations with Abu'l Khayr and the majority of the Small Horde, although in 1740 Abu'l Khayr did attack the Volga Kalmyks who were also under Russian protection. In that same year Abu'l Khayr was attacked by the Jungars at the Russian fortress at Orsk, and he was forced to take refuge under Russian protection in Orenburg.

In 1742 Urussov was succeeded by I. I. Nepluiev, who moved the site of Orenburg to its present site. During his administration, the Orenburg fortified line was completed and the Uisk line (between the Irtysh and Ishim rivers) begun. He also presided over the formation of the Orenburg *guberniia* (province), with its capital as Orenburg.[10] However, Nepluiev was not particularly successful in dealing with the Kazakhs, and he fell into Abu'l Khayr's bad graces when Nepluiev refused to permit him to exchange his son, Khoja Ahmad (Khodzha Akhmet), held as hostage, for a less-favored illegitimate son. Probably more significant was Nepluiev's refusal to permit Abu'l Khayr to use Russian authority to bolster his own weakening position in the Small Horde. Abu'l Khayr, by now an old man, was faced with challenges from within, most particularly from Batir Janibek. In 1743–1744 the relations between the Kazakhs and the Russians were quite strained; the Kazakhs attacked, the Russians counterattacked, and trade through Orenburg was sharply reduced. During this period Abu'l Khayr contacted Nadir Shah of Persia and received permission to migrate in the northern regions of the Khivan khanate; he was also assured that Nur Ali would succeed to the throne in Khiva. In April 1744 Nepluiev was authorized to encourage a Kalmyk (from Jungaria) attack on the Kazakhs but, before an attack developed, relations between Nepluiev and the Kazakhs improved. Abu'l Khayr sent his son to St. Petersburg to swear fealty to the new tsar, Peter II, and returned some 30 Russian hostages as a sign of good faith.

The improved relations between Russians and Kazakhs was shortlived. In 1746 hostilities resumed, caused this time by the Kazakhs' unlawful crossing of the Ural River and Abu'l Khayr's successful winter attack on the Volga Kalmyks. Within that year, however, Abu'l Khayr and his supporters suffered several major reversals when their attack on the Volga Kalmyks led to defeat. The Kazakhs were caught by an early frost and were unable to return to their lands via the Caspian Sea, as they had the year before. They traveled north through the territory of the Ural cossacks and recrossed the Ural River. The cossacks attacked, with apparent Russian approval, and the Kazakhs sustained heavy losses. In mid-1747 Tevkelev was sent to the steppe to try to close the widening gulf between Abu'l Khayr and Nepluiev; an agreement was worked out in 1748 that exchanged Khoja Ahmad for Ayshuak (Aichuvak) on Abu'l Khayr's promise to stop attacking the Russians. However, even improved relations with Russia could not halt the erosion of Abu'l Khayr's power base. Sultan Batir Janibek (whose son Qayip became khan of Khiva in 1747 instead of Nur Ali) undercut Abu'l Khayr's position in the southern part of the Small Horde's territory and drove Abu'l Khayr into the territory of the Karakalpaks, who were under the protection of Sultan Barak of the Middle Horde. This resulted in open conflict between Abu'l Khayr and Barak. Barak's troops proved superior; in August 1748 Barak killed Abu'l Khayr.

## THE SUCCESSION OF NUR ALI:
## THE SMALL HORDE AND
## THE PUGACHEV REVOLT

Nur Ali Khan (reigned 1748–1786) was elected to succeed his father with the connivance of the Russians, who made it clear to the elders of the Small

Horde that he was their preferred candidate. His position was precarious from the start, since most of the clans from the southern territory of the horde were allied with Sultan Batir Janibek, who was in at least tacit alliance with the Kalmyks (from Jungaria) and who enjoyed the support of Khan Ablai of the Middle Horde. Nur Ali was unable to strengthen his personal power; Batir Janibek and his son Qayip retained control of their clans and territory, while thwarting Nur Ali's attempts to gain influence in Khiva. Nur Ali also failed to gain control of Sultan Barak's Middle Horde territories, although he did successfully plot to poison Barak in 1750.

Within a year of becoming khan, Nur Ali quarreled with the Russians over his request that 1,000 men be sent to build a monument at his father's gravesite along the Kodir River. Russia agreed to help construct a suitable memorial, but only if Abu'l Khayr's remains were moved to a site near Orenburg. Nur Ali resisted this, believing it was proof of Russia's plans to annex the steppe.[11] There is no evidence that a mausoleum for Abu'l Khayr was ever built. Nur Ali's fears are another demonstration that the Kazakhs saw their relationship with the Russians as an expedient alliance and resisted efforts to create any permanent union between the two peoples. Because of this quarrel, Nur Ali agreed to receive the Jungar khungtaji's envoy, who sought the betrothal of Nur Ali's sister in accord with an earlier agreement with Abu'l Khayr. The Jungar ruler tried to woo Nur Ali away from Russia by offering him control of Turkestan (the former Yasi city, holy to the Small Horde because it was the site of their ancestors' bones), in lieu of a kalym (bride-price). Accepting the offer would require a break with Russia, a step Nur Ali feared because of his own precarious position within the horde. Fortunately for Nur Ali, the sister died before the marriage could take place, but, in the absence of a strong ally, Nur Ali and his supporters were frequently attacked by Batir and Qayip. Although Russia refused Qayip's request to cut into Nur Ali's lucrative privilege as khan of controlling the movement of caravans in the territory of the Small Horde, Batir and Qayip still collected tribute from all caravans that crossed their ever-expanding territory, thus denying Nur Ali a substantial percentage of the income his father had enjoyed. Batir and Qayip attacked those Russian caravans in their territories that were driven by Nur Ali's supporters, and Nur Ali attacked those passing through disputed territories if they paid tribute to Batir. Naturally, Russian-Kazakh relations deteriorated to the point where Nepluiev, desperate to keep this internal chaos from bringing a complete halt to Russian trade across the steppe, ordered the border troops to begin reprisal raids against the Kazakhs. In 1755, however, when the Bashkirs called upon the Kazakhs (as well as on the Kazan Tatars) to join their fight against the Russians, Nepluiev tried to enlist Kazakh support by ending the reprisal raids and promising that the Kazakhs could keep the Bashkir women and children living among them (a long-standing point of contention between Nepluiev and Nur Ali). Nur Ali accepted

Nepluiev's terms, fearing that a Bashkir victory would simply be a prelude to a Bashkir takeover of the steppe.[12]

Improved relations between Russia and the Small Horde were soon threatened by the 1756 ukase (part of the Russian settlement with the Bashkirs), which banned the Kazakhs from crossing the Ural River and so using the rich pasturelands between the Ural and Volga rivers (the so-called Inner Side). This ban, which remained in effect until 1801, when the Inner or Bukei Horde was formed and granted permission to occupy these lands, created constant tension between Kazakhs and Russians. The Kazakhs periodically violated the ban, since denial of this much pasturage put increased strain on their already depleting pastureland.[13] In addition to provoking Russian reprisals, the Kazakhs faced reductions of their herds, which placed further strain on the already weakened economy of the Small Horde.

Yet another tension between the Kazakhs and Russians was the configuration created in the steppe by the defeat of the Jungars and the appearance of the Ch'ing empire. Initially, the Kazakhs (both Nur Ali and Ablai) supported the Jungars against the Ch'ing, but when Manchu victory seemed assured both the Small and Middle hordes received envoys from Peking. Ablai swore fealty to the Ch'ing emperor in return for pastureland in Jungaria. Nur Ali remained somewhat more aloof, accepting presents but refusing to become a Chinese subject. When the Chinese threatened Russian fortifications in southeast Siberia in 1758, Nur Ali was ordered to attack the Manchus. Happy with the balance he had achieved between his two powerful neighbors, Nur Ali managed to delay his attack until the Chinese threat had receded and so was able to remain on amicable terms with both. The Russians' relationship with the Kazakhs deteriorated again, however, when Nur Ali had difficulty dealing with Nepluiev's successor, Davydov. St. Petersburg, fearful that a further breakdown of Russo-Kazakh relations might be perceived by the Chinese as an invitation for expansion, ordered Davydov to apologize to Nur Ali for any perceived injustices, to increase the recipients of annual stipends in the Small Horde from one (Nur Ali) to three (his brothers, Er Ali and Ayshuak), and to build sheds and stables for the khans' herds. In return Nur Ali was to discourage the Small Horde from joining the Middle Horde in occupying territory such as Jungaria, which was part of the Ch'ing empire. Russia feared that such occupation would leave the Russian traders traveling the steppe wholly at the mercy of brigands and thieves.

The next serious conflict between Russia and the Kazakhs came in 1762, following Catherine's ascendancy, when Nur Ali sent deputations to both St. Petersburg and Peking. The latter delegation was so well received that Nur Ali believed he could take a more independent attitude toward Russia, and he resumed attacks on the Russian caravans. Catherine's own goals rather quickly became apparent; her Russia was interested in an expanded presence in the East. In the first decade of her reign, this interest took the form simply of extended trade, both with and through the steppe. Semipalatinsk was established as a major trading post, and attempts were made to improve Russia's relations with the Middle Horde. N. M. Rychkov was sent on a lengthy mission to explore the expansion of trade routes through the steppe. At first Catherine was most concerned with eclipsing Turkish power in the Crimean and Black Sea regions, but in the 1780s she addressed pacification of the steppe territory, for which she favored the settlement of the nomads.[14] As early as 1767 Catherine had issued a ukase that provided for the building of fixed residences for Nur Ali and Dos Ali (yet another brother).

One of the problems Catherine faced in seeking to strengthen Russia's ties with the Kazakhs was that the end of the 1760s was a relatively rare period of unity within Central Asia. The Afghans, fearing Chinese encroachment, sought to strengthen their ties with the Kazakhs and the other Central Asian peoples, arguing that all Muslim states should work in concert. Although the hold of Islam was weak, the ruling families of all the hordes identified themselves as Muslims and were receptive to requests for aid from their co-religionists.

For his part, Nur Ali was growing increasingly disenchanted with Catherine and suspicious of her motives in dealing with the Kazakhs. In 1765, 1766, and 1767 Russian forces were dispatched in retaliation for Nur Ali's attacks against the Volga Kalmyks. His sense of ill treatment increased in 1768, when a second son died in hostage in Orenburg; Nur Ali feared, not without reason, that a conspiracy between Russia and his own brothers would prevent his son, Ishim, from succeeding him. Relations between Nur Ali and the Russian authorities improved briefly in 1771, when they permitted the Kazakhs to attack and attempt to drive back the Torguts (Volga Kalmyks), who were fleeing across the steppe to Chinese territory. After enjoying mixed success in the attack, however, the Kazakhs were soon at odds with the Russians again over the use of the abandoned Kalmyk land. Their claim to the Inner Side was once again rejected in favor of Bashkir claimants.

It was into this atmosphere of Kazakh-Russian hostility that, in 1773, the news of Pugachev's uprising filtered.[15] It is difficult to assess the involvement of the Kazakhs in the uprising, just as it is difficult to establish a direct link between the Pugachev forces and those of the Small and Middle hordes. Throughout the first year of the revolt (1773–1774), fighting was focused in territory adjacent to that of the Small Horde; the Kazakhs clearly took advantage of the Russian preoccupation with Pugachev, particularly during the siege of Orenburg in 1774, to attack Russian settlements and to graze freely on the pastures of the Inner Side. Archival materials show further that Dos Ali's son, Seid Ali, sent 200 armed men as a sort of amanat to serve with Pugachev, while Nur Ali allowed 400 Russian rebel fighters protection in his territory.[16] Whether the Kazakhs saw Pugachev as anything more than a convenient instrument in the service of their own demands, however, remains in question.

One Kazakh, N. E. Bekmakhanova, has argued that unrest in the Small Horde occurred in four stages and unrest in the Middle Horde in three phases. She believes that in the first phase of Kazakh rebellion, from September 1773 to March 1774, Pugachev served as a catalyst for the Kazakhs, inciting popular resistance against the Russians while inciting competing factions within the Small Horde as well. In the second phase, from March to late autumn, 1774 (which corresponds to Pugachev's siege on Orenburg), the Kazakh resistance to Russia took on a mass character. In the third phase, late 1774 to September 1775, the uprising within the Small Horde continued, despite the defeat of Pugachev. By this time the rebellion had taken on a life of its own; the Kazakh masses, perhaps seeing the potential benefits of violence, were not to be stopped until their grievances were met or a superior force encountered. Finally, from September 1775 to February 1776, the Small Horde was beset by internal division; Nur Ali's opponents were being led by an unidentified warrior, whose exploits are recorded in Kazakh folk history as tales of the Invisible Man.[17]

One difficulty in evaluating the relationship between Nur Ali and Pugachev is the nature of source materials for the period. The Pugachev rebellion, today and for most of the Soviet period, has been regarded as a positive phenomenon, a peasant uprising. Characterizing Kazakh involvement in the uprising has been more problematic: understood as assistance to a peasant revolt, Kazakh participation is considered good, but when resistance is understood as anticolonial and hence anti-Russian (as it has been since the late 1940s), it is bad. Even in the earlier years of Soviet rule, when it was considered good (the best example being Viatkin's 1941 history, which championed Kazakh anti-Russian resistance as progressive), the extent of actual Kazakh participation in the revolt has been difficult to ascertain.[18] One explanation may be that Nur Ali himself appears to have played a waiting game, reluctant to commit himself wholeheartedly to Pugachev until the latter proved himself able to prevail against the tsar's forces. Pugachev must have recognized the Kazakhs as both ally and potential rival for control of the Inner Side pasturelands. Although he promised land in return for Kazakh assistance, Pugachev also insisted upon using amanat to ensure the loyalty of the Kazakhs he recruited.

Nur Ali seems to have sided openly with Pugachev until after the latter's unsuccessful siege of Orenburg (October 1773), in which a few thousand Kazakh troops reportedly participated.[19] However, once Pugachev and his forces were routed from Orenburg, Nur Ali agreed to work with the Russians in seeking Pugachev's defeat, although his offers to lead patrols against Pugachev were refused. Not all of the Small Horde turned against the rebels; Sultan Dos Ali, who headed the Kazakh clans living closest to the Ural line, remained a supporter of Pugachev until his defeat.[20] A good deal of spontaneous support also came from the Kazakhs of the Bersh, Serkesh, Tama, Tabyn, Jagabail, and Baibakt clans, all of whom were interested in gaining Inner Side pastures. Kazakh attacks on Russian fortifications continued throughout 1774 and 1775.

By late 1775, however, it became clear that the Kazakhs would not gain access to land on the Inner Side. When the administrative districts were redefined, the Simbirsk (later renamed Ulyanovsk) and Ufa districts containing these pastures were placed under the control of Orenburg, and the lands were awarded to Russian cossacks in an effort to relieve some of the Russian land hunger that had provoked the Pugachev uprising in the first place. Further restrictions against Kazakh use of this land were enacted in 1782. Kazakh dissatisfaction over the repeated denial of the Inner Side lands and their anger at Russian treatment of them in general contributed to the disturbances of 1775 and 1776, when resistance was directed as much against Nur Ali, by now seen as a Russian lackey, as it was against the Russians themselves. By late 1775 the Kazakh resistance began to take on a more organized quality. For example, in the uprising of the so-called Invisible Man, nearly 2,000 armed Kazakhs from the Tabyn, Tama, Shekty, Shomekei, and Baibakt clans attacked the Russian and Bashkir lines on the outer side of the Ural River. Dos Ali was unable to quell the rebellion and so was forced to appeal to Nur Ali and Sirim Batir (Srym Datov; a rebel leader in the Small Horde). Ishim, Nur Ali's son, was sent to oppose the rebels, but he was unsuccessful. Russian forces were summoned; in February 1775 two detachments, 300 cossacks and 500 Bashkir, were dispatched. Fighting continued until summer 1776, when the rebellious clans moved en masse to pasturelands in the south.[21]

The Pugachev uprising, and the subsequent fighting within the Small Horde, gave ample evidence to Catherine of the disintegration of the khan's authority and of the personal weakness of Nur Ali Khan. Catherine was thus forced to pose the question of Russian rule of the Small Horde, if the steppe were to be pacified and the safety of Russian trade to be assured. The Pugachev uprising taught Nur Ali and the Kazakh leadership generally the painful lesson that Russia was a colonial empire whose first concern was protecting the interests of the Russian population; when the interests of the Kazakhs and Russians conflicted, as they did in the joint claims on abandoned Kalmyk pasturelands, the interests of the Russians would predominate. In addition, the Small Horde's failure to gain use of the pasturage further compounded the Kazakh economic problems, increasing demand on existing pastureland and placing even greater burdens on the diminishing powers of Nur Ali. Popular unrest and violent disturbances within the Small Horde became more common until, in the final decades of the eighteenth century, fighting within the horde became a constant.

## THE CONQUEST OF
## THE MIDDLE HORDE

After Abu'l Khayr had sworn his loyalty to the empress in 1731, Tevkelev, at Anna Ioannovna's direction, sent an emissary to Khan Semeke of the Middle Horde to offer him suzerainty under the same terms. The Middle Horde, which consisted of something less than 500,000 people (110,000 households), occupied the territory of what became the provinces of Semipalatinsk, Akmolinsk (later Tselinograd), and parts of the Syr Darya and Semirech'e regions. Semeke (like Abu'l Khayr a son of Tauke), who always had problems of control in the Middle Horde, swore allegiance to Russia in an attempt to minimize the external threats to his role posed by Ural cossacks and Bashkirs in the northwest and by Kalmyks in the southeast. Semeke probably viewed his alliance with Russia as simply expedient, since in 1733 he attacked the Bashkirs, Russian subjects with whom he had sworn to live in peace. Following his second unsuccessful campaign against the Bashkirs, Semeke sent a formal apology to Anna Ioannovna and agreed to receive patents of investiture as khan of the Middle Horde. When Kirillov arrived with the patent in 1734, however, he discovered that Semeke had been dead for over a year.

Semeke was succeeded as khan by his son, Abu'l Muhammad, who shared power with Sultan Ablai for two decades, until he was eclipsed. Abu'l Muhammad resisted the initial approaches of the Russians, choosing instead to cooperate with the Jungar Kalmyks, who gave him the freedom to attack the Bashkirs. In 1740, though, probably because of the re-emergence of a strong and hostile Jungar confederation, both Abu'l Muhammad and Ablai went to Orenburg with their deputies to kneel on the golden tissue, kiss the Koran, and swear fealty before Prince Urussov. The leaders of the Middle Horde promised safe conduct to the Russian caravans and agreed to reduce their attacks on the Volga Kalmyks, who were subjects of the tsarina. In return, Ablai, clearly the dominant Kazakh in the negotiations, demanded a higher rate than that being paid Abu'l Khayr's guides who led Russian caravans across his territory; Ablai also urged the Russians to exploit the trading potential of Semipalatinsk, sparing the Middle Horde the need of their month-long animal drive to reach Orenburg. The role of Semipalatinsk was expanded in the 1780s to become the capital of the western Siberian province, the territory of the Middle Horde.

In 1741, shortly after Abu'l Muhammad and Ablai swore loyalty to the Russian tsarina, the territory of the Middle Horde (as well as part of that of the Small Horde) was attacked by Galdan Chereng, khungtaji of the Jungars. Ablai was taken prisoner, and a Russian mission to arrange his release failed; Ablai was freed only after Abu'l Muhammad agreed to send a son as amanat to the Jungars. Once this was done, the Kalmyk forces pulled back. From this time forth Ablai maintained good relations with the Jungars and with their successors, the Ch'ing dynasty. This alliance served as a successful buffer for the internal rivalries that Ablai faced, posed by Barak of the Middle Horde and Abu'l Khayr of the Small Horde. Abu'l Muhammad accepted control of Turkestan from the Jungars, retiring there in 1744 with his khanate retinue and leaving much of the day-to-day management of the horde to Ablai, who lived with his retinue and associated clans close to the Russian fortified line near Semipalatinsk. By 1750, after the death of Barak (who was poisoned on the orders of Nur Ali), Ablai emerged as the pre-eminent figure in the Middle Horde (although not elected Sultan until 1771) and the most powerful Kazakh in the steppe.

Placing Ablai and his deeds in proper historical perspective is difficult. The ideological nature of Soviet historiography has further confused what little literature about him exists. The only contemporary accounts came from the travels of Captain Andreev and G. Volkonskii, who lived among the Middle Horde in the last quarter of the eighteenth century; Ablai is also discussed by both Veliaminsky-Zvernov and Levshin.[22] Still, it is difficult to estimate his power because his independent, probably anti-Russian stance made him a puzzling figure to Russian and Soviet historians. Although his precise genealogy is lost, it is likely that he was a direct descendant of Khan Shigai; it is certainly clear that he styled himself a great Kazakh khan in the tradition of Tauke or even Qasim. He was the last independent Kazakh khan, deriving his power solely from his people without dependence on Russian investiture to shore up his power base. In fact, he was wary of the Russians and their goals in the steppe, and so he tried to keep his people only loosely allied with the Russian state but on good terms with their Asian neighbors. Within the horde, Ablai enhanced the power of the khan at the expense of that of the biis and elders; thus, the heads of rival clans opposed him, but none ever became a serious rival.

In his lifetime and throughout the nineteenth century, Ablai inspired the Kazakh people in resisting the transformation of their economy and lifestyle by Russian colonial policy. Descent from Ablai gave authority to a grandson, Kenisary Qasimov (Khan Kene), who led a revolt against the Russians in the 1830s and 1840s. Ablai came to occupy a prominent place in Kazakh oral literature, as recorded by the poets of his day.[23] Yet, because he championed an independent (or more independent) Kazakh state, the Soviets have vilified him regularly, and his noble origins meant that his exploits were ignored in the late 1940s, when Kazakh historians revised other popular but nonaristocratic figures. Even in the immediate prerevolutionary period most Kazakh secular nationalists refused to glorify Ablai; he represented the aristocratic tradition, which they considered dangerously antiquated and antithetical to the interests of a modern, secular Kazakh state.

Whatever else he was, or failed to be, Ablai was assuredly an astute politician, generally able to emerge on the winning side. An example is the tenuous equilibrium he maintained among the Russians, Kalmyks, and Manchus in the 1750s and 1760s. At first, in 1756, Ablai asked refuge and support from the aggressive Kalmyks. He then briefly gave Davatsii, the Kalmyk pretender, protection in the Kazakh Steppe, but turned him out as soon as it became clear that the Chinese would conquer Jungaria. Ablai became so openly pro-Chinese that in 1757 he received an offer of Chinese citizenship, which it seems he refused, although the documents on the question are contradictory. Ablai did, however, travel to the Chinese ambassador in Semipalatinsk and offer a son as amanat.[24] Chinese sources claim that Ablai did become a tributory prince, which Russian sources deny.[25] Ablai unquestionably did pay a tribute to the Manchu emperor, Kien Lung, for a number of years, and he sided with the Chinese in their dispute with the Afghans. He also sent some of his clans to graze the abandoned pasturage in Jungaria, on land now in eastern Semirech'e, while he himself continued to graze close to the Russian line and periodically attacked the border settlements. Ablai's close ties with China enabled him to be bold with the Russian border authorities, although he told them that his submission to China had been involuntary. Ablai called himself khan as early as 1760 but refused Russian suggestions that he be formally invested in Orenburg, leave a son there as amanat, and receive an annual pension in exchange for his support.

Catherine, displeased with the special relationship that Ablai enjoyed with the Chinese, sought to bring him closer to the Russians. In 1762 the Russians built Ablai a palace and small village opposite the fort at Petropavlovsk, but Ablai, concerned both for his independence and his reputation within the horde, declined to occupy these structures; however, in this period (1761–1764) he did accept an annual allowance of 212 poods of grain from the empress. In 1764 he also agreed to receive a Russian delegation of ten farmers sent by Catherine to teach the Kazakhs how to farm. At this time there was serious debate over the issue of settlement of the nomads, since Catherine had been convinced that the nomadism of the Kazakhs would continue to deter trade across the steppe. There was already some limited Kazakh agriculture developing in both the Small and Middle hordes among the populations contiguous to the Russian line. Russia's embroilment in the Seven Years' War, however, prevented much attention from being paid to further pacification of the Kazakhs, although a mission led by Ia. Bouver was sent to the steppe to study the problem. Bouver concluded that the presence of the Russian fortified line had made traditional pasturelands inaccessible and had thus created additional economic hardships; Bouver recommended that precise areas of migration be marked out for every sultan, with a homestead and animal stalls established for each. He also proposed that the Tatars be invited to spread Islam among the Kazakhs and to establish Russian-Tatar schools in the steppe. Preoccupied with the Pugachev uprising and the expansion of Russian influence in the Crimea, Catherine set aside Bouver's recommendations, and little was done during her lifetime despite the bleak realities of the Kazakh economy that Bouver described, which gave ample motivation for Ablai's interest in the rich pasturelands of Jungaria and his consequent support of the Manchus. Only when the Middle Horde had fully occupied these pasturelands did Ablai begin to shun contact with the Ch'ings and to seek to improve his relations with Russia. In 1775 some chiefs of the Middle Horde, including Ablai's son and heir, Vali, approached the Russians for a grant of pensions. Catherine refused, demanding the loyalty of Ablai as a prerequisite. Ablai's main argument with Catherine at the time was her refusal to invest him as khan after he had formally assumed the title in 1771, at a ceremony in the city of Turkestan following the death of Abu'l Muhammad. Ablai was recognized as khan by the ruler in Jungaria, but Catherine denied him the honor, maintaining that it was she who must be approached with a request for the dignity of khan; she claimed that since Semeke's oath of fealty in 1732 the dignity of khan rested with St. Petersburg and not with the Kazakhs themselves. The Pugachev revolt intervened; although the Middle Horde was less involved than the Small Horde, Ablai's sympathies were clearly with the rebels, whom he assisted to a limited degree. Ablai did not approach Catherine again to request the dignity of Khan until 1777. It was not until October 22, 1778, less than three years before his death, that Ablai was offered a diploma, naming him as khan, and a pelisse, saber, and cap. Ever stubborn, Ablai refused to travel to a Russian post to swear his oath; a Russian officer had to be dispatched to Ablai's camp to confer the title. Ablai never claimed the remaining signs of office from the Russian fortress at Petropavlovsk, because he still feared insulting the Chinese. He also antagonized the Russians by attacking the Kirgiz and by refusing to return Russian captives of the horde. Catherine never completely came to terms with Ablai, who died in 1781 at the age of 70 and was buried in the city of Turkestan.

Toward the end of Ablai's life his power was already being challenged within the Middle Horde, in which, as within the Small Horde, the Pugachev uprising provoked a struggle for lands. Following his death, the unity that Ablai had achieved dissolved quickly. His son, Vali, nominally succeeded him as khan but only ruled over the northernmost clans of the Horde, and this only with Russian protection. The Naimans elected their own chief, Abu'l Ghazi, who ruled with the support of the Chinese; after his death, Khan Khoja (Barak's son) took control of this part of the horde. The southernmost part of the Middle Horde was absorbed by the Great Horde, which was also under Chinese control. The Russians thus controlled only about one quarter of Ablai's former territory. Throughout the 1780s a relative tranquility was maintained in the lands of the Middle Horde, in striking contrast to the situation in the Small Horde. Vali remained on relatively good terms with both the Small Horde and the Great Horde clans on which he bordered. In 1793 the Russians sent a detachment, led by General Strandman, to seek the release of captured Turkmen held by Vali. In 1794–1795 Vali countered by sending his son to offer submission to the Chinese emperor; at the same time, however, part of Vali's following broke with him and petitioned to be accepted as Russian subjects. Fearful of driving Vali irreconcilably to the Chinese, Russia declined to accept them.

Even so, by the end of the century Khan Vali had dispersed most of the power base established by his father, and the part of the Middle Horde under his control was riven with internal rivalry. In 1798 Russia, recognizing that the authority of the khan of the Middle Horde was largely honorific, established a tribunal at Petropavlovsk composed of both Russians and Kazakhs to settle disputes among the Kazakhs. This was Russia's first real attempt to administer the territory of the Middle Horde. It was, however, half-hearted. The Kazakhs chose not to bring disputes to the tribunal and thus it had no real function; the tribunal did not even hear cases until 1806, when Vali migrated briefly into Chinese territory. In 1816 Emperor Alexander nominated Bukei (son of Barak) to govern the Middle Horde jointly with Vali. Vali died in 1817, Bukei in 1818; with them the title of khan of the Middle Horde ended, for Russia had recognized that a more systematic form of administration had to be substituted for that of khanate rule.

## THE BREAKUP OF THE SMALL HORDE

Study of the final decades of the Small Horde, from the late 1770s until the formal end of the khans' rule in 1824, is complicated by Soviet historiography. The most recent editions of the official history of Kazakhstan suggest that this period was chaotic, with a number of unpopular localized revolts against the authority of the khan.[26] A more accurate view is probably that offered by M. Viatkin in his 1941 study of Kazakh history; Viatkin argues that the history of Russo-Kazakh relations from 1735–1869 was one of continuous popular opposition to Russian rule.[27] According to this argument, the great uprisings of the period—by Sirim Batir (Small Horde, 1780s and 1790s), Isatai Taiman uli (Inner Horde, 1830s and 1840s), and Kenisary Qasimov and Sadyk (Middle Horde, 1840s–1860s)—were all related. Each rebellion fueled the next, all caused by strong anti-Russian feeling among the Kazakhs, who saw the Russians as the cause of their deteriorating economic situation.

More recent accounts conflict with Viatkin. The present rulers of the Soviet Union require that Russian conquest and colonial rule be depicted as both beneficial and voluntarily acceded to. The national minorities in the Soviet Union are meant to recognize the superiority of the Russian tradition and the inevitability of the Russians' leading role in a multiethnic state government. Thus, Russian control of the Kazakhs is described as positive, not as a conquest at all but as unification of the Kazakhs with the Russian state or as the voluntary submission of the Kazakhs to Russian rule.[28] We know, however, from some prerevolutionary histories as well as from several Soviet studies, that Kazakh submission to Russian rule, particularly from the 1780s on, was anything but voluntary.[29] The leaders of the great Kazakh revolts, such as Sirim Batir and

Kenisary Qasimov, were extremely popular figures who commanded great devotion both during their lives and afterward, when localized opposition continued in their names and for their cause.

In fact, it could be argued that the only Kazakhs who voluntarily submitted to the Russians were the khans themselves. In the early years the khans needed the Russians to stave off the greater threat of the Jungars and, in the final decades, to lend legitimacy to their deteriorating authority. The irony was that, as memory of the Aqtaban Shubirindi dimmed, the authority of the khans declined largely because of their alliance with Russia. Some popular leaders, particularly Sirim, opposed the institution of the khan, which they saw as corrupt and incapable of exerting independent authority. Later, Kenisary sought to strengthen the khan's rule as an entity independent of any ties with Russia. Kenisary believed the steppe was Kazakh, to be ruled by the Kazakhs in their own traditional ways.

Certainly in the years following the Pugachev revolt the institution of khan in the Small Horde (as exercised by Nur Ali) no longer had any real power. Kazakh participation in Pugachev's revolt and the subsequent disorder in the steppe convinced Catherine and her advisers that the Kazakhs should not be left to govern themselves; the steppe would then be in no way secure for expanding Russian trade. The attempts at limited Russian government introduced by Catherine, as well as the subsequent reforms of Michael Speransky, were however both ineffectual. Neither produced a stable civil administration while both increased Kazakh wrath, proving correct those critics within the hordes who claimed that Russian intentions were to prevent Kazakh independence.

To the Kazakhs, the land question remained paramount. From 1775 to 1782 the Russian governor generalships of Simbirsk and Ufa barred the Kazakhs—under the jurisdiction of the Orenburg Frontier Commission—from using Russian-controlled land on the Inner Side. The Kazakhs continued and even increased the number of illegal crossings of the Ural River, further antagonizing the Russian authorities and clashing with the Ural cossacks who had been awarded this land. From 1782 until 1801 the Russians permitted Nur Ali and his family to cross the Ural River and pasture their animals on the Inner Side, but this did little to solve the land problem while further increasing tensions within the Small Horde; it justified the charges by Nur Ali's rivals that his alliance with Russia was solely to promote his personal interests. Nur Ali's crossings also encouraged numerous other Kazakhs, whole auls and clans, to make illegal crossings of the Ural, which angered the Ural cossacks. The winter of 1782–1783 brought widespread fighting in the westernmost part of the Middle Horde and on the Inner Side, first between Kazakhs and cossacks and then among the Kazakhs themselves. This was the revolt of Sirim Batir, who commanded some 6,000 fighters, 2,700 under his direct control. Nur Ali was requested by the Russians to put down this revolt, which also threatened his own power, since Sirim rejected both a Russian presence and Nur Ali as their agent. Sirim was supported by Nur Ali's major rival, Sultan Abu'l Ghazi, son of Qayip, who controlled the lands to the south of Nur Ali. Soviet historians Viatkin and Asfendiarov in particular have tried to cast this revolt as a peasant uprising against feudal Kazakh rule, but this seems an overstatement; Sirim's primary goal was to obtain more land for the increasingly impoverished Kazakhs who lived along the line of Russian settlement.[30] Although he certainly hoped to bring down Nur Ali, whom he regarded as greedy, Sirim showed no preference for a democratic form of government. Instead, he advocated only the end of the domination of clanic and tribal authority enjoyed by the white bone, the alleged descendants of Chingis Khan. Division of authority within Kazakh society became an increasingly important issue throughout the colonial period as the Russians tried to enlist the Kazakh aristocracy in the service of their own monarchy.

By the autumn of 1784 Nur Ali saw that Sirim posed a far greater and more immediate threat to his rule than did Qayip or any of his sons. He requested military assistance from the Russians. Two detachments, some 1,500 cossacks, were dispatched from Orenburg. They fought against the rebels throughout the winter of 1784–1785; a temporary stalemate was achieved when Sirim and his supporters fled south, from Russian territory to the area between the Aral Sea and the Syr Darya River. The widespread nature of the uprising led to the conviction expressed most forcefully by Baron Igel'strom, governor general of Orenburg, that Sirim Batir's revolt threatened not only the authority of Khan Nur Ali but also the stability of Russian control in the steppe. Igel'strom argued that the Kazakhs in their present mood should be considered enemies of Russia. The Kazakh threat to Nur Ali was clear. A meeting of 20 of the 25 leading Kazakh elders was held in the winter of 1785, at which time they disclaimed Nur Ali as their khan. The assembly did not agree on a successor.

Catherine was convinced that some degree of additional Russian control was required both to restore and to maintain order. In 1786 a ukase was issued that remained in effect until the promulgation of the Speransky reforms. This order to the governor generals of Simbirsk and Ufa, dated November 27, 1784, noted that Nur Ali had lost the confidence of his people and had served Russia poorly. The proclamation urged that Nur Ali be goaded into more loyal service, on pain of denial of refuge to him and his family. It also urged investigation of the background and attitudes of Qayip, to see if he would be a fitting replacement as khan. Implementation of the first two paragraphs, however, created the greatest changes. The second paragraph called for the creation of frontier courts in the steppe to try disputes between Kazakhs and Russians; these courts remained in effect until 1799. The first paragraph called for the introduction into Kazakh territory of mosques, religious schools, and caravansarais, to be organized by the Muslim clergy of Kazan. Since Christian missionaries clearly had not succeeded, it was hoped that Islam would serve as a civilizing force for the wild and unpredictable Kazakhs. Ironically, Islam had the opposite effect. By the middle of the nineteenth century it served as a new and more potent focus of anti-Russian sentiment.

Igel'strom himself, with the encouragement of Catherine, proposed a more extensive administrative reform that was meant to supplement Catherine's 1784 decree. Known as the Igel'strom Reform of 1787, it called for the abolition of the khanate and for division of the Small Horde into three sections (western, central, and southern), each to be administered by an elective administrative council of elders and a frontier court composed of Kazakhs and Russians. This idea was strongly opposed in the steppe by the family of Abu'l Khayr (Nur Ali, his brothers and sons) and by the family of Qayip, who hoped to supplant Abu'l Khayr's descendants. Khan Vali also opposed the reform, since he feared it would serve as a precedent for the introduction of Russian rule in the Middle Horde. The reform was, however, strongly supported by Sirim, who was pleased by Igel'strom's sweetener: 4,500 Kazakh families would be permitted to graze on the Inner Side, protected from cossacks by the Russian authorities. In the end the strongest opponent of the reform was Catherine, who had been made fearful of any form of popular rule by the French Revolution and who chose to side with the monarchs, as she termed Nur Ali and his family.[31]

The Igel'strom Reform was nominally in effect from 1787 to 1790, but many of the most important clans never participated in the elections or in the selection of representatives. It was therefore judged a failure, although 1787 showed a marked decrease in the unrest in the steppe. The explanation is probably that given by Pallas, a member of a geographical expedition in the steppe in the 1770s and 1780s, who wrote that, "It is my judgement that the Kirghiz hordes can have no internal structure."[32] Certainly during the period that Pallas was traveling among them the Kazakhs showed little evidence of being able to regulate their own disputes. The khanate system had proven ineffective, since no one had emerged in the families of Abu'l Khayr or Qayip who was able to lead the Kazakh people in this period of economic crisis. Similarly, the assembled tribal elders, who sought to strip both of these aristocratic families of their accumulated power, lacked consensus on solutions to the Kazakhs' problems or lacked influence to implement them. The leading figure of the day, Sirim Batir, was by his own description a fighter and had no claim to the title or authority of khan. Sirim argued for rule by the assembled elders, but even his prestige could not make them into an efficient or effective body.

Furthermore, Sirim's own interest in serving the Russian empire and his support of the Igel'strom reforms weakened during the Russo-Turkish war, when envoys from the emir of Bukhara appealed to him as a Muslim to support Turkey's cause. Sirim, like the other Kazakhs of his day, was far from a devout or even a practicing member of the faith, but like most Kazakhs he considered himself to be Muslim and was attentive to calls for the unity of the faithful. Some contemporary sources report, too, that such calls were accompanied by promises of material reward.[33] Although Sirim was in contact with the emir of Bukhara, no major anti-Russian effort was mounted in Central Asia; instead, 1788 and 1789 saw increasing factional rivalry as the boards of elders remained incapable of achieving effective control.

Igel'strom's experiment was abandoned in 1790, when Nur Ali died in exile in Ufa. Igel'strom was recalled to show support for Er Ali (Nur Ali's brother) and for the restoration of the khanate, with which his replacement, Governor General A. A. Peutlink, was charged. Er Ali's receipt of the patent of office on September 4, 1791, provoked renewed warfare among those Kazakhs who opposed his rule. Sirim called a meeting of elders in late 1791, at which time war against Russia was declared with the support of Shir Ghazi (from the family of Qayip). Shir Ghazi denounced Er Ali, arguing that no Muslim could legitimately serve a Christian ruler, although Shir Ghazi himself had previously shown strong interest in having his brother, Abu'l Ghazi, receive the dignity of khan from Catherine. In 1792 the uprising spread throughout the Small Horde, according to some reports, threatening the very existence of Russian rule; Sirim was attacking Russian settlements as well as those of Kazakhs supporting Er Ali. In September 1792 Sirim launched an unsuccessful attack against the town of Iletsk (later called Novo-Iletsk), after which his resistance became more partisan-like. On the death of Er Ali in the summer of 1794, however, Nur Ali's son Ishim declared himself the rightful khan. Sirim then countered with an attack on Ishim's aul. Ishim, long a personal enemy of Sirim, did not have his uncle's stature in the horde. The Russians remained neutral, refusing to back Ishim even after the tribal elders elected him khan in 1795. He finally received the dignity of khan in 1796, when he had proven to the satisfaction of the new Russian governor, General S. K. Vizamitinov, that he had some basis of support. Ishim was unable to institutionalize his own rule, however, and was unable to provide his tribesmen with enough land, partly because of the severe ice storms of 1795–1796 that sharply reduced the amount of available pasturage. Vizamitinov allowed additional auls to graze on the western bank of the Ural River, but this was not sufficient; Sirim and his supporters also launched numerous reprisal raids on Ishim's auls to capture much-needed livestock. Sirim's supporters increased; by early 1797 he had some 1,000 fighters under his direct control. This made him even more confident; he again attacked the aul of Ishim and this time killed the khan.

The next dignity of khan was initially denied to the family of Abu'l Khayr. Igel'strom was sent to Orenburg to replace Vizamitinov, and the 1787 reforms, modified, were reintroduced. The elected council of elders was now to be led by an elected president. Russia's candidate was Sultan Ayshuak, yet another of Abu'l Khayr's sons, but when the council was convened in August 1797 it quickly chose Sirim to head the assembly. This was unacceptable to Igel'strom, who had despaired of working with Sirim; on October 16, 1797, Sultan Ayshuak was elected khan by a hastily called meeting of Kazakh elders. He was presented with the dignity of khan by Emperor Paul I two weeks later.

Khan Ayshuak was never an effective ruler. He had been chosen by the Russians and had no real support among the Kazakhs themselves. The favored candidate of the sultans was Karatai Nur Ali uli (known to the Russians as Karatai Nuraliev), an illegitimate son of Nur Ali whom the Russians rejected because of his illegitimacy and, more important, his close association with Sirim. Ayshuak's son, Jhan-Tore, was also a candidate and maintained his own faction, as did Abu'l Ghazi, who ruled the southern part of the horde. The threat of Sirim Batir, however, soon faded. Sirim fled to Khiva at the end of 1797, where he continued for the next year or two to launch raids against the cossacks and the Bashkirs of the Inner Side. Although there is no precise account of Sirim's death, it is generally accepted that he was killed in 1798 or 1799. Even with this threat removed, Ayshuak could not muster any effective authority; he was a very old man at the time of his election, and Shir Ghazi, followed by Abu'l Ghazi (son of the earlier Abu'l Ghazi), challenged his position. Abu'l Ghazi became ruler of the Karakalpaks and attacked Ayshuak's clans and tribes. The Russians responded to the increasing disorder by placing the Kazakhs under Russian civil law in 1799, but with few exceptions Kazakhs were brought before the courts only when they were accused of crimes against Russians—that is, on the infrequent occasions when the Kazakh offender was caught.

The constant problem was that the Kazakhs simply did not have enough land on which to graze their animals. The average herd size was dropping and individuals without livestock had no alternative means by which to survive, since agriculture was both unappealing and relatively unknown. The poorest households did adopt a primitive form of farming, but only as last resort. Even when the Russians granted more Kazakh households the right to graze on the western side of the Ural River in 1797, there was still not enough pasture.

One recognition of the plight of the Kazakhs was the formal organization of the Inner or Bukei Horde, created by Paul on March 11, 1801. This ukase permitted some 7,500 Kazakh families under the leadership of Sultan Bukei, Nur Ali's son, to take control of the Naryn Peski region of the Ural-Volga region. These families were given permission to reside in the area, not simply to cross the river annually as had previously been the case. Bukei was independent of the Astrakhan and Orenburg governors but had to levy a cart tax of 50 kopeks per cart annually, for which in 1814 he was awarded householder status.[34] There are also some reports that he may have collected the *za'akat* (livestock tax) as well. After 1817 the aging Bukei ruled jointly with Khan Jangir, who succeeded to sole rule after Bukei's death in 1823. Initially, at least, the Bukei Horde provided relief for its members, or a little over 10 percent of the Small Horde;

these households flourished, with the number of animals increasing seven or eight-fold in twenty years and the number of households increasing to over ten thousand by 1825. Khanskaia Stavka, the seat of the khan, emerged as a major trading center in the steppe. As the number of animals increased and the families grew or were joined by relatives from the Small Horde, the pressure on the strictly defined amount of land grew; there was some migration back to the Small Horde in the late 1820s as well as, once again, increased internal disorder.

For the vast majority of the Small Horde, the formation of the Bukei Horde left the situation unchanged, and war within the horde increased substantially in the early years of the nineteenth century. The published archives of the Orenburg governor general for this period are full of dismayed accounts of the unrest around him. Barymtas (punitive raids) between rival clans became almost daily occurrences. In 1803 a meeting was held at a trading post near Orenburg, attended by most of the competing factions, which resulted in the unanimous decision to promote peace in the steppe and to halt the growing rift between the black and white bone (that is, between the clanic elders and the aristocracy). However, Sultan Karatai refused to attend the meeting and would not be bound by its decision. Instead, he continued to fight Ayshuak by attacking the auls of his supporters. Ayshuak rarely went far from the Russian lines; he was forced to abdicate in 1805. He was succeeded by his son, Khan Jhan-Tore. With the abdication of Ayshuak, Governor General Volkonskii in Orenburg recognized that the Russians had to take strong independent action to assert their own authority in the steppe; thus, on May 10, 1805, he issued a declaration to the Kazakh sultans, elders, and biis stating what would be considered acceptable conduct from that time forth. He urged sultans and elders to assume some control to prevent the high incidence of civil disorder, on the threat that the Russians would end the institution of khan along with the powers and privileges that the ruling family enjoyed. It was clear to the Russians, through their representatives in Orenburg, that a more formal civil administration was imperative if trade through Orenburg were not to be constantly disrupted.

Even the limited institution of the frontier court was constantly floundering on problems peculiar to governing the Kazakhs. This can be seen in a report from the Orenburg military governor Volkonskii to the state council on foreign affairs, about the refusal of the Kazakhs to obey the Russian injunction against selling their children into slavery in the Khivan markets. The Kazakhs argued that the children being sold were not Kazakhs but the children of captured Karakalpaks, Turkmen, and so forth—hence not Russian subjects and not protected by Russian law. The Kazakhs emerge in the report as either astute students of legal technicality or confirmed traders determined to avoid Russian control. The issue of slave trade was particularly thorny for the Russians, since the Kazakhs found the capture and sale of other peoples (as well as the children of Kazakhs in disfavor) to be highly profitable.

The Russians were still not willing to create a complete civil administration in the steppe, however. They knew that this would incite the full opposition of the Kazakhs, a price they were not yet ready to pay. Instead, they tried to placate the opposition to their favorite, Khan Jhan-Tore; on May 31, 1806, Tsar Alexander I created the institution of the khan's council to aid and advise the khan in the governing of the horde. This council, made up of the principal elders chosen by their tribes, was given a ten-point charge that included accompanying the khan, assuming the responsibility for trial and punishment within the horde, reducing internal enmity, and preventing attacks against the Russian border or Russian caravans.

Although this council placated many of Jhan-Tore's opponents, it did nothing to calm Karatai, who by now had launched an all-out war against the khan. In 1807 the elders acknowledged the weak position that Jhan-Tore maintained, even with Russian support, and so petitioned the tsar to have Karatai named khan. This petition was refused; instead, a punitive expedition was sent out against Karatai. This only goaded him to increase his attacks on the Russians and on Jhan-Tore. His opposition grew in strength and popularity until he succeeded in killing Jhan-Tore in 1809.

These were very difficult years for the Kazakhs. The land problem was growing ever more acute, as is suggested by the drop in the number of animals sold in Orenburg.[35] The Russians made a few token gestures, such as providing free seed, granting loans for implements and construction materials, exempting Kazakhs near the Russian defensive line from taxation, and permitting some Kazakhs to graze among the Cossacks. Such measures were not only insufficient, however, but were also countered by constant seizure of land for the strengthening of the Russian defensive line throughout the period 1811–1850. Seizure began in 1811 when the expansion of the Iletskii line took all the land between the Ilek and Ural rivers. This sharply reduced the amount of Inner Side land available for Kazakh grazing. The Kazakhs were also being pushed by both Khiva and Kokand, each of which was headed by an expansionist ruler during the first decades of the nineteenth century.

Even Karatai faded temporarily as a threat to Russia. The 1809 punitive raid against him and his followers was so harsh that there was real decline in support—or great fear to show support. Karatai himself fled to Khiva, where he was welcomed by the Khivan khan Muhammad Rahim, who saw an alliance with Karatai as a way to bring the Small Horde under the control of the Khivan khanate. In an attempt to promote order within the steppe, the Kazakhs were governed by the khan's council without a khan for just over two years. In 1812, however, the Russians felt that old angers had sufficiently died down to permit the renewed dignity of khan, which was awarded to Shir Ghazi, another of Ayshuak's sons; at the same time, Bukei was given the title of khan of the Inner Horde. Shir Ghazi was never a powerful figure. Meier, the nineteenth-century Russian historian, describes him as "cowardly, sly and closed-mouth; as the head of the party he had no significance at all. His power spread no further than the Russian outposts and the *baigush* [hired hands] who migrated there obeyed him only out of necessity."[36] Karatai returned to the steppe and led the opposition to Shir Ghazi until he emerged as his chief rival. In 1812 and 1814 punitive expeditions of Ural cossacks were sent against him. Volkonskii finally accepted the strength of Karatai's position and in 1814 held unsuccessful negotiations with him. A tentative accord was ultimately reached with Karatai by Volkonskii's successor, P. K. Essen. From then on, Karatai directed his efforts against Aryn Ghazi (Abu'l Ghazi's son and heir) and did not attack the Russians, who in turn pardoned him for the murder of Jhan-Tore. Essen tried to have Karatai made khan in 1818, but the ministry of foreign affairs would not consent. Although Karatai never achieved his dream of becoming khan, the Russians awarded him the position of sultan-administrator of the western part of the Small Horde at the time of the abolition of the dignity of khan in 1824.

In 1815 Aryn Ghazi inherited the position of head of the Shekty clan (located in the lower Syr Darya region), making him one of the most powerful individuals in the Small Horde. He sought an alliance with the Russians to protect his land against the aggression of Khiva. He reached an accord with Essen, as well as with Shir Ghazi, and promised the safe passage of Russian trade caravans through the steppe. Described as an honorable individual and a devout Muslim, his influence in the steppe grew; the Kazakh elders urged that he be made khan in 1817 and again in 1819.[37] Essen endorsed this request but it was turned down by the Asiatic department of the foreign affairs ministry, who argued that it would go against Russian colonial interests.

In this same period (1816–1820), Shir Ghazi was growing increasingly weak and corrupt; as a consequence, Khivan expansion along the Syr Darya went unchecked. For their part, the Khivans were advancing the candidacy of one Sultan Manenbai, nephew of Abu'l Ghazi, as leader of the Kazakhs. The Kazakhs did not accept his leadership, but in 1820 Aryn Ghazi, who headed the Kazakh opposition, was defeated by the combined armies of Manenbai and his Khivan detachments. This defeat substantially weakened Aryn Ghazi's position and led to growing discontent with his role in St. Petersburg. This discontent grew into opposition when Aryn Ghazi forcefully protested Negri's 1820 expedition to Bukhara. Negri, despairing of safe conduct, took with him 235 men and 2 guns, which Aryn Ghazi took as a violation of his authority. This assertion was rejected by Essen; Aryn Ghazi was called to St. Petersburg where he was stripped of his titles in 1821. He was sent to exile in Kaluga, where he died in 1833. Meanwhile, in the absence of any effective authority, Kazakh or

Russian, Muhammad Rahim was quickly able to gain control of the lower Syr Darya; in 1822 the entire Shekty tribe was absorbed into the Khivan khanate.

Shir Ghazi continued to hold the dignity of khan until his death in 1824, but he had no real power. Russia had suffered serious reverses in the years of his rule, first because of internal opponents of the khan, then because of the more serious threat to Russia's authority mounted by Khiva and the threat of increasing Kokand control of the Great Horde. The decisionmakers in St. Petersburg realized that if Russia did not assume greater administrative control over the Kazakhs, the future of Russian trade and expansion in Central Asia would be threatened. Shir Ghazi's disastrous rule, coupled with the inability of any other individual after the death of Ablai to exert control over the Middle Horde, made it clear that the institution of khan was moribund. In 1824 the title was formally abolished.

# THE KAZAKHS
# IN IMPERIAL
# RUSSIA

## PART TWO

# 3 The Development of a Colonial Apparatus

## INTRODUCTION

By the beginning of the nineteenth century, Russian administrators were confronted with the problems of the Kazakh Steppe. The internal rule of the khans had all but disintegrated. As Levshin describes it, Kazakh self-government was nothing more than an "anarchic combination of despotism with freedom for every individual."[1] Much of the day-to-day control of the steppe had devolved to the local clanic authorities who lacked effective judicial mechanisms and so resorted to such traditional institutions as barymtas (punitive raids) and the extractions of kuns (blood prices) for the regulation of conflict. Furthermore, entire areas of the steppe were in revolt against khanate rule. Opposition was greatest in the Small Horde, where the memory of Sirim Batir remained alive. Anti-Russian feeling was also exacerbated when Aryn Ghazi was taken hostage. Tolshan Tilenshi, an elder of the Tabyn tribe, organized opposition to the Russians after more land along the Iletskii line was seized.

The Tabyn clansmen were joined by fighters from the Argyn, Adai, Kete, and Ozhrai clans, all of whom had lost winter pasturelands to Russian policy. Raids against the Russian fortifications increased until the summer of 1823, when a punitive detachment was sent out from Orenburg.

By 1820 the problem of administering the steppe took on new importance, since Russian trade interests in the area had increased. The nascent Russian industries required markets; because of the relatively low quality of the goods they produced, Asian markets were potentially more lucrative than European ones. Trading caravans to Persia, China, India, and the Central Asian khanates had to pass through the Kazakh territories, but their safety could not be guaranteed and the frontier garrisons at Orenburg and Omsk lacked sufficient manpower or authority to safeguard passage.

A new form of administration was introduced in the steppe to resolve some of these problems. In 1824 a major modification of the khans' rule (along the lines outlined by Igel'strom in 1787) was introduced in the Small Horde. In the Middle Horde, khanate rule was abolished entirely; the region became known as the territory of the Siberian Kirgiz and was included as part of western Siberia in the Speransky reforms of 1822. These changes did not prove sufficient. Internal disorder, although initially somewhat abated, continued and spread, culminating in the large followings achieved by Kenisary Qasimov in the Middle Horde and Iset Kutebar uli in the Small Horde. At the same time the Russians grew ever more concerned about safeguarding their trading interests in Central Asia and western China. To this end they annexed the territory of the Great Horde, at that time under the rule of the khan of Kokand, and finally in the 1860s acquired control of the khanate of Kokand itself. After these conquests it became obvious that some sort of full-scale civil and military colonial apparatus had to be introduced. The Steppe Commission was formed in 1865 and its report, considerably amended, became the basis of the *Statute on the Administration of Turkestan* (including the *Provisional Statute on the Administration of the Semirech'e and Syr Darya Oblasts*) (1867), and the *Provisional Statute on the Administration of the Turgai, Akmolinsk, Uralsk, and Semipalatinsk Oblasts* (1868; called the Steppe Statute).

## THE SPERANSKY REFORMS
## AND ADMINISTRATIVE CHANGES
## IN THE SMALL HORDE

On June 22, 1822, the *Rules on the Siberian Kirghiz* came into effect. This legislation, which applied only to the Kazakhs of the Middle Horde (who were ruled from Omsk and not from Orenburg), was the product of the eminent Russian statesman, Michael M. Speransky. Speransky, then general governor of Siberia, devised a wholly new administrative structure for Siberia that extended the civil administration of western Siberia to include the Kazakhs of the Middle Horde. Until that time these Kazakhs had governed themselves, save for periodic mediating efforts by the Omsk frontier commission. The new reforms, however, divided the eastern portion of the Kazakh territory into territorial units, each with its own administration.

The smallest administrative unit was the clan or aul (*rodovaia uprava*), which consisted of 50–70 carts (approximately 15 families) and was headed by an elder chosen by the community. This unit was to be ethnically homogeneous as was the region, the *volost* (*inorodnaia uprava*), which was to consist of 10–12 auls and be administered by a sultan or member of the aristocracy chosen by the elders. At this time the territory of the Siberian Kirgiz was divided into 87 volosts spread between 4 *okrugs* (districts). Three okrugs were added by 1834. Each okrug was administered by a *prikaz*, a committee chaired by an elder, generally a sultan, and including two Russian representatives sent by the authorities in Orenburg and two elected Kazakh representatives, all of whom served two-year terms.[2] The okrug prikaz was expected to have both police and court functions, and the local cossacks were charged with policing the okrug.

No specific recommendation regarding the judiciary was included in the Speransky legislation, however. Speransky himself was much impressed with the thoroughness and suitability of the adat (the Kazakh customary law) for the adjudication of disputes not only of the Kazakhs but for all nomadic populations. He established a project for the codification of the adat, known as the *Code of Laws for the Steppe* and completed in 1841. Speransky was not able to get this code formally enacted into law, although some copies of the draft made their way into the hands of Russian officials who used it in making judicial decisions. No systematic codex was introduced until the 1860s. In 1842, however, a temporary committee was established to examine the problem of the Kazakh legal system, and in 1843 it reported that the adat was well suited to the adjudication of most civil disputes. Military courts were established to try criminal cases and by 1852 all cases involving murder, robbery, or barymta were to be tried before them. On May 19, 1854, when these courts were given responsibility for virtually all criminal cases, Russian law was extended to the Siberian Kirgiz.[3]

It was Speransky's hope that the Kazakhs could be induced to become farmers, for which several incentives were incorporated in the 1822 reform. Every Kazakh was given the right to receive free a fifteen *desiatin* (40-acre) plot, which would be his own private property, as well as free seed and implements with which to farm. As a further inducement, Kazakh elders who took up farming were awarded 30 desiatins and Kazakh sultans 40 desiatins of land. At the same time some restrictions were placed on the migration of the Kazakhs; each okrug and each volost (and later each aul) was assigned defined borders that could not be crossed by the migrating Kazakhs without the permission of local authorities. Such administrative restrictions did little to encourage the Kazakhs to become farmers, but they did greatly increase disorder in the steppe; illegal migration between volosts and okrugs, and even between the territories of the Small and Middle hordes, became quite common.[4] The main task of the Russian administration was to allocate pastureland to the populations under its rule. Local officials were also charged with maintenance of the free flow of trade, assuring the safety of caravans and traders alike. Russian traders were given the right to duty-free trade in the steppe and Kazakh traders to duty-free trade in the rest of the empire.

The cost of the local administration was borne by the Kazakhs themselves. A yearly yasak (tribute) of one animal per hundred owned, though suspended from 1822 to 1827, remained in effect until 1837. After that date the Kazakhs were subject to a yearly cart (or in this case household) tax of one ruble, fifty kopeks. The money collected was used to pay the salaries of all officials and their staffs from the aul through the okrug level.

The 1822 reforms recognized the special position of the Kazakh aristocracy while greatly undercutting its power. The Kazakh sultans could continue to use their titles, but they were not recognized as part of the nobility of the empire unless through service they were appointed to it. They could not own serfs but could own land; one-fifth to one-seventh of the Kazakh pastureland was reserved for the sultanic families.

The sultans were further charged with the maintenance of the clergy, mosques, and religious schools. The rights of Muslim clergy were not yet restricted; Baron Meiendorf had convinced the ministry of foreign affairs that the clergy was a positive influence. Still, the clergy could construct mosques only with the permission of the okrug administration.[5]

The change in administration in the Middle Horde came in 1824. It followed the failure of a special commission (consisting of seven elected officials, the khan, three mullahs, and three sultans) to strengthen the authority of the Khan. Shir Ghazi was then requested by the Russians to go to Orenburg and relinquish the dignities of his office. To substitute for the role of khan, the Orenburg governor general proposed a reform of administration to the Asiatic Committee that called for the development of a three-tiered system consisting of aul, clan, and regional administrations. Simultaneously, General Essen entered into negotiations with the three most powerful Kazakh leaders: Karatai Nur Ali uli, Temir Er Ali uli, and Juma Kudai Mendi uli. Each agreed to head a regional administration with the title sultan-administrator. Karatai Nur Ali uli, who styled himself khan, headed the western region, which included all Kazakh lands west of the Ilek River but east of the Aral Sea. Temir Er Ali uli (Er Ali's son) was sultan-administrator for the central region of the horde, east to the upper course of the Toguzak and Tobol rivers. The eastern section was headed by Juma Kudai Meni uli, a nephew of Qayip. His territory extended to the junction of the Kala and Syr Darya rivers and to the border with Bukhara; he, too, assumed the title of khan. Each sultan-administrator received a house and monthly stipend of 150 rubles in exchange for keeping order and supervising the collection of any taxes and duties due the Russian government.

In the western and central regions the office of sultan-administrator remained in the hands of the family of Abu'l Khayr. In the southern region the family of Qayip dominated, although a descendant of Ablai served as sultan-administrator for six years in the 1830s.[6] Over time, however, authority of the office was taken by the local, or black bone, leadership. E. Schuyler, an

American who traveled through Central Asia in the mid-nineteenth century, described the sultan-administrators as "mere Russian creatures entirely destitute of culture . . . themselves inclined to revolt at times, and neither they nor the annual military expeditions from Orenburg could maintain order in the Steppe."[7]

In an attempt to stabilize the civil order, several administrative adaptations were introduced. In 1831 each territorial subsection of the Small Horde was divided into *distantsii*, or range districts—8 in the western, 20 in the central, and 28 in the eastern regions. Subdivisions of the steppe continued until, by the mid-nineteenth century, there were 54 such divisions, the commanders of which were chosen by the local population and approved by Orenburg.[8]

On June 14, 1844, the *Statute of the Administration of the Orenburg Kirghiz* dissolved the Orenburg Frontier Commission and created the Orenburg governor generalship in its stead.[9] This was one more attempt to save the native-dominated administrative structure. The Orenburg Kirgiz (that is, the Kazakh Small Horde) were placed under the authority of the Asiatic department of the ministry of foreign affairs as well as of the Orenburg military commander, each body to function both jointly and individually. The change was intended to eliminate what had previously been an ambiguous chain of command, since the frontier officials in Orenburg had never been firmly integrated into the state bureaucracy. When there were dedicated administrators, this freedom gave effective administration of the Kazakhs, but when the local official in Orenburg was either ineffective or malevolent, the situation was almost uncontrollable. The new structure still left a great deal of administrative discretion in the hands of the governor general, but it did introduce a greater sense of accountability as well.

The general administration of the Small Horde was to be the responsibility of the Orenburg border commission, consisting of a chairman, his assistant, four Russian advisers, and four elected Kazakh representatives who were subject to Russian approval. To strengthen the authority of the sultan-administrators, they were given a detachment of 100–200 cossacks (under Russian command) to assure the maintenance of order. The work of the sultan-administrators was regularized; each was to have an assistant, a scribe, and a staff of five messengers, all of whom were salaried officials. A formal court system was established wherein all criminal offenders were brought before military courts and all civil offenders were brought before Kazakh courts of customary law. In 1837 the ministry of foreign affairs authorized the collection of a cart or household tax of one ruble fifty kopeks per annum. This tax was to support the legal and judicial apparatus as well as pay for a Kazakh school to be established by the Orenburg border commission.

In 1845, upon the death of Khan Jangir, a slightly modified version of this system was introduced in the Inner Horde. The dignity of khan expired with

Jangir's death and therefore a provisional council was established, headed by his brother, Adil Bukei uli. The council consisted of three other members: two sultans (Shuke Nur Ali Khan uli and Bukei Khan uli) and an official from the ministry of state property. At the same time, the territory of the Inner Horde was subdivided and a system of clan commanders introduced. By 1853 each commander had gained a seat on the provisional council; by 1858 they numbered 24 members, the majority of them sultans and of whom half were from the house of Bukei.

Thus, these reforms begun in the 1820s in the Small and Middle hordes ended the dignities of the khans while leaving the sultan and white bone aristocracy in control of the new civil authority. Neither the sultans themselves nor the administrative apparatus that had been introduced were capable of administering the Kazakh population; rather than being the period of stability and order that the officials in St. Petersburg had envisioned, the four decades following the introduction of the Speransky reforms were a time of increased disorder and disarray in the steppe. As Maksheev', a contemporary Russian observer in the steppe, concluded about the reforms of this period: "All these profound measures did not subjugate the Kirghiz but only increased their anger. With the sultan-administrators as with Abu'l Khayr one hundred years before, the Kirghiz fought between themselves, launched *barymtas* and attacked the settlements along the line."[10]

Finally, in 1858, Ignatiev was sent on a special mission to the steppe.[11] He reported to the Orenburg governor general and the chairman of the Orenburg border commission that bribery, extortion, and violence against the Kazakh population were a direct result of the weakness and corruption of the sultan-administrators.[12] Ignatiev's report was widely circulated in St. Petersburg and ultimately helped prompt the appointment of the special commission in 1863 to study a new form of administration for the Kazakh Steppe and for the newly acquired regions of Turkestan.

## CIVIL DISORDER IN THE STEPPE

The first important organized resistance of the early nineteenth century came not in the newly reorganized territories of the Small and Middle hordes but in the Inner Horde, where an increasing population on a restricted amount of land forced a rapidly deteriorating economy. The land available to the horde was further restricted by what Soviet historians have termed the excessive demands of Jangir's feudal ruling family, who controlled about eight percent of the 6.5 million desiatins of available land.[13] Whether Jangir was malicious or repressive would be difficult for a Western analyst to determine; certainly he was a ruler out of touch with the conditions of the population that he governed, raised as he was outside of the steppe among Russians, and not a livestock breeder himself. Upon assuming the title of khan in 1824, Jangir moved to Khanskaia Stavka, had himself built a wooden house in the Russian style, and turned his efforts to making Khanskaia Stavka into a livable, Russian-style settlement and trading post rather than to solutions for the worsening economic plight of his subjects.

The deterioration of the economic situation was hastened by the unusually severe winter of 1826–1827 and its aftermath, when many Kazakhs whose herds survived the winter had their animals seized by the Russians when they drove their herds westward into Saratov guberniia in search of grazing land. A group of more than 1,800 Kazakh families led by Sultan Qayip Ali (son of Ishim) tried to cross the Ural River and settle on the eastern bank in the land of the Small Horde. Qayip Ali had already made two unsuccessful attempts to cross the Ural River in 1818 and 1826–1827. In 1827–1828, however, he and his forces persisted after the initial skirmishes, and troops from the Russian garrison were sent to drive these Kazakhs back across the river. After a siege of several weeks, the Kazakhs were defeated. Most were driven back across the river; Qayip Ali fled to Khiva, where he was given asylum by the khan. Nearly 200 fighters were arrested and tried in the Russian frontier courts.

The ferocity of the Kazakh resistance worried the governor general in Orenburg; he dispatched A. Geins, chairman of the frontier commission, to investigate the situation within the Inner Horde. Geins concluded that most of the problems were of the Kazakhs' own making, caused by rivalries between the various branches of the white bone. As a remedy he suggested introducing territorial, rather than clanic, divisions, as had been done in the Middle Horde. He did however admit that there were severe economic difficulties in the Inner Horde, caused by the shortage of available pasturage. This shortage, he noted, was heightened by Russians taking advantage of the Kazakhs when they rented land to them. Geins recommended that the Russian government purchase the land that the Kazakhs were renting and turn it over to them on a rent-free basis. The request was refused, although some limited land belonging to the Ural cossacks was transferred over to the Kazakhs; this was not enough to defuse the situation. In 1829 another group of Kazakhs tried to cross the Ural River and were again countered only by armed force.[14]

For the next several years a relative stalemate held in the Inner Horde, since the presence of Russian forces east of the Urals and the absence of any strong Kazakh leader within the Inner Horde reduced the level of hostilities. Yet the economic crisis worsened as the number of animals held by the horde dropped and the population of the territory continued to increase. Worse still, the tax burden on the individual remained the same. Each household was charged with paying za'akat (religious tax) to the khan (generally one-fortieth of family livestock holdings annually) as well as their share of the aul tax to the Russians, which in the 1830s amounted to a total of some 400 horses and 2,400 rams annually. Many households were forced to sell off a part of their herd to meet their tax obligations. This only increased anti-Russian feelings. Many opposed the khan as well because he permitted taxation by the infidel. Finally, in 1836, popular discontent became so great that localized resistance overtook most of the Naryn Peski region.

The most prominent figure in this opposition was Isatai Taiman uli, an elder of the Bersh clan and a member of the black bone or local clanic leadership. Isatai, a proponent of local self-rule, had long struggled against the khan of the Inner Horde, for which he had been arrested in 1817 and 1823. He and his aide and chronicler, the noted akyn (poet) Muhammad Utemis uli (Makhambet Utemisov), organized opposition among their own Bersh clan and then picked up support from most of the other clans of the horde. The goal of this opposition, which Isatai termed a *gazavat* (holy war), was to free the people of Naryn Peski from both the khan and the Russians.[15] The rebels received direct assistance from the Khivan khan, who armed and dispatched troops commanded by Qayip Ali. Isatai also got help from Sultan Shin Ali Orman uli, the former sultan-administrator of the western section of the Small Horde. The movement grew almost unchecked throughout the remainder of 1836 and most of 1837. The rebels even succeeded in routing a detachment of 300 Ural cossacks sent by Orenburg. Finally, in July 1838 a new, strengthened detachment of Russian soldiers and Ural cossacks was sent in that broke up the resistance (at this time about 2,000 fighters) and killed Isatai Taiman uli. Although the uprising was crushed, Russian authorities were reluctant to continue their support of the khan of the Inner Horde. In 1840–1841 a temporary commission met to consider abolishing the dignity of khan in the Inner Horde but resolved to continue it only until the end of Jangir's rule. Upon his death in 1845 the dignity of khan was replaced by a provisional council.

During this same period, 1836–1837, there were several minor uprisings in the Small Horde. In 1837 the garrison at Orenburg dispatched three small detachments into Small Horde territory: one to punish the Kazakhs who lived along the Irgiz River for attacking Russian caravans; another to end Kazakh attacks on Russian interests along the Caspian Sea; and a third, including 300 Ural cossacks, to punish the Adai tribesmen in the Taisuigan Desert for their attacks on Fort Aleksandrovsk (present-day Shevchenko).

The greatest challenge to Russian authority, however, was the revolt of Kenisary Qasimov in the Middle Horde. The revolt itself lasted from 1837 until 1846 and was the culmination of nearly fifteen years of localized opposition by Qasim and his family. Qasim was the son of Ablai and was generally recognized in the Middle Horde as likely heir to Vali. Upon Vali's death, however, the dignity of khan was abolished. Qasim and his son Sarzhan both opposed the new administrative structure and led periodic skirmishes against the Russian authorities. Support of their opposition was fueled by the continually deteriorating economic situation in the Middle Horde. The traditional grazing lands of the horde, already considerably reduced, were being exhausted, and the Russian authorities refused to award additional lands to the Kazakhs. This, as well as the increased tax burden and the fact that Russian merchants were often taking advantage of Kazakhs in the newly established markets, hardened the popular attitude against the Russians.[16]

Discontent was transformed into violence when in 1825 Sarzhan Qasimov attacked cossack detachments sent to stabilize the internal situation of the Middle Horde. His opposition to Russian rule continued to gain support; at one point in 1826 his ranks numbered some 1,000 armed men. The pattern of his rebellion resembled that of Tolshan Tilenshi: periodic forays against both the Russians and those Kazakhs who supported the new administrative order. Because the warriors primarily sought new land, the uprising had only a quasi-political character. Russian efforts to put down the resistance were finally successful in late 1827 and Sarzhan fled to Kokand. He remained there until late 1830, when he launched a guerrilla-like campaign against the "loyalist" Kazakh auls. He was again defeated in 1834. From then until the end of his life in 1836 he fought Kokand expansion into the Kazakh steppe and died in battle in Tashkent.

After Sarzhan's death the leadership of the house of Qasim was assumed by his half-brother Kenisary Qasimov, a leader of great initiative and vision who is regarded by many Kazakhs today as the first Kazakh nationalist. Kenisary was born in 1802 in the Kokchetav region. As the self-styled heir of his grandfather, Khan Ablai, Kenisary believed that only he could unite the Kazakh people to withstand the twofold threat they faced: absorption by the Russians and defeat at the hands of the Kokand. Kenisary wrote the following in a letter to a supporter at the time of his campaign against the Russians:

> The Russians come from the North, Kokand from the South.
> Having established fortifications, they trample us,
> From whom would we have both this squeezing and this crowding
> We the children of the Kazakhs,
> What would be if we had unity?
> Until now we have been split
> Because we have no unity.[17]

Kenisary strove to make himself a popular leader, enlisting the aid of his entire family—brothers, half-brothers, uncles, and cousins. The claims of modern Soviet historians notwithstanding, Kenisary was able to achieve mass support; his movement marks the last occasion when the horde functioned as a unit, with all clans of the horde and all sectors of the society resisting the Russians. Most of the recent Soviet historians of Kazakhstan vilify Kenisary for leading a "feudal-monarchical movement," and they claim that the Kazakh masses resisted him with force.[18] This position is unsupported. As Bekmakhanov showed in his lengthy 1947 study of Kenisary (for which he was attacked in *Pravda* in 1950; the work was thus revised in 1957), the movement was a popular one, supported by the whole of the Middle Horde.[19] There seems little doubt that Kenisary was in fact a popular hero among the Kazakhs, loved in his lifetime and revered after his death. His life and exploits were the subjects of numerous poems and songs, and he was praised by all the leading akyns of his day, including Dos Khoja, Nysambai, and the blind Hassan. Even Jambul, the much-celebrated people's akyn of the Soviet period, wrote a now-suppressed tribute to Kenisary. The Kazakhs today are rediscovering him as well, most notably through the recent novel by Il'ias Esenberlin.[20] Although it is clear that Kenisary was popular, it is difficult to assess the reasons for his success. Kenisary was able to surmount tribal antagonisms, but it is not known whether his support represented a new Kazakh political consciousness or simply a more apolitical expression of discontent with Russian rule and its concomitant economic dislocation.

Kenisary began his opposition to the Russians in 1837. At the height of his movement he had over 20,000 fighters under his command. Kenisary and his supporters were fighting to restore the power of the Kazakh khanate and to vindicate the memory of Khan Ablai, in whose name they often went to battle. The Kazakhs of the Middle Horde had accepted Russian protection largely as a military expedient; they were pressed between stronger powers to the east and to the south. The khans of the horde valued their independence and had tried to remain as distant as possible from their new protector. The Russians had gradually strengthened the economic tie with the Middle Horde and so understood the Speransky reforms of 1822 as a natural extension of the earlier relationship. The family of Qasim and their supporters did not share this understanding. They had been denied the dignity of khan and supplanted by what they regarded as an unlawful and corrupt form of government that operated contrary to the interest of the Kazakh people.

In 1838 Kenisary sent five lieutenants with a letter of protest to Prince Gorchakov, Governor General of West Siberia. In this letter he argued that the rule of the Kazakhs should be returned to the Kazakhs themselves and the institution of the khan restored. He maintained that the new political administration was corrupt and was merely an excuse for the cossacks to exploit the Kazakhs; he cited as proof many cases of unlawful slaughter of Kazakh livestock and the imprisonment of innocent Kazakhs by the local militia.[21]

The Russians turned down Kenisary's requests and redoubled their efforts to defeat him, since his resistance had all but destroyed Russian trade with the

Middle Horde and had disrupted all trade across its territory. It has been estimated that Kenisary's revolt cost the Russians 8 million rubles in lost trade for 1838 alone.[22] Furthermore, as the grandson of Ablai, Kenisary had stature throughout the steppe, not just within the Middle Horde. The situation within the Small Horde remained tenuous; Orenburg feared that the continued success of Kenisary's movement could imperil the stability of Russian rule there as well. These fears were strengthened when Kenisary sought and received sanctuary from the Small Horde in 1838. He remained in the territory of the Orenburg Kazakhs for nearly two years and was granted amnesty by the Russians on the condition that he leave the territory of the Small Horde.

Soon after returning to the Middle Horde Kenisary resumed his opposition, this time over the placement of Russian settlements in the Irgiz and Turgai regions on lands that were traditionally used to graze the Kazakh livestock. Most of his activities in the next four years (1840–1844) were directed against these settlements, but the goal of his movement remained the same: to restore the khanate of the Middle Horde. During these years Kenisary was the effective ruler of most of the Middle Horde with the aid of a council of tribal elders and leading batirs. His chief aide was his brother, Sultan Nauribai. Kenisary supported his rebellion through direct taxation and by exacting payment from all caravans passing through his territory. Kenisary's rule was based on law; he attempted to devise a code, which was based on Tauke's *Jhety Jharga* with modifications from *Shari'a* law. He was also influenced by the efforts of Sultan Aryn Ghazi (reigned 1815–1821) to regularize the biis' authority. Kenisary established a system in which juridical authority was divided between customary courts headed by local biis and courts of Islamic law chaired by *qazis*. He seems to have accepted assistance and guidance from Polish nationalists exiled to the steppe. Most of his weapons were fashioned by craftsmen who lived among the Kazakhs and smelted rifles for them.[23] He received additional arms from the emir of Bukhara.

The Russians viewed the existence of a rival authority as intolerable. Finally, in 1844, they dispatched sufficient troops to the Middle Horde territory to defeat Kenisary. Once it became apparent that the Kazakhs could not defeat this superior force, Kenisary and his fighters accepted amnesty from the Russian authorities. Kenisary himself left the Russian-controlled territory of the Middle Horde and joined Jan Khoja Nur Muhammad uli in the latter's struggle to liberate the Kirgiz from the rule of Kokand. Kenisary died in battle in Kirgizia in 1847. Following the defeat of Kenisary, the Russians strengthened their military presence in the territory of the Middle Horde and increased the number of Russian settlements throughout the steppe. These two developments had the desired effect; although resistance to the Russians could emerge, it was forced to be more localized. As a result, the two subsequent challenges to Russian authority—the revolt of Iset Kutebar uli (1853–1857) in the Emba region and that of Jan Khoja Nur Muhammad uli (1856–1858) in the Syr Darya region—were more easily defeated.

Iset Kutebar uli was a leader of the Shekty clan of the Small Horde, which resided primarily in the middle section of the Orenburg Kirgiz territory, and his uprising was restricted to this area. Fighting broke out there in 1853 when the Russians demanded an additional 4,000 camels from the Kazakhs, over and above the 4,200 animals already requisitioned that year, to aid them in their siege against Kokand at Aq Mechet (or Ak Mechet, later renamed Perovsk and now known as Kzyl-Orda). The requisitions were begun by Sultan-Administrator Araslan Jantiurin and proved to be the catalyst in what was already an extremely unstable situation. Since 1847 the Russians had been demanding large numbers of camels annually, first to aid in their activities in Central Asia and later to send to troops in the Crimea as well. All these requisitions were dutifully executed by Sultan Araslan, increasing local discontent with his rule. Much of the Shekty displeasure with his rule was a continuation of the old struggle of clanic authorities (black bone) who resented the domination of the aristocracy (white bone); they especially resented the exclusive control exerted by the descendants of Abu'l Khayr. Such descendants came to be seen as lackeys of the Russians, and it was widely believed that they ruled contrary to the best interests of the Kazakh people. Unarguably, in the years of the sultan-administrators the basic economic situation of the Kazakhs had not improved. Pastureland was still in short supply, the average (and more importantly, the median) number of animals per family continued to drop, and the poor conditions had been exacerbated by bad jut in the winter of 1849–1850. The Kazakhs of the central part of the Small Horde were also not particularly supportive of Russia's efforts to defeat Kokand, let alone willing to give aid.

The rebellion of Iset Kutebar uli was primarily directed against the rule of Araslan Jantiurin, and Araslan was expected to defeat him with the assistance of 100 cossacks and arms to supply 100 fighters. Iset had over 1,500 fighters and proved difficult to defeat. He managed to withstand Araslan's offensive drive by taking refuge in Khiva. In 1855 Iset led another strong attack against Araslan, and he also declared all Russian caravans fair game. His attacks continued through 1856; in 1857 Orenburg dispatched a large punitive expedition armed with cannons and rifles. The Russians were convinced—without any supporting evidence—that Iset's rebellion was part of a grand anti-Russian design by Khiva and Turkey. Finally, in 1858, Iset was forced to surrender.

At the same time that the Russians were trying to disarm resistance among the Shekty, Jan Khoja Nur Muhammad uli was organizing a resistance movement among the Kazakh farmers living along the lower course of the Syr Darya River. Fighting broke out there after the Russians, concerned with strengthening their fortified line, forcibly evicted some 3,000 Kazakh families and sent them across the Syr Darya without any allocations of land or seed. Warriors from six separate Kazakh clans joined together to attack the Russians. These Kazakhs were from a part of the Small Horde that had only come under direct Russian control in the 1840s. From the very outset, relations had been difficult; the Russian military command seized land first in 1850 (after the harsh winter), again in 1852, and again in 1855. The final insult came in 1856, when the Syr Darya line was completed and cossack families were settled on the former Kazakh homesteads. Twice-displaced, the Kazakhs, who had only begun farming that region in the 1820s and 1830s when they had lost their herds, now resorted to violence. Jan Khoja and his fighters, fewer than 1,000 men, were joined in 1857 by supporters of Iset. After defeating Iset, however, the Russians were also able to put down Jan Khoja's resistance. Thus ended the last major organized threat to their rule.

## THE GROWTH OF RUSSIAN TRADE WITH CENTRAL ASIA

Formal Russian trade relations with Central Asia began in 1738, when the Russian government decided to permit the export of gold and silver coin as well as iron and grain to this area. Earlier Russian trade with the Kazakhs and the khanates of Central Asia had occurred on a local and informal basis. With the development of an all-Russian market in the eighteenth century, Russian merchant companies became more interested in trading with the Kazakhs and in exporting Russian goods through the steppe territory to the markets of Central Asia, Persia, and China. During this period Russian traders representing the large merchant companies dominated trade with this region, and over two-thirds of the goods went through Orenburg or Semipalatinsk, destined for markets to the south or east. Russian merchants bought livestock and related products from the Kazakhs; a document from October 31, 1785, reported that in a three-month period of that year livestock valued at over 200,000 rubles had changed hands.[24] The Kazakhs bought sugar, cloth, grain, and some metal goods from the Russians. Nonetheless, most of this trade remained localized, whereby Kazakhs traded their goods with neighboring Russian peasants.

At the beginning of the nineteenth century the Russian government adopted a new tariff structure designed to make the terms of trade with Asia more favorable. In 1817 legislation governing imports from Asia levied a 1 percent duty on service goods and a 2 percent duty on all intermediate products. Inexpensive manufactured items were taxed 10–20 percent and luxury items 25 percent. There was no duty placed on cotton, livestock, fish, and medicines. These latter items were the goods that Russia hoped to import from Central Asia. Regular trade routes through the Kazakh Steppe were established during the first half of the nineteenth century, based on established caravan routes. Before the coming of the railroad there were three major water routes that brought goods from the Volga River to the Caspian Sea and then either across the steppe to Bukhara and points further east or south to Persia. This form of transport was costly, about two rubles per pood (36 pounds avoirdupois) depending upon the destination, and the goods were in transit an average of two months.[25] It was far easier to send goods overland to Orenburg and then via camel caravan to their destination. From Orenburg goods sent to the seasonal Kazakh markets in the western part of the steppe (the largest of which was in Khanskaia Stavka) were separated, some put on caravans for Khiva and the rest sent in large caravans to either Semipalatinsk or Petropavlovsk. From Semipalatinsk goods were dispatched to the seasonal markets of the Middle Horde and sent on caravans to Kokand, Kuldja, and Kashgaria. Caravans were organized from Petropavlovsk to Tashkent, Bukhara, and Turkestan as well as to Kuldja and Kokand. During the first half of the nineteenth century, the trading settlements established by the Russians nearly a century before (in Orenburg, Orsk, Uralsk, Semipalatinsk, Petropavlovsk, and Troitsk) took on the character of European towns. Merchants from European Russia came annually and increasing numbers of Russian artisans set up workshops in Orenburg and Semipalatinsk, the largest of these towns, either fashioning metal goods to be traded to the Kazakhs or curing and tanning Kazakh leather for sale in the European provinces.

The caravan trade was seasonal, since the dirt trails that traversed the steppe were impassable after winter snows. Crossing the steppe was dangerous at any time of year, however, because of the constant risk of internal dispute among the Kazkahs or some sort of anti-Russian display, in spite of the fact that all caravans were escorted by members of the Kazakh clans that controlled the territory. Because of the dangers and difficulties inherent in travel, only a few caravans—but each with up to several hundred carts—made the journey across the steppe each year. There was an annual or biannual caravan from Orenburg to Bukhara, a journey of 75–80 days in 1850, and one caravan each year from Orsk to Bukhara, which took 40–50 days; these caravans returned with raw cotton. There were three caravans sent each year (in May, August, and November) from Petropavlovsk to Tashkent, and two caravans from Troitsk to Tashkent. The merchants of Tashkent sent their goods—mostly fruits, rugs, silks, and crafts—to market in Troitsk once in winter and two or three times in summer. Khivan merchants sent the majority of their goods, the most important of which was raw cotton, to Orenburg in two or three caravans per year; they also sent one caravan to Astrakhan annually. Although the Russians built some roads and highways in the years following the 1867 Turkestan statute, the difficulties of transport were not relieved until the construction of the Trans-Siberian railroad at the end of the nineteenth century. The high cost of caravan transport was reflected in the price of the items sold in Russia, particularly that of cotton.

These problems might have slowed the expansion of Russian trade with Central Asia, but they did not dampen the interest of Russian merchants and manufacturers. During the period 1825–1830 there was a sharp increase in Russian exports to Asia, and when in the 1830s there came a rapid drop in the amount of goods exported to Persia, increased trade with Central Asia and China took up the slack. In 1840, 36.8 percent of all Russian goods sent abroad went across Russia's Central Asian borders.[26] Most nineteenth century Russian economists echoed G. P. Nepolsin's conclusion that Russian goods were not competitive in the markets of Europe or North America, making Central Asia the logical outlet for Russia's new clothing and metal industries.[27] Furthermore, as Russian merchants themselves noted, the markets of Central Asia and particularly those of Kazakhstan would accept goods of average or even poor quality that could not be sold elsewhere.[28] From 1791 until 1853 Russia's trade with Central Asia grew by more than 350 percent; by 1853 over 75 percent of the Russian goods exported to Central Asia were manufactured items. Exports were valued each year at only slightly less than the imports, over 90 percent of which from Central Asia were raw materials. During the mid-nineteenth century almost half of the Russian trade with Central Asia was with the Kazakhs, who were becoming consumers of Russian grain and, to a lesser extent, of manufactured items.[29]

With the growth of the Russian cotton industry in the 1850s and 1860s, the demand for Central Asian cotton increased; the total number of poods of cotton imported annually went from an average of 527,000 in 1841–1845 to an average of 2,421,000 in 1857–1860. When the American Civil War brought an embargo on U.S. cotton, Russian merchants were left in a precarious position. The price of Central Asian cotton at the Nizhni-Novgorod (present-day Gorky) market quickly rose from 4–5 rubles per pood in 1860 to 12–13 rubles in 1862, then to 22–24 rubles in 1864. Completion of the Russian conquest of the Kazakh Steppe in the 1840s and 1850s eased the conditions of transport somewhat but did little to encourage the local khans of the Central Asian states either to produce more cotton or improve the terms of trade with Russia. After the Turkestan territory was conquered in 1864–1865 there was an immediate explosion in the cotton trade. Russia imported massive amounts of raw cotton, and exports of cloth to Kokand went from 74 rubles in 1864 to nearly 12 million rubles in 1867.[30]

## THE SUBJUGATION OF THE GREAT HORDE AND THE CONQUEST OF CENTRAL ASIA

The first stage of the expansion of Russia's control of Central Asia was the conquest or annexation of the Great Horde. In the 1730s, when the khans of the Small and Middle hordes swore their fealty to the Russian empress Anna Ioannovna, one part of the Great Horde joined the clans of Er Ali, Abu'l Khayr's son, and became Russian subjects. The majority of the Great Horde, however, remained under the control of the Jungar state. When the Jungar empire was defeated in 1756, vast new pastures were opened up for these Kazakhs who were now under Chinese rule. One group migrated to Jungaria; another remained in the Tashkent area and adopted a semisedentary life-style, some of them joining the agricultural Karakalpak population. This second group became subjects of Kokand when the troops of Alim Khan captured Tashkent in 1808. A third group camped in the eastern Semirech'e region, and quickly established their independence from China.

By the first part of the nineteenth century this third group, ruled by Sultan Suiuk (son of Ablai), found itself forced to choose between two powerful, expansionist states, Russia and Kokand. Suiuk decided that rule by Kokand was the greater evil and so in 1818 swore his loyalty to Russia. This brought an additional 55,000 Kazakhs under Russian rule. The Russians were quick to build on this advantage; in 1820 the governor general of western Siberia sent a military detachment of 120 cossacks to the territory of the Great Horde to secure the trade routes and to gain Russian control over the area without force. In 1824 an additional 50,000 Kazakhs accepted Russian administration. The population was ruled in accordance with the 1822 reforms but was released from the yasak (annual tribute). By 1826 the Russians controlled the entire Karatai region as well. Further expansion among the Great Horde was stalled by the threat of Kenisary Qasimov. It was not until June 1846 that a new okrug of western Siberia was created in the region just north of Lake Zaisan. In 1847 the Russians consolidated their hold over the Kopalsk region when all of the Kazakhs migrating between the Lepsi and Ili rivers, an additional 40,000 families, accepted Russian administration. This resulted in the formation of a council on January 10, 1848, to administrate the Great Horde; in 1854 this territory was made part of the newly created Semipalatinsk guberniia.[31]

The Russians also consolidated their hold over the Kazakhs of the Middle and Small hordes by building a series of military outposts throughout the steppe; Kokpekty was built in 1820, Kokchetav and Karkaralinsk in 1824, and Baian-Aul in 1826. Fort Aleksandrovsk was constructed in 1834 on the Mangyshlak Peninsula and a new military line was established between the Emba and Ui rivers. During this same period Khiva, under the rule of Khan Muhammad Rahim (reigned 1806–1825), was expanding northward into the Syr Darya and Aral Sea regions.

In the 1820s and 1830s the Russian authorities at Orenburg and Omsk sent several military missions to explore the steppe and recommend the course of Russia's future military strategy. One of the results of these missions was the ill-fated campaign against Khiva in 1839, led by Governor General V. A. Perovskii of Orenburg. Told of the military weakness of the Khivan forces, Perovskii overestimated the strength of his own forces and wholly ignored the problems of a remote desert campaign. Perovskii's expedition lost nearly 1,000 men and most of its transport; Perovskii himself was forced to flee for his life across the desert and steppe. This travesty led him to conclude that the successful military conquest of Central Asia could only succeed if the Russian military presence were extended deep into the steppe. Military outposts were therefore built in Turgai (now Amengel'dy) and Irgiz in 1845 and Atbasar in 1846. In 1847 Perovskii began an ambitious project to build two fortified lines, one (the Novo-Aleksandrovsk line) from the northeast corner of the Aral Sea for 300 miles along the Syr Darya, and the other to run southward from Semipalatinsk. The construction of these two lines began with the building of a fort at Raim (Aral'sk) and Kopalsk (in the region north of the Ili River) and ended six years later with the construction of Kazalinsk in 1853 and the founding of Vernyi (later renamed Alma-Ata) just south of the Ili River in 1854. After this the Russians began their campaign against Kokand, taking the fort at Aq Mechet, which they renamed Perovsk (later Kzyl-Orda).

Russia was not the only state interested in gaining control of the Kazakh Steppe. Khan Omar of Kokand (reigned 1809–1822) was himself following an expansionist policy toward the Kazakhs. After the conquest of Tashkent the armies of Kokand moved on to Turkestan, then crossed over to the right bank of the Syr Darya. They acquired territory northwest of the Ili River, annexing all of present-day Kirgizia and placing many of the Kazakhs of the Great Horde under their rule as well. The advance of Kokand into the steppe proceeded in two directions: from Tashkent to Chimkent, Aulie Ata (Dzhambul), Pishpek (Frunze), and Lake Issyk-Kul; and along the Fergana Valley, then across the Naryn River and north into Kazakh territory. Many of the sultans of the Great Horde supported Kokand because Khan Omar permitted them to collect their customary taxes from the Kazakhs in return for collecting the za'akat and ushur in Omar's name. The Kazakh herdsmen and farmers were less pleased, for conquest by Kokand meant the beginning of a dual tax burden that required them to sell off ever greater shares of their property each year. In 1821 a group of some 12,000 Kazakhs from the Turkestan, Chimkent, Sairam, and Aulie Ata regions, led by Tenek Tore, revolted against the khan of Kokand. Nevertheless, Omar was handily able to defeat them. In the 1830s and 1840s there were periodic skirmishes between the Kazakhs and the troops of the khan of Kokand, and in 1858, after an increase in taxation was announced, Kazakhs attacked Kokand's fortresses at Tokmak and Aulie Ata. Still, despite the claims of present-day historians, the vast majority of the Kazakhs seem to have been unopposed to Kokand rule and were not strongly in favor of being joined to the Russian empire. They undoubtedly sought relief from the heavy burden of taxation that Kokand imposed upon them, which the Russians promised them as Russian subjects, but for many Kazakhs the Kokand argument that they should be ruled by a Muslim ruler as part of a Muslim state had considerable weight. The Kazakhs of the Great Horde, who lived in close proximity to the Muslim centers of Central Asia, had by this time assumed a stronger identification with Islam than their kinsmen to the north. They were persuaded by the arguments of the khan of Kokand, supported as he was by the khans of Khiva and Bukhara, that as Muslims they had an obligation to resist rule by the infidel. Although the majority of Kazakhs must have had conflicting emotions, some clearly preferred Kokand rule, for the Russians encountered Kazakh resistance when they moved to take the Ili and Chu river valleys.

The Russian authorities themselves put off moving against Kokand for nearly a decade after the completion of their new military lines. They were not united as to what strategy should be followed in Central Asia. St. Petersburg was committed to the expansion of Russia's role in the area, but the problem of timing was a critical one; Alexander II wanted to counter England's influence in the region without antagonizing London. The administrative structure in force at the time also ceded a great deal of military control to the local military governor general. In 1861, when Kokand made the first move by attacking Vernyi, the two men with authority to order reprisals against Kokand disagreed on an appropriate strategy. Governor General Diogamel of western Siberia believed that the Russian-Kokand border was not stable but favored the continuation of peace negotiations between the two states being held at Omsk. The officials in Orenburg disagreed, arguing for immediate military action against Kokand and urging a unified Russian attack on Tashkent under the commands of Siberia and Orenburg. A compromise was reached; on September 23, 1861, the Kokand fortress Kurgan was attacked, and in March 1862 plans were laid for a major attack on Kokand to occur in the unspecified future. These plans were forwarded to St. Petersburg with the recommendation that a campaign against Kokand, although costly to outfit and equip, would allow Russia to control the entire Chu valley within a year of the attack's commencement.

In late 1862 Great Britain signed a treaty of alliance with Emir Dos Muhammad of Afghanistan, which supported rumors in St. Petersburg that England planned to acquire Bukhara and Khiva. This further swelled popular sentiment, expressed with increasing frequency in journals and political commentary since the advent of the American Civil War and the embargo on cotton, that Russia should move to take over Central Asia and Transcaspia. Such an action would guarantee sufficient cotton to the Russian mercantilists and would effectively bar England from further expansion in the region, thereby safeguarding Russian borders and maintaining a strong Russian presence in the region. The unsuccessful Polish uprising in 1863 led to a further loss of Russian prestige abroad and consequently to St. Petersburg's increased interest in achieving a foreign policy coup. In March 1863 a single detachment was dispatched to take Aulie Ata. This mission failed, which strengthened the belief that Kokand could only be defeated by a major military campaign.

On December 20, 1863, Tsar Alexander II signed a ukase ordering that a concerted attack be made on Kokand during 1864. Preparations for the attack were completed in May and two separate armies were dispatched; Colonel Verevkin left Perovsk with some 1,500 men and marched toward Turkestan, and Colonel Chernaiev was sent from western Siberia to Turkestan with about 2,500 men and 22 guns. On June 4, 1864, the combined armies (under the command of Cherniaev) took possession of Aulie Ata and on June 9 began a successful three-day siege against Turkestan. After the fall of that city they attempted to take Chimkent but failed until September 21, after an additional Russian detachment had been sent. St. Petersburg directed Chernaiev to maintain his defensive line at the Arys River, but on September 27 Chernaiev defied orders and marched against Tashkent. After an unsuccessful attack he was forced to retreat.

Almost immediately upon the conclusion of this campaign the famous Gorchakov Circular was sent to the various European powers; in this document Gorchakov, the imperial foreign minister, articulated his version of a Russian manifest destiny, arguing that:

> The position of Russia in Central Asia is that of all civilized States which are brought into contact with half-savage nomad populations, possessing no fixed social organization.
> In such cases it always happens that the more civilized State is forced, in the interest of the security of its frontier and its commercial relations, to exercise a certain ascendancy over those whom their turbulent and unsettled character makes most undesirable neighbours.[32]

Gorchakov then went on to argue that the goal of the Russian government was to create a safe, stable border in Central Asia. This required the creation of a single fortified border, which the Russian conquests of 1864 permitted. Although not specifically stating so, the circular implied that Russia's recent conquests marked the end of her territorial expansion in the area. In 1865 the oblast of Turkestan was formed under the administration of a military governor. Chernaiev was appointed to the post. Although told to leave Tashkent untouched, Chernaiev was also ordered by Kryzhanovskii, his superior in Orenburg, to improve Russia's military position in the oblast. Chernaiev took this to mean that he *could* (not should) invade Tashkent, which he did on June 9, 1865. The city fell to the Russians on June 14, but Chernaiev was removed from his post and returned to St. Petersburg to be both criticized and promoted. Britain was placated and St. Petersburg content.[33] The power of the khan of Kokand was broken and the city of Kokand surrendered to Russians in 1876. Brief military campaigns were subsequently launched against Khiva and Bukhara, and both these khanates became Russian protectorates in 1873. However, the conquest of Tashkent was the key, for after this was accomplished the Russians could turn their attentions to the administration of the new territory.[34]

## THE TURKESTAN AND
## STEPPE POSITIONS

The successful military campaigns of General Chernaiev exacerbated the problem of administering the Kazakh Steppe and the newly acquired Turkestan region. Ignatiev had traveled to the Orenburg oblast to consider the problem in 1858–1859 and concluded that the existing system of sultan-administrators had to be replaced. Other distinguished experts, including A. A. Levshin and the Kazakh ethnographer Chokan Valikhanov, were also asked to make suggestions. The widespread rioting in the steppe following the jut of 1862 increased the pressure on the administrators in St. Petersburg. Finally, in July 1865, shortly after the conquest of Tashkent, the minister of the interior appointed a four-man commission, headed by Colonel F. K. Geiers, to travel to the steppe and report on a government suitable for the Kazakh and Turkestan regions. This report, which was two years in preparation, concerned itself exclusively with the question of the Kazakh population. The commission found that the existing system of dual authority, by which part of the population was administered from Orenburg and the rest from Siberia, was ineffective: "The study of the demands of the local conditions and life of the people convinced the commission that the Kirghiz by origin, by faith, language and form of life constitute a single people and therefore it is necessary for them to have a single administration."[35]

The report went on to argue that both the Siberian and Orenburg systems of administration had some basic flaws. The problem with the Orenburg system was that it relied on sultans and khans who no longer enjoyed support; the Russian government, therefore, was being discredited by association with the Kazakh aristocracy. The Siberian system was flawed in its creation of two separate administrations, one for the Kazakhs and one for the cossacks, which was driving these two populations farther apart. The commission argued that, particularly with the acquisition of Turkestan, the Kazakh Steppe had become an integral part of the empire and hence a *Russian* administration had to be introduced, albeit one that would take into consideration the unique characteristics of the native population. The Kazakh Steppe should be set up as a guberniia, divided into a number of oblasts and they in turn into *uezd*s and volosts, just as in the rest of the empire. At the guberniia and oblast levels the administration would be dominated by Russians, while the uezd and volost administrations should be elected from the local population, with boundaries drawn up that would minimize clanic hegemony. A system of parallel courts would be maintained, subjecting the Kazakhs to Russian criminal law but also permitting customary law to adjudicate civil disputes.[36]

The Steppe Commission spent a long time investigating the problems that resulted from the nomadic basis of the Kazakh economy. It concluded that it was desirable for the Kazakhs to become sedentary, but through persuasion, not force. Noting that the Russian government had not yet decided the question of the ownership of the land on which the Kazakhs migrated, the commission held that the Kazakhs were entitled to use their traditional pastureland with the agreement of volost officials. The commission did acknowledge the difficulties that nomadism produced, in particular the problem of large groups of people crossing volost, uezd, and even oblast boundaries during their annual migration. Commission members counseled that the Kazakhs were ill-equipped then to adopt a sedentary economy and that the steppe itself, save for a part of the Atbasar volost in Semipalatinsk, was largely unsuitable for agriculture. The steppe could be profitably developed only by skilled farmers who knew how to maximize the arability of the land.

When the Steppe Commission completed its work in July 1867, its report was forwarded to a special committee composed of the ministers of war, interior, and foreign affairs, each of whom had an interest in maintaining control over this territory. The committee studied and made several changes in the report, most significant of which was the decision to separate the Syr Darya and Semirech'e regions from the rest of the Kazakh Steppe and join them to the Turkestan territory, thus creating two separate guberniias. Kryzhanovskii, governor general of Orenburg, strongly opposed this division of the steppe, which he argued would create numerous unnecessary administrative difficulties as well as personal hardships for the Kazakhs. His position was supported by the former members of the Steppe Commission. Kryzhanovskii further objected to the nature of the proposed administration to be introduced, arguing that the administrative structure was too sophisticated for the primitive Kazakhs. He believed that having two governors-general would create potential rivalries and that it was being done only to assuage competing interest groups.[37] Kryzhanovskii himself favored the appointment of a military governor for the region who would serve under the governor-general of Orenburg.

The report of the special committee was allowed to stand, however, and the recommendations became the basis of the *Provisional Statute on the Administration of the Semirech'e and Syr Darya Oblasts*, July 11, 1867, and the *Provisional Statute on the Administration of the Turgai, Akmolinsk, Uralsk, and Semipalatinsk Oblasts*, October 21, 1868. Unsuccessful attempts to revise these pieces of legislation, which were designed for a two-year trial period, were made in 1871, 1872, 1874, and 1876. They were finally superseded by the *Statute on the Administration of the Turkestan Region*, July 2, 1886, and the *Statute on the*

*Administration of Akmolinsk, Semipalatinsk, Semirech'e, Uralsk and Turgai Oblasts*, March 25, 1891 (known as the Steppe Statute of 1891).

The 1867 and 1868 legislation divided the Kazakh Steppe into six oblasts, each headed by a military governor. The two Kazakh oblasts in Turkestan—Syr Darya and Semirech'e—were under the jurisdiction of the governor-general of Turkestan. Until 1891 there was no governor-general of the steppe; Uralsk and Turgai were under the Orenburg governor-general and Akmolinsk and Semipalatinsk were administered by the governor-general of western Siberia. The oblast military governors were the commanders of the troops stationed within each territory. Each oblast was divided into uezds headed by Russian officers who were assisted by local Kazakhs, usually drawn from the aristocracy. The uezds were divided into volosts and the volosts into administrative auls, with these authorities elected from the Kazakh population. The volosts and auls were formed on a territorial principle. Each volost consisted of between one and two thousand households, each administrative aul of between one hundred and two hundred families. Each volost and uezd was to have a native court and a Russian criminal court, in which the judges of the former would be elected and those of the latter appointed. The cost of this administrative apparatus was to be met by the Kazakhs themselves, for which the one ruble fifty kopek cart tax was raised to three rubles in the four northern oblasts, and two rubles seventy-five kopeks in Turkestan. These taxes were quickly raised again, to three rubles fifty kopeks in 1872 and to four rubles per household in 1892. The Kazakhs were also subject to local (*zemskii*) taxation to maintain post roads, prisons, and schools, as well as to any traditional or religious taxes that they might choose to levy on themselves.[38]

Probably the most controversial aspect of these pieces of legislation was the treatment of the land question. All land was declared to be the property of the Russian state: "The land occupied by the Kirghiz nomads belongs to the state and is granted in common use to the Kirghiz." The uezd and volost administrations were charged with assigning winter and summer pasturage to the Kazakhs, by volost and aul respectively. Within each aul the elder was to apportion land to each household, guided in his decision by the size of the household. It was assumed that auls and even volosts would migrate as a unit, remaining year round within their uezd if possible and certainly within their oblast. Naturally, what occurred was far different; the Kazakhs maintained many of their traditional migratory patterns until the arrival of widespread Russian settlement at the end of the nineteenth century. Nevertheless, this legislation did hasten the breakup of the Kazakh livestock breeding economy. The Russian government offered a private plot of fifteen desiatins per household, nearly 40 acres, to any Kazakh family willing to farm the land or build some sort of permanent residence on it; funds for seed and construction materials were set aside to aid the Kazakhs in becoming homesteaders. All land that was used in common was to be allocated annually.

The new administration also regulated the religious authorities under the jurisdiction of the ministry of the interior.[39] The Kazakhs were limited to one mullah per volost; the volost officials were the only ones with the authority to permit the construction of either mosques or religious schools. Once built, these structures were under the jurisdiction of the Orenburg muftiate, a subsidiary of the ministry of the interior. This was designed to reduce the growing influence of Islam in Kazakhstan, since one of the charges to the Steppe Commission had been to investigate how the Kazakhs could be encouraged to become Christian subjects. The Steppe Commission had recommended that the Russians not intervene directly in the religious affairs of the Central Asians, but rather should restrict the spread of Islam. General Kaufman, the first governor-general of Turkestan, was strongly against Christian missionary activities in the steppe. Although Muslim clergy in the sedentary regions lost power under the new law, the Muslims of Turkestan were able to continue their missionary activities among the Kazakhs of Semirech'e and Syr Darya.[40] The Orenburg muftiate also engaged in the active spread of Islam by funding the construction of legal and illegal schools and mosques throughout the northern part of the steppe.

## KAZAKH RESPONSE
## TO THE NEW LEGISLATION

News of the provisional statutes aroused a strong burst of anti-Russian feeling among the Kazakhs. Uprisings broke out among the Middle Horde, the Small Horde, and the Adaev Kazakhs of the Mangyshlak Peninsula. Opposition in the Middle Horde was led by Sultan Sadyk, son of Kenisary Qasimov. After the defeat of his father he had gone south, to fight with the Kirgiz in their quest for independence from Kokand. Following Russia's attack upon Kokand in 1864 Sadyk decided that Russia was the greatest enemy of the Central Asians. He wrote:

> I cannot go over to the Russians, as this would be breaking the path of my ancestors. If the Russians take Kokand, I will go over to Bukhara, if they take Bukhara I will go to some other Muslim state. There are many. But I will not depart from the path of my father.[41]

After the defeat of Kokand Sadyk joined forces with the emir of Bukhara, after whose capitulation he lived out the rest of his life in the desert of Gissar, surrounded by his entourage.

The most significant opposition to Russian rule was among the tribes of the Small Horde, first in the Uralsk and Turgai oblasts and then in the Mangyshlak region. In December 1868 the Orenburg governor general organized a special commission to travel throughout the steppe and inform the Kazakhs of the provisions of the new legislation, which was to go into effect in 1869. The commission (a group of former sultan-administrators traveling with some Russian civil servants and escorted by 25 cossacks) was to travel from aul to aul, take a census of the population for the tax rolls, and prepare the communities for the upcoming elections. However, it was forced to retreat when it was attacked by a group of Adaev fishermen. The commission was dispatched again in February 1869, this time accompanied by 200 cossacks and 2 guns. Instead of placating the Kazakhs, the presence of the military escort only encouraged resistance. The Kazakhs interpreted the military force as a sign of Russia's intention to extract the now widely publicized increase in taxation and to enforce the Steppe Statute's restrictions on migration.[42] Although the Kazakhs seem to have disliked virtually all the provisions of the new legislation, these two items appear to have been the most hated. Within a month Kazakh resistance overtook all of the Uralsk oblast as well as the western and southern parts of the Turgai oblast. A majority of the fighters were the poor Kazakhs, who were most directly threatened by the tax increase, but they were led by the biis and elders whose power base was threatened by the administrative reform. The rebels were apparently supported by all sectors of Kazakh society. The only people who supported the Russians, or were at least willing to fight with them, were the remaining descendants of Abu'l Khayr's family, who had benefited from the Russian administration of the previous 40 years.

The resistance was so widespread that almost all trade in the area was halted; its resumption was slow because the rebels destroyed virtually all the postal roads and telegraphic communication. An expeditionary force of 5,300 men and 20 guns was sent out in mid-June 1869 under the command of General V. A. Verevkin, the military governor of Uralsk, to the Russian fortresses in the steppe. This turned fortune against the Kazakhs, and by the end of the year the rebellion had been put down; reconquest of the steppe had required over twice as many men as had been employed in the defeat of Kokand.[43] Some 71,000 carts had been destroyed and hundreds of thousands of animals had been killed by the Russian troops in the course of putting down the uprising. Russia set strict punishments for the rebellious Kazakhs. Prominent fighters were arrested and sentenced to death, and many Kazakhs were sentenced to terms of between twelve and fifteen years (among these was the father of the future Kazakh communist leader, Turar Ryskulov). A fine of one ruble per household was levied against the participants, from which the civil administration collected nearly 150,000 rubles in fines in the course of 1870.

Almost immediately following the defeat of the Kazakhs in the Turgai and

Uralsk oblasts, the Russian authorities were faced with an outburst of equal magnitude by the Adaev Kazakhs. These people, who lived in the desert and semidesert regions of the Mangyshlak Peninsula, were to be subjected to the provisional statute effective January 1870. The tribes of the region, which included Adaev Kazakhs and Turkmen, had existed as a sort of buffer zone between the Russian and Khivan states for most of the first half of the nineteenth century. In 1846 the Russians had strengthened their military presence in Mangyshlak without opposition, since Khiva was then at war with Bukhara. The Khivans had helped incite some Kazakh resistance in 1847, but by 1848 the first frontier districts had been organized. Almost all of the Adaev Kazakhs had come under Russian control while the Turkmens remained part of the Khivan state.

The Adaev had proved themselves to be difficult subjects, and several times in the 1850s the Russians had been forced to send troops to collect the required taxation. The Russian authorities knew that the 1868 Steppe Statute, which caused even traditionally passive populations to revolt, was sure to produce a violent response by the Adaev Kazakhs; the legislation, which barred migration beyond oblast boundaries except with official permission, effectively cut these tribes off from their traditional summer pasturage along the Emba. Thus when the statute was announced, troops from Orenburg and the Caucasus were already in residence to guard the roads and seize the wells, in order to deny Kazakhs who refused to accept the legislation water for their animals. The new legislation required the Adaev Kazakhs to pay a one-ruble zemskii tax in addition to the three-ruble fifty-kopek cart tax that they were already paying. In addition, two years' back taxes were demanded from every household, which was extreme since the Adaev had no hard currency; they were far from the Russian markets and had little to trade. Without cash they were liable to have their livestock seized by the often-corrupt tax collectors, who took the best animals and sold them for amounts far in excess of the taxes due.

In spite of their preparation, the Russians were met in March 1870 by a massive and uncontrollable Adaev uprising. By the end of the month the Russian troops had been routed and the second-in-command killed. In June a new Russian commander, Major General Komarov, was dispatched and the newly rearmed Russian troops inflicted heavy losses of lives and property on the Kazakhs. Although some rebels continued the fight until the end of October with assistance from Khiva, by September the Russians were in sufficient control to force payment of the annual tax, which had been raised to five rubles in 1870, to pay the cost of the military operation against the Kazakhs. In December Komarov organized a meeting with representatives of each of the major clans to work out a compromise permitting those communities that paid their tax peacefully to cross into Uralsk and Turgai and so travel to their traditional summer pasturage.

For the next two and a half years Russian trooops lived among the Adaev to enforce order. These troops were withdrawn in 1873 to participate in the Russian campaign against Khiva, and the Adaev, again led by the same fighters, were quick to join the Khivan and Turkmen resistance. The Russians, however, had prepared themselves adequately for the campaign by sending troops to the front from Orenburg, Turkestan, and Transcaspia. The conquest of Khiva was completed by the spring of 1874. The Adaev resistance was defeated for the final time. As punishment for Adaev involvement with the Khivans, the Mangyshlak region was severed from Orenburg and joined instead with the newly acquired Turkmen territory centered around Krasnovodsk. This region was organized as the Transcaspian oblast and placed under the direction of the governor-general of Caucasia. The Adaev were thus again cut off from their summer pasturage.

Although it took the Russians over a decade to subjugate the Turkmens, the conquest of Khiva did lead to the rapid capitulation of Bukhara. Both these khanates remained nominally independent of Russia but in effect were protectorates. The conquest of Turkestan was thus virtually complete and the new administrative authority established. Now the task facing the Russians was to integrate the steppe and Turkestan regions into the government and economy of the empire.

# 4 The Land Problem

## INTRODUCTION

The pastoral livestock breeding economy of the Kazakhs never fully recovered from the Aqtaban Shubirindi (Great Retreat) of the eighteenth century, since the new grazing lands were never adequate for even a diminished Kazakh herd. In the eighteenth and early nineteenth centuries there was a constant struggle for land, both within the Kazakh community and between Kazakhs and Russians. In the 1820s and 1830s some Kazakhs seem to have started sowing grain to supply as animal feed; others turned to agriculture as a living after they lost their livestock holdings. Following the introduction of restrictive land policies in the years 1867–1870, the transformation of the Kazakh economy accelerated rapidly. By the time widespread seizure of land began in the 1890s, the economic situation was dire; the settlement of nearly 3 million Europeans in Kazakh territory during the decade prior to World War I made things even worse. By the Russian Revolution in 1917 the traditional Kazakh economy of pastoral livestock breeding had ceased to be viable.

The whole question of the economic transformation of the Kazakhs, particularly the subtheme of the development of agriculture, is controversial in modern Soviet scholarship. The issue of agriculture is really an extension of the problem of Kazakh feudalism. Soviet scholars who have sought to depict the Kazakh aristocracy as feudal landlords have been forced to employ a very loose definition of agriculture to be as inclusive as possible. Consequently, official histories generally discuss the widespread character of Kazakh agriculture without providing specific information about either the meaning of agriculture or the extent of its use. If agriculture is defined as the cultivation of crops or raising of livestock on both fixed and privately owned land (private ownership would appear to be a necessary precondition for a feudal society), then agriculture was not a significant part of the Kazakh economy in the first half of the nineteenth century.[1] Even in areas where agriculture may have been relatively widespread, less than 10 percent of the Kazakhs were actually engaged in agriculture when the land policies of the 1860s were introduced, and nothing in these areas resembled a Kazakh landlord.[2]

Not only were there few Kazakh farmers, but the Russian administrators themselves were divided as to whether it was even desirable to introduce agriculture to the Kazakhs. One important group, led by Governor Sukhtelen, the military governor of Orenburg in the 1830s, argued that it was better for the steppe lands to serve as rich pasturage than as poor farms and that the Kazakh people were of great use to the Russians as livestock breeders who could provide animals and animal products to the Russians in exchange for surplus grain. In 1833 General Perovskii and the Asiatic department went so far as to prohibit members of the Small Horde from farming within fifteen *versta*s (approximately ten miles) of Russian settlements. Agriculture had been encouraged since the time of Ablai within the territory of the Middle Horde, but limited to lands along the Irtysh River that adjoined the Russian settlements. After the Kenisary Qasimov uprising the Russians became more fearful of encouraging the development of Kazakh agriculture, since the majority of the rebels were eginshi (poor Kazakh farmers); many officials felt that the unrest stemmed from the problems the Kazakhs experienced in becoming self-sufficient farmers.[3]

Still, in the 1860s, despite some hesitation by members of the Steppe Commission, the Russian government opted for a land policy designed to encourage the Kazakhs to become sedentary, to combine farming with livestock breeding. The experience of the 1830s and 1840s convinced the Russians that nomads were difficult to rule and that the short-term risks of encouraging the development of agriculture among the Kazakhs would be worth the long-term gains that pacification of the steppe would provide. This view was vindicated at the end of the century when the steppe came to be seen as a rich source of land with which the demands of the Russian peasantry could be satisfied.

Even before the shift in Russian policy, however, agriculture was becoming an economic force in the steppe, particularly among the Kazakhs who lived close to the Russian lines along the Ural and Irtysh rivers. The decline of pastoral livestock breeding seemed irreversible. It was impossible to maintain large herds without finding some source of food to supplement free grazing. In the middle of the century the demand for Kazakh livestock was greater than ever before; this was particularly true for cattle, which required larger amounts of feed than goats, sheep, or horses. Thus, large numbers of Kazakhs turned to agriculture to produce surplus feed, not because they had lost their animals and needed farming to survive but so that they could raise more cattle. This need provided employment for hired hands (*baigush*) or hired farmers (*eginshi*). One prominent Kazakh economic historian has argued that the introduction of agriculture among the Kazakhs should be dated from the beginning of farming by the rich in search of fodder, for only then did farming become permanent.[4]

Many contemporary accounts describe the creation and development of agricultural communities among the Kazakhs in the period 1830–1860. Among the most important are the reports of Major General Bronevskii, who traveled through the steppe in 1833 and again in 1848. He noted that the Kazakhs farmed along the rivers from the Orenburg line south, following the line of Russian settlement; it was reported that there were about 6,700 Kazakh farming families in the Orenburg jurisdiction in the late 1830s. Agriculture was slowest to develop in the south, where Bronevskii observed fewer than 1,500 Kazakh farming families on his 1848 trip through the Syr Darya and Semirech'e regions, although these areas had long supported agricultural populations.[5] Still, once Kazakh agriculture began to develop along the Syr Darya in the 1850s, it spread quickly; by 1860 some 10,000 Kazakh households were sedentary.[6] The farms themselves were small, only two or three desiatins on the average, and were generally located on unirrigated lands. Prior to 1870 agriculture made little or no gain among the populations of the Inner Side or in southwestern Kazakhstan. In both areas the saline content of the soil was high and there was a shortage of water.

Virtually all sources agree on the relatively primitive quality of Kazakh agriculture. Kazakh farming was almost entirely restricted to the growth of cereal grain on unirrigated lands. The few implements Kazakh farmers possessed were wood; metal implements were found on only a few farms located close to Orenburg and Omsk. A few Kazakhs who farmed close to the Orenburg line were able to become moderately successful at farming, even having surplus grain to sell in the Russian markets, but most of the Kazakh farmers barely produced enough fodder to make agriculture worthwhile. Those few who did produce a surplus often fell prey to unscrupulous Russian and Tatar middlemen who traveled the steppe buying up Kazakh grain for substantially less than the market value.[7]

Nevertheless, those Kazakhs who began farming voluntarily and allowed livestock to be stalled in the winter did not regret their decision. They were able to take advantage of rapidly expanding Russian trade in the steppe by raising cattle for sale to the traders and merchants of the growing markets in the north. For these Kazakhs a transformation of lifestyle had begun. They raised cattle and horses rather than sheep and goats, became employers of hired help, and ultimately increased their wealth. Many built permanent winter campsites, most of which were in the north; at first these sites had only simple dugouts to store grain, then animal shelters, and finally dirt and even wood and stone houses. Even these Kazakhs, however, remained nomadic. Even the wealthiest members of the community and their entire households migrated to summer pastures, leaving only a few old women and young guards at the winter campsites. The yurt remained the residence of the migrating Kazakh, and cultural practices remained influenced by seasonal migration. The Kazakhs still did not recognize personal ownership or even clan ownership of land, and so even those wealthy sultans who did erect some sort of permanent structures could lose the right to graze on these lands if they fell from favor or were pushed out by a rival clan.[8]

The temptations of the market began changing the Kazakh economy in fundamental ways, and the transformation sped up in the 1850s, after Russia grew more interested in trade through the area. For most Kazakhs the economic changes of the first half of the nineteenth century were not beneficial. The expanding Russian military line encroached upon their migratory paths and even the pastures themselves; although only a few thousand additional European households moved into the area, they took some of the richest pasturelands and blocked access to other grazing. Finally, as some Kazakhs introduced fields and permanent structures on their lands, the traditional rule of free grazing for all was threatened. Rivalry for the better lands increased as each tribe and clan tried to control a specific piece of land. The Russian tax burden was further straining the Kazakh economy, since few Kazakhs had the one ruble fifty kopeks in currency necessary to pay the tax collectors. They thus fell prey to Russian or Tatar middlemen, if not to the tax collectors themselves, who bought the animals for the price of the taxes due and often resold them for three or four times the sum paid.[9] After the new land policies were introduced, the situation grew worse.

## THE RUSSIAN LAND POLICY

The Turkestan and Steppe statutes established the principle of state ownership of the Kazakh lands and the right of Kazakhs to graze in common on lands awarded to them by the civil authorities. The Kazakhs could only achieve permanent control of land by farming it and erecting permanent structures. Russian law subjected the Kazakhs to the principles of land ownership that were in effect throughout the empire and made little concession to their nomadic practices. The Turkestan and steppe territories proved more difficult to govern than had been expected; it was hard to attract qualified administrators to the region, and so the civil administration, particularly at the volost and uezd levels, became riddled with corruption. Simple payment of salaries annually overdrew the budget, and there was little money to invest in the incentives promised to the Kazakhs in the statutes to begin farming, such as free seed and construction loans.

Although the initial statutes were intended to be in effect only two years, they stayed for nearly twenty. The *Provisional Statute on the Administration of Turkestan* (1867) was replaced by the July 2, 1886, *Statute on the Administration of the Turkestan Region*, which applied to the Kazakh population of the Syr Darya oblast.[10] Semirech'e was separated from the governor-generalship of Turkestan and included with the steppe region.[11] The statute was designed to strengthen and regularize the colonial administration in Turkestan. It called for the creation of uniform types of volost administrations, expanded the role of the government to cover medical and social services, and mandated an increase in the number of secular schools. An attempt was made to exert greater control over the formal structure of religion by limiting the number of mosques and madrasahs to one per volost; further restrictions on people's courts were also introduced. Land policy from the 1867 and 1868 statutes remained almost entirely unchanged, save that a new provision restricting the expansion of *waqf* (clerically owned) lands. Because this statute focused on the needs of the sedentary population of Turkestan, not the nomadic one, the lifestyle of the Kazakhs was little changed. Of the three oblasts that composed this territory (Fergana, Samarkand, and Syr Darya), only the last had a sizable nomadic population.

The Steppe Statute of 1891 was exclusively concerned with administration of the Kazakh population and paid particular attention to expanding Russian control of land usage.[12] For the Kazakhs, the most damaging aspect of this legislation was Article 120, which stated that all land in "excess of Kazakh needs" was to be given over to the control of the ministry for state property. Each Kazakh household was entitled to fifteen desiatins (about 40 acres) of land for their personal use or for use in common with the other members of their aul. All land in excess of this amount was to be given over to the Public Land Fund, administered by the ministry of state property. Whereas the 1868 statute had established the principle of state ownership of the steppe lands, the 1891 statute established the mechanism by which this control would be exercised. Article 120 also asserted that the government had the power to seize lands forcibly from Kazakhs who refused to comply with the provisions of the act. This 1891 statute was the result of a new position on the question of internal resettlement. On July 13, 1889, a law was passed enabling any peasant to petition for permission to resettle, contingent only upon the availability of free land at the desired destination. People requesting settlement in Asiatic Russia were entitled to receive an allotment of fifteen desiatins per household. The oblasts of Akmolinsk, Semirech'e, and Semipalatinsk were covered by this provision, which in 1891 and 1892 was extended to the Uralsk and Turgai oblasts respectively.[13]

Steppe authorities were quick to act on this provision, for there was already a great demand for homesteads by Russians and Ukrainians who had moved into the territory illegally and farmed on lands rented from the Kazakhs; after the 1891 legislation Kazakhs continued to have the right to rent their lands, but only up to the fifteen desiatins that they could personally control. In July 1893 the governor-general of the steppe decreed a procedure for seizing lands along the Trans-Siberian railroad on which to establish Russian settlements; this would further secure the safety of the railroad.[14] In 1896 a resettlement administration was formed to award homesteads to settlers from European Russia, publicize settlement in the steppe among the already land-hungry Russian peasants, and facilitate their journey to this region. However, until the decree on June 6, 1904, permitting the free movement of Russian subjects throughout the empire, the resettlement administration was more concerned with the seizure of land from the Kazakhs than with the allocation of plots.

Although there was considerable disagreement within Russian administrative circles over the legality of the concept of excess lands, it very quickly became clear that, legal or illegal, the seizure of lands was badly hurting the Kazakh economy, since the government was taking the best pastureland. In 1895 the noted Russian agronomist, A. A. Kaufman, was sent on a fact-finding mission throughout the steppe to study both how the seizure of lands was being conducted and how it could be improved. He made five recommendations for modification of the 1893 decree, among them the requirement that seized land should truly be excess and not used by the Kazakhs either as grazing land or as irrigated farmland. Kazakh gravesites and holy places were to be inviolate, and those communities that for one reason or another had to lose their traditional pastures were to receive new pasturelands from excess Kazakh land, preferably from their own clan. These recommendations became law on May 31, 1896. However, Kaufman's observation that fifteen desiatins per household was too small in the topography of much of the steppe was ignored.

Following his work in the steppe region, Kaufman was sent to study how Russian settlement could best be achieved in Turkestan. On June 10, 1900, the tsar decreed that the nomads of the Syr Darya oblast should be settled and that Russian settlements in this territory, previously banned, were permitted. Kaufman was also charged with examining ways in which irrigation could be improved. He observed that the rental of land to the Russians from the Kazakhs was quite commonplace in Turkestan; Kazakh landlords profited by both receiving rent and learning how to farm. Kaufman believed that better use should be made of the land in this region, which with adequate water was quite fertile; for this to be achieved the Kazakhs must however relinquish their pasturage. He strongly believed that any scheme to redistribute land must consider the needs of the Kazakhs as well as the demands of the Russian peasants. This he felt could best be achieved by declaring as excess reasonable amounts of irrigated land and land close to sources of water. The Kazakhs should be left all lands unsuitable for agriculture and irrigation as well as the forest and desert regions.

Kaufman's report makes clear how imprecise and unworkable most of the land provisions of major statutes were for the steppe. He felt that good examples of this were the provisions concerned with the category of worked land. According to the provisions of the law, only those lands containing permanent residential or agricultural structures could be considered private property and thereby used in perpetuity by oneself and one's heirs. By the end of the nineteenth century, however, many Kazakh families planted feed grain on the same plots year after year and erected temporary sheds annually. The individuals were semisedentary and were in compliance with the spirit, but not the letter, of the law; their fields could therefore have been declared excess, although these fields should more accurately have been considered worked lands. A further problem was the hundreds of thousands of acres of pasturage that had worked land holdings scattered throughout them. According to a strict reading of the new rules, such land could not be used as pasturage, nor could it be used for anything else. Kaufman concluded that pastoral livestock breeding was doomed; the Kazakhs of Syr Darya and Semirech'e could only withstand the loss of pasturage envisioned by the Russian authorities if a substantial part of the community were to become farmers.[15]

In the first decade of the twentieth century, particularly after the agrarian revolts of 1906–1907, the Russian authorities became very concerned with satisfying the land hunger of the Russian peasantry, even at the expense of the economic well-being of non-Russian peoples. Therefore the problems of the Kazakhs became comparatively less important. Stolypin argued that the needs of one group, such as the Kazakhs, could not come before the interests of the empire as a whole. In Stolypin's terms, the greatest good for the most people would be achieved if the steppe region were to become a net exporter of grain, made possible by the new Trans-Siberian railroad line.[16] The Kazakhs were not, in Stolypin's opinion, being mistreated. Fifteen desiatins of land were quite reasonable for a farm; peculiarities of culture and temperament could not be valid arguments to slow the progress and development of the Russian state. Because the settlement of the nomads did not impede the development of large-scale cattle breeding, which was needed to feed the growing cities of European Russia, Stolypin's views provided a justification for the more vigorous land policy followed in the final quarter century of tsarist rule.

## ECONOMIC CHANGES IN THE STEPPE UNDER COLONIAL RULE

The Russian land policy led to the destruction of the nomadic economy practiced by the Kazakhs. By 1917 some 17 million desiatins of land were awarded to nearly 3 million Russian settlers in 500,000 families, and the Public Land Fund contained an additional 20 million desiatins of land intended for future homesteaders. This Russian settlement changed the character of life in the steppe. Although only 35,000 settlers came to the steppe from European Russia between 1865 and 1895, and the 1897 census reported only 15.7 percent of the population as Russian or Slavic by nationality, by 1916 these same population groups constituted 41.6 percent of the population of the four northern oblasts.[17] In some of the northernmost districts, Slavs were an absolute majority of the population.[18] The line of settlement was moving southward; by World War I there were nearly 250,000 Russian settlers in Semirech'e and over 100,000 in Syr Darya, where from 1910 on land seizure was concentrated.[19] In the Syr Darya oblast in 1916 Kazakh families owned (as distinguished from used in common) less than 700,000 desiatins of land, while Russians owned some 1.5 million desiatins; another 1.7 million desiatins were in the Public Land Fund. This is even more remarkable since the governor-general of Turkestan forbade the seizure of any Kazakh lands until 1905.

In theory, European settlement in the Kazakh territory was supposed to take advantage of potential farmland and, in the south, irrigated farmland. This land was to be seized with the approval of the Kazakh local authorities, and full compensation would be given to those few Kazakhs who would be inadvertently forced off their land. The reality of seizure was quite different. Most important, a nomadic economy really has no excess land. Pastoral livestock breeding depends on the existence of large amounts of free grazing lands, so that when the grass is eaten there is still plenty of available pasture. Furthermore, the only protection such an economy has against harsh climatic conditions—jut and drought, for example—is other unused lands. Rather than enjoying surplus pasture, the Kazakhs had suffered a shortage of pasturelands ever since the Aqtaban Shubirindi. Russian policy was devised solely in terms of a farming population, and so the settlement of the nomads was a foregone conclusion as early as the 1867–1868 statutes. The Russians themselves did not abide by the terms of seizure that they had set out, however; land acquisition by the resettlement administration completely disregarded patterns of Kazakh land usage. The Russians were interested in acquiring the best farmlands for new European settlers, particularly since the Kazakhs themselves showed little or no interest in farming. The result was the loss of some traditional pastures and the inaccessibility of others.

This destruction of traditional life did not disturb even the most charitable of the Russian officials, such as Count K. K. Palen, whose 21-volume report on conditions in Turkestan is openly sympathetic to the plight of the natives.[20] Palen felt that the Kazakhs were being fairly treated, since on average they were left thirty desiatins per household, twice the allotted norm of the Russians. The only realistic appraisal of the situation seems to have been by A. A. Kaufman, who wrote that the nomadic Kazakhs required an average of 145 desiatins per household in Syr Darya and 110 desiatins per household in Semirech'e in order to permit pastoral livestock breeding. Kaufman's report pointed out that the earlier and lower estimates were arrived at by studying the patterns of land usage by the Kazakhs within uezds only, whereas actual migratory patterns typically took the Kazakhs far beyond their own district boundaries. He argued that these faulty estimates explained the hardships experienced by the Kazakhs of the steppe region after land seizure began there. Yet even Kaufman felt that there were about 10 million desiatins of surplus land in the steppe, and therefore the then-present average of nearly 300 desiatins per household was double the actual needs of the Kazakhs. Still, such lands were excess only after the Kazakhs were relocated, since they grazed upon the very lands most suitable for agriculture.[21]

Estimates of how much land the Kazakhs had at their disposal vary considerably. As Kaufman noted, it is extremely difficult to measure the amount of land used by a people practicing the free ranging of livestock. The fifteen-desiatin standard applied only when those who had their pastures seized requested compensatory new lands. Although, as Palen noted, the Kazakhs were typically granted holdings double the approved size, even thirty-desiatin plots were still much too small to allow free grazing. Kazakhs whose lands were untouched enjoyed control of much larger amounts of land; many Kazakhs had enough land to be able to rent parcels to the Russians, which suggests the unequal patterns of land distribution within the Kazakh community. The Russian settlers were technically permitted to rent no more than two desiatins per household member, but it was easy to get around the restrictions and was not uncommon to find Russian settlers with homesteads of 100 desiatins or more. While Kazakhs with land enough to rent were clearly the exception, their existence was taken as proof that the Kazakhs indeed held excess lands.

The Russian policymakers were generally ignorant of the needs of the nomads. They were committed to the most rational economic use of the newly annexed lands, which they honestly thought would be to the long-term advantage of the Kazakhs as well as the Russians. They failed to appreciate how determined the Kazakhs were to preserve their nomadic way of life, which naturally held great social, political, and economic meaning for this people. To the Russians, nomadism was simply a stage beyond which the Kazakhs should pass; the Russian policy of land seizure insured that they must. Denied sufficient pastures, the vast majority of the Kazakhs had no choice but to adopt a semisedentary lifestyle that combined limited agriculture with a restricted annual migration.

The policy of land settlement was therefore an important element hastening the end of Kazakh nomadism. It greatly speeded up the process of the breakdown and transformation of Kazakh livestock breeding, although this process was already quite irreversible at the time that the decision to seize large quantities of land was made.[22] What made the Russian policy of allocating and assigning pastureland to the Kazakhs truly effective was the willingness of most administrative aul and volost officials—that is, Kazakhs themselves—to cooperate with the policy. The unsuccessful rebellions of 1869 and 1870 had convinced most clan leaders that the Russians were well able to impose their will if they so desired; compliance, therefore, seemed easier. In addition, a new group of pro-Russian officials was emerging, many from the ill-utilized Kazakh aristocracy, who were more concerned with the satisfactory performances of their own jobs than with the good of the Kazakhs. Still, submission of the Kazakhs was not complete. Many clans, especially among the Adaev in the Mangyshlak region, continued to migrate across uezd, oblast, and even province boundaries. Nevertheless, the increasing number of Russian forts, defense outposts, and small settlements, often sited on traditional trails and near sources of water, did alter the patterns of migration. The major tribes and clans were forced to use the same lands year after year, a practice that had been hitherto unknown in the steppe; overuse further depleted the soil, making the Kazakhs evermore vulnerable to the vagaries of nature. The harsh winter of 1879–1880, known in the steppe at the "Great Jut," turned many Kazakhs exclusively into farmers; this one winter shortage of fodder was so acute that in the Akmolinsk oblast alone over 800,000 head of cattle died, while Turgai lost over 300,000 horses and more than 1 million sheep.[23] The Kazakh economy received another jolt with the drought of 1890–1891, which led to the death of hundreds of thousands of animals throughout the steppe and increased the Kazakh demand for plots of land. Still, in spite of all the difficulties of livestock breeding, the eve of the Russian Revolution found nearly one quarter of the Kazakh population still dependent upon animal husbandry as their sole economic pursuit.

The incentives to alter the traditional practice of livestock breeding were not wholly negative. The development of a trade network throughout the steppe with local exchange posts, seasonal markets, and permanent markets all increased demand for livestock and livestock products, particularly for beef cattle. As of the 1870s there was considerable local agitation for the construction of a railroad to link Siberia with the rest of the empire. Construction of the Trans-Siberian rail link with Omsk and Orenburg began in 1892 and was completed in 1896. Most of the Russian residents in the steppe had pushed unsuccessfully to have the railroad placed further south; they then began agitating for a link between Orenburg and Tashkent. The Orenburg-Tashkent railroad was opened in 1906. Because transportation in the eastern part of the steppe, the former territory of the Middle Horde, was largely by water on the Irtysh River system, a rail link through this territory was not begun until the construction of the Turkestan-Siberian railroad in 1926–1927.

The difficulties of transportation slowed the development of a semisedentary form of livestock breeding in the eastern parts of the steppe, where most of the livestock breeders continued to maintain herds of horses, sheep, horned cattle, and camels; however, it was uncommon for even a wealthy breeder to possess more than ten or fifteen head of cattle. Where railroad linked the western regions of the steppe, particularly Turgai and Uralsk, with the markets of Russia, a wealthy cattle breeder might have a herd of several hundred and in some cases even several thousand head. In 1906–1914 the quantity of animals shipped increased four fold, the total value of exports from the steppe increased to nearly ten times that of imports, and already the steppe region was able to export grain to European Russia.[24]

The development of agriculture among the Kazakhs accelerated rapidly in the first years of the twentieth century. A study of one region in the Kustanai district shows that in the seven years between 1898 and 1905 the percentage of Kazakh households planting grain went from 72 percent to 94 percent, while the size of their holdings increased from 2.4 desiatins to 7.6 desiatins per household. For Kustanai as a whole, the percentage of households engaging in agriculture went from 77 to 89 percent.[25] Similar trends were observed in Aktyubinsk and Uralsk. In contrast, the percentage of Kazakh households engaging in agriculture in the Semipalatinsk oblast grew from 36 to 48 percent, which demonstrates both the economic incentive the railroad provided and the effect in areas where Russian settlement had proceeded more slowly. In the two southern oblasts, Syr Darya and Semirech'e, where Russian settlement proceeded more slowly still, Kazakh agriculture was less developed; yet even there it spread rapidly, once introduced.[26] Whereas in 1877 only about one third of the Kazakh population had farmed the land, by 1916 more than 80 percent of the population depended upon agriculture for part of their economic livelihood.[27]

Kazakh agriculture was most developed in the districts of Omsk, Kustanai, Aktyubinsk, and Uralsk, where a minimum of 90 percent of all Kazakh households were engaged in at least limited agriculture. Although most of these alleged farmers were really livestock breeders who planted grain to serve as feed for their herds, at least a quarter of the population were truly farmers. The European settlers provided the Kazakhs with a model of successful farming and produced a marketable surplus; in northern Kazakhstan markets were easily accessible. Just south was another tier of districts, including Kokchetav, Atbasar, Saisan, and Petropavlovsk, where the markets were not as close and the soil not as rich. In this region only about half the Kazakhs engaged in even limited agriculture. Here the herd was typically a mix of sheep, goats, and cattle. The Kazakhs in this region were generally less successful than those in the north; many in fact had moved south to this region in search of pasture. Those who failed to find adequate pasturelands anywhere had only the choices of becoming hired help, farming, or moving south. Some Kazakhs began searching for pastures at the northernmost borders of the steppe and ultimately ended their search only in southern Syr Darya. Even there many did not find open range, and those who did had already lost most of their animals to hunger and thirst en route.

The economic situation of the Kazakhs in the northern part of the steppe varied widely. Successful cattle breeding for sale required a minimum number of animals, fewer than which it was impossible to profitably prepare fodder and stalls. Those who managed to stay above this threshold did well and were often able to expand their herd and thus their profitability. This group provided an important source of work for that part of the community (estimates go up to one-third) that was without animals and lacked the means even to begin to farm. These people, the baigush or hired hands, were very poor. The resettlement administration was only able to process about one-third of the requests made by prospective Kazakh homesteaders, and most of these were in the northern regions, close to the example provided by Russian settlers. Yet these northern Kazakhs were scarcely better off; they were subsistence farmers who generally lived on plots of fewer than ten desiatins and owned only the most primitive implements with which to farm. Most Kazakhs combined agriculture and livestock breeding; with a small herd and some grain they got by, but less successfully than a generation before.

The situation in the southern region, Semirech'e and Syr Darya, was somewhat less bleak. Here fewer Kazakhs were able to profit from the expanded markets and become wealthy, but fewer were forced into poverty, although there was a poor stratum composed primarily of Kazakhs who had migrated south in an unsuccessful search for land. There are several reasons for this relatively easier adjustment by the Kazakhs of these two southern oblasts. Although these Kazakhs were subjected to the same bad climate that had hurt their clansmen to the north—the Great Jut of 1879–1880 killed off almost half the herd in some regions, followed by the drought of 1891 and the harsh winter of 1892–1893—poor conditions were not further exacerbated by immediate seizure of millions of acres of land. The Russian officials, who had already seen the negative side effects of their policy in the north, paid more attention to the prior relocation of Kazakh communities when they seized land in the southern oblasts. There were also important differences in the topography of the two regions; much of the Semirech'e and Syr Darya oblasts are in the Hungersteppe (Betpak-Dala Desert), which is suitable for irrigated farming.

The Russians were long interested in exploiting the agricultural potential of the Hungersteppe, for which irrigation schemes were put forward as early as 1865. These plans sought to rationalize the existing system of irrigation ditches, make better use of the great rivers and their tributaries flowing through this region, and thus water hundreds of thousands of previously unirrigated acres. Irrigation experts discovered many untapped underground water reserves. In the 1870s and 1880s over 3,000 verstas of irrigation ditches were dug in the Kazalinsk and Perovsk guberniias alone. By 1900 more than 600,000 desiatins of irrigated land were open for settlement. During the two decades before the Russian Revolution plans were made for massive irrigation in the Hunger-steppe, but the outbreak of World War I ended further efforts. The newly irrigated lands were awarded to both Kazakh and Russian settlers; by the revolution, 10 percent of the Kazakhs in Turkestan were engaged in irrigated farming. Most of these grew grain, but there was also some truck farming as well.

In the late eighteenth and early nineteenth centuries the economy of the Kazakhs in Turkestan followed two separate paths of development. One was followed by those clans who lived and migrated in Semirech'e and the northern districts of Syr Darya (Perovsk and Kazalinsk), who were fully integrated into the economy of the steppe region. These people were primarily nomads who began to grow grain in the mid-nineteenth century only as a last resort. They were scarcely interested in breeding cattle because they were at least a month's drive away from the markets of Omsk and Orenburg. The percentage of cattle in the total livestock in Semirech'e went only from 1.3 percent in 1865 to 9.7 percent in 1915.[28] In the 30 or 40 years preceding the revolution, decreasing pasture forced the vast majority of Kazakhs in these areas to go from a pastoral nomadic economy to one that was seminomadic; they grew some grain to be used as fodder while they continued to drive their animals as much of the year as possible, which in practice was only about four or five months. These communities often still migrated several hundred versts to summer pastures in Uralsk or Turgai, then returned to their winter campsites in Turkestan in time for the fall harvest. This was in contrast to the virtual end of north-south migration within the steppe, where freedom of migration was hampered by Russian settlement and land seizure as well as by the reluctance of the Kazakhs to drive cattle over long distances.

A second, distinct path was followed in Turkestan by the clans of the Great Horde who lived in the Aulie Ata and Chimkent uezds. These people had been part of the Kokand state until the mid-nineteenth century and so were exposed to an agrarian economy much earlier than the Kazakhs to the north. At the time of the Russian conquest, these Kazakhs were fully integrated into the Turkestan economic region. Many of the Kazakh sultans had accepted parcels of land from the khan and become indistinguishable from the Kokand princes themselves (which gives the feudal school of historiography the only evidence it may legitimately claim). Here the Kazakhs were quite willing to become farmers; nearly 90 percent of them adopted at least limited farming. Many of the Kazakhs differed from their Russian neighbors only in the size of their plots, generally about half that of the Russian average of ten desiatins per household, about 50 percent more than the Russians. Unlike in the north, where it was easy to distinguish classes or economic groups among the Kazakhs, the Kazakhs of Turkestan were essentially undifferentiated. Here the livestock breeders were not particularly wealthy and could not afford to imitate the lifestyle of the European settlers. In many ways the Kazakh farmers, although they did not own much land or livestock, were still the best off since they were truly self-sufficient and integrated into the economy of their territory. Social integration was also strengthened by the success of Kokand missionaries in converting the Kazakhs to Islam, thus providing a cultural link between the Kazakh farmers and their Turkestani neighbors.

## THE KAZAKH ECONOMY
## ON THE EVE OF THE 1916 REVOLT

The policy pursued by the tsarist colonial authorities in the steppe and Turkestan regions irreversibly affected the Kazakh economy and the society as a whole. It transformed the steppe from an ethnically homogeneous to an ethnically diverse society and introduced nearly 3 million Europeans into a society of fewer than 5 million Kazakhs. The Russian peasants were generally successful farmers, since those who could not adjust to the life simply returned to European Russia. The new settlers provided much-needed grain to the markets of European Russia while adding millions of rubles in taxes to the state treasury. For the Kazakhs, the impact of Russian policy was more varied and less positive. Certainly many Kazakhs—estimates vary from 5 to 25 percent of the population—enjoyed a greatly raised standard of living because of the switch to cattle breeding. The price of all forms of livestock, particularly of cattle, rose spectacularly in the first decades of the twentieth century, and the European settlers introduced the Kazakhs to a wide variety of goods that could be purchased at the newly constructed markets and seasonal bazaars. The volume of trade in the steppe grew yearly. Figures for Akmolinsk indicate that the value of goods that changed hands in this oblast alone went from 6.6 million rubles in 1882 to 18.5 million rubles in 1900.[29] All the northern trading towns recorded similar increases, and by the end of the century these steppe towns were becoming cities in their own right. The 1897 census reports that 36,446 people lived in Uralsk and Vernyi, while Semipalatinsk and Petropavlovsk each had approximately 20,000 residents. The census also reported that more than 40,000 people traded in the steppe. With the development of cities came the development of trades. Russian joiners, blacksmiths, carpenters, and glaziers all came east to help build the settlements, and some trained Kazakhs in their trades. The newly trained Kazakhs in turn went back to their auls to practice their new crafts. The new markets also encouraged a flourishing of more traditional Kazakh handicrafts; Kazakh silversmiths and tanners sold their wares to Russian merchants, who also bought native rugs and embroideries for shipment west.

Toward the end of the century Russia, with English financial backing, became interested in exploring the mineral wealth of Siberia and the northern steppe region. Coal and copper mines were opened; in 1916 these employed a total of 18,747 Kazakhs.[30] Almost all of these workers were employed seasonally, since in the winters they migrated with their auls and clans. There was also an expansion of salt mining during these years. The Adaev Kazakhs near the Aral Sea were encouraged to develop a fishing industry. The Kazakhs of this region had always lived in part on fish, but now this became the sole economic pursuit of several thousand people. Probably the most striking change in Kazakh employment patterns was that by 1914 one-fifth of all Kazakhs received wages for part or all of their income. In 60 years the steppe had been transformed from a barter to a cash economy.

Although more than 90 percent of the Kazakhs continued to earn their living from livestock breeding, farming, or some combination of the two, the Kazakh rural economy changed dramatically under Russian colonial rule. Kazakh livestock breeding was placed on a fundamentally new basis. It was no longer possible for any but the smallest Kazakh herds to be maintained solely by free ranging. Farming had become essential. The degree of dependence upon agriculture varied by region and even from community to community. For some Kazakhs, agriculture was simply an ancillary pursuit; the entire community farmed land in common to produce the needed feed to get through the winter. However, in many communities the Kazakhs accepted the thereto alien philosophy of private ownership of land. In the north, in communities close to the railroad, and in the south on lands irrigated by the Syr Darya and its tributaries, many Kazakhs could already be considered sedentary. They viewed their winter campsites as their homes and their land as something to be worked and protected. They farmed with members of their family or hired help, and at least part of the family remained at the winter site year round.

By the time of the revolution almost three-quarters of the Kazakh population kept the same winter campsites from year to year. They had begun to erect structures on the land, which ranged from primitive shoshalas (dirt mounds) for grain storage to wood and even brick structures for both animals and humans. The principal residential unit of the Kazakh remained the yurt. All Kazakhs lived in these felt tents in summer, and most lived there year round. Three stages of non-nomadic households merged in this period. The earliest group of Kazakhs to become sedentary were the poor, who ceased migration because they owned no animals and so had no reason to wander. The second group to settle were the wealthy livestock breeders of the north, who remained year round at their winter sites; in the summer their animals were driven to pasturelands, generally not too far away, by relatives or hired hands. In the south there was a comparable economic stratum of settled Kazakhs who were somewhat less wealthy. Really farmers rather than livestock breeders, they produced a surplus for market and maintained some livestock both for sale and for their personal needs. The third group—by far the largest, about 70 percent of the Kazakhs—could make a living neither through farming nor livestock breeding and so combined the two; they sowed grain for winter feed and migrated in the summer. It has been estimated that in 1919 50 percent of the Kazakhs migrated only from May to September and that 90 percent of the Kazakhs planted some grain at their winter campsites.[31]

Although the Kazakh economy certainly underwent major transformations during the 50 years preceding the Russian Revolution, it is difficult to evaluate the impact or importance of the changes that occurred, both for the Kazakh society and for the economy of the region as a whole. In this period steppe territory became integrated into the market economy of the empire as a whole, but only a part of steppe society did—that is, the Russian farmers and the large livestock breeders. The vast majority of Kazakhs achieved little from the Russian policy. Although the Kazakhs formed at least 50 percent, and in some areas 75 percent, of the farming population, they owned only 20 percent of the sown fields. Furthermore, in the 10 years preceding the revolution, the total acreage sown by the European population increased nearly sixfold while that cultivated by the Kazakhs increased only twofold. Agriculture continued to occupy a subsidiary role in the Kazakh economy, producing fodder for livestock rather than being a primary economic function.

The composition of the Kazakh herd was affected by the availability of fodder. Previously, a Kazakh household required 150 desiatins of land to maintain 150 animals, a herd that supported a comfortable life with no need for additional food or income. In areas where the animals were stalled all winter, only 30 desiatins of open range land were required. As Kazakh grazing land shrank, the relative importance of small animals for subsistence declined and cattle became the primary animal in the herd, bred for profit. Whereas in the mid-eighteenth century sheep and goats had accounted for over 90 percent of the total herd, by the revolution they made up only about half the herd. Average herd size dropped from about 150 animals per household to 10 or 15 animals, and only 5 percent of the population owned more than 50 head.[32] Despite this, the total herd size increased from some 17 million animals in 1885 to 30 million in 1916.[33] Obviously, differences in wealth were increasing in the Kazakh community. Real fortunes could be made by successful cattle breeders. Norman Fell, an American mining engineer working for a Russo-English mine in Baian-Aul, reported that once when the post failed to receive the payroll, the factory manager brought in the local *bai* who ripped open the lining of the *khalat* (robe) to lend the manager several million rubles. Kazakhs such as this bai did exist, but their economic situation was unusual; the reports of Palen and F. Shcherbina are filled with accounts of the desperate plights of most Kazakhs, and both concluded that the economic situation of the Kazakh livestock breeders was bad and growing worse. An increasing percentage of the total herd was held in an ever smaller number of hands. Farmers were little better off; Kazakh methods were primitive and, save along the Syr Darya River, most Kazakh farmers showed little interest in adapting themselves to the needs of a sedentary lifestyle.

The economic changes were paralleled by a social transformation of Kazakh society. Most of the social and political structures that had governed the Kazakhs during the period of the khanate grew from the needs of pastoral nomadism. Even before tsarist colonial rule, the authority of the khans and sultans had eroded and been replaced by an increased dependence upon the clanic, or black bone, authorities. The introduction of Russian civil administration as well as the disruption of migratory paths hastened this process, since they increased Kazakh dependence upon the aul and lessened ties between auls and clans. By the end of the nineteenth century some tribes reorganized; the Kipchak, Kerei, and Naiman tribes all subdivided, and clan ties became more localized. A new social organization appeared in Kazakh society, the *aul obshchina* or *aul-commune*, a semisedentary residential community based on common ownership of land and livestock and communal income derived from both farming and livestock breeding. These more localized clan ties were very important and were often the sole factor in choosing aul and volost officials. The power of the local clan and aul authorities was strengthened by the economic advantage that some of them enjoyed. The richest Kazakhs, typically from the old noble families, became so well-to-do that they aped the ways of their conquerors by sending their children to Russian schools and building homes in the cities of the northern steppe. These were the exception, however. Most of the local authorities combined economic and political power; some of them augmented this power through close alliance with the increasingly vocal and influential Muslim religious authorities, who had been actively proselytizing among the Kazakhs throughout the nineteenth century. Clan and family ties seem to have remained the primary orientation of the Kazakhs, and these were strengthened by the new importance of Islam. Rather than seeking their own personal profit, the Kazakh leadership seems largely to have remained committed to the notion of a Kazakh community; they pressured the Russians to expand the economic opportunities of the majority of Kazakhs. They argued, fruitlessly, that the steppe should be populated by Kazakhs for their own benefit. Discontent in the Kazakh community increased, and thus the Kazakhs were receptive to the revolutionary fervor that grew nearly universal in the empire in the first decades of the twentieth century.

# 5 The Growth of Discontent Among the Kazakhs

## INTRODUCTION

The Kazakh community had grown increasingly unhappy with Russian policies in the steppe until discontent climaxed in the 1916 uprising. The most serious problem in the decades before the revolution had been the shortage of accessible pastureland; good grazing land had always been in short supply, but the imperial policy of land seizure for distribution to European settlers had greatly exacerbated the situation. The Kazakhs in the north had been particularly hard hit. Some had become grain growers while others, unable or unwilling to adapt to the changing economic situation, had migrated farther south and tried to graze their animals in pastures in the Syr Darya and Semirech'e oblasts. Among the generally burdened Kazakhs these northerners had been especially affected by the increase of taxation and animal requisition quotas imposed by government policy at the start of World War I. It was not surprising, therefore, that these Kazakhs reacted strongly to the draft edicts of 1916; Semirech'e in particular was a site of violent Kazakh opposition.

Tsarist colonial policies had weakened the traditional authority structure in the Kazakh community. Although the Russian officials had attempted to create a native service class that could dominate the Kazakh community, these efforts fell short of their goal. During the quarter century that preceded the Russian Revolution, several forces vied for control of the Kazakh masses, among them secular reformers, Kazakh bureaucrats, the Muslim clergy, and Pan-Turkic reformers. However, each group encountered difficulties in legitimizing their authority.

Since the 1880s an ever-increasing Kazakh intelligentsia had expounded its views, first within the steppe and then, after 1905, in the new national forums provided by the State Duma and the legalization of parties, caucuses, and privately-owned press. Many of these intellectuals were graduates of the state schools (the Russian-Kazakh aul and volost schools) who then went on to gymnasiums in Orenburg, Omsk, or Semipalatinsk. There intellectuals appeared first on the pages of newspapers in the 1880s—the *Akmolinskii Listok*, the *Orenburgskii Listok*, and the *Kirgizskaia Stepnaia Gazeta/Dala Vilayeti*—where they expressed horror at the suffering and narrow economic straits of the Kazakh nomads. Their criticism grew more pointed after hundreds of thousands of Russian families settled in the territory; the liberalized press and publication laws permitted them to be openly critical of many of the colonial policies in the final decade of imperial rule. Most supported Kazakh demands that a certain amount of well-situated pasturelands be reserved exclusively for Kazakh use.

The last half of the nineteenth century witnessed one other major change in Kazakh society: the spread of Islam among the Kazakh masses and the emergence of Islam as a major social and moral force in Kazakh society. By the last quarter of the century there were a large number of Kazakh intellectuals who had been educated in Muslim schools in the steppe and were committed to the merging of Kazakh culture and Islam. They turned to Kazan or Istanbul for their intellectual direction and were much influenced by Pan-Islamic and Pan-Turkic teachings. After the 1905 revolution these intellectuals began to form a working relationship with the secular reformers who had graduated from the Russian-Kazakh schools. Both groups believed that the improvement of the Kazakh economy was a necessary first step for any subsequent policy changes in the steppe, and both saw the Russian social and religious policy in the steppe as an indication of the disdain the colonial ruler had for those colonized.

The changes introduced after 1905–1906 also provided these intellectuals with a forum in which to make their appeals. Mass meetings were held that were organized by the clergy and publicized by the intellectuals who controlled the newly sanctioned typography machines. The new Kazakh press provided a forum for a wide variety of political views and so helped politicize the atmosphere in the steppe in the decade preceding the revolution. This atmosphere was so highly charged that the June 1916 draft decree set off an explosion.

## THE SPREAD OF ISLAM IN THE STEPPE

The Russians had social as well as economic impact on the Kazakhs. The new colonial rulers introduced a network of secular schools into the steppe and so exposed some Kazakhs to the ideas of Western civilization. Yet because the Russians considered such secular education to be for the few, useful primarily to develop a pro-Russian elite, they were willing at least initially to allow the masses more traditional education through Islam. In the late eighteenth century Catherine had become convinced that the nomads of the steppe could best be civilized by Muslim rather than Christian missionaries. The Tatars, whom Catherine saw as the most likely intermediaries, had the necessary language skills and were far better equipped to understand the culture and values of the nomads than were Russian missionaries. Catherine also hoped that conversion to Islam would be quickly achieved and thus make pacification of the steppe relatively speedy.

Catherine's policy had mixed success. The Kazakhs became Muslims; those in the northern part of the steppe were converted by the Tatars but those in the south received their religious instruction from the uninvited Central Asian missionaries. The Kazakhs of the Great Horde were converted under the rule of the khan of Kokand; they accepted a conservative form of Islam that was very critical of the Russian infidels who conquered them.

By the mid-nineteenth century the Russians had ceased to regard the conversion of the Kazakhs as entirely positive, and they had begun to view Islam as a potential rival for the loyalty of their subjects. The Steppe and Turkestan statutes legislated that the construction of mosques and religious schools required the approval of the civilian authorities, who were reluctant to give it. This did not seem to impede the construction of religious establishments; mullahs simply opened "secret" schools and mosques. Because the Kazakhs had no clerically owned lands to support the religious establishments, these schools and mosques had little to tax and were quite capable of avoiding detection by the Russian authorities. Later, the Russian authorities introduced more serious restrictions, which did hamper the clergy in the towns, on the operation of legally constituted schools and the application of Shari'a law. By this time the authorities perceived the greatest threat as coming not from the traditional Central Asian clergy but from the Pan-Turks. The *Jadidi*, Tatar proponents of the new-method (*Jadid*) Muslim school, gained many supporters among young Kazakh intellectuals, particularly in the north.[1] Like their Tatar teachers, the Kazakh Pan-Turks showed an increasingly strident political undertone in their teachings and writings, a tone that became more critical as they came in contact with many other groups of opponents of the regime in the decade before World War I. On the other hand, they stayed within the law and so there was little that could be done to curb their activities.

By World War I the Russian government no longer considered Islam as either a positive or a progressive force but rather as neutral at best and dysfunctional at worst. This was primarily an instinctive and emotional response to a force that Russians could not wholly understand. They had simply seen that the Tatars were orderly and loyal while the Kazakhs were wild and unruly. Russia had hoped that, if converted, the Kazakhs would settle down and become more like the Tatars. What the administration failed to realize was that the process of settlement was complex and that conversion need not result in the sedentarization of the nomads. Worse, the Russians seem to have understood conversion as some sort of mass baptism ceremony; they did not recognize that the introduction of Islam would require cultural conversion as well or that a Muslim Kazakh population might well find more in common with other Muslims than with the Russians who had encouraged their conversion.

It is difficult to judge precisely how successful the Muslim missionaries were; the successfully converted had little reason to boast of their new faith to the Russian authorities, while the Russians, with a small number of conspicuous exceptions, were unequipped to accurately record let alone evaluate the influence of Islam in the steppe. A general picture, however, can be traced. All information supports the conclusion that until the first decades of the nineteenth century the Kazakh masses were Muslims in name only, with no knowledge of Muslim rituals or beliefs. By the 1820s and 1830s travelers among the Kazakhs encountered some clergy, especially among the sultanic retinues. This clergy seems to have used the decline of the khan's authority as an occasion to strengthen its own influence. Chokan Valikhanov reported that in the 1840s Islam was making inroads in the cultural practices of the Kazakhs. This was especially true among the aristocracy, who were making pilgrimages to Mecca and practicing the partial seclusion of women. Some of the richer sultans and biis were paying to establish Quran schools in their territories, but these were still few in number. Nevertheless, some folksongs and even the spoken language of Kazakhstan of this period show signs of Islam's influence.[2]

By the 1860s there was already a sort of formal Muslim religious establishment. Geins noted the existence of Quran schools in Karkaralinsk, Petropavlovsk, and Semipalatinsk; schools in these latter two enrolled over 700 students.[3] Nonetheless, travelers in the rural areas in the 1870s, the most knowledgeable of whom was V. V. Radlov, reported that the Kazakh understanding of Islam was still primitive, characterized by the practice of customs with no knowledge of dogma.[4]

The Kazakh understanding of Islam seems to have changed quite rapidly during the last half of the century. Shcherbina reported 1,659 mullah-teachers in 10 volosts surveyed, at a time when there were nearly 100 Kazakh volosts. It is difficult, however, to know how many students were enrolled in Muslim schools. A study from 1886 reports that in Akmolinsk, Semipalatinsk, and Uralsk there were 7,688 students in Quran schools,[5] yet Ali Khan Bukeikhanov (Ali Khan Bukei Khan uli) claims that the number of students varied from 2 percent to 9.4 percent of Kazakh males; this would make the number of Kazakh students in 1910, the time of his writing, anywhere from 50,000 to 100,000. Bukeikhanov's figure includes students in both legal and illegal schools.[6]

Not only did the number of Kazakh Muslims increase in the last half of the nineteenth century, but the degree of their religiosity did as well. For the first time, a large number of mosques seem to have been built, most of them in the native quarters of the new towns. In 1900 there were 61 mosques reported in the town of Akmolinsk. The Kazakhs who could afford it tried to make the pilgrimage to Mecca; in 1910 alone the Russian government received 500 visa requests.[7] The Kazakhs also adopted many Muslim customs governing marriage, burial, circumcision, inheritance, and the treatment of women. There was a great deal of support from within Kazakh society to have Shari'a law serve as the basis of adjudication in the peoples' courts, and in 1893 the Russian government finally gave the auls some local option in application of this law.

It is difficult to specify the effect that all of this had on Kazakh life during the last decades of tsarist colonial rule. Certainly there was political impact since many of the demands made in 1905–1906 were for greater religious freedom. The 1916 uprising too makes little sense if religious issues are ignored. Unquestionably the spread of Islam changed the structure of Kazakh society. Religious schools produced graduates able to read and understand religious books as well as to assimilate the ideas of Muslim thinkers from outside the steppe. Most such graduates had only rudimentary knowledge of the Quran and of Arabic, yet a minority did go on to receive higher education and so to serve as the reading public for the over 200 religious books published in Kazakhstan in the 40 years before the revolution. Many of these people tried to use their education in the service of their community and for the betterment of the Kazakhs in general.

## THE CREATION OF SECULAR ELITES

The first half of the nineteenth century saw the effective destruction of the Kazakh aristocracy without the creation of anything to replace it. The most serious pretenders were the clan authorities, who had been instrumental in the popular uprisings in the first decades of the century. The colonial administration introduced by the Russians did little to strengthen the power of such authorities. They were able to retain control of the aul-level administration, and some clans managed to gain representation at the volost level as well. Clan leaders, however, were almost by definition excluded from holding power above that level; they lacked the Russian and worldview necessary for service in the higher administration, where the sole entry was appointment by the Russians. The power of the clan leaders declined during colonial rule, largely because they could not perform their primary duty—the allocation of pastureland.

The Russians saw the decline in the authority of the biis and elders as positive; it was a necessary step for the creation of a loyal, peaceful Kazakh population. They intended the graduates of the Russian-Kazakh schools to serve in the colonial administration and in time to replace the clan authorities as respected community figures. The Russians particularly encouraged aristocratic families to send their children to these schools, since they mistakenly believed that aristocratic heritage would lend further legitimacy to the new government. They seemed unaware of the small respect paid to members of the aristocracy, especially to descendants of the family of Abu'l Khayr, which left most Kazakhs reluctant to serve the colonial administration in any capacity other than educator. Consequently only the most self-serving Kazakhs went to work for the volost and uezd governments; the majority, mostly scribes and translators, were corrupt or corruptible and often compounded the problems of administration by having lied about their skills. Thus, the efficiency of the colonial administration in the regional centers was very low, and the Kazakh officials who served in the administration became objects of derision.

Not all—or even most—of the graduates of the new Russian-Kazakh schools were incompetent or corrupt. Many biis and tribal elders sent their children to these schools for a few years to learn Russian, in order better to represent their people upon assuming their fathers' positions. Still, the number of Kazakhs who were educated in the secular schools was quite small; in the 60 years the schools existed, only a few hundred Kazakhs achieved what could be regarded as a high school education in the secular schools. These individuals formed a new secular elite.

The role that this new elite played is difficult to evaluate, but in general they seem to have increased Russian understanding of the Kazakhs rather than the reverse. Several of the individuals educated in these schools came to prominence within the steppe, and three in particular—Chokan Valikhanov (1835–1865), Ibrahim Altynsarin (Ibirai Altinsarin, 1841–1889), and Abai Kunanbaev (Abai Konanbai uli, 1845–1904)—have been elevated to the stature of national heroes by the Soviets because of their secular pro-Russian worldview.[8] Although their importance while alive has certainly been exaggerated, the three were influential figures. They and their followers, the early pedagogues and the first Kazakh writers, helped shape the attitudes of the Kazakh intellectuals who came to maturity just before the revolution. This first secular elite had only slight contact with the Kazakh community and certainly held no positions of importance. The second generation, however, were those intellectuals raised and educated under colonialism, and they were committed to restructuring the authority relationships within the Kazakh community. Unlike their predecessors they wanted not only to understand the Kazakh plight but also to change it.

The writings of Chokan Valikhanov are probably the most articulate expression of a wholly secular Kazakh worldview.[9] Valikhanov, a direct descendant of the khans of the Middle Horde, received a primary education at home and completed his formal studies at the Omsk Cadet Academy. He then took a commission in the imperial army and traveled to St. Petersburg, where he lived for several years. He returned to the steppe to lead scientific expeditions through Russian and Eastern (Chinese) Turkestan. Although an unqualified supporter of all things Russian, he was deeply committed to the elevation and purification of the Kazakh culture. He felt that the Kazakhs stood between two strong cultural traditions: the Russians, who represented enlightenment; and Islam, which reinforced conservative cultural tendencies and prevented the Kazakhs from enjoying the full advantages of citizenship in a European empire. He was not alarmed by the changes occurring in the Kazakh economy because he believed that the Kazakhs should understand their nomadic lifestyle as atavistic and so settle down to a combined form of agriculture and livestock breeding.

Valikhanov was dead before the Steppe Statute was introduced in 1868, and so he never witnessed the economic dislocation that the tsarist land policy occasioned. He also wrote exclusively in Russian, and so when his works filtered back to the steppe the few Kazakhs who might read them would undoubtedly have been struck by their dated quality. This was also true, but to a lesser extent, of the writings of Ibrahim Altynsaryn.[10] Altynsaryn, the son of a Kazakh judge, completed his secondary education in Orenburg. Altynsaryn laid the foundations of the first Kazakh secular school system, organized the first Kazakh-Russian district school in Turgai in 1867, and ultimately rose to the position of inspector of schools for the Turgai oblast. He believed that only through education could the Kazakhs assume equality with the Russians in the steppe, and he saw survival as adaptation to the realities of Russian rule. Not a devout Muslim himself, Altynsaryn believed that the Kazakhs must concentrate on secular education and the acquisition of technical skills. He was the author of the first Kazakh grammar and the first Kazakh-Russian dictionary. He too believed that Kazakh nomadism belonged to the past and that the Kazakhs should learn from the Russians how to combine agriculture and livestock breeding. Like Valikhanov, he also died believing the Russians a benign influence.

Abai Kunanbaev is without question the best known of the group; his memory was popularized by a two-volume historical novel written by Mukhtar Auezov.[11] Abai was the son of Kunanbai, the leader of the Tobikty tribal confederation of the Middle Horde. After graduation from the district school in Karkaralinsk and primary education in a local Quran school, Abai began to criticize the traditional Kazakh way of life in the lyric poems he composed; if Soviet reports may be believed, these poems became widely recited in the steppe. Although he published several volumes of poetry, Abai's ideas are probably most clearly expressed in a book of essays called *Edifications*;[12] most of these essays were written during the 1890s when the Russians were beginning to seize large amounts of land and thousands of European settlers were moving into the steppe. Abai could offer no real solutions for the Kazakhs' economic woes, but he encouraged them to accept the reality of the situation and to gain the technical skills necessary to adjust, to become farmers and cattlemen rather than wandering livestock breeders.

Unlike Altynsaryn and Valikhanov, Abai was unable to offer solely praise for his colonial ruler. Certainly by the 1890s even the most pro-Russian Kazakh intellectual would have been alarmed by the tens of thousands of Kazakhs who had almost no livestock and little land, about whom the imperial government must have seemed wholly ignorant if not actively malevolent or, worse, simply incompetent.

By the 1890s virtually all educated Kazakhs agreed with the criticisms constantly voiced in articles in the *Kirgizskaia Stepnaia Gazeta/Dala Vilayeti*, a weekly, dual-language supplement to the *Akmolinskie Vedomosti*, which was published from 1890 through 1906. This official gazette published articles on Kazakh history and ethnography, original works of fiction, and pieces designed to provide technical assistance to the Kazakh farmers. The writers stressed the need for secular education and called for the curtailment of the power of the mullahs in the education of Kazakh youth. Although the Russian economic policy was not always criticized, the desperate condition of the Kazakh masses was often illustrated; a series of articles titled "Hunger in the Steppe," published in 1890, was often quoted in contemporary analyses. Clearly, the educated Kazakhs no longer approved the Russian administration uncritically. Although this change in attitude cannot be precisely dated, the relaxation of censorship that followed the 1905 revolution brought into wide circulation the views of a new group of younger and more articulate writers who were far more critical of Russian rule. They were also more aware of the important role played by Islam. Not only had Islam brought mass conversion, but it had also led to the creation of a Kazakh Muslim elite, in which Muslim and Kazakh cultural values were fused. Unlike the secular reformers, this elite did influence the lives of most Kazakhs.

## ISLAM AND THE KAZAKH INTELLIGENTSIA

The Central Asian and Tatar clergy were opening Quran schools at the same time that the imperial government was sponsoring a network of secular schools. Throughout the late nineteenth and early twentieth centuries, the number of graduates of religious schools increased, although most received only a rudimentary knowledge of Islam. Still, over time a small Kazakh reading public developed, which served as the audience for the evergrowing number of poets and essayists who wrote in Kazakh. In the 1860s Kazakh had become a literary language, based on spoken Kazakh with Arabic and Tatar influences. Until the 1905 revolution there was no typographer of Arabic script in the steppe; the work of these Kazakhs was printed in Kazan, which served as the Kazakh intellectual center. There may also have been Kazakh language printing done by the Central Asian typographers, although no evidence of such has yet been found.

The most prominent of this first group to write in Kazakh were Shortambai Kanai uli (1818–1881), Dulat Babatai uli (1802–1871), Murat Monke uli (1843–1906), and Abubakir Kerderi (1858–1903). They were committed to the perpetuation of the Kazakh way of life based on pastoral livestock breeding, which they believed Russian conquest and imperial policies seriously threatened. Although they were Muslims, these writers venerated the values and teachings of Islam primarily because they preserved and strengthened most Kazakh cultural values; still, as Muslims they also objected to the Russian presence because the Russians were infidels whose economic and political policies menaced Kazakh society.

Collectively, these writers are known as the *Zar Zaman* (Time of Trouble) poets because of how they characterized Russian annexation, which they held had harmed the Kazakhs by depriving them of much-needed grazing lands and stripping clan authorities of the ability to regulate the lives of their clansmen. As Shortambai lamented, "the Kazakhs are encircled on all sides."[13] Both Shortambai and Murat openly fought the Russian advance and sided with Kenisary Qasimov and his fighters. Dulat, who did not participate in the resistance himself, commemorated it in his poems, the most famous of which was his "Khan Ablai," the inspiration for Kenisary's warriors.

All these men believed that the hard times made the preservation of their faith all the more important for the Kazakhs. In times of economic hardship and physical need Islamic doctrines served to keep the community together. As the traditional clan authorities had less and less authority to exercise, these writers' call to Islam became evermore urgent and the increasing number of mullahs became a growing social force in the steppe.

As the century ended, however, new ideas began to appear in the poems and essays of the Kazakh religious writers, of whom Abubakir is a good example; his later writings display familiarity and sympathy with the Pan-Turks and new-method reformers of Kazan. The crisis in the steppe had become so severe that to call only for a return to the past or the spiritual rejuvenation of the Kazakh people seemed hopelessly inadequate. Thousands of Kazakhs starved in the famines of the 1890s; when land seizures began it became even more painfully evident that the traditional pastoral economy could never be revived. Such conditions strengthened the Tatar reformers who found religious commentaries to prove that Islam sanctioned scientific education; Abubakir took up their program and urged the introduction of new-method schools in the steppe. The Kazakhs could then simultaneously remain good Muslims and gain the skills necessary to survive in the changing economy of the steppe, which required them to compete with the Russians. A new group of Kazakh writers emerged, all of whom grew up under colonial rule and were influenced by the Zar Zaman poets, especially by Abubakir. These younger writers, including Shakarim Kudaiberdi uli (1858–1931), Aqmolla Muhammadiar uli (1839–1895), and Mashur Zhusup Kopei (1857–1931), were all devout Muslims who gave considerable time and energy to the propagation of the new-method Muslim schools. Although they were concerned with the spiritual life of the Kazakhs, they were more interested in improving the temporal. They accepted the passing of Kazakh pastoral nomadism and urged economic reforms very similar to those urged by more secular Kazakhs, with whom they began to work more closely. The political events of 1905–1910 encouraged such closeness, and Kazakh activists of all persuasions were brought together in new political forums.

## THE 1905 REVOLUTION
## AND THE STEPPE

Soviet scholars are chary of writing about Kazakh unrest in the nineteenth century, which creates problems for Western scholars. Whereas Soviet historians have in some periods risked recording Kazakh resistance before complete colonial rule, Kazakh opposition to Russian colonialism is definitionally negative in that it contradicts the supposed "voluntary" nature of Kazakh submission to Russian rule. The first detailed history of the 1869–1870 civil disorders was published only in 1977, under the innocent title *The Kazakhs of Mangyshlak in the Second Half of the Nineteenth Century*.[14]

Although the defeat of these uprisings brought comparative quiet to the steppe until the 1916 draft riots, the peace was at best uneasy. The Kazakhs accepted Russian rule because they acknowledged Russia's superior military force, which they were shown in the 1840s and again in 1869–1870, but they remained hostile. Almost all Kazakhs of any stature refused to serve in the new administration, and taxes were collected only by force or its threat.

The colonial government did little to inspire Kazakh confidence. A post in Turkestan or the steppe was normally a sign of official disfavor, and so civil and military posts were filled by unsavory characters. As one Russian officer observed:

In the eyes of the natives we are far from being on the moral height where we ought to have placed ourselves as soon as we arrived in Central Asia. We have not been able to inspire the natives with the confidence, which should be the principal source of our moral influence and political preponderance. The high moral qualities which ought to have carried Russia's civilizing mission to the natives are lacking, and most of the functionaries of our administration in Central Asia are distinguished by their bad characters.[15]

The Kazakhs who served in the civil administration, mostly as translators, were generally no better. Since all official business was carried out in Russian, the translators were quite powerful; without their cooperation the complaints of the local Kazakh authorities could not receive a hearing. Many of the Kazakh translators were corrupt, demanding favors for their services, and others were simply incompetent, mangling the messages they were supposed to convey.

Although poor administration and inefficiency exacerbated Kazakh dissatisfaction, it was caused by Russian land policies and restrictions on Kazakh migration. Prior to the large-scale settlement of European peasants in the steppe, dissatisfaction was directed toward the government alone, but by the end of the nineteenth century the Kazakhs had begun to vent their frustrations on the European settlers directly, raiding their homesteads and stealing their animals and grain. No precise information is available on the frequency of such attacks, but Count Palen reported in 1910 that several thousand Kazakhs were arrested for crimes of violence against Russians during the 40 years of colonial rule.[16]

Increased education, both secular and religious, gave the Kazakhs new means for communicating their grievances to one another and to the Russian government. The spread of Islam served to increase Kazakh dissatisfaction. The Kazakhs were now subjected to two sets of restrictive rules—those designed for "natives" and those for Muslims—and during the last decades of the century the latter set of laws became even more restrictive as the state sought to curtail the power and influence of Islam. Conversion made it even harder for the Kazakhs to identify with many of Russia's aims, since the Muslim minority in the empire became a larger and more vocal constituency.

There is not much information about Kazakh political activity in the steppe prior to the 1905 revolution. The writings of Ali Khan Bukeikhanov (1869–1932), as well as other pamphlets from this period addressed to the "Children of Alash," urged protest against the government's encroachments on Islam.[17] How widespread such protest meetings were is in question, but the tsarist regime was quick to strike back; the first searches of Kazakh auls for seditious materials began, and Kazakh leaders were arrested on political charges. The large increase in the literate Kazakh population seems to have caught the Russian authorities by surprise. They increased the restrictions on Muslim clergy and tried to curb the spread of illegal Quran schools. Soviet historiography of 1905–1906 focuses on workers' protests in an attempt to show the influence of Marxists in general and Bolsheviks in particular.[18] Since there were few Kazakh workers and no Kazakh Marxists, the Soviet literature speaks little of Kazakh activity during those years.

Although Kazakh dissatisfaction was widespread, the events of Bloody Sunday (January 22, 1905) in St. Petersburg seem to have had no immediate effect in the steppe. This was in part because the Russian rural population on their new homesteads had fewer complaints than their compatriots west of the Urals. In addition, the 1905 revolution was worker-led, particularly at its onset, and the overwhelming majority of what tiny working class the steppe possessed was Russian, not Kazakh; in the early months of 1905 protests in the steppe were confined to the virtually all-Russian railroad industry. The few Kazakhs who might be called proletarian worked in menial capacities in the mines, and so Kazakh participation was largely anomic violence. Nevertheless, the unrest was sufficiently severe in the Syr Darya region to prompt requests for additional aid from the ministry of war.

Kazakh protest acquired a more organized and political character in the summer of 1905, when the more sophisticated of the Kazakh elite realized that, although the Kazakhs shared few of the workers' demands, it was in general a propitious time to press their own demands. The traditional religious elite and the new Kazakh intelligentsia seem to have realized simultaneously that their differences were best put aside in 1905–1906, in pursuit of common goals.

The religious elite played the primary role in organizing popular protest in several significant rallies. In response to the show of Kazakh strength, the government gave in to some longstanding Kazakh demands in an attempt to stop the spread of popular unrest. On April 17, 1905, Kazakh–language religious instruction was permitted in primary schools. More important was the June 18 recommendation by the tsar's council of ministers to broaden the powers of the local Muslim clergy in the steppe (at the expense of the Tatar clerics), which in 1906 resulted in the creation of the muftiate of the Steppe region.

Such concessions were not sufficient to halt rising Kazakh dissatisfaction, however. The unrest was also fed by a growing Pan-Turkic political caucus, the *Ittifak al Muslimin*, which maintained cells in Orenburg, Omsk, Petropavlovsk, Semipalatinsk, and Vernyi.[19] Their activities encouraged the Kazakhs to organize concerted action. A petition campaign sponsored by a group of Muslim clerics led to a bais' congress, which was held in the summer of 1905 in the Kuiandinsk market of Karkaralinsk. This meeting of some 14,500 people from 31 volosts drew up a petition to the tsar that protested government interference in the practice of Islam, official prohibitions against the construction of mosques, denial of a universal right of pilgrimage, and the transfer of jurisdiction over family and marital disputes to the civil courts. The petitioners demanded that Islam be granted the same legal position as that which the Russian Orthodox church enjoyed, and that Orthodox missionaries cease their activities among the Muslims. The petitioners also demanded the return of all land seized from the Kazakhs and protection from further seizures, the return of control of forests and fisheries, and the assurance that mineral extraction would be solely by the Kazakhs for the benefit of the Kazakhs.[20]

There was no immediate response to the petition, and rural violence intensified throughout the summer; disturbances were reported in Semi-palatinsk, Turgai, Uralsk, Baian-Aul, and Pavlodar uezds. Most of these began with Kazakhs forcibly resisting seizure of their land for allocation to Russian peasants, but many grew into protests against Russian authority itself. The governor-general of Akmolinsk reported that the local population refused to provide fresh horses while he was out on an inspection tour. By the end of the summer violence had been reported throughout the Syr Darya and Semirech'e oblasts.[21]

Another mass meeting came in October 1905, this time in Kazalinsk; the resultant petition called for an end to government persecution of Islam and demanded that the adjudication of family and marital disputes be returned to courts of Shari'a law. Greater stress was put on the Kazakhs' economic complaints; the signatories demanded the allocation of adequately sized plots with full rights of ownership to all Kazakh heads of households. They also sought unlimited access to all lakes and rivers and the elimination of the "oppressive laws" that controlled the use of pastureland by Kazakh cattle.

Creation of the State Duma gave the Kazakhs additional occasions to voice their indignation, both in election meetings and when they petitioned the new representatives. Two of these meetings were particularly noteworthy. The first, held in Uralsk in December 1905, drew representatives from five oblasts of Kazakhstan; it was at this meeting that the Alash Orda party was formed, and it ratified the program of the Constitutional Democrats (KDs) with the addition of the following provision: "In the Kirghiz [i.e., Kazakh] Steppe no one other than the Kirghiz has any rights; the laws which declare that the Kirghiz Steppe belongs to the Crown, and that peasants and cossacks can be settled on it at no cost need to be revoked."[22] Little was done to realize such ideals until after the revolution, but this attempt to establish a Kazakh national party reinforced the use of concerted action throughout the steppe.

The second meeting was a conference held in January 1906 in Kazalinsk that drew widely from the steppe population. This meeting was called to draw up a list of Kazakh demands for the forthcoming all-Muslim congress, and the resolutions of this conference mirrored those of earlier meetings.[23] Ultimately more important than any of these demands, however, was the precedent established of the Kazakh population acting in concert. During these decades straddling the turn of the century, the Kazakhs increasingly thought and acted as a homogeneous community. This was partly because of the Russian policy of secular education, which led to the development of a self-aware Kazakh elite, and partly a product of the spread of Islam, which introduced another definition of community and provided a literate clergy who could maintain a communication network throughout the steppe. Of course, there were divisions within the Kazakh community between the secular nationalists and those Kazakhs who maintained a strongly Islamic worldview; even the religious community was split between traditional Muslims and Pan-Turkic reformers, but most Kazakhs felt that such rifts should be bridged when presented to the outside world, particularly before Russian audiences in St. Petersburg, where the Kazakhs argued their case in the newly created State Duma.

## THE POLITICAL CLIMATE ON THE EVE OF THE FIRST WORLD WAR

The creation of a State Duma ultimately had little effect on the development of colonial policy as applied to the steppe. The Duma proved a great disappointment to the Kazakh elite. A total of eight Kazakhs served in the Duma. They failed to get any legislation passed that was of benefit to the Kazakhs, although they did use the Duma as a forum to attract increased attention to the Kazakh economic plight.

Four Kazakhs and four Russians represented the steppe in the first Duma.[24] The land question in the steppe was not considered in this session despite an impassioned speech on the special needs of the Kazakh nomads by T. Sedelnikov, delegate from Orenburg and former member of the Shcherbina expedition, which had investigated the steppe economy.[25] The second Duma included eight Russians and five Kazakhs; like the first session, the Kazakhs allied themselves with the Kadets and participated in the Muslim caucus.[26]

Sultan B. Karataev, a Kazakh lawyer from Uralsk and a member of the land commission, managed to get the economic situation of the Kazakh nomads placed before the second session of the Duma. He urged the creation of a special commission with Kazakh members to investigate the problem of land distribution in the Kazakh Steppe. Such a commission received the support of the Octobrists, the Kadets, and the Muslim caucus, but was rejected by the Council of Ministers. The Kazakh representatives then petitioned Stolypin directly; they requested an end to Russian settlement in the steppe and asked that land be awarded to the existing settlers only after the needs of the Kazakh population were met. This proposal was never acted on.[27] Although denied membership in the third and fourth sessions, Kazakh lobbyists drafted legislation awarding all Kazakh plots large enough to sustain either the free grazing of cattle or feed lands for their support. This law was never enacted, although it had received the endorsement of 60 deputies.

The most important result of Kazakh participation in the Duma was that it helped strengthen Kazakh unity and political awareness. The limited number of seats meant that in order for all sectors of Kazakh society to be represented, the elected representatives had to be acceptable to the local religious authorities, the Pan-Turks, and the secular nationalists. All three groups continued to send lobbyists to St. Petersburg after the Kazakhs were barred from membership in the Duma. The Duma served as a sort of living laboratory for the Kazakh representatives and lobbyists to observe the more experienced political actors in the empire, both Russian and Muslim. They learned how to organize political caucuses and how to approach the government with their demands. Those who journeyed to St. Petersburg came home even less in awe of the government than when they had left, having learned how many other nationalities and social groups had serious complaints about Tsar Nicholas II.

Few of the Kazakh representatives to the Duma adopted a party affiliation, but almost all participated in the Tatar-dominated Muslim caucus. These Kazakhs strengthened their allegiance to a common Muslim cause, which they transmitted to their constituents when they returned to the steppe. The activities of the Muslim caucus, which was dominated by Pan-Turks, served to demonstrate the effectiveness of its ideology; its members were able to define common goals for the various Muslim nationalities, and the new-method schools had graduated spokesmen articulate enough to debate in Russian on the floor of the Duma as equals or near equals with the other delegates. From this time forth, Pan-Turkism became an increasingly important ideological strain in the steppe that influenced Kazakh writings until the mid-1920s.

A few Kazakh deputies chose not to work with the Muslim caucus. The most prominent of these was Ali Khan Bukeikhanov. Bukeikhanov was born in Samara, son of Barak, former khan of the Inner Horde. After completing his studies in the Higher Institute of Forestry in Omsk he became a faculty member at this same institute and then an official of the Agricultural Bank of Samara.[28] Best known as the founder and leader of the Alash Orda party, Bukeikhanov was an active member of the Constitutional Democrat party and served as a member of its central committee. An active opponent of the tsar, Bukeikhanov was twice arrested on political charges while the Duma was in session. From 1905 on he was a steady contributor to Kadet party publications as well as to the budding Kazakh press.

Bukeikhanov's 1910 essay for the Kadet volume on nationalities is an eloquent statement of the prerevolutionary Kazakh situation. About imperial policy he says in the opening paragraph:

> As in the other regions of Russia, so too in the Kirghiz [Kazakh] Steppe a policy of Russification has from time immemorial been conducted by those who shine neither in educational qualifications nor in knowledge of the local population. The customary attendant of this Russifying policy is coarseness, rudeness, and the unceremonious slighting of us by those who constitute the sacred population.[29]

Bukeikhanov claimed that the Russian policy was a form of national antagonism against the Kazakh people, because they denied Kazakhs ownership of their traditional pasturelands and asserted instead that all land belonged to the Russian tsar. Bukeikhanov maintained that the goal of Russian policy was not solely to force the settlement of the nomads but to achieve the destruction of a unique Kazakh culture. He believed that the Kazakhs had to mount a political offensive to protect their heritage and their right to remain a distinct people. For this to be successful, the Kazakhs had to transcend their tribal loyalties and realize that they were a people with common interests and common goals who must work in concert.

Bukeikhanov's beliefs were shared by many of his generation. The intellectuals, secularists, and Pan-Turks were committed to working together to save the Kazakh people from absorption by the dominant culture of the empire. They organized newspapers and journals to spread this message to the literate Kazakhs, who in turn were charged with spreading these ideas to the illiterate masses.

Three journals appeared briefly, without wide circulation: *Serke*, *Qazaqstan*, and *Alash*. Of the three, *Alash* was the most long-lived; it published 22 numbers between November 26, 1916, and May 25, 1917.[30] Two other Kazakh publications were more successful. *Ai Kap* first appeared in 1911 and ceased publication in 1915, issuing 88 numbers in all. It appeared monthly for two years, then switched to a bimonthly format and enjoyed a circulation of between 900 and 1,200 copies per issue. This gazette published articles by Kazakhs, Tatars, and Russians and tried to present a variety of viewpoints on any given issue, under the editorship of Muhammadjan Seralin (1871–1929). The other periodical, *Qazaq*, printed its first issue in 1913 and its last in 1918. After the February Revolution it became the official organ of the Alash Orda party and had a circulation of about 8,000 per month. Its editorial group consisted of Ali Khan Bukeikhanov, Mir Yakub Dulatov (Dulat uli, 1885–1937), and Ahmed Baitursunov (Baitursin uli, 1873–1937).

The editorial positions of the two gazettes were quite similar, differing only because the editors of *Qazaq* defined their purpose as a more consciously political one. Both staffs were dominated by young poets and writers, some of whom, like Dulatov and Sultan Muhammad Toraighir uli (1893–1920), are better remembered for their literary contributions. Seralin (1871–1929) was himself a poet. The educational backgrounds of the editors varied and included graduates of both the secular and Koran schools, but virtually all were the children of old noble families who were attempting to exercise the traditional noble role of leading the Kazakh masses. Yet their ideas were not traditional.

Both gazettes devoted considerable space to the severe economic problems of the Kazakh nomad and suggested ways that they could be alleviated. The editors of *Ai Kap* gave qualified support to the settlement of the Kazakh nomads, since they believed that the Kazakhs could retain control of even a part of the steppe only by adopting a mixed economy; Kazakh resistance to such change was leading to their own impoverishment. This new generation of reformers distinguished between Kazakh culture, which they felt was a real force within the Kazakh community, and the nomadic way of life, which had created the culture but was no longer vital to it; Kazakh culture could survive in the absence of pastoral livestock breeding. As Omar Karashev wrote:

> Eternal nomadic livestock breeding was not ordered as the eternal Kazakh fate. There comes a time when we are able to live as agriculturists and as traders. The present-day Russians and Tatars and other settled peoples first led nomadic lives, raising livestock. How they are occupied in the present day is known by all. We are no worse off than they are and we are the children of humanity. We are also able to live as they do.[31]

Although the editors of *Ai Kap* endorsed the idea of the settlement of the nomads, they opposed what they felt was the government's uneven treatment of the Kazakhs, alleging that one standard was used for Russian peasants and another for Kazakhs. They requested an all-Kazakh conference, to be held in the winter of 1913–1914, to discuss how the sedentarization of the Kazakh population could best be achieved. The governor-general of the steppe ruled that Russian economic policy was not a problem to be resolved by a group process—settlement was a personal matter for the Kazakh families involved—and so he denied the request.

The editors of *Qazaq* also believed that the Kazakh nomads had to give up their migratory existence and adopt a more rational and lucrative economic pursuit. However, they were bitter about the government treatment of the Kazakhs and claimed that both the size and location of the land allotments made to the Kazakhs were inequitable; the allotments were based on standards suitable to farming, not to livestock breeding. The editors of *Qazaq* were quite clear on this point:

> the transition of the local population to a sedentary way of life means the voluntary giving over of land to the settlers from the central guberniias of Russia. In order to maintain in their hands sufficient land masses the local residents ought to receive land parcels according to the so-called "nomadic norm" and so land parcels in that norm would be twice as great as according to the sedentary norm. . .
> The opinion of the newspaper *Qazaq* on the agricultural question is to support the position of seizing the Kazakh land according to order and law. The expropriation of land according to order means not to destroy the existing economic order of the Kazakhs: that is, if the Kazakhs live by agriculture, then give them land according to livestock breeding norms and take the remaining surplus. To take away land means to have some sort of

legal position, published so that the resettlement officials do not get out of hand. When the resettlement officials take away Kazakh land, they are unable to depart from the framework of this legal position.[32]

The editors of both gazettes believed that much that was positive would be achieved by the settlement of the nomads, especially if done in a reasonable and fair manner. Many of the intellectuals were critical of some of the customary Kazakh practices, particularly the treatment of women, which had become much worse with the increased influence of Islam. The dependent position of women was a common theme in the Kazakh press, and several Kazakh writers wrote poems and novels on the subject, including the very popular novels *Sad Maria* by Kashirov and *The Girl Jamilia* by Donentaev. These authors argued that the question of women's roles was only a manifestation of the opposition by the traditional leadership to such changes as would enable the Kazakhs to revive their shattered economy. Worse still was this leadership's opposition to the secular and new-method schools; to the young intellectuals, education was the key to the successful transformation of the Kazakhs.

The government, too, was criticized for failures in this sector. The Russians had introduced too few schools—only 157 aul schools existed in 1913—and the program was insufficient to allow the Kazakhs to develop the level of linguistic or technical skills necessary to gain admission to the district full primary and secondary schools. The religious authorities were chastised for their objections to the new-method schools and for their reluctance in allowing scientific subjects to be taught in the Quran schools. However, the intellectuals split on the issue of secular versus religious education; some—and these views were more apt to be represented on the pages of *Ai Kap*—were committed to a religious education for the Kazakhs, despite the strong Tatar influence in the religious schools. Nevertheless it was stressed that a religious education should not prevent the introduction of progressive social themes.[33]

Kazakh intellectuals were influenced by Pan-Turkic ideas and sometimes contributed to the progressive Muslim journals like *Terjuman* and *V Mire Musul'manstva*. Yet they were also committed to the idea that the practice of Islam should adhere to Kazakh cultural needs, rather than the reverse, which clearly showed that they were late and incomplete converts.[34] The Kazakhs in general were split about the role Islam should be allowed to play; the editors of *Ai Kap* saw the religious leaders as valuable allies in the fight to modernize the Kazakh community, whereas the editors of *Qazaq* believed that the Kazakh people should seek leadership within the traditions of their society. Thus, the issue that divided the two editorial staffs was whether Shari'a or adat law should be used in the Kazakh people's courts. *Ai Kap* advocated the use of Shari'a law, while *Qazaq* supported the use of the adat because, as Bukeikhanov wrote, "The Kazakhs are non-Muslims or at very most half-Muslims. The preservation of customs and traditions is useful to the Kazakhs. The *Shari'a* is harmful to the Kazakhs."[35]

The editors of *Qazaq* had as their primary goal the preservation of a distinct Kazakh people with a consciously political purpose; they claimed that the Kazakhs were entitled to political as well as cultural concessions. They understood their "Kazakhness" as a form of national identity, to which they devoted their gazette. Baitursunov wrote in the lead article of the first issue, "Our newspaper is named *Qazaq*, our slogan is the preservation of our national character . . . "[36] The very name *Qazaq* was a political stand, for this was the Kazakhs' own name for themselves as opposed to the Russian misnomer, "Kirgiz." Baitursunov and his co-editors were trying to preserve their language, culture, and history, fight the assimilationists among them, and argue that one could be Kazakh and speak Kazakh while still being progressive, modern. They maintained that the Kazakhs could achieve economic parity with the Russians through technical education in the steppe and the subsequent spread of modern (that is, Russian) agricultural and livestock-breeding techniques. All this could be achieved without becoming Russified, whereas assimilation would buy modernization only at the price of national identity. Baitursunov wrote:

> From the Volga to the Irtysh, from the Urals to Afghanistan, a solid mass of us lived, Kazakhs, and now when different people penetrate into our midst, why are we not able to live as such, a Kazakh nation, not losing our name, our national character? This question occupies us day and night, disturbing our sleep. When such a mixing with our peoples comes about, only a nation that has its own language, its own literature will be preserved. The national character of a people who speak their own language never disappears.[37]

The gazettes and their editorial staffs remained a lobbying group in the steppe until the Russian Revolution, when they established and staffed a short-lived Kazakh autonomous government. It is difficult to assess their precise role in the prerevolutionary period. These writers may have helped frame public opinion, but they were only one force and were more successful in harnessing popular fury than in preventing it. They were forced to stand helplessly aside during the popular unrest in the summer and fall of 1916.

## THE 1916 UPRISING

The overall economic situation in the steppe was deteriorating rapidly in the years immediately prior to World War I. Of course some Kazakhs were getting help, but most of the population was feeling the impact of the continuing land seizures, which by this time were concentrated in the Syr Darya and Semirech'e regions. In these oblasts the total number of animals was declining at an approximate rate of 5 percent annually.[38] The adverse economic conditions were further exacerbated by the war conditions that were introduced in late 1914. War led almost immediately to the breakdown of the empire-wide market, and Kazakhs and Russians alike were forced to trade their goods almost exclusively locally. This led to a sharp drop in the price of livestock and a variety of shortages in the steppe economy. As their contribution to the war effort, the Kazakhs were "requested" to make "donations" of meat and hides and to provide horses to the imperial cavalry; in 1914 and 1915 alone some 260,000 head of livestock were taken without remuneration. Although exempted from the draft, the Kazakhs were required to donate work on the homesteads of the Russian peasants who had gone off to war. In addition to these strains, the tax burden on all households was increased by 3–5 percent. During these years the government also continued to increase the size of the Public Land Fund.

These measures worsened existing tensions. As early as 1913 the steppe authorities had warned that they could not guarantee the safety of the Russian settlers if Kazakh lands were seized and if the Kazakhs were treated inequitably by the resettlement administration; nevertheless, the treatment of the Kazakhs grew even worse during the war.[39] The imperial authorities were engaged in an uphill battle and needed the cooperation of all subjects, so appeasement of the Kazakhs or any other subject population was never a consideration. When a policy seemed to serve the war effort, it was simply implemented.

In late June 1916 the Russian government made a new and disruptive demand. The tsar called for conscription into labor brigades of the indigenous population, aged 18 through 43, from the Caucasian oblasts and Turkestan and steppe regions; this was at a time when the Russian army was seriously understaffed and the front was collapsing. The manifesto was a response to mounting military pressures, without regard to complaints from Central Asia that violence against Russians was increasing. Compliance was not difficult to obtain in the Caucasus, but in Central Asia opposition was immediate and violent. An uprising rapidly spread throughout the affected regions, worsening the economic situation and further alienating the already-hostile subject populations.

The ukase called for the conscription of 390,000 men from the Turkestan and steppe regions. In the Kazakh regions 87,000 men were to be drafted from Semirech'e, 60,000 from Syr Darya, 50,000 from Uralsk, 40,000 from Akmolinsk, 60,000 from Turgai, and 8,500 from the Semipalatinsk oblast; the first wave of conscription was to concentrate on 18- to 31-year-olds. Mobilization began with the dissemination of the ukase, and so too did violent resistance. It took some time for word of the conscription order to spread throughout the Steppe. Word of the order reached Semipalatinsk on June 28,

1916, and Akmolinsk on June 29, accompanied by a statement from the governor general of the steppe that conscription was to begin on June 30.

In the uezds of Semirech'e and Syr Darya mobilization began on July 2, when men in the immediate vicinity of uezd centers who seemed to be the appropriate age were rounded up to demonstrate the seriousness of the conscription order. In Tashkent 13,182 men were drafted, in Chimkent 9,682, in Aulie Ata 13,104, in Perovsk 6,670, and in Kazalinsk 9,744.[40] Plans for the systematic extension of conscription throughout the countryside were dependent on the support of the indigenous leadership. Russian officials expected to disseminate the proclamation by having the mullahs read to the congregants in their mosques; these mullahs and elders were also expected to generate lists of draft-eligible youth from their communities. Some officials did cooperate but used their authority for personal gains by, for example, forgetting to include the names of their relatives and those of their allies while having no lapse of memory with those of their rivals. However, strong popular sentiment quickly dissuaded those Central Asian officials who tried to cooperate; they became the first victims of the violence caused by the draft decree. Accounts of Kazakh attacks on elders employed by the Russians (primarily aul administrators and scribes) appear on police blotters in the Birmola volost (Akmolinsk) on July 11, Karam volost (Vernyi) and Bistiubinsk volost (Kustanai) on July 12, and Akkargin volost (Vernyi) on August 22.[41] Nevertheless, the most fierce Kazakh resistance was saved for the Russian officials.

Organized open resistance began first among the Turkestani population. On July 4 Russian officials in Samarkand reported pockets of fighting throughout the city, while the local garrison was encountering heavy and organized resistance in the old city. The uprising quickly spread, first engulfing the Samarkand uezd and then the oblast. Organized resistance began in the old city of Tashkent on July 11 and spread to Fergana and throughout the Fergana oblast. The Tashkent uprising was an important spark for both Kazakh and Kirgiz resistance. Kazakhs living in or traveling through Tashkent from Syr Darya hurried home to help organize resistance to this latest Russian outrage; among them was Turar Ryskulov, who later rose to fame and then fell to ignominy as a Bolshevik leader in Kazakhstan.

The Russian authorities tried to intimidate the Central Asian insurgents into submission by announcing stiff penalties on July 19. Any attack on Russian property or on a Russian official in the course of duty (which included all those making lists of potential conscriptees) became a punishable offense. This strategy seems only to have strengthened the popular will to resist. By early August the uprising had spread throughout the Syr Darya oblast, and detachments of between 5,000 and occasionally even 8,000 armed natives—Kazakhs, Kirgiz, and Uzbeks—attacked Russian troops along the Tashkent-Orenburg railroad.[42] Russian troops battled the insurgents throughout September; by mid-October the uprising in Syr Darya had been reduced to sporadic attacks. Groups of Kazakh fighters fled to the Irgiz and Turgai uezds, where organized resistance to the Russians continued.

The native uprising in Semirech'e was of similar duration but Kazakh resistance there was even more widespread and better organized. On July 10 Kazakh representatives from eleven volosts gathered near the ancient city of Otrar to organize their plans for concerted attacks on the Russian forces. At this same meeting the Kazakhs also decided to send thousands of draft-age men into exile along Lake Balkhash.

On August 7 coordinated attacks were made on the postal and telegraph stations along the Tashkent-Vernyi road. Shortly after, on August 13, another all-oblast planning session was held, this time in the Jail'mysh volost. By mid-August there was fighting throughout Semirech'e, even in remote mountain areas of the Lepsinsk uezd. Kazakh resistance was massive; over 30,000 fighters were reported to be in the Kopal uezd alone.[43] Tokash Bokin, a Kazakh from outside Vernyi who later died fighting for the Bolshevik cause in 1918, was an important leader in the Kazakh resistance. The Kazakhs threatened Russian control of the railroad lines throughout August; local Russian garrisons required reinforcement from cossack detachments.

In September, Russian forces throughout the steppe were reinforced by the arrival of a special expeditionary force; under the command of Lieutenant-General Lavrent'iev, nine companies of the imperial army and seven detachments of cossacks gathered from military outposts in Perm, Kazan, and Saratov. The troops treated the native population of Semirech'e harshly. Throughout September and October punitive detachments were sent from aul to aul to hunt out participants of the uprising and arrest draft resisters. In many cases whole villages were judged collaborators and all the yurts burned. By the end of October thousands had died and some 300,000 Kazakhs and Kirgiz had been driven from their traditional camping places. Some stayed in the oblast awaiting resettlement, some fled north to join the fighting, but most migrated to China with what remained of their possessions.

The Kazakhs of the northern oblasts of the steppe also offered substantial resistance to the tsar's ukase. By mid-July disturbances had been reported in the Zaisan, Ust-Kamenogorsk, Karkaralinsk, and Semipalatinsk uezds of the Semipalatinsk oblast and in the Akmolinsk, Atbasar, and Petropavlovsk uezds of the Akmolinsk oblast. The Kazakh leadership began to gather and plan a concerted strategy as early as July 16, when a congress of aksakals from four volosts met in Atbasar. Local meetings continued throughout the summer, and the bands of Kazakh fighters ranged from small groups of a few dozen men to detachments of 400–700. By September Kazakh resistance was fully organized, and colonial officials in Omsk reported that nearly 30,000 Kazakh fighters camped in the Akmolinsk region. In addition there were groups of 7,000 fighters each in the Zaisan and Semipalatinsk uezds, two groups in the Pavlodar uezd (one of 4,000, the other of 2,000), and several groups of around 3,000 men each in Ust-Kamenogorsk.[44]

The Kazakhs made a major assault on the city of Akmolinsk on September 26–27, again on October 3–4, and a final attack on October 6. These attacks were repulsed by reinforcements from Lavrent'iev's expeditionary forces. Organized resistance collapsed; by the end of the month the northern region was again under the control of the Russian garrison at Semipalatinsk, which supervised the conscription of Kazakh forced laborers. By mid-November 50,479 people (59 percent of the quota) in the Semipalatinsk and 43,316 people (55 percent) in the Akmolinsk oblasts had been conscripted, although always with violent resistance. Troops from the Tomsk garrison had to be called in to help, because some of the Russian peasants who served in the Semipalatinsk garrison were in sympathy with the Kazakhs and refused to shoot the resisters.[45]

In mid-July reports of disturbances began to come in from the Inner Horde and from the Temirtau and Guryev districts in the western part of the steppe. The heaviest resistance in the steppe region was in the Turgai, Irgiz, Aktyubinsk, and Kustanai uezds in the Turgai oblast. The key figure of the Kazakh revolt in this area was Amangeldy Imanov (1873–1919), later to become the first Soviet Kazakh hero because he commanded pro-Bolshevik Adigei troops during the Civil War. Amangeldy's forces were certainly the best organized during the Civil War; by October 1916 they numbered some 20,000 men, of which 5,000 were under his personal command and the rest under a group of allied commanders. He was responsible for the greatest Kazakh victory of the uprising; on October 23 some 15,000 Kazakh fighters surrounded the city of Turgai, cutting off telegraph and railroad connections. The siege did not end completely until mid-November, when Lavrent'iev's troops arrived; these troops had virtually deflated all Kazakh resistance en route between Semipalatinsk and Turgai. The Russian army regulars launched a three-prong attack on the Kazakhs and inflicted heavy casualties; by November 30 only about 6,000 Kazakh fighters were left. They fled to the more remote steppeland of the Irgiz uezd, where in ever-dwindling numbers they continued to resist the Russians. By mid-January only some 2,000 rebels were left, and they melted further and further into the steppe. Finally, on February 27, only days before the abdication of the tsar, the punitive detachments of Russian soldiers were withdrawn from the Irgiz and Turgai uezds.[46]

There has been much debate in Soviet sources about the precise nature of the 1916 uprising. This debate centers on whether the uprising was a response to harsh economic conditions and thus a progressive prelude to the fall of tsarism, or whether it was a reactionary attempt by a worn-out and moribund clergy and traditional (so-called feudal) leadership to fight for a false faith and to preserve power in the face of ever-increasing challenges. At least in the

Kazakh case all sources—pre- and post-revolutionary, Kazakh and Russian—seem to agree that economic motivations were great. Following the suppression of the revolt, a special commission was dispatched to the region to examine causes of the uprising and recommend punishment for the arrested rebels and their supportive townsmen and clansmen. Although the full protocols of the committee have never been published, those parts that have been argue persuasively that the government's land policy was the single best explanation for the magnitude of hostilities in the Kazakh territory. The military governor of Semirech'e testified that:

> The causes of the displeasure of the local nomads is still not precisely clear, but unquestionably one of the leading causes was the widespread colonization of Semirech'e by Russian elements, which entailed the restriction of their former space, and in places loss by the natives of formerly settled land and previously controlled water.[47]

The greatest Kazakh resistance came where the Kazakhs had been especially harshly treated by the Russians and where few economic resources were left at their disposal; for example, in the Merkes region of the Syr Darya oblast large numbers of Russian settlers had moved in, thereby driving the Kazakhs toward the mountains and into the deserts. In Semirech'e Russian settlements had been planned to hamper use of traditional migratory paths and were often placed on irrigation canals, making traditional water supplies inaccessible to the Kazakhs; they were deliberately designed to drive the Kazakhs from the area to facilitate subsequent Russian migration. Although Russian settlement ceased with World War I, the Public Land Fund continued to confiscate Kazakh lands to accommodate future European homesteaders.[48]

Resistance was especially violent in those regions where large numbers of landless nomads had watched their animals die of starvation. Such desperate people had nothing to lose by their resistance. One observer of the situation in the Kokcheri Valley in the Semirech'e oblast said: "There is already almost no grain among the Kirghiz [Kazakhs] and they are unable to supply themselves with it. So since the Kirghiz could neither migrate nor harvest . . . there was no answer to the question of what further to do."[49]

Still, economics can be overemphasized as the sole cause of the revolt. The Muslim clergy played on the religious discontent of the population, which was characterized by a feeling of official inferiority to the Christian community; the clergy encouraged resistance in the areas of Syr Darya and Semirech'e (for example, Aulie Ata, Lepsinsk, and Przhevalsk), areas of sedentary Kazakh agriculture. The devout Turkestani, and the more deeply religious Kazakhs of southern Kazakhstan, had tried to ignore the fact that Russia was at war with Turkey, which was a traditional friend of Central Asia and the home of the caliph. Yet when the Russian government demanded their assistance in fighting the war, such religious obligations took on a renewed importance. A good Muslim could not fight with the infidel against the true faith. Many Turkestanis had long been uncomfortable about their domination by the infidel state, and although the imperial government had made some concessions to the Islamic religious establishment in the period 1906–1914, the Muslim consciousness and sense of political purpose had also strengthened in these years. Even further north, where doctrinal Islam and connections with Turkey were weaker, the clergy tried to use religious themes to mobilize the population; they declared a *jihad* (holy war) against the Russians and promised that all casualties would be considered martyrs to the faith.[50]

When the revolt was finally put down in late 1916, virtually all sectors of Kazakh society had united in protest against Russian authority. Even the Kazakh stagecoach and mine workers had joined in the protest.[51] The only group that had come with reluctance to support the revolt was the Kazakh nationalists of the newspaper *Qazaq*. As early as 1915 there had been rumors of the impending conscription; in February 1916 Baitursunov and Bukeikhanov went to Petrograd (formerly St. Petersburg) to discuss Kazakh conscription, and they urged that the Kazakhs be drafted into the cavalry and receive the customary land grants at the conclusion of the war.[52] They were disheartened by the terms of the June 25 manifesto, which to them was yet another demonstration of the Kazakhs' second-class status, but in *Qazaq* issues no. 188 and no. 192 they urged compliance and good performance in order to convince the authorities that the Kazakhs merited better treatment. They also hoped that the tribal leaders' unsuccessful attempt to encourage popular resistance would discredit the traditional leadership. Once the widespread support of the revolt became plain, however, the young Kazakh intellectuals became alarmed that it would discredit them, not their rivals; Baitursunov, Dulatov, and Bukeikhanov maintained a cautious editorial line, attacking all forms of excess violence to prevent being closed down, but in private making it clear that they supported the rebellion. Soviet sources continued to publicize *Qazaq*'s support for the tsar in the early days of the revolt as an effort to discredit the Alash Orda.[53] Several maverick Kazakh intellectuals supported the rebels from the outset, including Turar Ryskulov in Syr Darya; Alibai T. Dzhangil'din (Ali Bai Jangel'din, 1884–1953), the organizational genius behind Amangeldy Imanov in Turgai; Seitgali Mendeshev (1892–1937); and Abdul Rahman Aitiev of the Inner Horde. For these men, all future Bolsheviks, their participation in the revolt and in its violent suppression proved a critical radicalizing experience.

The same widespread nature of the revolt that enabled the Kazakhs to resist for several months also ensured the severity of the Russian response. The Kazakhs had made it clear that they were involuntary subjects of the tsar whose future loyalty might be suspect. Governor General Kuropatkin warned the tsar that the truce achieved by the Russian troops was a temporary one; he counseled that "it is impossible to rely on the fact that a part of the Kirghiz [Kazakh] of Syr Darya and Semirech'e *oblasts*, with the appearance of ready fodder, would not make a new attempt at armed demonstration. Measures against such a demonstration are being taken."[54]

The revolt proved to be very costly to the Kazakhs. It is impossible to find precise figures on the loss of life directly or indirectly (for example, through subsequent famine) attributable to the revolt. There is relatively good data on population decline for only one oblast, Semirech'e. The population of the Dzharkent uezd declined by 73 percent in the period between the onset of World War I and January 1, 1917, in Przhevalsk by 70 percent, in Lepsinsk by 47 percent, in Vernyi by 45 percent, and in Pishpek by 42 percent.[55] Many who chose not to fight or who wanted to avoid subsequent retaliation fled with their families to the deserts, and those who could tried to migrate to Khiva and China. Ryskulov estimates that about half a million Kazakhs fled to China. Thousands of these died en route, and those who did reach China found the Chinese inhospitable. Immediately after the revolution nearly 53,000 of these Kazakhs, the better part of the surviving migrants, returned to the steppe.[56]

In the course of the revolt Kazakh rebels had often plundered Russian property and killed Russian animals; the Russian forces retaliated by destroying Kazakh property. During 1916 the number of horses in the six Kazakh oblasts declined by 50 percent, the number of cattle by 39 percent, the number of camels by 55 percent, and the number of goats and sheep by 58 percent; the area under crop cultivation was reduced by 163,000 hectares.[57] The government then chose to impose a harsh peace and again placed the needs of the empire before the needs of its subject populations. As Kuropatkin wrote, "I have come to the conclusion that it is necessary, where possible, to separate these nationalities (from the Russians) for a long time."[58] The uprising strengthened the already prevailing Russian view that rational economic use of the steppe could best be achieved by the settlements of Russian farmers. The Kazakhs were demonstrating themselves to be both poor farmers and a people impervious to change.

The postrebellion truce was designed to push the Kazakhs deeper into the desert and away from potentially irrigatable farmlands. One part of the truce called for the creation of an all-Russian zone in the Chu River valley and around Lake Issyk-Kul (that is, all of the Przhevalsk and parts of the Dzharkent and Pishpek districts). To accomplish this, about 200,000 Kazakhs and Kirgiz (the population from the new all-Russian zone plus returnees from China) were resettled in the barren, hilly Naryn region, which was declared off limits to Russians. The justification of this measure was that the Russian and native populations had to be kept separate for their own protection and that each had been awarded lands they were most fit to use—farmland for the Russians and grazing land for the Kazakhs. The fact that the territory the Kazakhs had originally inhabited was better grazing land was not addressed.

Much of the postrebellion truce was strictly punitive; it was designed to show the untrustworthy indigenous population of Central Asia that disloyalty to the government was unacceptable, particularly in times of war. Group fines were levied on the Kazakh population (as on all natives of the Turkestan and steppe regions) in the hopes that this would make tribal and clan leaders more willing to control their clansmen. Those rebels who were caught were made examples of. At a special tribunal convened on February 1, 1917, 347 Kazakhs were sentenced to death although only 51 were actually executed before the February Revolution, when the remainder had their sentences commuted. Nearly 170 were sentenced to hard labor and 129 were imprisoned.

Ultimately, the 1916 uprising accomplished little. Forced labor brigades did form, albeit with only half the requested number of conscripts, and both the uprising itself and the punishment it occasioned only exacerbated the Kazakhs' economic crisis. It did increase Kazakh hatred for the Russians, but demonstrated that the tribal and religious leaders were incapable of defeating the Russians. The 1916 uprising occurred in the last days of the old regime; when the imperial government fell, the Kazakhs did not mourn its loss. Many were now willing to accept guidance from the new elite, the educated and articulate journalists and poets who seemed able to function in the confusing world of Petrograd and who offered to mediate a solution favorable to Kazakh interests.

For Soviet purposes, the vehemence with which the Russian government attacked the Kazakh rebels made clear that the latter were not tsarist sympathizers, but the extraordinary hatred the natives showed has made the uprising controversial for Soviet historians. Only on the first jubilee celebration—the tenth anniversary of the uprising—was the revolt painted solely in positive terms as an important precursor to the revolution that had a wholly economic genesis.[59] By the fifteenth anniversary, native challenges to Russian rule were no longer seen as positive, and the revolt, although still an important precursor to the revolution, had become a movement for "the restoration of the rule of Khans and sultans; for the restoration of the old; subjectively the uprising was a counterrevolutionary movement."[60] By the twentieth anniversary, the Soviet regime was already actively engaged in rewriting history to serve the needs of the present, and so the Kazakh revolt was recast as a classic "peasant" revolt, that is, as anti-Tsar but not anti-Russian.[61] After Stalin's death scholars were given greater flexibility in reproducing contemporary documents from the revolt, but the conceptual framework of the 1936 studies has never been entirely rejected.[62] Thus the rebels of 1916 suffered two distinct defeats: first beaten in battle, then denied a hero's place in the history of their people.

# REVOLUTIONARY AND SOVIET KAZAKHSTAN

## PART THREE

# 6 The Revolution and Civil War in the Kazakh Steppe

## INTRODUCTION

News of the February Revolution in 1917 was greeted enthusiastically by all sectors of society. The event was seen as marking the beginning of a new era, one in which the Kazakh grievances would receive a fair hearing and former wrongs would be righted. The Kazakhs supported the Provisional Government and many young intellectuals worked to establish a Kazakh nationalist party, the Alash Orda, to represent and articulate their interests in Petrograd. Their optimism quickly faded as the Provisional Government, too, was overthrown and the Bolsheviks disbanded the democratically elected constitutional convention. Most Kasakhs found it difficult to support the new Bolshevik regime and chose instead to create the Alash Orda autonomous government. This government, which attempted to govern the steppe from December 1917 through mid-1919, fought with the various White forces to defeat Bolshevik rule. As the White cause faded in late 1918 and throughout 1919, increasing numbers of Kazakh nationalists sought accommodation with the Bolsheviks; by the end of 1919 virtually all sectors of Kazakh society had acquiesced to Bolshevik rule. Many joined the new Soviet government hoping to convince the Bolsheviks of the Kazakhs' need for cultural and limited political autonomy, but by late 1919 the economic chaos of the steppe made peace and stability the preeminent concern of all Kazakhs.

## THE KAZAKH STEPPE
## DURING THE PERIOD OF
## THE PROVISIONAL GOVERNMENT

Joseph Castagné, a Frenchman residing in Turkestan, wrote that no one there regretted the overthrow of the tsar: "Pacifists par excellence, the Kazakhs welcomed the revolution which promised them a new life and reparation for the losses inflicted upon them by the former methods of colonization."[1] The Provisional Government quickly sent a representative to the steppe, a certain Petrov. He was charged with organizing regional meetings to gain popular support for the February Revolution and overseeing the local colonial authorities to insure that they exercised their power in a manner conforming with the interests of the new rulers in Petrograd.

At the same time there was little indication of the policies that the government was going to adopt on those issues most directly concerning the Kazakhs, that is, economic reconstruction of the steppe and Kazakh self-rule. Nevertheless, the meetings and rallies after the revolution heightened Kazakh interest in achieving a solution to those problems and increased their sense of unity and group identity.

A generation of young Kazakh intellectuals quickly took the foreground. Most had already been active in the new Kazakh youth groups, including *Birlik* (Unity), formed in Omsk in 1915, and *Erkin Dala* (The Free Steppe), formed in Orenburg in 1916. These groups were discussion circles that helped increase the political awareness and unity of the educated Kazakh youth. Almost immediately after the revolution these young intellectuals took advantage of their new opportunities to form some twenty new youth societies, including *Igylikti Is* (Good Deeds) in Orenburg and *Umyt* (Hope) and *Jas Qazaq* (Young Kazakh) in Uralsk. The Kazakh intellectuals who staffed the journal *Qazaq* (and who then became leaders of the Alash Orda) were the inspiration, and often the direct sponsors, for all these societies. The editorial line of *Qazaq* set the agenda of discussion for all literate Kazakhs; most agreed with the arguments on the journal's pages, but even those who did not agreed that the journal posed the questions that must be answered. *Jas Qazaq*, the most popular of the youth groups, closely followed *Qazaq* in its own journal, *Sary Arka*, even though some of its members (such as Saken Seifullin) went over to the Bolsheviks in the Civil War.

The major questions before the Kazakh elite were whether or not to support the Provisional Government and what price in policy concessions to demand for their support. This involved the question of Kazakh autonomy and whether it should be defined as political independence or as cultural and political autonomy within a federative structure. This issue was not resolved until the defeat of the Kazakhs in the Civil War in 1920. In February and March 1917 the issue was wholly moot, since the Provisional Government had neither the legitimacy nor the power to establish its authority fully, nor did the Kazakh leaders have the broad political support or the economic self-sufficiency necessary to establish an independent region.

From March through November 1917 people of all political persuasions organized wide-ranging debates throughout the steppe in the attempt to fill the obvious political void in the Kazakh territories. Probably the greatest problem facing the Kazakh intellectuals and the Provisional Government was how to bring some sense of political order and unity to the Kazakh community. Although the Kazakh intelligentsia wrote about the Kazakhs as a single people, the general population and the traditional leadership were more inclined to think in parochial terms, accustomed as they were to the 60-year division of the Kazakhs into steppe and Turkestan regions. Most plans for creating political legitimacy were based on consolidating authority in a particular locality and then extending control; this was the strategy of the Provisional Government, the Kazakh nationalists, and the pro-Soviet forces. It was not until July 1917, at the time of the nationalists' all-Kirgiz (Kazakh) congress, that an attempt was made to unite the two regions.

Tashkent was the center of what Provisional Government existed in Central Asia. The formal apparatus of administration, the Turkestan Committee of the Provisional Government, was not created until April 19, 1917, and most of the governmental structure this committee intended to introduce was still being drafted when the October Revolution occurred. Despite several other committees established in the summer of 1917, the Provisional Government in Turkestan was never more than an attenuated executive branch of a still-theoretical administration; it supervised what little policy came down from Petrograd through the chain of regional commissars.

In an attempt to legitimate the revolutionary overthrow of the tsar in the eyes of the indigenous population, the government chose several Kazakhs who had worked with the Kadet party to be commissars; these included Ali Khan Bukeikhanov, Turgai oblast commissar; Muhammad Tynyshpaev, Semirech'e oblast commissar; and Mustafa Chokaev, a commissar in Turkestan. Ahmed Baitursunov also worked for the Provisional Government. Yet nowhere did the Kazakhs have exclusive authority; they continued to work in a Russian-dominated administration. Still, this administration attempted to make at least token gestures to appease the hostile Kazakh population.

The Provisional Government quickly ended the forced conscription of Central Asians and declared an amnesty for those arrested and charged during the uprising. Nevertheless, the level of popular discontent remained high, and sporadic attacks on Russian settlers continued. In March 1917 the Provisional

Government ordered 2.5 million hectares of land recently seized in Semirech'e to be restored to the original owners.[2] However, the government was not yet willing to take up the larger question of how to use the pre-1916 Public Land Fund—that is, whether to use this land for further settlement of Europeans or to return it to the original owners, as the Kazakhs were pressuring it to do. Despite their attempts throughout the spring of 1917, the Kazakh Kadets were unable even to have Tynyshpaev appointed to the ministry of agriculture in Petrograd, a post that they hoped would have given them greater visibility.

Conditions in the steppe remained severe. No systematic efforts were made to help those Kazakhs and Kirgiz who had lost their property before the fall of 1916, and so their economic distress worsened. By the fall of 1917 much of southern Kazakhstan had been declared a famine region, but there was no relief aid available. In mid-summer 1917 the ministry of agriculture of the Provisional Government at least implicitly agreed to take up the Kazakhs' problems when it directed the economic subcommission of the commission for settlement and colonization to consider "the native economy and the foundation of normal rational land guarantees of appropriate land use in regions such as the Kirghiz, Buriat, and so forth."[3]

Kazakh representatives of the Muslim caucus visited Kerensky twice while the matter was under consideration, August 8 and 24, 1917, and the commission's decision was partly to their satisfaction. On September 22, 1917, the economic subcommission reported that areas seized by the resettlement administration but not yet allocated to homesteaders should be restored to their former economic use; in addition, plots in Semirech'e that were now found too costly to irrigate should be reassigned to native livestock breeders. A. A. Kaufman, who was still attached to the ministry of agriculture, argued that the decisions did not go far enough and that it was the government's responsibility to fund and direct the restoration of unused Public Land Fund land everywhere in the steppe to the indigenous population.[4] Still, at about the same time the Provisional Government allocated over 11 million rubles (up to 100 rubles per household) to aid Kazakhs and Russians who had lost property in the 1916 uprising. Despite government support, actual implementation of these measures was still pending when the October Revolution broke out.

During the late spring and summer of 1917, when the Provisional Government was fumbling with the economic problems not only of the steppe but of the entire country, the Kazakh elite began to wonder whether they might try to seize upon the political uncertainty and resolve their economic dilemmas by snatching government and economic management out of Russian hands and taking it into their own. To this end several meetings were held in the spring of 1917, in or near the regional steppe centers; the largest meetings were in Uralsk and Turgai. Saken Seifullin (1894–1938) describes the first meeting in his memoirs and offers a vivid portrait of the chaotic political environment that faced the Kazakh elite. The Uralsk meeting, like the others held in the oblast, were intended to permit the Kazakh population to air their grievances while the various elite groups unified and mobilized the population behind some purpose. Seifullin makes clear that such unity was not only not achieved but that the assembly was bitterly divided before the meeting could even begin. He describes how the clerical representatives indignantly refused even to take their seats, since women were present; when these women were discretely reseated in a separate and remote section of the town circus (where the meeting was held), the clerics agreed to sit, but then balked at having to speak with the western-dressed secular elite, whom they deemed indecently clad. These ominous preliminaries were accurate indicators of the more serious differences that surfaced once the meeting was actually brought to order. The mullahs and *chinovniki* (functionaries) of the former government were able to block the initiatives of the secular intellectuals but were not themselves able to get any type of unifying program passed. The meeting adjourned with little of substance accomplished.[5]

The conference held in Turgai April 2–8, 1917, was far more successful. Some 300 delegates attended, representative of all sectors of Kazakh society, but most of them were handpicked by the *Qazaq* editors who had organized the meeting; they were chosen both because of the constituencies they represented and because, in accepting the principle of Kazakh unity, they seemed willing to negotiate and compromise. A precursor of the Alash Orda, the meeting was chaired by Ahmed Baitursunov, who was assisted by Bukheikhanov and Dulatov. The resolutions passed by this body bore the stamp of the secular nationalists but also showed how influential the reformist clerics were. Kazakh religious affairs, they resolved, were to be directed by a muftiate in Orenburg, which was to insure proportional Kazakh representation; this clerical administration was to be chosen directly by the populace and they in turn would select the *qazis* (judge) who would staff the courts. The total number of religious officials would be a function of the number of mosques, which would be determined by the popular demand for them. The conference recognized the continued separation of church and state, but education was to be a function jointly shared. There was a demand for mandatory universal education (in Kazakh for grades one through three), and the state was to fund the religious schools. The resolutions also recognized the jurisdiction of both civil and religious law.[6]

The conference delegates generally agreed about the seriousness of the economic problems facing the Kazakhs and about their cause: the government seizure of land. However, in these early days of the Provisional Government the assembled Kazakhs were still inclined to let the new government resolve the economic injustices inflicted by its predecessor. The congress resolved only that illegally seized lands should immediately be taken away from Russian homesteaders and returned to the Kazakhs; legally seized lands could remain under

Russian cultivation until the entire question of land in the steppe could be taken up by a specially appointed extraordinary commission.[7]

The conference also considered other pressing political matters, including Russia's continued participation in the First World War. They recognized the need of the "motherland" to pursue the war to a victorious conclusion and so the responsibility of the agrarian sector to provide labor, food, and livestock for the war effort. They even supported the resumption of labor conscription (which had stopped with the February Revolution), but demanded that the conditions of conscription be changed: those already drafted were to be treated better; sole supports of families were to be returned for the planting and harvest seasons; and Kazakh laborers should be permitted to organize, given medical aid, and assured a decent wage. The delegates also called for the Provisional Government to name a new commission to investigate conditions in Turgai during the 1916 uprising.[8]

Although the meeting had been called to help instill a greater sense of Kazakh unity, the participants were not prepared to take the next step of creating a political format for such unity; therefore they continued to support the Provisional Government. They did, however, call for the creation of two local supervisory committees: a Turgai Military-Industrial Committee, to consist of Ahmed Kirai Kosvakov, Seid Azim Kadirbaev, and Sirlibai Bekbaev; and an inspection committee, to consist of Mir Yakub Dulatov, Saridik Doshanov, Gali Ibrahimov, and Isen Turmuhammadov. All these men were either attached to Qazaq or sympathized with it. The meeting also affirmed the need for an independent press in Russia and resolved that Qazaq served as the guardian of the interests of the Kazakh people.[9]

Many of the people at the Turgai meeting also attended the all-Russian Muslim congress held in Moscow in May 1917. The political role of national minorities was one of the central issues discussed at this meeting. Halel Dos Muhammadov, subsequently an Alash Orda leader, became one of the most vocal defenders of what emerged as the majority position—that the national minorities should be accorded territorial rights rather than cultural autonomy. The Kazakh representatives—Resul Zadeh, Zeki Validi, and Abdallah Hojaiev—joined on the question to produce a combined Azeri, Bashkir, Kazakh, and Central Asian majority over Tatar opposition.

From the conclusion of the all-Russian Muslim congress until the defeat of the Alash Orda during the Civil War, the Kazakh press focused on creating a distinctly Kazakh political entity and recording the debate over what form this entity should take and what role it should play in the Russian-dominated state. In mid-June 1917 Qazaq published a series of articles that advocated political autonomy for the Kazakh people. But the editorial staff recognized the complexity of the problem, as the following excerpt from an editorial printed in the June 24 issue of Qazaq makes clear:

if it is decided that autonomy is needed, what form is more acceptable to the Kazakhs; state autonomy or regional autonomy? If we come to a formula of regional autonomy what shall be its basis, territoriality or the peculiarities of culture (nationality)? Can the Kazakhs lay claim to an independent autonomy or establish it in unity with other peoples?[10]

Resolution of this question was the central theme at the all-Kirgiz congress held in Orenburg July 21–28, 1917. At this meeting both Mir Yakub Dulatov and Ahmed Baitursunov called for the creation of an independent and autonomous Kazakh state.[11] Ali Khan Bukeikhanov spoke in favor of what became the majority position for Kazakh national territorial autonomy in a democratic, federative, and parliamentary Russian republic. The congress organized itself as a Kazakh national party. The meeting passed a series of resolutions that were to serve as the party program; this platform was to be put into effect four months hence at an all-union congress scheduled for Turgai on November 21, 1917, when the Kazakh autonomous republic was to be declared.[12]

The central plank in the party platform was a plan to redress Kazakh economic grievances. It demanded that further migration into the steppe cease until after a census had been completed and that all confiscated but as yet undistributed land be returned to the previous holder, whether livestock breeder, merchant, or religious institution. All land that had been distributed but not yet "worked" was also to be returned, and further seizures were prohibited. Kazakhs whose private holdings were being cultivated by Russians were to receive equivalent land parcels. All grazing lands (that is, lands of common usage) still in the custodianship of the Public Land Fund were to be returned to the communities that traditionally used them; they were to be managed by newly created communal land societies. These provisions were to apply to the Kazakhs of the steppe region; the Kazakhs of Turkestan were to be reimbursed through cash payments.[13]

The remainder of the program that was adopted by the congress showed how strong the influence of the *Qazaq* intellectuals had been at the session. The delegation sought to curtail sharply the Muslim clergy. Women were to receive full legal rights. The payment of kalym was forbidden. All marriages were to be with the consent of the parties involved, and both bride and groom must have reached majority. Widows were to be free to remarry as they wished, and only a first wife could authorize the polygamy of her husband. The clerically run Kazakh peoples' courts were to be disbanded and a new legal structure substituted for them, which could include but was not to be dominated by the clerical establishment. Education was to become mandatory and the responsibility of the civil authorities. The first two grades were to be conducted in Kazakh, with the written (Arabic script) language to reflect Kazakh, not Tatar, spelling. The section on ecclesiastical administration also reflected the delegates' desire to reduce Tatar influence; the program supported a call for an independent muftiate in Orenburg to administer the oblasts of Akmolinsk, Semipalatinsk, Turgai, Uralsk, and the Kazakh districts of the Transcaspian oblast (present-day Mangyshlak).

The congress laid out procedures for obtaining popular support for its program. The November 1917 founding session of the Kazakh autonomous government was to be attended by delegates popularly elected at oblast and district sessions throughout the steppe. Although representatives of all political groups were invited to participate, it was nonetheless the hope of the Orenburg convenors that a single unified all-Kazakh party would emerge that would run the Kazakh autonomous oblast, participate in the *Shuro Islam* (the all-Russian Provisional Muslim National Council), and represent the Kazakhs in the activities of the Provisional Government. They believed that the existence of such a party would strengthen Kazakh domination of the oblast government. Moreover they demanded that this government have the right to raise and maintain its own militia and to create *zemstvo* (elected district council) governments in both sedentary and nomadic regions.[15]

Throughout the summer and early autumn of 1917 regional conferences were held to affirm the July resolutions and elect delegates for the November meeting.[16] However, although the July resolutions did achieve widespread support among secular and even religious leadership, this support was far from unanimous.

Those Kazakhs who rejected the Provisional Government also rejected the decisions of the all-Kirgiz Congress. Many of these people came to rally around the person of Kolbai Togusov, who had been active in Birlik circles since their founding. After the February Revolution Togusov, by now editor of the Kazakh journal *Alash*, began to take an active role in organizing the Turkestan Kazakhs of southern Kazakhstan who had never been involved in the activities of Bukeikhanov and the *Qazaq* group. Togusov organized a meeting in Tashkent on March 12, 1917, which was attended by Turar Ryskulov, who was already active in the Tashkent Soviet.[17] This meeting does not seem to have gone well for Togusov; by the end of the month he apparently moved his center of operations to Kazalinsk, where on March 27 he presided over a meeting of some 5,000 Kazakhs, Uzbeks, and Tatars (whom later Soviet sources incongruously report as Muslim soldiers).[18] Whatever these peoples were by occupation, they chose three Tatar, three Kazakh, and three Uzbek delegates to attend the May 1917 all-Russian Muslim congress.

Togusov's influence continued to grow throughout the months that followed. By the time the Alash Orda government was constructed in November 1917 he was in charge of what was probably the most serious Kazakh oppositionary faction. This faction included Saken Seifullin and Shaimerdin Alimzhanov, who with Togusov formed the *Ush Zhuz* (Three Horde) party based in Tashkent. Although much has been written about the socialist impulses of this group, especially by Seifullin, it is more likely that personal rivalry with the Alash Orda leadership, undoubtedly heightened by the Alash Ordists aristocratic origins, explain the desire of Togusov and his friends to strike out on their own. Whatever the cause, the Togusov faction was quick to support Bolshevik rule.

In the region where the descendants of the Bukei Horde lived, there was another large group of Kazakh intellectuals who also chose not to go along with the *Qazaq*-led Alash Orda government. They included Abdul Aziz Musa Galiev, Shafkat Bek Muhammadov, Batir Khayr Niazov, Ishan Ali Mendikhanov, and S. M. Mendeshev (who eventually became a buro member in the Kazakh Communist Party).

From February through November 1917, soviets (popularly chosen workers' councils) were being organized throughout the Kazakh territory. In the winter and spring soviets were established in Tashkent (by far the largest), Orenburg, Omsk, Petropavlovsk, Aktyubinsk, Vernyi, Semipalatinsk, and Perovsk; by late summer there were additional soviets in Akmolinsk, Atbasar, Karkaralinsk, Turgai, Irgiz, Kustanai, Lepsinsk, and Dzharkent. Between the February and October revolutions, however, these soviets were not the "largely Russian" institutions that Soviet sources like to depict but were almost exclusively Russian. These men called a mass meeting on April 21, 1917, at which the delegates declared themselves a provisional government and resolved that the Inner territory should be removed from the steppe region and made a separate unit under the administration of Astrakhan.[19] This resolution was probably influenced by a century-old drive for new land to the west. For a brief period after the October Revolution many Kazakh leaders decided to support the Bolsheviks because of their promises of land reform (never delivered), rather than permit their fate to be decided by representatives from the eastern Kazakh territories, the populations of which had long been unsympathetic to the western regions and who were allied with Ali Khan Bukeikhanov. Yet no Soviet source has offered evidence of significant mass support for the Soviets in the prerevolutionary period (whether Menshevik or Bolshevik), nor even for support of Soviet activity among the disaffected Kazakh elites.

Had the second revolution not occurred, the Alash Orda government would still have faced an uphill struggle to gain legitimacy for its policies, but it was Bukeikhanov and his supporters who emerged from the October Revolution with as broad a consensus as any Kazakh group of the day was likely to achieve.

## THE RISE OF THE ALASH ORDA GOVERNMENT

The Bolshevik takeover in Petrograd occurred only a week before the pre-congress planning sessions of the long-awaited second all-Kirgiz congress were to be held in Orenburg. These planning sessions, which were to set a final agenda for the congress, began as scheduled on November 14, 1917. The Bolshevik philosophy had not yet had an impact on the lives of the Kazakhs who gathered in Orenburg, since there were few people then in the steppe with first-hand knowledge of the new regime. However, the Bolshevik coup did force the minimal representations of the Provisional Government to close, which left in its place what was essentially anarchy.

The Kazakhs who gathered, and these included most of the prominent Kazakh intellectuals, now faced a new and more serious task than they had planned for all summer and fall. Initially the question of Kazakh autonomy had supposed the existence of the Provisional Government—a government committed to ruling Russia according to democratic principles and pledged to full participation by minority nationalities. This government was a logical extension of the liberal democratic ideas that had circulated widely in salons from St. Petersburg to Orenburg, where even Kazakhs had taken part. It had been assumed that the new Kazakh autonomous unit would support and represent the Russian regime. When that government was overthrown, however, the continuation of Kazakhstan within Russia came into question. The Kazakhs felt that they had to determine the political agenda for the steppe themselves, not simply because of their philosophic commitment to the principle of autonomy but because if they didn't, economic conditions in Kazakhstan would deteriorate further and threaten what civil order remained.

The agenda these Kazakhs set for the second all-Kirgiz congress was published in *Qazaq* no. 251 on November 21, 1917. They advocated their commitment to the ideals of the Provisional Government, which were that Kirgizia (they were still reluctant to use "Kazakh" as a legal term) should be an autonomous republic within a Russian federative parliamentary republic. All citizens of this republic were to be assured freedom of speech, press, and assembly. This republic was to have the right to organize its own militia, and to be funded through a system of graduated taxation. The Kazakhs proposed that there be a separation between church and state; a Kirgiz ecclesiastic administration would adjudicate questions relating to birth, death, marriage, and divorce, and the state would retain the responsibility for providing and maintaining a system of free universal Kirgiz (that is, Kazakh) education. They also recommended that all Russian-seized land be returned and that Kirgiz (Kazakhs) be given first priority in all subsequent land-related decisions.[20]

These items were discussed at the congress that met in Orenburg December 5–13, 1917, with representatives from the Uralsk, Turgai, Akmolinsk, Semipalatinsk, Semirech'e, Syr Darya, Samarkand, and Altai guberniia. The presidium of the congress was Bahit Kirei Kulmanov (chair), Ali Khan Bukeikhanov, Halel Dos Muhammadov, Azim Khan Kenisarin, and Omar

Karashev. Dauletshe Yusep Galiev, Mir Yakub Dulatov, and Seid Azim Kadir-baev served as secretaries.[21]

Halel Gabbasov, representing the Provisional Kirgiz Commission, delivered the keynote address, which advocated Kazakh autonomy, the creation of a supervising soviet (the actual word used), and an independent militia. The formal protocol of the meeting, itself a political statement, records that this address was received with great interest.[22] The congress delegates shared a concern that the absence of government was permitting a daily rise in anarchy in the cities and towns of the steppe, thereby threatening the safety of the Kazakh-Kirgiz. They believed that this could only be remedied by the creation of a government that had moral authority and popular support. They maintained that only a Kazakh-dominated government would gain this mass approval and unanimously resolved to create a Kazakh-Kirgiz autonomous region, to be called *Alash*, which would own (presumably in the sense of eminent domain) all land, water, and underground mineral rights in the oblast.

The executive body of this oblast was to be a provisional peoples' soviet, to be called *Alash Orda*, which was to consist of 25 members, 10 of whom would be Russian or other non-Kazakh nationalities. This membership would ensure minority rights within the oblast, including cultural autonomy and legal extra-territoriality. The Alash Orda was empowered to form a militia to collect taxes, contract loans, conduct negotiations with neighboring autonomous groups, draft a constitution, and supervise local elections of representatives to attend the constituent assembly.

All assembled agreed that the Kazakh autonomous oblast should be composed of the former steppe territory (the oblasts of Uralsk, Turgai, Akmolinsk, and Semipalatinsk), the Kazakh districts of Transcaspia, and the Kazakh-dominated regions of Turkestan—the oblasts of Syr Darya and Semirech'e and Kirgiz regions of the Fergana, Samarkand, and Amu Darya oblasts. The congress nearly dissolved, however, over the question of how to achieve this unity and what to do if the inhabitants of the Turkestan territory did not agree to this incorporation. The delegates from Uralsk, the Inner Side, and part of the Syr Darya oblast argued that the declaration of Kazakh autonomy should be made immediately and that unification of the steppe and Turkestan regions would follow once the Alash Orda government was created. This minority refused to submit to the will of the majority, which sought to announce the formation of the government of Alash only after negotiations with the Kazakh and Kirgiz populations of Turkestan were successfully completed and a militia had been organized. A compromise allowed the congress to continue. The announcement of the new Kazakh government, to be chaired by Ali Khan Bukeikhanov (from the minority group) was delayed a month, while negotiations with the Turkestani autonomists proceeded. The new government, whether representing a united Kazakh community or only the steppe territory, would be declared as of that date. This would also give Bukeikhanov time to move from Orenburg and establish his administration in Semipalatinsk, which was designated the capital.

The remainder of the congress was devoted to the pragmatic issue of creating a Kazakh militia. There was to be a detachment for each oblast, to be raised and supplied (food, clothes, and horses) by uezd, with arms provided by the central administration bought with money they anticipated raising through taxation. The Kazakhs expected to use the Orenburg cossacks to train their officers. They correctly assumed that the success of their experiment depended upon their ability to mount the superior military presence in their area. By early January 1918, when the Alash Orda government (formed only from the steppe region) came into formal existence, the pro-Alash Orda factions had already been forced to flee Orenburg prematurely because they were no match for the newly organized pro-Bolshevik Red Guard detachments.

In these early months of their regime, the Bolsheviks were most concerned with maintaining power in Moscow and Petrograd in the face of a growing German threat. In places such as Kazakhstan they left pro-Bolshevik activity to their local supporters, who concentrated on agitating among and, if possible, arming Russian workers in order to create a Bolshevik presence in the cities and larger settlements. Kazakh public opinion seems to have been divided between being pro-Alash Orda (apparently the majority view everywhere but in the Bukei region) and being indifferent.[23] Only a negligible percentage of the population supported such exceptional and isolated pro-Bolshevik Kazakhs as Turar Ryskulov in Syr Darya and Amangeldy Imanov and Alibai Dzhangil'din in Turgai. In fact, when Dzhangil'din ran as a delegate for the constituent assembly he received only 41 votes as compared to 54,897 for the Alash Orda ticket.[24]

Five years later, in a history of the Civil War, Turar Ryskulov wrote that "the *Alash Orda* in the first period following its formation was a progressive and revolutionary force and it was supported by the masses in large measure."[25] Ryskulov (who was charged with being a bourgeois nationalist in the 1930s) went even further. He argued that the Alash Orda takeover of the steppe was the only political event in the Civil War that had any real meaning to the Kazakhs and that millions of Kazakhs were simply unaware of the developments in Moscow and Petrograd during the entire revolutionary period.[26] Ryskulov's eyewitness account says plainly that those Kazakhs who supported the Bolsheviks in the early days broke away from the Kazakh masses.[27] This contradicts traditional Soviet historiography, which maintains that mass enthusiasm greeted the news of the Bolshevik victory.

The local Bolshevik organizations recognized how isolated they were in both the Russian and the Kazakh communities. Virtually all post-1930 accounts of the Civil War period go to great lengths to conceal this isolation from their readers, just as at the time the Bolshevik cells in the steppe tried to conceal or at least downplay their lack of local support.[28] The third west-Siberian congress of soviets, with delegates from Kokchetav, Atbasar, Semipalatinsk, and Pavlodar, was held in Omsk, December 2–10, 1917, with the hope of diverting attention from the Orenburg all-Kirgiz congress going on simultaneously. In fact, when the Omsk meeting broke up, members of the self-styled "Union of Working Muslims" cabled Lenin that "the autonomy of the *Alash Orda* was unnecessary to the Kirgiz Muslims."

In these early months some local Bolshevik authorities sought to use the Ush Zhuz, Kolbai Togusov's caucus, as a way to cut the Alash Orda's support within the Kazakh community. Yet Bukeikhanov was so confident of his control over the the Kazakh elite that he had the following appeal from Togusov published in the November 21 issue of his journal, *Sary Arka*:

> Kazakhs who are not pleased with the policies of the political party *Alash* [*Orda*], created by the well-known *kadet* Bukeikhanov, have organized an independent socialist party, *Ush Zhuz*, whose goal is to defend the federation, and write Turko-Tatar tribes.[29]

The Ush Zhuz was more a caucus than a political party. Togusov drew his membership from those former Birlik supporters who preferred the Bolshevik alternative to the Alash Orda government. There were Ush Zhuz caucuses in the soviets in Omsk, Petropavlovsk, Semipalatinsk, and Akmolinsk. In fact, the Provisional Revolutionary Committee created in Akmolinsk on December 25, 1917, included two leading Ush Zhuz figures, Abdulla Asylbekov and Saken Seifullin. Within a month, however, both men were dropped from membership when an all-Russian executive committee was named to head the Bolshevik administration in Akmolinsk. Both Asylbekov and Seifullin soon joined the Communist Party and again assumed active roles in the Bolshevik efforts during the latter stages of the Civil War. The Ush Zhuz soon ceased to be a factor in Kazakh politics. Its newspaper, *Ush Zhuz* (published in Petropavlovsk), was later closed down when the Ush Zhuz platform was attacked as being influenced by the Left Socialist Revolutionary (Left SR) party. The Ush Zhuz members (labeled petty-bourgeois) were permitted the right of reconstruction through membership in the Communist Party.

The Kazakhs were attempting to create an autonomous government that owed its loyalty to a nonexistent parliamentary regime in Petrograd. At the same time, officials in Moscow were allowing the Bolshevik name and authority to be invoked by self-proclaimed and self-regulating cells that were springing up throughout the steppe. On November 14, 1917, pro-Bolshevik social democrats seized control of the local Orenburg soviet. The executive committee of this soviet made a determined effort to administer the city and to serve as a regional center of Bolshevik rule; by mid-January they had managed to re-open the banks and re-establish some local commerce. However, their commitment to Moscow's antibourgeois nationalization campaign guaranteed them the enmity they quickly earned. Although Bolshevik authority was invoked throughout the steppe, it was ineffective as a political force and did not dampen hostility to its rule. Nevertheless, pro-Bolshevik soviets were organized in Chimkent, Aulie Ata, and Perovsk in mid-November, and these cells faced no local resistance. On November 30 the Bolsheviks forcibly replaced the existing soviet in Omsk; on December 2 Soviet rule was declared in Khanskaia Stavka; and on December 25 the Bolsheviks took control of the soviets in Kustanai and Akmolinsk, in Turgai a few days later, and in Aktubinsk on January 8, 1918. The soviet in Atbasar was forcibly reconstituted on January 12, as were those in Pavlodar and Kokchetav on January 15. A pro-Bolshevik soviet was formed in Semipalatinsk on February 17 and in Vernyi (soon after renamed Alma-Ata) on March 3.

In several cities (Orenburg, Akmolinsk, and Semipalatinsk being the best examples), Bolshevik and Alash Orda representatives claimed authority simultaneously, neither recognizing the other's legitimacy. In the cities of the Syr Darya and Semirech'e regions, Alash Orda representation was minimal, but the virtually all-Russian makeup of these soviets ensured Kazakh hostility to them. In these areas the Bolsheviks sought control over both the Russian and Kazakh populations. When instances of nationalization of land and livestock became commonplace in southern Kazakhstan in March 1918, hostility toward Bolshevism spread throughout the steppe.

The nationalization drives also strengthened the Russian peasantry's support for Russian alternatives to Bolshevik rule. Cossack-led provisional governments sprang up around the cossack garrisons and settlements in the months following the fall of Kerensky's regime. Ataman Dutov declared himself military governor of Siberia in Orenburg on November 14, 1917, and by December he could claim authority over much of the Uralsk oblast. Ataman Annenkov declared himself in control of Akmolinsk on December 24, 1917. Within six months the combined military forces of these men dominated northern Kazakhstan. A short-lived, cossack-led Turkestan military organization was created in Tashkent in November. Cossack troops from the Sofia barracks held Vernyi from mid-November 1917 until March 1918. In March the Petropavlovsk garrison took control of the city, and in mid-April a group of officers from northern Semirech'e who termed themselves the "Turkestan Union for the Struggle with Bolshevism" established a local authority that remained in control for more than two and a half years.

The primary goal of the cossack commanders was the military defeat of Bolshevism, first in the various localities and then in the entire steppe. They also attempted to serve as interim administrators, trying to preserve order among the Russian population and to raise enough money and volunteers to arm a force capable of defeating the Red troops. In these early months the cossack leadership expressed little direct interest in the Kazakh experiment in autonomy. Their only concern was that the Kazakhs help control periodic outbursts of anomic violence against the Russian settlers by other, impoverished Kazakhs who still wandered the steppe in large numbers. So long as the common threat of Bolshevik domination existed, cossack-Kazakh toleration was encouraged. Attempts to coordinate their efforts came later; for each the challenge of establishing authority within their national communities was sufficient responsibility for the moment.

Because of cossack indifference and Bolshevik weakness, the Alash Orda government was left more or less on its own to govern the Kazakh community. Bukeikhanov and his supporters used the months immediately following their organizing conference to create an administrative structure that could raise and disperse revenue; they tried with mixed success to form a Kazakh militia and in general struggled to keep the steppe economy afloat. It is impossible to reconstruct with any precision what occurred within Kazakh society during these months. Alash Orda activities were reported in great detail in their newspapers—*Qazaq* (its printing plant in Orenburg was destroyed by the Bolsheviks on March 4, 1918), *Sary Arka* (published in Semipalatinsk in 1918 and 1919), and *Ablai*, a newspaper for youth—but postrevolutionary issues of these papers never made it to the West and are today unavailable in Moscow; even Kazakh scholars in Alma-Ata are given only limited access to them.

Available sources detail the promotion of several Alash oblast committees in late 1917 and early 1918.[30] The Alash Orda central executive body consisted of eight Kazakh members—one representative from each of the six oblasts and the Inner Side, plus Ali Khan Bukeikhanov as chairman—and fifteen deputies of non-Kazakh origin. The Omsk committee, which had its regional center in Akmolinsk, consisted of fourteen members chaired by Asylbek Seitov, a physician. Its membership included Aidar Khan Turlibaev (jurist and lawyer), Migadachka Ablai Khanov (former officer in the tsarist army), Musulman Seitov (translator), Erezhep Itpaev (okrug court translator), and Smagul Sadvakasov (student and subsequently a senior Bolshevik figure). This committee claimed to have organized uezd groups as well.[31] The Turgai committee also consisted of fourteen elected members, including Mir Yakub Dulatov, Sagindyk Dosjanov, Abduh Rahman Dosjanov, and Ahmed Baitursunov as chairman.[32] Halel Dos Muhammadov and Muhammadjan Dos Muhammadov shared responsibility for the Uralsk organization, and Halel Gabbasov chaired the Semipalatinsk committee. By late February 1918 the Alash Orda was the effective responsible authority for the Kazakh populations of Semipalatinsk, Uralsk, Akmolinsk, and Turgai. An active Alash Orda organization also existed in Semirech'e, chaired by Muhammad Tynyshpaev.[33]

The Alash Orda had immediately rejected the Bolshevik takeover as a violation of the principles of parliamentary rule to which they had committed their existence. However, Lenin and Stalin knew that recognition by the Kazakh autonomists would legitimate Bolshevik rule within the Kazakh community. Thus, in March 1918, while the local Bolsheviks were engaged in armed struggle with the Kazakhs in Orenburg, Uralsk, and Akmolinsk, Lenin and Stalin invited the Alash Orda to come to Moscow to negotiate their differences. No protocols of the meeting ever appeared, but part of the discussion can be reconstructed from Stalin's published correspondence. Lenin and Stalin apparently tried to assure the Dos Muhammadov brothers, who had been sent as Alash Orda representatives, that the Bolsheviks were committed to the principles of national self-determination and that the aims of Kazakh autonomy could be attained within the confines of Soviet rule.

It is difficult to ascertain what occurred next. One account has it that the Dos Muhammadovs were offered and accepted 40 million rubles to fund an Alash militia to oppose the cossack forces, only to have this money seized from them by the Saratov soviet authorities, who arrested the brothers as counterrevolutionaries and thieves on their way back to Uralsk; the argument was made that no Bolshevik would fund the Alash Orda.[34] The story of funds changing hands may well be apocryphal, concocted well after the event by some creative Soviet historian to further discredit the by-then-deceased *Alash Orda* leadership; yet Moscow's overtures unquestionably created serious debate and raised divisive issues for the Kazakh autonomists. Mir Yakub Dulatov was the most vociferous opponent of cooperation with the Bolsheviks; he wrote an article, "Who is a Friend, Who is an Enemy," published in *Sary Arka* (March 3, 1918), which argued that the Bolsheviks were as great an enemy as the tsar and the Christian missionaries had been, since they attacked the idea of Kazakh autonomy and rule by freely elected members of the Alash Orda.

The members of the Alash Orda continued until the end of April 1918 to debate the question of whether to support Lenin and his followers. In mid-April Halel Gabbasov went to Moscow and met with Stalin. While these negotiations were in progress, Stalin received a telegram from Togusov, dated March 21, 1918, which urged the arrest of the "counterrevolutionary" Gabbasov and claimed that only the Ush Zhuz could legitimately represent Bolshevik interests within the Kazakh community because they endorsed Lenin's ideals.[35] It is hard to know whether the telegram did anything other than make Togusov look foolish, because he never did receive Lenin's trust or an assignment of responsibility. Stalin's discussions with Gabbasov broke off inconclusively in late April, apparently because Gabbasov became convinced that the Bolshevik and Kazakh aims were not the same and that Bolshevik rule would prove short-lived.

Certainly the military situation in the steppe during the spring and summer of 1918 did not augur well for Lenin's cause. White (anti-Bolshevik) forces took control of Uralsk on March 28, 1918 and then began a drive eastward across northern Kazakhstan; at the same time, local cossack commanders joined by some of the Czech legion combined their forces in the name of the provisional Siberian government. This campaign was not well organized; in some cities the Bolsheviks and Red Guards kept the White troops occupied for several weeks. Still, in each case the professional soldiers ultimately defeated the amateur ones. The Bolsheviks were driven from Petropavlovsk on May 31, Semipalatinsk on June 3, Ust-Kamenogorsk on June 9, and Kustanai on June 23. On June 28 they surrendered in Orenburg after a six week siege, and seven days later the Bolsheviks in Omsk also surrendered. In May the Semirech'e cossacks had gone on the offensive, capturing Lepsinsk in early June and driving the Bolsheviks out of northern Semirech'e. They had also surrounded Aulie Ata, Dzharkent, and Alma-Ata. Nevertheless, the Bolsheviks successfully withstood the siege, and by late summer Red forces were in control of nearly all of Syr Darya and the southern half of the Semirech'e oblast.

By that time, however, anti-Bolshevik forces controlled all of the Akmolinsk, Uralsk, and Semipalatinsk oblasts, most of the Turgai oblast, and northern Semirech'e. There were several thousand Bolshevik troops in Syr Darya and southern Semirech'e, but in the north of Kazakhstan the Bolsheviks held only southern Turgai (Adaev territory) and the Inner Side; here their military presence was largely restricted to Alibai Dzhangel'din's Kazakh regulars, who were armed with Bolshevik funds but supplied with horses and provisions by the local Adaev tribes.[36] By now Moscow had recognized the severity of the threat Whites posed in the steppe region. In July 1918 they declared the existence of the Eastern (Aktyubinsk) Front and dispatched regular Red Army troops to recapture the area; these troops had to spend six months fighting their way across the Urals and western Siberia before they could even begin to engage the White forces in the steppe.

The Alash Orda leadership believed that Kazakh autonomy could be maintained only if defended by a Kazakh-led militia. As early as January 1918 they had turned to the White forces for assistance in arming the Kazakh population; the provisional Siberian government, the committees of constituent assembly in Ufa and Samara, and Ataman Dutov in Orenburg were all approached but were either too preoccupied or simply not eager to aid the fledgling Alash Orda regime.

By May 1918 Bukeikhanov and his colleagues had become completely convinced both that the Bolsheviks threatened Kazakh autonomy and that a successful White counterrevolution would only respect Kazakh self-rule if the Kazakhs helped them achieve their victory. The military situation in the steppe contributed much to this attitude. The Bolshevik forces in the north numbered only a few thousand men and were virtually cut off from European Russia; ambushes and localized fighting halted rail travel and caravans, making communication across the steppe so dangerous and irregular that by May 1919 the Alash Orda in Semipalatinsk and its committee in Uralsk (in Dzhambeity) were forced to function as self-sufficient centers, and each required protection.

For their part the local White commanders appreciated the need to pacify the Kazakh population, since they couldn't fight Bolsheviks and Kazakhs simultaneously. Furthermore, an armed, pro-White Kazakh force would be yet another impediment to a Bolshevik takeover. Beginning in May 1918 and continuing throughout the summer a number of accords were signed between representatives of the Alash Orda and local cossack forces; these accords provided for White military assistance in arming Kazakh militias and coordinating military campaigns of Kazakh and White Guard troops.

The first formal military accord was signed between the Alash Orda and the Uralsk White Guards at the White Congress, May 18–22, 1918.[37] On the opening day of the congress, 300 armed Alash Orda party members for the first time joined the Semipalatinsk White troops in battle. Later in May, a certain Grishin-Almazov of the cossack troops in Omsk began to distribute arms to local Alash Orda members.

The Dzhambeity Alash Orda committee established a military command center at the newly renamed Uili Oliaiat (formerly, and again later, Dzhambeity village) just outside the city. On June 9, 1918, the Uralsk Kazakh military commander formally requested the commander of the Orenburg cossacks to send arms as well as cossack officers to assist in the training of a Kazakh officer corps.[38] By late June armed Kazakh bands were regularly fighting alongside White forces in Semipalatinsk, Turgai, and Akmolinsk, and three Alash Orda divisions (so-called "hundreds," after the Mongol usage) had even been dispatched to aid the Semirech'e cossacks. By mid-summer the first Kazakh military school was established in Uili Oliaiat and its graduates were sent to staff the first Kazakh mounted regiment, which was a part of the Uralsk military corps of the Orenburg military district.[39] From July 29 to August 3, 1918, military negotiations were carried out between representatives of Bukeikhanov and Ataman Dutov. Shortly afterward, the forces at the Alash Orda center (Semipalatinsk) were formally joined with the autonomous Siberian troops, and the Alash Orda recognized the provisional Siberian government as a legitimate representative of the February 1917 revolution.[40]

Although the cossacks and the Alash Orda fought side by side from mid-1918 through 1919, there is no evidence to suggest that the White Guard leaders in the steppe ever accepted the philosophy of Kazakh autonomy or gave any thought whatsoever to the problem of what role the indigenous population should be accorded once Bolshevism was defeated. However, through the course of the Civil War in the steppe, the White leadership made no attempt to interfere with the policies of the Alash Orda. Thus, the institutionalization of Alash Orda authority continued through the summer and fall of 1918.

Because Soviet sources have long sought to both reduce and discredit the impact of this Kazakh experiment in Kazakh autonomy, it is impossible to chronicle precisely how far Kazakh self-government extended. There were at least three full sessions of the Alash Orda soviet convened from June to September 1918 for purposes of drafting legislation. One session met June 11–24, at which time it declared that all Soviet decrees were to be considered null and void on the territory of the Alash and resolved to establish a court to try Kazakh Bolsheviks for treason.[41] They also issued a statute, "On Provisional Land Utilization on the Territory of the Autonomous 'Alash.'"[42] This statute, signed by A. Bukeikhanov, M. Tynyshpaev, and H. Gabbasov, sought to implement and expand upon the land decisions made by the Provisional Government. The statute supported the principle of private ownership of land but state (Alash) ownership of water resources, and it sought to set up a system for the adjudication of land dispute. It stipulated that within the Kazakh community all disputes over privately owned lands were to be worked out by aksakals who represented each of the aggrieved parties. Disputes over rightful ownership involving Kazakhs and Russians were to be handled by zemstvo committees (whose membership had been sanctioned by the Provisional Government). There were a number of new provisions to cover return or restitution of Kazakh lands seized by the colonial resettlement administration: any land awarded to Russian settlers after February 1917 was to be immediately returned; all land listed for seizure or seized but still a part of the Public Land Fund was to be returned to its owner; and any seized land already awarded but as yet unsown (whether awarded to private farmers, livestock breeders, schools, churches, or monasteries) was to be returned to the previous Kazakh owners; and the Russians who had received these parcels were to receive just compensation from the zemstvo officials. All other seized land was deemed unrecoverable. Those Kazakhs who had lost land that was deemed unrecoverable were to receive just compensation from the government. The Alash Orda also recommended that the zemstvo officials expand their distribution of agronomical and veterinary assistance. In particular, they were urged to take immediate steps to develop an improved system of supplying breeding grounds for horned cattle.

Another full session of the Alash Orda convened in Orenburg on July 24, 1918. At this meeting the participants focused on local administration (creating uezd soviets of 3–5 members each), taxation, and the organization of local militia (30 mounted cavalrymen per volost). The meeting ended with a call for unity with the Siberian and Bashkir autonomists.[43] Shortly after the meeting, *Sary Arka* published a call to arms for 2,000 additional Kazakhs.

The Alash Orda met again on September 11, 1918, in Ufa, to legalize the de facto split between the Alash Orda central body and the Alash Orda west, now formally designated an autonomous branch of the Alash Orda. The new branch was to be headed by a group of commissars including the Dos Muhammadov brothers, Kulmanov, Turmuhammadov, and two Russians to be chosen subsequently.[44] The Alash Orda west would regulate Kazakh activities in the Inner Side, Uili Oliaiat, Mangyshlak, Aktyubinsk, and Turgai. The meeting reaffirmed that both Alash Orda organizations, their uezd subdivisions, and the zemstvo officials under their supervision would be governed by the legislation of the former Provisional Government and the pronouncements of the central Alash Orda. Again, because of the severe lack of source material, it is difficult to know how deeply into the Kazakh localities the Alash Orda government was able to penetrate. It is known that the Alash Orda was generally successful in its efforts to collect taxes. After defeating Gubaidulla Alibekov's attempt to introduce a system of graduated taxation, Halel Dos Muhammadov received support for an annual flat tax of 100 rubles per household. In 1918, 3 million rubles were reportedly collected in Akmolinsk alone.[45]

In the summer of 1918 it looked as though the Alash Orda government was beginning to handle successfully its administrative challenges, and the Kazakh leadership might have continued to stabilize its rule if it had been left unchallenged. However, Moscow's decision to open the Eastern Front forced military concerns to the fore.

In mid-1918 the White forces held a clear advantage in the western Siberian Kazakh region, but they never successfully consolidated their advantage through the creation of a single unified anti-Bolshevik regime. Although Admiral Aleksandr Kolchak claimed authority over the entire territory, local commanders such as Ataman Dutov and Ataman Annenkov were in reality far more important in maintaining order. These men shared common aims, but none of them were willing to see their own authority diminished.

In the summer and fall of 1918, the situation in Kazakhstan worsened. In July the connection between Orenburg-Aktyubinsk and Tashkent was cut by White forces trying to unite armed resistance across the Fergana, Semirech'e, and Transcaspia regions. Most of the newly created five armies of the Eastern Front, commanded by S. S. Kamenev, were occupied fighting in the Volga region. Yet M. V. Frunze's Fifth Army and M. N. Tukhachevsky's First Army were both ordered to break through to Aktyubinsk to relieve the overwhelmed first Orenburg and twenty-eighth Ural regiments (under the command of G. V. Zinoviev), although success was far from certain.

The economic situation in Kazakhstan had been desperate even before the 1917 revolution, but it grew much worse when the fighting broke out in 1918. Conditions were particularly harsh in the Soviet-controlled regions. The nationalization decrees of early 1918 nullified most legal title to arable land, and openly marketed food invited only confiscation, since the markets themselves were regulated to force the sale of foods at artificially low prices. In August the

Bolshevik authorities responded by calling for forced grain requisitions all along the Eastern Front, but they lacked the manpower to enforce their policy. In early September the Bolsheviks further reduced their popularity by demanding conscription of all those males who had become eligible since 1915. Although they mustered few recruits, these still had to be fed, clothed, and transported. On October 23 the Aktyubinsk Bolsheviks again increased local animosity by requisitioning winter clothes and forage from the local population.

The Kazakhs of Syr Darya and southern Semirech'e were under the control of the Turkestan Bolsheviks. For more than fifteen years these areas had attracted a swelling immigration of Kazakhs, whose ranks were now being further strained by the thousands of propertyless Kazakhs who were returning from China, where they had fled in 1916. Thousands of Kazakhs and Kirgiz died of starvation throughout the summer of 1918. Many of these were more properly victims of the tsar than the Bolsheviks, because they had lost or fled their land in the 1916 uprising and had lived by slaughtering their animals over the ensuing eighteen months. In most of southern Kazakhstan and northern Kirgizia no crop was even planted in 1918. Because the Turkestan ministry of health predicted widespread epidemics if more food was not found, on November 28 the Turkestan central executive committee (TsIK) called for the creation of regional famine committees throughout Syr Darya and southern Semirech'e; however, few communities had any surplus to share. In Aulie Ata, Kazalinsk, and Perovsk, local soviets organized food distribution points to feed 6,500, 1,250, and 1,050 people respectively, but this was a small fraction of the starving population. For the most part, Soviet officials had little choice but to watch the local population starve, knowing that the situation would only grow worse. As the following excerpt from an official report makes clear, the revolution in Kazakhstan succeeded, at least in destroying class distinction, because it made everyone a beggar:

> in this way even the Kirghiz [Kazakhs] who were previously considered prosperous have now become almost mendicant. Therefore in the Steppe districts it is a rare Kirghiz family who will not have to depend upon economic assistance until summer of next year.[46]

The Bolshevik failure to respond successfully to the Kazakhs' economic hardships made it easier for the White forces to consolidate their position in Semirech'e. In late August 1918 the White forces drove the Bolsheviks from Lepsinsk and laid siege to the Bolshevik stronghold of Sarkand (near present-day Alma-Ata). The White forces continued to rout the local Bolsheviks in northern Kazakhstan as well. In October Ataman Dutov attacked Aktyubinsk in an attempt to link up with the British in Transcaspia, but he was held at Ak

Bulak. In the fall of 1918 Dutov had some 10,000 rifles and 5,000 sabres under his command as well as 500 armed *jigits* (warriors) of the newly formed second Kazakh mounted regiment. In early December Perm fell to the Whites, and Kolchak arrived to coordinate White operations in Central Asia and Kazakhstan.

On December 17, 1918, Moscow created the Siberian buro of the central committee to coordinate activities in northern and northeastern Kazakhstan. This group overlapped with and supplanted the Kazakh Peoples' Commissariat of Nationalities (*Narkomnats*) appointed in May 1918. F. I. Goloshchekin came to the area to serve in the new buro and was then named to the Turkestan Commission (*Turkkomissiia*). However, Goloshchekin's authority was soon overshadowed by the arrival of the Red Army. On January 10, 1919, the Bolsheviks began their campaign to retake Uralsk. Using the first and second brigades of the thirtieth infantry division and the twenty-fifth infantry division of the Fourth Army, they took Uralsk on January 24, only to lose it again two days later. The Bolsheviks finally took the city on February 11 after the arrival of Frunze's Fifth Army. During the battle for Uralsk the twenty-fourth Simbirsk division of the First Army defeated the White forces in Orenburg. The capture of Orenburg and Uralsk allowed the first supply wagons to go westward in nearly six months. On February 22 nearly 1 million poods of grain were shipped. This grain was gathered through forced requisitions, as were livestock and agricultural implements.[47]

Kolchak's White forces tried unsuccessfully to recapture Uralsk on February 15. The Bolsheviks retained control of the city, but the countryside remained in the hands of the Whites and the Alash Orda. The Kazakhs continued to hold nearby Dzhambeit (Uili Oliaiat) to the southeast. Frunze continued to drive westward across the more populated regions of northern Kazakhstan and captured Orsk on March 5. He then headed north to engage the White forces in the southern Urals. This left the remaining Red Army troops vulnerable. On April 6 Kolchak recaptured Orsk, and Ataman Dutov simultaneously attacked the Bolshevik forces at Aktyubinsk and Turgai. Turgai fell quickly, by April 20. The Whites arrested 337 Bolsheviks, including Amangeldy Imanov. On April 21, the Whites captured a detachment of 400 soldiers en route from Kustanai. The White forces bivouacked in Turgai found virtually no food in the city, testimony to the support the Reds had enjoyed. Aktyubinsk fell to Kolchak and Dutov on April 18. This allowed the White forces to establish their control of the Orenburg-Samara railroad, and so Central Asia and Kazakhstan were again cut off from Moscow.

Although the Bolsheviks were taking a terrible beating in northern Kazakhstan, they did succeed in consolidating their hold over the famine-struck regions of Syr Darya and southern Semirech'e. In the spring of 1918 communication between Tashkent, Semirech'e, Fergana, and Samarkand was restored.

However, the Bolsheviks could waste little time enjoying their improved position, since they faced the deteriorating economic situation. In late January 1919 U. Dzhandosov, head of *Natsotdel* (the department of nationalities) of Semirech'e, urged his subordinate department to give its full attention to famine relief; in March 1919, in the brief period when communication with Moscow was possible, the Bolsheviks in Alma-Ata received 42 million rubles for famine relief, but there wasn't enough grain available even to exhaust this small sum.

## THE DEFEAT OF THE ALASH ORDA

Despite the severity of the famine, ending it was not considered as important as consolidating Soviet rule. In the late spring of 1919 Moscow's primary goal in Central Asia was to reverse Kolchak's gains of April. On March 4 Frunze had launched a new offensive, using the 277th cavalry and thirty-first infantry divisions to regain control of the Orenburg-Samara railroad. The Red Army troops did secure the railroad but were repulsed in their attempt to regain control of Turgai, the capture of which was necessary to insure the westward movement of grain across northern Kazakhstan. On May 22 Frunze received an additional 7,300 riflemen, several large guns, and 3 armed cars.

Additional forces shifted the military balance to favor the Soviets; thereafter Frunze remained on the offensive, and by late June he had driven the Whites out of the city of Uralsk. Now optimistic, the Bolsheviks created the *Kirrevkom* (Kirgiz Revolutionary Committee) on July 11 to administer the oblasts of Uralsk, Turgai, Aktyubinsk, and Semipalatinsk as well as the Kazakh population of the Inner Side. S. S. Pestrovskii headed the Kirrevkom with the participation of A. T. Dzhangil'din, S. M. Mendeshev, A. Aitiev, and A. D. Adveev, among others.

Even before Frunze routed the White forces in June and July 1919 they had had problems maintaining unity, but now they faced administrative as well as military challenges to their internal cohesion. Never based on mutual trust, Kazakh-White relations had become far more strained on November 4, 1918, when Kolchak had ordered the Ufa directorate of the provisional all-Russian government to abolish the Kazakh autonomous government and demanded, on threat of withdrawal of military assistance, that the Alash Orda submit to White Guard leadership in their anti-Bolshevik struggle. Over the next few months relations between the Whites and the Kazakh leadership had been regularized and again improved, and Kolchak worked in concert with the Alash Orda in the Akmolinsk, Atbasar, and Kokchetav oblasts.[48] Yet the constant demand to recognize Russian supremacy was resented by the Kazakhs; when the military fortunes of the Whites collapsed in late 1919, the bad feelings created in 1918 and 1919 made it that much easier for the Kazakhs to approach the Bolsheviks. This tendency was growing clearer in June 1919, when the hard-pressed Kolchak could not honor the western Alash Orda's request for aid; Kolchak also met resistance among the Russian peasants. Although things were better in northern Kazakhstan than in the south, it still grew ever more difficult for the Russian peasants to feed both themselves and the White Army. In April Kolchak had successfully faced a peasant uprising in the Atbasar uezd village of Mariinskoe, but the military defeats of June and July, coupled with the general decline of support, forced Dutov and Kolchak to withdraw to Semipalatinsk, where they made the defensive outpost of Cherkasskoe their center of operations.

By mid-July the Bolsheviks controlled most of the Uralsk oblast. The Red Army prepared to advance across northern Kazakhstan, and the Bolsheviks in southern Kazakhstan enforced a draft of all males who had reached mobilization age in 1910–1911, in order to prevent a White retreat south. In Alma-Ata the communists were forcing laborers into farming to keep the army provisioned.

In early August 1919 the Bolsheviks captured Troitsk, which allowed the army to bring reinforcements across the Orenburg steppe. By mid-August the Third Army was in western Siberia, fighting its way to Tobolsk, and the First and Fifth armies were besieging the White Ural-Orenburg army. The first, second, and third Kustanai regiments and the first Akmolinsk regiment of the Fifth Army engaged Kolchak's forces along the Trans-Siberian railroad. The Bolshevik forces were now strong enough to divide and successfully attack the Whites at several points simultaneously. On August 19 the Fifth Army seized Kustanai, and shortly thereafter the Fourth Army took control of the Iletsk-Ozernoe line, captured the city of Iletsk, and then took the Orenburg-Akmolinsk railroad as far as the Ak Bulak station. On August 29 they captured Orsk. By late August, the Red Army had control of all the territory between Orenburg and Uralsk and were able to return the Tashkent railroad to use.

On September 2 the First Army entered Aktyubinsk and for eight days fought their way across the city. On September 10 they captured the easternmost part of the city and with it some 20,000 of Kolchak's men. On September 14 Frunze announced that the First Army had joined up with the Red troops of the Turkestan front. This permitted the Red forces based in Aulie Ata to send troops further south into Turkestan to fight the Basmachi, who controlled the mountain approach at Tekmen Tiube, and to drive the Turkestani rebel leader Irgash's bands out of the Aulie Ata uezd.

Part of the Fourth Army remained in Uralsk and continued to eat away at the Alash Orda west; on September 21 the forty-ninth division captured the village of Dzhambeity, leaving the Kazakhs isolated in their outpost at the nearby Dzhambeity settlement. The bulk of the Red forces moved eastward to engage the Whites at their outpost of Cherkasskoe in Semipalatinsk.

On October 8, 1919, Moscow announced that the Eastern Front had been liquidated and the next day the Turkkomissiia was named, which was to complete the conquest of the territory and supervise the firm establishment of Soviet rule. Membership included M. V. Frunze (chairman), V. V. Kuibyshev, Ia. E. Rudzutak, Sh. Z. Eliav, G. I. Boukii, F. I. Goloshchekin, and T. Ryskulov, who was named to head the *Musburo* (Muslim bureau) of the Turkestan region. On October 10 the first grain shipments in eight months left Uralsk, one train westward and the other to feed the Bolsheviks of Aktyubinsk and Tashkent. The Bolsheviks continued to drub the White forces. The Fourth Army and the Iletsk group in Uralsk, some 19,000 men with bayonets and 3,000 with sabres, continued to battle some 17,000 White fighters (including 10,000 on horseback). On October 14 the outpost at Cherkasskoe was taken, leaving the way open for the Red forces to advance to Taldy-Kurgan and northern Semirech'e. On October 30, after heavy battle, the 307th, 308th, and 309th infantry regiments of the Third Army took Petropavlovsk. This victory gave the Bolsheviks access to the Ishim River and the road to Omsk. The Fifth Army remained occupied with fighting along the Kustanai-Troitsk line. Altogether there were 60,000 Red Army men with bayonets and another 7,000 with sabres in northern Kazakhstan at that time.

In November 1919 the Bolsheviks launched a two-pronged attack on Omsk. The Fifth Army, led by Tukhachevsky, dropped south, captured Kokchetav, and then turned north. The Third Army fought its way toward Omsk along the railroad line. Kolchak entered the city with his White forces when the Irtysh River froze on November 10, and on November 14 he loaded seven trains with troops and valuables and fled eastward just ahead of the Fifth Army.[49] Tukhachevsky took control of the city on November 19 and captured some 45,000 of Kolchak's men, 2 armoured trains, 100 machine guns, and thousands of rounds of ammunition. The Fifth Army continued to fight in Omsk until November 23, when the Petropavlovsk-Omsk operation was declared successfully concluded. However, there was a large-scale forced labor mobilization in Petropavlovsk to provide manpower to move troops and supplies along the railroad.

On November 21 the Red Army took control of the Alash Orda outpost at Dzhambeit. The First Army then moved southeast. They captured the city of Atbasar on November 23 and Akmolinsk on November 26. They then attacked the White forces at Semipalatinsk, which fell to E. M. Mamontov's pro-Bolshevik peasant army around midnight on November 30. The Fifth Army arrived in Semipalatinsk on December 10 and then quickly moved on to Karkaralinsk, captured on December 12, and Ust-Kamenogorsk, which fell to the Bolsheviks on December 15. The Third Army continued to fight its way across the Trans-Siberian railroad, and reached Tomsk on December 17. The Bolshevik capture of that city on December 20 marked the end of organized

White resistance in eastern Siberia. White forces continued to oppose the Red Army in northern Semirech'e, but even there the major urban stronghold of Sergiopol (Ayaguz) was taken by troops from the First and Fourth armies on January 20, 1920. On that same date the Fourth Army also captured Guryev and began consolidating its authority in western Kazakhstan. However, the Red Army was strapped for manpower and, while these battles were being fought, the Bolsheviks in Alma-Ata were augmenting the Red forces by conscripting the 1914, 1916, and 1918 draft-eligible population.

Although it would be many months before the defeat of all resistance on Kazakh territory, in late 1919 Moscow and the local Communists began to face the problem of postwar administration. The creation of the Kirrevkom and Turkkomissiia were seen as first steps in the regularization of administration of this area; these executives were handpicked by Moscow rather than by the local Bolshevik cells. The problem confronting Moscow in administering this territory was not solely one of personalities; it was also a question of philosophy of rule. In the steppe the Bolsheviks made a conscious choice to differentiate between Russians and Kazakhs. They punished Russians who supported the White Guard while rewarding those former members of the Alash Orda who agreed to sponsor or serve Bolshevik rule.

On November 5, 1919, the Military Revolutionary Soviet (*Revvoensovet*) had passed a resolution on amnesty for the Alash Orda. The text of this resolution, signed by Frunze, expressed sympathy for the Kazakh desire for autonomy and blamed much of local hatred for the Bolsheviks on the excesses of local Communist Party and Soviet cells in their nationalization and anti-religious programs. Moscow was thus able to dissociate itself from those policies that were still opposed by what even the Soviets called "a not insignificant" part of the Kazakh population of Astrakhan, Orenburg, Uralsk, and Turgai. Frunze accurately perceived that the task of subduing the Kazakh population would be substantially reduced if the Alash Orda leadership supported Soviet rule, and so the resolution promised complete amnesty for all leaders and fighters for Alash who would dissociate themselves with the White cause.[50]

On December 10 the Alash Orda sent a delegation to Orenburg to negotiate with Frunze and his staff. The Alash Orda leaders who attended these two weeks of meetings agreed to sever all ties with the Whites and to surrender their arms to the Bolsheviks.[51] By December 16 some 300–400 Alash fighters had been rearmed and reconstituted as "Red Communards," and they were being used in the campaign in Turgai.[52] However, the process of surrender and rearming the troops of the Alash Orda did not go as smoothly as the Red Army might have liked. A December 22 Revvoensovet document from the campaign against the Whites in the Ural-Emba oilfields notes that, although the surrender of the Alash Orda leadership was assured, the Red Army command was less confident that the Kazakhs could guarantee that their troops would surrender, let alone fight for Bolshevik rule.[53]

The Bolsheviks conducted further negotiations with the Alash Orda on January 11–20, 1920. At the conclusion of these meetings the Kirrevkom announced that the Alash Orda had merged with the Kirgiz revolutionary government, that all laws of the Alash Orda were null and void, and that all their property was to be seized. The Alash Orda was called to return those arms captured in battle, but until the end of hostilities on the Uralsk front the troops of Alash could continue to bear arms as part of the third Tatar regiment.[54] The Bolsheviks endorsed the principle of Kazakh self-rule, and to demonstrate this they invited Ahmed Baitursunov to join the Kirrevkom, named Ali Khan Bukeikhanov an oblast commissar for Turgai, and appointed Muhammad Tynyshpaev a commissar for Semirech'e, although these last two territories were not yet securely held.

Beginning in January the Bolsheviks began to hold party and soviet organizing conferences throughout Kazakhstan, while continuing to battle partisans in the countryside. On January 20 there was a guberniia party conference in Uralsk and on January 23 a meeting of volost *revkom*s (revolutionary committees) in Akmolinsk. In early February Moscow ordered all state and party organs in Kazakhstan to establish separate bureaus for handling Kazakh affairs.

Additional organizing conferences were held on March 13 in Aktyubinsk and March 11–16 in Semipalatinsk. On March 27 the Adaev territory was formally annexed to Kazakhstan. More important, however, was the consolidation of control the Bolsheviks achieved in eastern Semipalatinsk and in northern Semirech'e. On March 21 Frunze began his final campaign in Kazakhstan. He fought his way across the Kopal-Abukumov-Lepsinsk line, capturing Urdzhar on March 22, Arasan on March 28, and Kopalsk on March 29, and he watched with satisfaction as Dutov fled to China. Frunze then continued southward with his Third Turkestan Army to fight the Basmachi, who were entrenched on the Kirgiz and Uzbek lands.[55] With the surrender in early April of some 6,000 soldiers who had served under Dutov and Annenkov, the Bolsheviks declared the Semirech'e front completely liquidated. On April 30 the *Orgburo* (organizational bureau) announced the formation of the Kirgiz oblast bureau (*Kirobburo*) of the Bolshevik Russian Communist Party—RKP(b)—to supercede the Kirrevkom. The Kirobburo in turn planned for the complete transfer to civil authority, which was achieved with the formation of the Kirgiz (Kazakh) Autonomous Socialist Soviet Republic (KazASSR) on October 4, 1920.

Government and Communist Party institutions were now formally in place. The Bolsheviks then had to address the problems of economic and political stability in the Kazakh territory, which had been a famine-plagued battleground for nearly four years. The population yearned for relief, but even with the Civil War over the Kazakhs had before them the hardships of war communism. In spring 1920 forced seizures of grain, livestock, and clothing began throughout the steppe. Victory gained, the Bolsheviks began to teach the Kazakhs the meaning of Soviet rule.

# 7 The New Economic Policy in Kazakhstan

## INTRODUCTION

In 1920, when peace was finally reached in Kazakhstan, the Bolsheviks faced a set of very complex tasks to legitimate their authority. They needed to create Kazakh loyalty for the new order and at the same time maintain their commitment to a program of radical social and economic change. Kazakh support depended on the redress of economic grievances that the Kazakhs believed had grown from a colonial policy that placed the interests of Russian settlers before those of the natives. However, because the Bolsheviks were at least theoretically committed to an internationalist policy—that is, one that would treat Russians and natives alike—by definition they were unable to favor the needs of the natives over those of the Russians. Moreover, most Bolshevik officials were Russian, and those in Moscow had little direct experience with this part of the empire. Not only did the Bolsheviks hold many of the traditional antinative biases, but their very data was drawn from many of the same specialists who had served in the colonial administration.

Thus, for a variety of reasons, the Communist Party leaders could not begin to understand the strong cultural and social consequences of further economic change in the steppe. The Kazakhs, like other Central Asians, viewed all efforts at economic transformation as threats against the old order. The Kazakh government leadership exacerbated the tension by using a rhetorical style that only increased the Muslim population's sense of being besieged.

The already desperate economic plight of the Kazakhs had grown considerably worse during the Civil War years. Matters required quick and strong address, but the Soviet government lacked both the legitimacy and the administrative capacity to restructure the economy of the Kazakhs. They chose not to undertake a major land redistribution, which was proposed by Georgi Safronov and backed by the Kazakhs and which would have returned seized land to Kazakh control. Instead, the first five years of the 1920s, the heyday of the New Economic Policy (NEP), saw little direct governmental intervention in the Kazakh economy. The steppe population was given some assistance in land reclamation and irrigation projects, but in general recovery was achieved by allowing the economy to readjust itself. The Bolshevik governmental forms of party and soviet bureaucracy were simply superimposed upon the existing local social and political hierarchies; traditional authorities merely assumed the new titles, and the Kazakh intelligentsia was visibly represented in the territorial bureaucracy.

In effect, the new government managed to subdue the Kazakh population and achieve a modicum of cooperation only because the Soviet authorities seemed inclined at first to leave life much as it was within Kazakh rural society. As Moscow swung from right to left, however, the central leadership grew less willing to maintain the status quo. Once again the needs of the Kazakhs had to be defined in terms of the greatest common good of the multinational state, which in this instance was the willingness to subscribe to Soviet revolutionary goals. The countryside had to be mortgaged to achieve the needs of rapid industrialization. Agriculture was to become efficient and scientific, despite the objections of both the Russian and non-Russian rural sectors. All who stood in the way were to be removed, and so many of the Kazakh Communists were dismissed.

There was little in the policies of the day to inspire the loyalty of the local population. The 1928 campaigns to confiscate livestock and seize grain were resisted by Kazakhs and Russians alike. Kazakhs who served in the administration became increasingly isolated. This was a period in which Moscow, as the center of Soviet government, was seeking to maintain control over the local governmental and party organs; the Soviets did not trust the Kazakhs. By the time of collectivization, the Kazakhs had been transformed from actors in a revolutionary struggle into people who were acted upon, but what was forcibly achieved in the 1930s had already well begun by the late 1920s.

## FAMINE IN THE STEPPE

The economic consequences of the First World War and Civil War were disastrous for the population of the steppe, both Russian and Kazakh. Yet the hardships were far worse for the Kazakhs, many of whom had suffered economic hardships since 1916 or even earlier. The Civil War destroyed the internal market system of the empire. The Kazakhs had nowhere to trade their animals; herd size dropped and, with it, the need for herdsmen. There was less and less grain to be bought as farmers planted ever fewer hectares; this was both because war had turned some fields into battlegrounds and, more to the point, because there was nowhere to sell grain nor anything to buy if a crop were sold. Since the Kazakhs could only feed animals so long as fodder was available, those who depended on the purchase of grain were forced to reduce their herds; slaughter and starvation reduced the number of animals throughout the period.

Conditions grew no better after the Civil War ended. Famine began in 1920 and was made worse by the harsh winter of 1920–1921. That winter virtually all seed on hand was eaten, leaving nothing to plant the next spring. In 1921 there was almost no harvest; although relief aid was requested, little arrived.[1] Hundreds of thousands of Kazakhs camped by settlements and railroad stops, begging for food and waiting to die.

There is no reliable demographic picture of this period, but the population decline was well over a million people. There were several hundred thousand emigrants, mostly Russians, as entire villages packed up and tried to return to their native regions. The Soviets are still reluctant to release precise figures on the number of people who perished from hunger or disease in the aftermath of the Civil War, but reliable sources estimate that there were nearly three-quarters of a million hunger-related deaths in the steppe. Ryskulov, in an article titled "Famine in the Steppe," claimed that famine touched everyone and that the average Kazakh lived on the point of starvation through these years.[2]

The decline in both livestock breeding and agriculture was not reversed until the harvest of 1923. By late 1922 the herd size was only one-third that of 1916, while the number of sown hectares was 40 percent of the 1913 figure. Moscow had distributed grain and encouraged the population to save part of the harvest for seed to plant the following season and for fodder to help preserve the herd. However, as statistics bear out, starving people do not save for a next season, and so the spiral of economic collapse was not halted until late 1922.

The economic hardships fell hardest on the seminomadic Kazakhs, those who depended on some combination of livestock breeding and agriculture. As seed became scarce they found it increasingly difficult to feed their herds, and yet the size of such herds was generally too small to permit the resumption of a free-grazing economy. The greatest losses of livestock occurred in the semi-nomadic communities; in the Uralsk oblast the herd size declined by 72 percent, and in the Karkaralinsk and Lepsinsk uezds of the Syr Darya oblast 81 percent and 87 percent of the herds were lost respectively.[3]

Where possible, the Kazakhs tried to keep their animals alive by free grazing, but local fighting and the establishment of numerous unplanned settlements cut the Kazakhs off from many of their traditional migratory paths.[4] This exacerbated the search for pasture lands. As pastoral nomadism became less viable, the trend toward involuntary settlement grew. These newly sedentary Kazakhs had few options.[5] Those auls that had rich bais were more fortunate, since communal responsibility required them to assist needy relatives. Of those without bais, the more fortunate settled in abandoned Russian villages, while the least favored either camped in the towns and along the railroad lines, waiting for assistance from the Russian authorities, or wandered the steppe until they died.[6] As one local Bolshevik official described the situation in 1923: "In these conditions this dilemma was placed before the Kirghiz [Kazakh] people, either agricultural settlement or complete annihilation."[7]

In Kazakhstan, as in much of rural Russia, the immediate needs of the population preempted any attempts at radical social or economic reform; by the spring of 1921 it was clear that if economic collapse was not soon reversed, the Kazakh Steppe would cease to exist as an economically self-sufficient part of the country.

## SOVIET ECONOMIC POLICY
## IN KAZAKHSTAN, 1921–1925

Soviet economic policymaking in 1921–1925 was contradictory. Although much was written about the importance of sustaining the revolution in the outlying areas and national regions, the regime concentrated on the establishment and stabilization of Soviet rule in Moscow and in the Russian bread-basket regions. The Bolsheviks were most comfortable with their familiar constituents, the Russians, for they realized that the Bolshevik experiment depended on winning the support of Russian proletarian and peasant society. The non-Russian areas were thus again peripheral to the state; the needs of the non-Russian populations received more attention on paper than in practice.

The Bolshevik rulers grew more aware of the limits of authority as they found that economic plans were difficult to formulate and harder still to administer. When riots broke out in early 1921 throughout the countryside, the peasantry proved that they too could be inflexible. Russian and non-Russian populations alike made it clear that social and economic experimentation would not be tolerated until economic recovery had been achieved—itself a monumental task. The resources at the disposal of the state were still severely limited, and even the greatest effort could not guarantee rapid success. To get the national economy in motion again the cities had to be fed, which required the rapid recovery of the traditional grain-exporting areas. Therefore the problems of the Kazakh economy, grave though they were, received relatively little attention. Although Moscow, and even on one occasion Lenin himself,[8] was called upon to mediate local disputes, the authorities in the republic capital (first Orenburg and then Kzyl-Orda) were expected to solve their own problems as best they could, using general guidelines and their own resources.

The new authorities did not debate the issue of the settlement of Kazakh nomads, since events had made pastoral nomadism no longer viable. Both land and livestock were in short supply. Again the government was asked to mediate the rival land claims of Russians and Kazakhs, in which the Kazakhs demanded the return of all land seized by the colonial authorities. The Kazakh party leadership, including Turar Ryskulov, a leading figure in Narkomnats and someone who enjoyed access to Lenin, took up their cause and demanded the expulsion of the Russian settlers from the steppe. First the Turkkomissiia, then a party plenum, and finally Lenin himself refused to agree, claiming that the settlers were not land-hungry kulaks but poor peasants near starvation themselves, so that only the unworked portions of the illegally seized lands could be redistributed. The unworked lands were to be given out to Kazakhs who had no livestock, no land, no seed, and no knowledge of farming.[9]

Despite what is claimed in some Soviet histories, economic recovery in the steppe was not impeded by Kazakh refusal to abandon their pastoral nomadic lifestyle.[10] Rather, the failure was of the state, which was simply unable to provide the sufficient land, seed, and equipment necessary to introduce agriculture in any systematic way. Sedentarization was a foregone conclusion from the Kazakh point of view; what the Kazakhs wanted was an economic recovery that would enable them to continue as livestock breeders and preserve their traditional social structure and cultural practices. The Kazakhs became increasingly committed to maintaining the status quo during the first half of the 1920s, when rural recovery led to the reassertion of local social and economic control by many of the traditional authorities.

These authorities were able to reassert themselves largely because of the weakness of Soviet rule during this period. The limited authority and resources enjoyed by the central regime meant that Moscow had to delegate initiative and control to the local government, even to private households. Recovery was predicated on the restoration of some local initiative and the partial restoration of free market forces. In Kazakhstan this meant a return to a mixture of livestock breeding and agriculture, combined with state-regulated commercial livestock breeding for the more privileged (and soon to be state-controlled) sector. The regime feared that economic recovery might lead to a revival of pastoral nomadism, whereby the Kazakhs would return to migration when they managed to accumulate herds large enough to sustain their families. Consequently, Moscow intended to provide the newly settled Kazakhs with more land, as well as with sufficient seed and agricultural implements, to allow them successfully to adjust to being farmers. Yet the regime soon discovered quite another reality in attempting to provide the countryside with the necessary agricultural assistance (of which the Kazakhs were only one recipient) to implement its policy. The real threat to the goals of the regime was not that the Kazakhs would resume migration, which few did, but that in failing to direct the economic recovery in the steppe, Moscow would lose its chance to gain control of the Kazakhs' economy and, with it, Kazakh society.[11] Thus, although nomadism was not restored, it was replaced by a traditional rural economy, in which livestock breeding acquired its former prominence. Those who could afford it migrated part of the year and stalled their animals in the winter, while those who could not support themselves solely through livestock breeding practiced subsistence farming as well.

In other words, the traditional authorities emerged from the Civil War period with their authority enhanced. Ten years previously, on the eve of World War I, Kazakh intellectuals and even relatively uneducated youth had distrusted their elders because traditional society appeared unequal to the challenges presented by the colonial power. Now, when the seemingly invincible Russian monarchy had been crushed and its successor was weak, most Kazakhs (97 percent of whom still lived in the countryside) saw the old clan system and the traditional leaders as offering at least the hope of stability through the continuation and strengthening of a subsistence-based, livestock-breeding economy. When compared to the alternative of starvation, the old ways took on new popularity. The tribal system had been destroyed and was not able to restore itself,[12] but clan and sub-clan ties, which had remained strong, now took on a new vitality. Furthermore, although the new, more decentralized structure of traditional authority impeded the formation of a unified Kazakh people, it was well suited to traditional Kazakh social patterns. Clan, village, and aul authorities simply reconstituted themselves as soviets and governed their population much as before.

This tendency was further strengthened by the provisions of the NEP, which restored limited private ownership in agriculture. Even before the NEP was announced in February 1921, the "Provisional Statute on Land Use" had recognized the claims of prior users in determining the control of land and explicitly endorsed the rights of clans. The Bolsheviks saw the NEP as a temporary expedient, only one facet of their land program, since it was to be accompanied by a more elaborate program of land redistribution and agrarian reform. Local Russian authorities, however, were generally reluctant to label their fellow nationals as kulaks and so did not seize Russian-controlled land. The only other potential source of arable land was the former Public Land Fund, but this held only a fraction of the land necessary to resettle homeless Kazakh and Russian peasants.[13] In the end very little was actually done to achieve the redistribution of land. The task was designated as more appropriate to the local authorities than to Moscow, and each guberniia was asked to establish a committee on land and water reform although they (and in turn their uezd subcommittees) were given little specific direction on what was to be done. In the Kazakh areas very little redistribution seems to have occurred. The public land reserves were gradually turned into common grazing land, but no systematic program was introduced. Recovery was achieved gradually—by 1926 the herd size had almost been restored to its prewar level—but this was a result of the efforts of local authorities, not of socialist planning.

Probably the most valuable incentive for recovery in Kazakhstan was the exemption or sharp reduction of tax on meat and wool produced in the nomadic and seminomadic regions.[14] This allowed the Kazakhs to regulate the sale of livestock as they thought best and relieved them of the pressure to sell young animals prematurely, solely to raise revenue. This abatement did not last long, however, for the regime assumed that Kazakhs were withholding marketable livestock in an attempt to drive up prices. In March 1922 the Soviets reintroduced taxation in an attempt to force animals into the market. This misguided official optimism about the upturn in Kazakh livestock breeding was typical of what would become a pattern of dealing with the Kazakhs: scant information combined with bad judgment. Predictably, restoration of taxation on animals and their products further slowed the recovery process, and this was compounded by an accompanying demand for a census of animal holdings designed to seek those who would deny the state its due.[15]

The regime tried to compensate for the increased tax burden by introducing a loan program that was to provide money for increasing and improving stock, buying fodder, and irrigating land on which to grow fodder. The problem with this generous program was that no source of capital was specified, and so although thousands of households requested assistance, little was available. What little money there was went to purchase seed and animals for heads of households that had received land allotments; such individuals numbered only a few hundred per uezd. Nonethelesss, the regime continued to maintain that it was committed to providing land and loan assistance for any Kazakh who voluntarily ceased migration to begin farming. In fact, the local authorities had only very limited amounts of land at their disposal, even in December 1923, when the state forests of Kazakhstan were open to grazing for the first time in nearly 50 years.[16]

Finally, in 1924, Moscow seems to have recognized at least something of the plight of the local officials. It was announced that each region would be awarded parcels of land for distribution. To provide the needed land, the fourth Kazakh congress of soviets in January 1924 resolved that all lands seized from kulaks should be awarded to the Kazakh People's Commissariat of Agriculture for distribution among the newly sedentary nomads.[17] However, hostility between Russians and Kazakhs was great, and both the republic government (which included a large and vocal Russian representation) and Moscow remained opposed to any policy that sought Kazakh recovery at the expense of the Russian peasantry. Only a fraction of the land reserves that local officials were meant to have to comply with the "Resolution on Land Construction Among the Nomadic, Semi-Nomadic, and Transformed to Sedentary Population of the

KazASSR," issued in Moscow in April 1924, were ever set aside. The resolution called for the regional governments to establish a norm for the amount of land necessary to permit a household to be self-sufficient, then to provide this amount to every household that agreed to stop migrating. In addition, the household was to be given free construction materials, ten-year loans for the purchase of farm implements and work animals, agronomical assistance, and a release from all state and local taxes for a five-year period.[18] The norms were debated, but never established;[19] the absence of precise norms was only a small impediment compared to the lack of material resources and the inability of local authorities to redistribute land.

The problems of redistribution were monumental. Before redistribution could occur, precise land ownership had to be established, a task that the patterns of traditional land usage made nearly impossible; this was further magnified because Kazakh grazing patterns had changed during the Civil War. The Russian settlers, too, had shifted fields and even moved entire settlements to escape conflict. There had also been a great deal of illegal Russian settlement throughout the Civil War and the first half of the 1920s. Even when problems of ownership could be surmounted, nationalization of property was still not always attempted. Russian soviet authorities were willing to nationalize and redistribute Kazakh-owned property and sometimes even Russian-owned property, but Kazakh soviet authorities were rarely willing to seize property from their kinsmen. Guidelines for redistribution were established by members of the old resettlement administration who had remained and now served in the new Soviet bureaucracy, but they were ordinarily not followed. Because of prevailing cultural attitudes it was difficult to find Kazakhs willing to seize land and livestock from the so-called privileged classes, who were generally the traditional clan leaders as well as often the local soviet leaders, especially since these allegedly privileged classes had no real surplus to share.

Many Kazakhs found the early Soviet policies difficult to understand. They could not comprehend why they had to pay taxes to a state that would then provide them with economic assistance. It seemed more logical to the elders that the Kazakhs should save their money and aid themselves, which they tried to do whenever possible.[20] Because the Kazakhs refused to redistribute land within the community, the only other source of land was the limited amount of unused land allocated by the state; because of intense competition for land following the Civil War, unused definitionally meant unworkable.

Although subsequent generations of Soviet historians argue that the feudal character of Kazakh society impeded economic recovery and subverted the NEP, such a conclusion is not supported by facts.[21] The regime did not have the resources to direct the process of economic recovery and could not offer the assistance necessary to the Kazakhs to become sedentary. In fact, many Kazakhs seem to have been happy, even eager, to become farmers, especially when there was no real alternative.

For example, reports from the Pavlodar regional committee of the Communist Party show that in 1925 the local party organization was unable to provide the land and resources necessary to settle the large number of Kazakhs who were willing, even desperate, to seize the opportunity granted them by the 1924 "Resolution on Land Construction."[22] Land was still in such short supply that in 1925 the regime reversed itself and encouraged communal use of land to give Kazakh communities more responsibility in directing self-recovery.

Economic recovery did occur, however slowly; until 1925 there were still widespread complaints that the markets were empty.[23] Both livestock breeding and agriculture in Kazakhstan were being reinvigorated. By 1925 the sown area in Kazakhstan was almost two-thirds (64.8 percent) that of the prewar level, and in 1925–1926, almost 400,000 metric tons of grain from Kazakhstan were made available on the internal market.

The annual agricultural growth rate, however, was only 5.6 percent, despite the fact that the number of Kazakhs engaged in agriculture increased annually; 25 percent of the fields were sown by Kazakhs in 1926 as compared to 15 percent in 1920.[24] Livestock breeding was recovering at about the same rate; in 1925 the herd size was 62.8 percent of the 1917 level. The network of internal communication was being restored very slowly, and the difficulty of marketing livestock lessened some incentive for the Kazakh livestock breeders. Still, herd size grew annually from 1924 until 1929, when the policy of collectivization was introduced.

## THE SOVIETIZATION OF THE KAZAKH AUL, 1925–1929

Kazakh economic recovery, however limited, did encourage the regime. Rather than sit aside and allow the economy to stabilize itself, however, Moscow chose to strengthen its political hold on the Kazakh community. To some degree the events in Kazakhstan simply mirrored those elsewhere in the Soviet Union, since this was the period of the power struggle in the Kremlin and of the retreat from the NEP. The policy of the sovietization of the Kazakh aul (that is, to achieve the loyalty and cooperation of the fundamental Kazakh societal unit; for further discussion see Chapter Nine), which was pursued in Kazakhstan from 1925 through 1929, was in part a product of the political events in Moscow but was also influenced by the same biases that the Russian colonial administration had held. It was a policy directed solely toward the

Kazakhs and was not applied to the other Central Asian nationalities. Kazakhstan, although a national region, was also a grain producer (with as-yet-unrealized potential) and so better integrated into the Russian economy than was the rest of Central Asia. Long a frontier people on the outskirts of Russian civilization, the Kazakhs were considered more malleable and cooperative than the other Central Asian nationalities; thus, the Kazakh aul was expected to adapt to the conditions of social revolution more readily than the *kishlak* (village) of the sedentary Central Asian Muslims.

The policy of sovietization of the Kazakh aul was adopted at the fifth all-Kazakh conference of the Communist Party, held in December 1925. The policy stated explicitly the previously only implicit assumption that the dictatorship of the proletariat was more difficult to achieve in Kazakh society than in the Ukrainian or Russian settlements of Kazakhstan, which thus required a special campaign of persuasion aided by restricting the powers of the traditional authorities. The policy was a result of a year-long discussion and debate provoked by a TsIK KazASSR resolution of December 1924, which highlighted the weakness of Bolshevik rule in the Kazakh areas. The timing of the December 1925 policy was deliberate, for it came at the beginning of the campaign for election of delegates to the 1926 Supreme Soviet; this was to be the first mass-elected Supreme Soviet. Conscious of how little had been done hitherto to disturb the power of the traditional rural authorities in the Kazakh community, the Soviet regime wanted to ensure the election of someone who would reflect its ideas and goals.

The decision to begin a campaign to control and restrict the power of the traditional authorities came at a time when the central leadership in Moscow, Stalin in particular, was growing restive with the NEP and beginning to move toward more direct supervision of the economy by the state and party. The fourteenth party congress, held in Moscow in December 1925, marked the beginning of the decline of the NEP by endorsing a policy of rapid industrialization, although no means for achieving it were spelled out for another two years. A necessary prerequisite for the successful functioning of a state-directed economy is a loyal, cooperative citizenry, which the policy of sovietization of the Kazakh aul was to achieve in Kazakhstan.

This policy was political and not very successful; over 90 percent of the officials elected in 1926 were nonparty candidates—represented, it is true, more in lower levels than in the higher. Such election results led the party to intensify its propaganda efforts in the countryside, restrict participation of nonparty candidates in the election process, and further limit the franchise among property owners. The goal of these policies was to limit the authority of the traditional leadership, who were seen as inimical to Moscow's drive to harness the economy for industrialization and rapid economic development.

Throughout the period 1925–1929, the government of Kazakhstan strove to increase agricultural efficiency and assume state control of the economy by reducing the hold of the traditional authorities over the economic life of the Kazakhs. The April 1926 plenum of the *Kazkraikom* (Kazakh regional committee of the Communist Party) attacked the rural party organizations as weak and without understanding of how to ensure the survival of a nomadic or semi-nomadic livestock breeding economy. The issue of land reform was approached anew, and the absence of local resources to achieve redistribution was acknowledged. The plenum called for more active intervention by the state and greater use of state lands to achieve a shift in land-usage patterns. The decisions of this meeting formed the basis of the May 1926 resolution by the TsIK KazASSR, which took the power to redistribute land away from the aul soviets and awarded it to official land committees, based on the argument that the auls were dominated by clan elders, hence untrustworthy; the land committees, composed of members of the aul soviets, the Koshchi Union, and the working population, would distribute newly acquired lands in accordance with socialist norms.[25] Ironically, the Koshchi Union was dominated by the same traditional forces that dominated the aul soviets. Of course, the greatest impediment faced by local authorities was not so much popular resistance as the absence of distributable land, a situation that was not rectified by the decisions of the plenum.

At the April 1926 Kazkraikom plenum, the leadership addressed and then dismissed the long-standing premise of the Kazakh intellectuals that the nomadic economy was unique. The intellectuals' argument—that nomads should not be treated as sedentes because livestock breeders were not like wheat growers—was discounted primarily because many of the most visible proponents, men like Bukeikhanov and Baitursunov, were now falling victim to Moscow's drive against nonparty members of national republic governments (see Chapter Nine). Many government agronomists also argued that the needs of nomads were distinctive, but since most of them were former Socialist Revolutionaries they too were soon barred from participation. However, in 1926–1928 they often argued that the traditional Kazakh livestock-breeding economy, which combined free grazing with stall feeding, was well suited to the conditions of the steppe and that any move to substitute grain growing for livestock breeding would reduce the economic productivity of the steppe. They warned that any dramatic and rapid change in the practice of Kazakh livestock breeding was likely to result in severe economic depression.[26]

In 1926 the policymakers in Alma-Ata seem to have been briefly swayed by these arguments and to have readjusted their thinking about how land redistribution could best be accomplished in the steppe, but it was becoming increasingly difficult to regard either Kazakhstan or the Kazakhs as a special case. The regime rejected the contention that the Kazakh aul was some sort of primitive commune, and it chose instead to understand the traditional society as feudal; traditional leadership was painted in increasingly negative terms as the decade went on. The regime could not afford to treat the Kazakhs as a special case, since the Soviet economy was evolving toward a centralized economy; such an economy demands the assumption that general economic policies may be applied equally well across mega-regions, if not across the whole expanse of the Soviet Union. To make the Kazakhs a special case was to open the possibility that most nationalities, and even subregions of the Russian Soviet Federated Socialist Republic (RSFSR), might want to be considered regions of the special cases as well. If that happened, it would become almost impossible for the regime to devise general policies to achieve rapid economic development.

Furthermore, to the regime agriculture meant grain growing, and so the entire rural population was expected to behave like Russian peasants. Trained agronomists disagreed, but they were a declining force in economic decision-making as the 1920s ended. The regime held that livestock breeding was important because meat was good for people and both skins and wool were valuable. Still, grain was more important; after all, meat was a luxury and bread was a necessity.

Despite a bumper crop of grain in 1926, a higher price was offered on the free market than by the state, which meant that only the minimum required was sold to the state. For livestock, price differences were even greater, with market prices often several rubles higher than the official rate.[27] After the 1926 harvest the official purchase price of grain dropped from 2.8 rubles to 1.3 rubles.[28] However, the 1927 harvest and lower official price encouraged many growers to withhold grain from the state market and use it as animal feed or sell it to private traders. As a result, much less grain reached the cities than had in the two previous years.

The reduced supply of grain was felt quite quickly and may well have contributed to the hardened attitude toward agriculture shown by the Fifteenth Party Congress, held in December 1927. The proceedings made plain that peasant-controlled agriculture was both inefficient and untrustworthy and that small, privately owned farms could not produce large surpluses. The congress resolved that the state had to achieve greater control if agricultural productivity was to increase. The party adopted a program that called for the eventual transfer of all agricultural enterprises to cooperative control, thus ending private ownership in the countryside. The collectivization of agriculture was to create a state-controlled grain surplus, which in turn would provide the capital necessary to launch the massive industrialization effort. The actual timetables for both collectivization and mass industrialization were to be set by the State Planning Board and incorporated in the (first) Five-Year Plan, which was also mandated at this meeting.

This new hard line was coupled with an attack on supporters of the so-called right position, which defended the NEP and some private ownership in the countryside. Because there was increased difficulty in procuring grain, the regime was intolerant of peasant resistance.[29] Beginning with the 1927–1928 harvest, peasants found with grain stores could be charged with illegal hoarding; teams of party workers were sent from the cities to secure the grain procurements for the authorities. This policy of what in effect were grain requisitions was applied to all grain-growing regions of the USSR save the desert regions of Kazakhstan. Again Kazakhstan became important as an under-utilized source of grain, particularly after 1927, when the government managed to procure only 80 percent of the grain desired from this region.[30]

The program adopted at the Fifteenth Party Congress set the agenda for the republic-level administrations, so the Kazkraikom took up the burden of grain requisitions. The sixth Kazakh regional party conference, held in November 1927, passed a six-point program that called for equalization of land holdings, sovietization of the aul, reduction of the power of the bais, introduction of cooperative organizations among Kazakh livestock-breeding households, improvement of party work in the localities, and greater integration of the Kazakh population into the government (*korenizatsiia*).

By early 1928 it was apparent that this new economic line was being actively pursued. Grain requisitions became commonplace for both Kazakhs and Russians, although many Kazakhs burnt their grain stores rather than turn them over to the regime. The regime began to use more active social policy in support of their economic goals; in Kazakhstan this took the form of an attack upon the Kazakh bais as feudal elements, now slated for elimination. A drive was begun to confiscate and redistribute the bais' livestock, following the Marxist logic that if they lost their animals they would lose their power. This policy underestimated the power of the Kazakh traditional leadership; the Kazakh masses did not see themselves as oppressed by their leaders and so saw the attack on the bais as an attack on themselves.

In 1928 the regime made yet another attempt at land redistribution. The hold of large and now even mid-sized landowners was to be broken in preparation for the introduction of a collectivized agriculture. For the first time in a decade land was seized, by force if necessary, yet the drives of 1927–1928 and 1928–1929 still did not produce the desired results. One published report from the Kustanai oblast highlights some of the problems encountered. Many of the people assigned to allocate land were not competent and did not carry the authority to convince the population that they had to be obeyed. This problem was compounded by the refusal of most members of the Koshchi Union to participate in the redistribution drive. There were also complaints that the volost land committees were given no money for travel and so remained ignorant of the situation in their territory.[31]

A report from Aktyubinsk paints a similar picture. In this oblast some 165,736 hectares of land were distributed among 68,859 households during the redistribution drive of 1927–1928.[32] This means that each household was awarded fewer than three hectares, an amount too small to permit any substantial change. The chairman of the provincial land committee argued that without additional support from Moscow, new sources of land for allotment, and additional executive power, the land committees could not hope to succeed with their task.

The drive to confiscate livestock from the Kazakh bais was even less successful than the land redistribution effort. As soon as the decree became public the Kazakhs began to sell and slaughter their animals in large numbers, and many bais fled to China, Uzbekistan, Siberia, and Astrakhan to avoid losing their animals.[33] In June 1928 the regime claimed the Kazakhs had overreacted, for only "large" bais would lose their animals; when this still failed to quell popular discontent, more precise guidelines for confiscation were published in late August 1928. In nomadic regions individual heads of household could own up to 400, in seminomadic regions 300, and in sedentary regions 100 head of livestock. Still, the guidelines did not stop the capricious seizure of animals, for local officials often "nationalized" holdings of "small or middle bais" in order to meet their regional quotas.[34] According to the August guidelines, only 700 households were liable to confiscation and, in the end, only 548 households had animals seized—in all 135,710 animals or 56 percent of their holdings. Only 4 percent of total holdings in the republic changed hands during this period.

Although the drive was relatively unimportant economically, it did feed the political gristmill; at the seventh Kazakh party conference in May 1930, 85 prominent party members were dismissed for having aided the bais during the 1928 drive.[35] Not all the charges against Kazakh party members were unfounded, for many had found the confiscation policy unusually harsh and difficult to enforce. Many regional executive committees had simply refused to provide assistance to those sent to carry out the campaign and had closed their eyes to Kazakh evasions of the law. Many bais had sold their "excess" animals before they could be confiscated. Still others had arranged fictitious transfers of ownership, nominally reducing their herds to below the legal limits, only to reclaim their animals when the danger had passed.[36]

## SOCIAL POLICY IN THE 1920s

Although the focus of government activity in this period was on rebuilding the economy and stabilizing Soviet rule in the localities, the Soviets did not abandon their goal of social revolution. They knew that the old order must be destroyed before any attempt to introduce socialist values could hope to succeed. Lacking the resources and support base to attack the old order, the

Soviets chose a strategy of so-called Soviet enlightenment, by which they taught the Kazakhs about societal alternatives and so tried to convince them that their customary way of life was deficient.

Education was not the only strategy, however; the most harmful of the Kazakh customary practices were quickly outlawed. In December 1920 the Supreme Soviet of the Kazakh ASSR passed a resolution banning kun, or blood revenge. Kazakh customary law demanded that the death or injury of a relative be avenged by comparable harm to a member of the offender's community. After 1920 those who took justice into their own hands were liable to arrest for murder.[37] A resolution was also passed that outlawed the payment of kalym, the bride price. In the following years laws were passed against a wide variety of traditional practices; barymta, marriage of minors, levirate and sororate, and marriage contracts of any type were all illegal by the end of 1923. Yet because the customary authorities were themselves practitioners of tradition, these laws were never enforced.[38]

The Soviets did see education as the principal agent of socialization and as the way to provide the technological basis necessary for the construction of socialism. In July 1922 the Kazakh government called for the mobilization of all literate Kazakhs in a massive campaign to eradicate illiteracy. At the same time permission was given for the reopening of the madrasahs to increase the number of schools, but the *muallim* (teachers in Muslim schools) proved themselves untrustworthy. Most of them used knowledge gained at retraining courses to better combat Bolshevik propaganda, and they counseled the Kazakhs to send their children to (legal and illegal) religious schools instead of to state-run primary schools.[39] Despite the ambition of the literacy campaign, less than 10 percent of the Kazakh population was literate by the end of the decade, and over 90 percent of the aul schools still lacked adequate buildings and supplies.[40]

The social programs of the party were to be popularized by several auxiliary agencies. At the end of 1921 the Kazkraikom of the RKP(b) called for the organization of peasant mutual-aid societies in the Kazakh population, the so-called Koshchi Union. Initially formed to help distribute relief aid, the Koshchi Union was intended as a local representative of the regime and its goals; the membership was intended to join the party. Instead, the Koshchi Union became dominated by the same people who dominated the local soviets, that is, the traditional clan leaders.

In 1922 the Kazakh government established Red Caravans; each district had to send its Red Caravan to tour auls and deliver lectures on the goals and programs of the Communist Party in Kazakhstan. Shortly thereafter Red Yurts were organized to eradicate female illiteracy and provide for the political enlightenment of women. The Red Yurts traveled year-round, spending two or three weeks in a community and migrating with it as necessary. There were technical specialists attached to the Red Yurts to distribute medical, veterinary, and agricultural assistance to the population, but the number of technical experts did not meet the demand; the Kazakh press throughout the 1920s complained about the needless loss of both human life and livestock in epidemics.[41]

None of these organizations were particularly effective. Following the disastrous defeat of Communist Party–backed candidates in the 1925 Soviet election, the Koshchi Union was disbanded and reformed under closer party supervision. But once cleansed of "dangerous elements," the new Koshchi Union was both smaller and less effective than its predecessor. In February 1925 a new civil code was introduced, which provided sentences of 40 days to one year at hard labor for the payment of kalym, forced marriage, polygamy, or child marriage. Over the next five-year period a variety of social campaigns were introduced, but fewer than 1,000 convictions for social crimes were obtained annually. In the end, neither the new organizations nor legal sanctions managed to eliminate customary practices. Kalyms were paid when the parties involved could afford to pay them, and child marriage remained common.[42] Some customary practices, especially barymta, became more, rather than less, common as harsh economic conditions made cattle rustling a lucrative activity for Kazakh and Russian alike.[43]

The reports of field expeditions of the late 1920s recount the failures of Soviet efforts to reconstruct Kazakh society. Rudenko's expedition of 1927–1928 to Semipalatinsk reported that the central role of the family in Kazakh society remained unchanged and the authority of the aksakal, or elder, remained undiminished. Customary practices were as important as before the revolution, and justice was still largely administered by adat and Shari'a courts.[44]

Rudenko's conclusions are sustained by other ethnographers of the period. Some sources suggest that the Islamic religious hierarchy became more firmly entrenched in the steppe during this period, which may in part have been due to the improved communication and transportation links between Kazakhstan and neighboring Muslim regions.[45] Another reason was that localities preserved jurisdiction to disqualify members of the clergy from serving in local and district governments, but often such self-policing was never done.

The composition of the local authority structure definitionally doomed Soviet social policy to failure. All sources agree that before collectivization—and even after it in many regions—the local power structure was controlled by the traditional clanic leaders. Aul soviets were formed in every community, as legislation required, but they were dominated by traditional leadership, both clanic and clerical. The same was true of the aul party cells; many communities had neither a party cell nor any aul Communists. However, where cells did exist the membership was indistinguishable from the traditional leadership groups.

Both the general members and the local party secretaries often had no secular education and knew nothing about either party ideology or party programs.

## THE FAILURE OF SOVIET POLICYMAKING IN THE 1920s

The social and economic policies applied to Kazakhstan in the 1920s not only failed to achieve the desired social and economic transformation, but all evidence suggests that traditional forces became more, not less, firmly entrenched. The regime was committed to increased exploitation of the agricultural and industrial potential of the region, particularly after the decision to allocate 200 million rubles to build the Turkestan-Siberian railroad.[46] The violent resistance that met redistribution and grain procurement drives helped convince the regime that complete control of the economy could not be achieved by half measures; they remembered this lesson when the collectivization drive of 1929–1930 was launched. Other lessons to be found in the failure of the policies of the late 1920s were not, however, so well learned.

In part this failure was the result of the regime's inability to create new political structures in the countryside that could legitimize Soviet authority and policies. Much of the fault, however, lies in the contradictions inherent in the economic policies themselves, which were predicated on the existence of a surplus in the steppe economy that was allegedly being withheld from the market. Examination of the actual economy in 1928–1929 quickly shows that there was no surplus. Total herd size in Kazakhstan did not return to prewar levels until 1927, and in 1928 it had increased to 110 percent the size of the 1917 herd. Furthermore, the growth rate began to slow in 1927, dropping to less than 4 percent for 1928–1929. The average holdings per family also dropped precipitously throughout the period; whereas in 1915 the average Kazakh household had owned 26 animals, by 1929 half the households owned 5 animals or fewer and individuals who owned 25 or more animals were classified as "small" or "mid-sized" bais.[47] Although the bais may have owned more than their fellow Kazakhs, it hardly seems fair to depict them as greedy feudal lords. Recovery in livestock breeding was uneven, and in many of the formerly nomadic regions the number of sheep and goats fell far below prewar levels.

Recovery in agriculture was also slow. In 1929 the total area sown still had not reached the prewar total, and the rate of return on land had declined. The Kazakhs were taking up agriculture in increasingly larger numbers; in 1929 they accounted for over 30 percent of the farmers in Kazakhstan. According to the 1926 census, 24 percent of the Kazakh population at that time was engaged solely in agriculture while another 33 percent combined agriculture with livestock breeding.

The Kazakhs generally were not as successful at farming as their Russian counterparts. Their traditional culture was not directed toward agriculture, and the Soviets were unable to compensate for this with adequate seed, implements, and technical assistance. Kazakh land was often arid, and official efforts at land reclamation were woefully inadequate throughout the period. Lack of water was probably the greatest concern to most Kazakh farmers. Although many irrigation projects were proposed to the Soviet authorities, very little seems to have been done to introduce an effective irrigation program.[48] Many new agricultural settlements had to disband and the settlers forced to return to the steppe, when the one well went dry.[49]

The increase in the amount of land under cultivation seems largely to have been due to the increased cultivation of marginal farm land, but there was also an increase in the number of farmers, most of whom were Kazakhs who had suffered the loss of their herds. Because of many new farmers and insufficient land, the average plot size in the republic dropped; in many predominantly Kazakh regions the average fell below the subsistence level.[50]

Agriculture had begun to recover some of its prewar momentum, but the rate of this recovery had slowed by 1929, due in part to the harsh winters of 1927–1928 and 1928–1929. Another reason was a self-imposed cutback in grain production by both Russian and Kazakh farmers to reduce the amount of grain available for requisition. Because the sale of meat was subject only to limited regulation, it was more profitable for a farmer to raise livestock, even if only a few head, than to reap bumper crops of grain; not surprisingly, this is exactly what many farmers began to do.[51] Therefore, although the regime depended on it to provide surplus grain, Kazakhstan on the eve of collectivization remained primarily a livestock-breeding economy. About 90 percent of the Kazakh population earned some of its income through livestock breeding, while nearly 40 percent were occupied with livestock exclusively. In 1927–1928 more than 80 percent of the value of all goods traded in the republic came from livestock-related products.

The 1920s saw recovery but no real economic growth in the region. Moscow's much-desired agricultural surplus was not created, and huge areas of poverty remained in Kazakhstan, mostly in the nomadic and seminomadic regions. The Soviet policies had failed to deal with the unique problems of the Kazakhs. Year-round migration was a thing of the past for all but the 10 percent of the Kazakhs who lived in the remote desert and semidesert regions of central Kazakhstan. Nearly two-thirds of the Kazakh population were seminomadic (engaged in a combination of livestock breeding and subsistence agriculture) and had looked to the regime to provide them with assistance, but the Soviet bureaucrats in Moscow had proved little better than the colonial civil servants in St. Petersburg. The Soviets had not found a formula to allocate land equitably between competing Kazakh and Russian claimants, nor had they been able to make the large investment necessary to reclaim new lands and introduce a more efficient form of agriculture. Despite this demonstrated inability to finance and execute any rational, integrated program of economic recovery, the regime next chose to make even greater economic demands on the region by collectivizing the rural economy.

# 8 Collectivization and the Stalinist Economic System

## COMMUNAL OWNERSHIP IN KAZAKHSTAN PRIOR TO COLLECTIVIZATION

Stalin's anniversary speech in November 1929 endorsed the principle of collective ownership of agricultural enterprises, and he called for that to become the principal basis of ownership in the countryside within the period of the (first) Five-Year Plan.[1] So much has been written about the reasons for Stalin's policy departure that there is little this book need add on the subject, except to point out that the decision to collectivize agriculture assumed that a basis for collectivized agriculture had already been developed.

The Bolsheviks had been committed to a policy of communal ownership of land since the revolution. In 1918 they had begun a large-scale drive to nationalize land but quickly backed off when they saw its widespread lack of popularity. The NEP had made limited private ownership the principle of agricultural organization, but still the regime clutched the dream that a communally based agriculture could become reality and so devoted some of its scant resources to establishing collective and state farms throughout the Soviet Union. After late 1925 increased material assistance was made available for communal enterprises; at this same time the Communist Party, long suspicious of the peasantry, began to seek more active control of the rural sector.

The program adopted at the Fifteenth Party Congress in December 1927 included the formal decision to move toward a collectivized economy, which was to be achieved gradually. The goals of the (first) Five-Year Plan, announced in April 1928, called for only 12.9 percent of the population to be collectivized within the period of the plan. Moreover, the rate of collectivization did not have to be uniform throughout the Soviet Union; it was expected that the process would proceed more slowly in the backward national regions, of which Kazakhstan was one.

At the time of Stalin's speech in 1929, agriculture throughout the Soviet Union was primarily in private hands, overwhelmingly so in Central Asia and Kazakhstan. It is difficult to state with any certainty what percentage of the Kazakh population was engaged in collective agricultural pursuits before the 1929 collectivization drive. Data is contradictory and imprecise, further complicated by a lack of agreement about what constitutes a collective farm. Three distinct types of agricultural cooperatives were introduced in the Soviet Union in the 1920s: the commune, the agricultural *artel*, and the *TOZ* (a society for the communal working of land).[2] In the commune, all property was owned in common; in the TOZ, land was worked commonly but livestock were privately held. In the agricultural artel, some private ownership of land and livestock was permitted but the principal income of the community was to be based on common labor. In addition, the state sponsored the creation of *sovkhozy* (state farms), in which the state owned all the property and the farmers were paid as laborers. Finally, the state also encouraged the development of communal attitudes by sponsoring cooperative supply and market networks for small-scale farmers and livestock breeders.

The most authoritative information on the degree of collectivization prior to 1929 is found in the works of the Soviet scholar F. I. Kolodin, who reports that as of January 1, 1928, 18.2 percent of the population was involved in some type of collective enterprise. The overwhelming majority of these individuals, however, were associated with the TOZ movement, and most of the TOZ enterprises were only nominally communal, with land and livestock still effectively under private control. His conclusions were based on archival records for 1927 from the Kzyl-Orda region, where of 105 TOZ farms, only 4 could accurately be classified as collective. Kolodin argued that this situation was common to other regions of Kazakhstan as well.[3]

Furthermore, these collective farms made an insignificant contribution to the economy of the republic. Nearly 20 percent of the population participated in collective enterprises, but only 6.4 percent of the land was cultivated in common by *kolkhozniki* (artel farmers) and 0.9 percent was sown by *sovkhoz* workers. The remaining 92.7 percent of the cultivated land was privately owned. Although precise information on the national composition of these early collective farms is unavailable, fragmentary evidence supports the conclusion that the artels were disproportionately Russian in makeup and were often formed as settlements for deported kulaks, generally on marginal agricultural lands.[4] The livestock-breeding sector was even less affected by the early efforts of the regime to introduce collective ownership than were the grain-growing regions; 99.1 percent of all livestock in the republic was still privately held in January 1929.[5]

Before 1929 the Kazakhs had had little exposure to the principles of collective ownership. They were underrepresented in the loosely structured cooperative supply and market network system. Very few networks were established in the livestock-breeding regions, where the only collective organizations were consumer cooperatives, most of which were ill-equipped and poorly supplied. Published reports from the Semipalatinsk oblast record a myriad of complaints about the functioning of these networks: for example, that the societies had not received seed or agricultural implements to distribute, that they could not provide adequate transport to take goods to market, and that the prices paid by the trading cooperatives for agricultural commodities were far below free-market rates.[6] The local authorities were as unprepared as the Kazakhs for the introduction of collectivization, and they were taken unaware as well; there was neither a collective nor a state sector of the agricultural economy upon which they might build.

Collectivization was to proceed by stages; the state plan of 1928 called for the individual peasant household to be gradually replaced by the communal household. There was to be an immediate increase in the number of consumer cooperatives, which in turn would pave the way for the domination of the market by goods produced at cooperatively or state-run farms. Most of Kazakhstan, including virtually all the Kazakh-dominated regions, was considered socially and economically backward; therefore, in the first years of the plan the republic administration concentrated on expanding the most loosely defined collective organizations, that is, the cooperative trade networks.

The government in Alma-Ata understood the difficulties of achieving collectivization in Kazakhstan. A TsIK KazASSR report from mid-1928 listed many of the specific problems of kolkhoz (artel) formation in the republic, including the weak political, organizational, and economic leadership previously shown by the local party apparat, the slow rate of kolkhoz formation in the past, the small size of the existing kolkhoz, and the lack of cultural work among the kolkhozniki.[7] Because all of these problems were most severe in the formerly nomadic regions, collectivization within the timetable of the (first) Five-Year Plan was considered possible only in the grain-producing regions.

Almost immediately the (first) Five-Year Plan began to fall short of its goals. By October 1, 1929, although the number of collective farms was four times greater than a year previously, only 7.4 percent of the population of the republic had been collectivized; this suggests the level of success a voluntary policy of collectivization could expect. Also troubling was that the Kazakh authorities had not been able to devote complete attention to the collectivization drive because they had to collect the required grain procurements; popular resistance to forcible requisition was great and the Kazakh party had to get help from Moscow to meet local quotas. There was little in the economic policy of 1928–1929 to build Kazakh trust in either the government or the economic policy process. Without such trust, as the Kazakh authorities perceived, the restructuring of the agricultural sector through collectivization would be nearly impossible, and so it proved.

Despite the resistance encountered throughout the USSR during the grain requisition drive and the opposition to collectivization mounted in Moscow by Bukharin and his associates and in Kazakhstan by Russian economists and Kazakh party leaders alike, Moscow remained adamant that the collectivized household was to become the basis of future Soviet agriculture.[8]

Stalin remained committed to the idea that agriculture must be collectivized, and so throughout Kazakhstan local authorities linked the redistribution of land to the creation of collective farms. The number of collective farms increased from 1,072 in 1927 to 2,315 in 1928, finally reaching 4,343 by late October 1929, when Stalin called for a mass drive to achieve collectivization.

Kazakh preparedness for collectivization remains a highly controversial subject in the Soviet Union; most contemporary accounts are rarely cited by modern scholars.[9] A. P. Kuchkin's book, *Sovietization of the Kazakh Aul*, which concludes that the Kazakh countryside was ill-prepared for collectivization, has met severe criticism.[10] Even so, most recent Soviet historians conclude that the livestock-breeding areas of Kazakhstan were not prepared for the mass, forced collectivization of 1930.[11] There had not been sufficient indoctrination on the meaning of and necessity for collective farms, and there were virtually no working models.

The situation was not much better in the grain-producing areas, although a small number of collective enterprises had been introduced, including kolkhoz, sovkhoz, *MTS* (Machine Tractor Stations), communes, and artels. In some regions of at least two oblasts (Kustanai and Petropavlovsk), up to 70 percent of the population was engaged in some form of cooperative activity, but many of these cooperatives were not economically viable.[12]

If the success of collectivization is judged not by the number of collective farms but by their economic significance, the evidence is overwhelmingly one-sided: all sources agree that before November 1929 collective enterprises played only a minor role in the economy of the steppe. In 1928 only 120,000 hectares of land were cultivated as communal property; most collective farms were very small, averaging only 128 hectares,[13] as well as inefficient, with a lower per-hectare yield than on privately owned land. It was on such a shaky foundation that Stalin wished to build an economy that would yield a massively increased surplus of grain.

## MASS COLLECTIVIZATION
## IN KAZAKHSTAN

The collectivization drive in Kazakhstan occurred in four distinct phases: the campaign for rapid collectivization, November 1929–March 1930;

retreat and experimentation with different types of collective farms, March 1930–August 1932; the use of the TOZ for the reintroduction of collectivization, September 1932–November 1934; and the reconstitution of TOZ farms as agricultural artels, December 1934–December 1938.

The mass collectivization drive formally began with the publication of Stalin's November 7, 1929, article, "The Year of the Great Turn," which, after noting the influx of large numbers of peasants into collectives, called for a "great breakthrough in the countryside." Shortly after this article appeared, the Central Committee plenum called for the formation of a committee on collectivization to consider how the goal of mass collectivization could be achieved. Soon after the plenum the various member parties convened and they too reaffirmed the program. The Kazakh party held their meeting December 11–16, 1929, and resolved that collectivization could only be achieved if the settlement of the Kazakh nomads occurred simultaneously. Collectivization and sedentarization were definitionally linked, because Stalin was determined to achieve the final destruction of the nomadic economy and so end the political authority of the old social order.

A detailed plan for the settlement of the nomads was included in the revised (first) Five-Year Plan, and a special committee on settlement was created. However, the Kazakh party plenum in December noted fearfully that rapid collectivization had already begun, albeit without adequate provision for the needs of the newly collectivized households and particularly without providing for the settlement of the nomads.[14] Despite this tone of official caution, collectivization was raging throughout Kazakhstan and keeping pace with the "prepared" regions. During November 1929, over 500 new collective farms were created in the nomadic and seminomadic regions of Kazakhstan.[15] On January 5, 1930, more precise details on the tempo of collectivization were made available; the Soviet Union was divided into three regions, the first to be completely collectivized by the spring of 1931, the second by the spring of 1932, and the third by the end of 1933. The grain-producing regions of Kazakhstan were included in the second group, and the rest of Kazakhstan was in the third category, along with the "backward" national regions of the east, north, and Siberia. That Kazakhstan was included in both the second and third categories indicated the ambiguous nature of that region; it was both a grain- and a cattle-producing area, both the first link of the food-supply chain for the Siberian cities and also a backward national region.

This January 1930 resolution did little to halt the rapid tempo of nationalization. The collectivization drive in Kazakhstan, as everywhere else, proceeded at a frantic pace. By February 1, 35.3 percent of the population was collectivized and by March 1, 42.1 percent.[16] At first the collectivization drive was carried out by urban Communists mobilized in January. Included in their ranks were young Kazakh students eager to effect social change through the destruction of the old order.[17] In early spring 1930 these were joined by some 1,200 "25,000ers," mostly from Moscow.[18] Gains were achieved at great cost, against stiff opposition, as they nationalized Kazakh property and forced the former nomads to settle onto the new collective farms.

It is impossible to recreate the details of the Kazakh opposition, but scholars with access to the archives conclude that resistance was widespread and often well organized. Party activists entered Kazakh auls to collectivize or arrest the so-called kulaks at risk of their lives, because they were often met with armed resistance. Roving bands of Kazakhs attacked newly created kolkhozy, rustling or killing the kolkhoz livestock. In some regions the aul leaders grouped together to plan concerted action to thwart the Soviets, including mass migration to Turkmenistan, where collectivization was reported to be proceeding more slowly.[19] A number of clan elders organized patrols to warn Kazakhs living in more remote areas not to join the new collective farms, on the reasonable grounds that these often lacked water and arable land. Although resistance in Kazakhstan, and in Central Asia generally, was stiffer than in most other parts of the Soviet Union, the collectivization drive was out of control throughout the country. On March 2, 1930, Stalin's famous "Dizzy with Success" letter was published in *Pravda* to signal a change in policy, which was formalized by the March 15, Central Committee resolution "On Distortions of the Party Line with Reference to the Collectivization Movement." This resolution reasserted the party's commitment to collectivization but stressed that the January 5 guidelines were not to be exceeded.

It is difficult to know precisely what percentage of the rural population was in fact collectivized at the time that the policy reversal occurred, but just under 60 percent seems to be a reliable estimate.[20] The pace of collectivization was uneven; in some parts of the Petropavlosk, Syr Darya, and Uralsk oblasts 70 percent of the population was collectivized, while in nomadic areas, where there were few collective farms to expand, fewer than 20 percent of the Kazakhs were in the collective sector.[21]

Collectivization was not only proceeding more rapidly than the peasantry desired but it had also outpaced the capacity of the regime to allocate resources to the new communities. This was particularly true in Kazakhstan, where the authorities not only lacked money, construction materials, seed, and farm implements to supply the new collective farmers but were also so inefficient that they could not distribute even those supplies on hand.[22] In addition, many of the new collective farms could never become economically viable since they were in the desert or semidesert and thus lacked enough water to support free grazing of livestock. Without the supplies to farm what was untillable land, these Kazakhs were unable even to graze sheep.

The organizational structure of these first collective farms was often poor. An average kolkhoz encompassed a territory of 200 square kilometers and was composed of anywhere from 10 to 20 separate auls, each with 10–15 families. The first kolkhoz chairmen were generally illiterate, unable even to understand simple directions from Moscow let alone prepare and follow the production plans that they received. The party officials at the regional level were little better trained themselves and received little or no assistance from specialists.[23] Not surprisingly, then, the first months of collectivization showed great confusion about the meaning of the campaign and how it should be achieved. On some collective farms the animals were confiscated and later returned, while on others livestock was slaughtered to forestall seizure, after which officials apologized and called the confiscation a mistake.[24]

The March 1930 pronouncements by Stalin and the Central Committee did not correct these problems. Although the pace of collectivization slowed, there was still great confusion that was unaddressed until the Sixteenth Party Congress convened in late June 1930. It was then decided that the type of collective introduced was to be determined by the economic needs of the region; the TOZ was chosen as suitable for Central Asia and Kazakhstan. These recommendations became the basis of the resolution "On Kolkhoz Construction and Measures for Strengthening It," adopted in July 1930 at the seventh all-Kazakh party conference. This resolution mandated that in Kazakhstan the agricultural artel was to be the basis of collectivization for the grain-producing regions, the incomplete artel (where limited private ownership was preserved) for regions of commercial crop cultivation, the TOZ for seminomadic areas, and cooperative market and supply networks for nomadic areas. The agricultural artels previously organized in nomadic areas were to be reconstructed as TOZ. By the end of 1930, 69 percent of all collective farms in Kazakhstan were TOZ.[25]

This policy change still left many Kazakh officials uncertain about which path they were to follow, and lacking other instructions local authorities began to recollectivize both people and livestock. The percentage of the population of Kazakhstan that lived on collective farms increased from 33.2 percent in November 1930 to 62.7 percent in November 1931, and to over 70.0 percent by late 1932.[26] The economy failed to reorganize, however, since the "restructured" collective farms were little better than those they had replaced.

The local officials were then made scapegoats for Moscow's policy failures; hundreds of local officials were rebuked and dismissed.[27] The fear of job loss or arrest served effectively to stifle any initiative that local cadres may have felt, and many collective farms were simply abandoned, stripped of their movable resources. Worse, the slaughter of livestock and destruction of seed stores resulted in famine throughout the rural sector.

The failure of the Kazakh economy was a central theme at the Seventeenth Party Conference held in 1932. The disasters of collectivization were ascribed to inadequate preparation for the settlement of a half million nomads that had occurred during these years.[28] At the time of the conference 25 percent of these people, termed *otkochevniki* (former nomads), had already fled their collective farms, were without livestock, had no means to feed themselves or their families, and were wandering the steppe aimlessly, simply awaiting death.

Although in 1930 the number of people targeted for settlement during the following five-year period had been reduced, the figure in 1932 was raised above even the original target. The TsIK KazASSR resolved that, while it was wrong to collectivize the Kazakhs forcibly, it was perfectly correct to settle them by force. F. I. Goloshchekin, first secretary of the Kazakh Communist Party, argued that:

> Settlement is collectivization. Settlement is the liquidation of the *bai* semi-feudals. Settlement is the destruction of tribal attitudes. . . Settlement is simultaneously the question of socialist construction and the approach of socialism, of the socialist reconstruction of the Kazakh mass without divisions by nationality under the leadership of the vanguard of the proletariat and the Communist party.[29]

Conditions in the Kazakh collective farms deteriorated between 1930 and 1932. Everywhere there were severe shortages of livestock, seed, agricultural implements, and construction materials. Livestock were dying in droves; in February 1932 only 48.5 percent of all private households and 13.0 percent of all collectivized households possessed animals of any sort.[30] The number of livestock breeders fell by over 200 percent in a six-year period, and the agricultural sector was expanding at an insignificant rate. Famine was widespread among the Kazakhs.

In September 1932 the regime finally assumed responsibility for redirection of the Kazakh economy in its resolution, "On the Correct Line for the Settlement of the Kazakh Nomads." The resolution maintained that without the settlement of the nomads it would be impossible to "eradicate the economic and cultural anachronisms" of the Kazakh economy and consequently impossible to collectivize the Kazakh people.[31] Collectivization thus far, it was claimed, had proceeded without regard to sedentarization; the blame for this and for the allegedly inadequate supervision of the local authorities was laid on Goloshchekin and the Kazakh party leadership, who were dismissed.

The September 1932 resolution stressed that the TOZ was to be the sole collective form in the livestock-breeding regions, thus recognizing private ownership as a prerequisite for the recovery of the herd and of economic stability in Kazakhstan. In addition, specific recommendations were given. On October 19, 1932, a Kazkraikom resolution designated 39 nomadic and seminomadic regions where the TOZ was to be the basis of ownership; each household would be permitted to own one hundred sheep, eight to ten cattle, three to five camels, and eight to ten horses. In agricultural regions the agricultural artel was reaffirmed as the appropriate type of collective; all animals were to be owned by the artel, but the kolkhozniki were permitted small herds of animals for personal use.[32]

After these resolutions economic recovery slowly began, albeit unevenly. The new collective farms simply could not accommodate all the homeless, since the number of otkochevniki increased constantly; by the end of 1933 they constituted 22 percent of the Kazakh population.[33]

Throughout the recovery, the private sector improved more rapidly than did the collective farms. In spite of heavier taxes on privately held animals, in 1934 barely half of all livestock were publicly owned, which threatened Moscow's goal of recollectivization of the herd.[34] In December 1934 Moscow simply decreed a reduction in the number of privately held animals, which was to be accomplished in two stages: first the transfer of livestock to the collective sector, followed by the reconstruction of the TOZ as agricultural artels. To promote the economic viability of the collective farms, the TOZ were exempted from required milk and grain deliveries in 1935 and 1936, required meat deliveries for 1935 were halved, and collectivized households were excused payment of an agricultural tax in 1935. The former Kazakh nomads, however, were still permitted private ownership of forty sheep and goats, five cattle, and one horse.[35]

It was this use of the TOZ that collectivized Kazakhstan. The Kazakh otkochevniki and private householders were gradually resettled; the percentage of rural households in the collective sector jumped from 67.3 percent in 1934 to 90.7 percent in 1935.[36] By December 1935 the regime felt confident enough to introduce the Model Artel Charter, which further reduced permitted livestock holdings for former nomads to 40 sheep or goats, two beef cattle, and one cow, and kolkhozniki and all others were limited to the livestock necessary to meet their personal needs. Such restrictions, however, were usually ignored in Kazakhstan during this period. At the end of 1938 approximately one-third of all livestock in the republic were still privately held.[37]

After the announcement of the Model Artel Charter, the Kazakh government called for all the TOZ to be converted to agricultural artels. This process began in 1936 and was completed by the end of 1938, by which time more than 98 percent of the rural population lived on collective farms. Collectivization was considered to have been achieved.

## THE COSTS OF COLLECTIVIZATION

The Kazakh economy paid dearly for the collectivization drive, particularly in its first years. Comparing figures from the 1926 and 1939 censuses, Naum Jasny has estimated that more than 1.5 million Kazakhs died during the 1930s and nearly 80 percent of the herd was destroyed between 1928 and 1932.[38] The actual losses were probably even greater. Recently published archival data show that the number of Kazakh households declined from 1,233,000 in 1929 to 565,000 households in 1936, and famine-related deaths were still being reported in 1938.[39] Some of this drop can be explained by out-migration, since 300,000 Kazakhs moved to Uzbekistan and a group of 44,000 Kazakhs fled to Turkmenistan, where they provided much of the leadership for a revived Basmachi revolt.[40]

Other Kazakh lives were lost to violence, not starvation. Party activists who tried to collectivize the Kazakh auls were often forcibly resisted, which cost many party workers their lives. Kazakhs died too, sometimes at the hands of special OGPU (Soviet secret police; after 1934 known as the NKVD) detachments, but many died when other Kazakhs fell upon newly created kolkhozy and rustled or killed the kolkhoz livestock.

The overwhelming majority of Kazakh deaths, however, must be attributed to starvation or related diseases. Throughout the republic settlements and railroad lines were bordered with starving Kazakhs, often otkochevniki who could walk no farther. Thousands of Kazakhs set out for China, but less than a quarter of them survived the journey. Not surprising, infant mortality rates rose dramatically while the birth rate plummeted. Loss of human life was proportionately greater in Kazakhstan than anywhere else in the Soviet Union.

The Kazakhs who chose to move to the collective farms did not fare much better than those who refused; the few first-hand accounts available all concur that conditions on the new collective farms were dismal. The Kazakhs had no shelter for themselves or their animals, no means to cultivate land, and often no land worth cultivating, since the regime failed to allocate arable land to the new kolkhozy. Many of the settlements were in desert or semidesert areas, far from water supplies, and inadequate even to sustain the existing livestock. Some collective farms were without seed, livestock, and capital. There was an acute shortage of construction materials, particularly of glass, iron, and nails. The state plan for 1930 fell drastically short of completion; only 15 percent of the residential units and 32 percent of the livestock barns that were planned were actually erected.[41] Most of the money allocated in 1930 for the settlement of Kazakhs was never spent.

The agricultural sector was not expanding rapidly enough to absorb the displaced livestock breeders. In the period 1928–1932 the area under cultivation in Kazakhstan increased by only 17 percent, and the average yield per hectare decreased.[42]

The destruction of the Kazakh herd, reduced by nearly 80 percent in the decade following the beginning of the collectivization drive, was the greatest economic hardship. This destruction was caused first by the slaughter of animals to prevent their nationalization, later to prevent their starvation. Widespread slaughter began in March 1930; in some areas over 50 percent of the herd was destroyed within a few weeks. The slaughter did not end until mid-1932, and the number of animals in the republic continued to decline through 1933. Precise figures are difficult to obtain, but one reliable source reports a loss of 2.3 million beef cattle and 10 million sheep during 1930 alone.[43] Another concludes that 35 percent of the Kazakh herd died during 1929–1930.[44] Livestock breeding went into a slump that continued for more than two decades. The proportionate loss of animals in Kazakhstan was far greater than in the other nomadic regions or in the USSR as a whole.[45]

Economic conditions in Kazakhstan did not improve appreciably during 1933–1934. Moscow was not able to provide much material assistance, and most Kazakhs were unable to acquire the maximum herd they were permitted to own. It was very difficult to settle the otkochevniki. There were not enough preexisting collective farms to absorb them nor sufficient materials on hand to allow for construction of new, properly equipped settlements on the necessary scale. Most of the new farms were on such marginal land that livestock often had to be driven year-round. Some order seemed to be emerging from the chaos, however, because conditions in the steppe slowly improved, albeit more rapidly among the Russians than among the Kazakhs. In mid-1936 it was announced that most people were no longer on the point of starvation and that now there was also enough grain to feed the livestock of the republic. The herd was beginning to rebuild; by late 1936 almost 90 percent of all collectivized households owned at least one animal.[46] Still, average holdings were small and the distribution was uneven; in some regions, especially in central Kazakhstan, many households remained without livestock. In 1935 Kazakhstan was 18–20 million animals short of an acceptable minimal herd size for the territory, and in 1940 the third congress of the Communist Party of Kazakhstan revealed that a large number of collective farmers still lacked even a cow of their own.[47] Despite the steady herd increase, the herd size did not return to pre-collectivization dimensions until the 1960s.

It was not until 1939 that Moscow saw sufficient economic recovery to dare nationalize the means of production on the new collective farms. Until that time, virtually all Kazakhs lived on artels where land and animals remained under private control, and the few kolkhozniki farmed privately, on plots rented from the collective farm, to feed their personal animals. One measure of this is that in 1938 approximately 75 percent of all kolkhozniki in the republic failed to work the required number of days for the collective, and over 8 percent of them failed to work in the collective sector at all.[48]

In 1938 Moscow called for a program to increase the common or collectively owned herd while increasing the yield of grain. The first goal was to be accomplished by improving the conditions of animal husbandry to raise the young animal survival rate and the general health of the herd. Such attention did have the desired effect; the size of the collectively owned herd more than doubled between 1938 and 1940, by the end of which two-thirds of all animals were communally owned. Increased grain yield was to be achieved by more rational use of land and by enlarging the collective farms, which still averaged fewer than 100 households during this period, but World War II intervened before this goal could be accomplished. Grain yield was not addressed with any seriousness until N. S. Khrushchev introduced his Virgin Lands Policy in the mid-1950s.

The failure of collectivization in Kazakhstan was a failure of planning. Stalin and the authorities in Moscow underestimated the complexity of transforming a nomadic, livestock-breeding economy into a sedentary, agricultural one, and they underestimated the commitment of the Kazakhs to preserve their traditional economic and social way of life. They also failed, in Kazakhstan and in the rest of the country, to understand that force alone cannot achieve economic change, although it did bring social change. The collectivization drive ended Kazakh pastoral nomadism by settling nearly 400,000 Kazakhs between 1930 and 1937.[49] By late 1936 there were only 150,000 Kazakh nomadic households left in the republic, most in the deserts of central Kazakhstan. However, fewer than 40,000 residences were constructed for the newly settled people, and most of these were in marginal areas.[50] Nearly 70 percent of the Kazakh population was settled in grain-growing regions, but few of the new collective farms had seed, work animals, or agricultural equipment, sharing as they did ill-equipped Machine Tractor Stations (MTS).[51] Only in three years (1934, 1938, and 1939) was the republic able to meet its targeted yield of seven centners (one centner equals 220.46 pounds) of grain per hectare sown.[52]

## THE KAZAKH ECONOMY, 1941–1953

As difficult as it is to document, the history of collectivization is an open ledger by comparison with the period of World War II and the final years of Stalin's rule. The problems posed by official secrecy are multiplied tenfold by the hysteria of intellectual life during this time. Even now Stalin's influence continues in the official ambivalence about him and the role he played in Soviet history, and this has done little to encourage any of the present generation of Soviet academics to consider researching this period. In turn, the lack of Soviet sources has discouraged Western academics from spending much time on Soviet policy processes during Stalin's last years. The history of the Eastern nationalities in those years, including that of the Kazakhs, has been utterly ignored in the West.[53]

Traditionally, World War II and the final years of Stalin's life are considered two distinct phases in the history of Kazakhstan. Analytically, however, 1941–

1952 is a unified subperiod of Stalin's rule, because throughout these years the authorities in Kazakhstan were required to maintain and even increase agricultural productivity. Since the cost of failure was frighteningly clear to those in responsible positions, enormous pressure was used to wring the required productivity from an exhausted and, in many ways, insecure peasantry (both Kazakh and Russian). In addition, during the war available manpower evaporated, and victory was followed by official reluctance or incapacity to invest in the rural sector.

The major problem facing the leaders of Kazakhstan during the war years was how to grow more food and yet use fewer farmers. By November 1941 over 40 percent of the Soviet population, 38 percent of total land used to grow grain, and 38 percent of all cattle had fallen to the Germans; this naturally placed great pressure on the remaining agricultural regions to feed what remained, as well as to stoke the rapidly expanding war machine. As an agricultural area far behind the lines of battle, Kazakhstan was expected to make a major contribution to the wartime economy, essentially from good will and thin air.

The manpower drain was severe; over 450,000 Kazakhs were mobilized for military service during World War II. The Kazakhs contributed five national divisions to the war effort: the 100th and 101st infantry divisions and the 96th, 105th, and 106th cavalry divisions. In addition, Kazakh soldiers served in many other divisions—most important, in the 38th infantry and the 316th, the so-called Panfilov Division—and fought in every major battle of the war. As a consequence, only 302,100 able-bodied workers remained in the countryside, most of them inexperienced or totally untrained. Kazakh women and teenagers had to manage the day-to-day running of the farms. By the end of the war nearly 80 percent of all agricultural workers were women; women had even penetrated the once all-male technical (agronomists, veterinarians) and mechanical (tractor and truck drivers) positions, although most supervisory positions (brigade leaders, kolkhoz chairmen, and party first secretaries) remained in male hands. However, the qualifications of the supervisory personnel declined precipitously, since nearly 80 percent of all kolkhoz chairmen were sent to the front and replaced by older, infirm, or otherwise unfit cadre. Matters on the MTS were even worse, since all experienced mechanics and drivers were of course transferred to the military sector. In 1945 only 34 of 1,445 station directors had any technical or higher education.[54]

Yet the lack of manpower was only one of the problems Kazakh agriculture faced. Beleaguered Moscow was simply unable to provide the material or technical assistance necessary for the expansion of Kazakh agriculture. Seed was in extremely short supply since, as commonly occurred in times of famine or near-famine, most available grain was milled, leaving inadequate reserves to plant a crop for the following season. The low level of mechanization in Kazakh agriculture now became painfully constricting as well. Throughout the 1930s the MTS and MSS (Machine Seed Stations) had been inadequately supplied with both parts and updated machinery, but because of the war supply problems became disastrous. Despite a call for increased tractor production, the emergency plans of 1942 gave clear priority to the production of military hardware; thus, heavy equipment factories produced tanks, not tractors, while all available spare parts went to trucks that moved war materials. By the end of the war only 24 percent of all trucks in the Kazakh S.S.R. functioned. The supply system created by the wholly nationalized economy of the 1930s was linked virtually all the way from farm to table and remained so during the war, in spite of the need to feed the troops at the front. No effective system was introduced either to harvest or to move grain quickly in regions such as Kazakhstan. In spite of the obvious need, machinery lay unused for want of parts or sometimes merely for want of drivers, while grain rotted because of inadequate storage or lack of transportation.

There was an acute shortage of all construction materials during this period, but no shortage of housing. A large number of evacuees were sent to Kazakhstan, nearly 400,000 by the summer of 1942. Some were sent to work in evacuated factories, but most were women and children from the besieged cities of European Russia, dumped in the towns along the railroad in southern Kazakhstan, and expected to serve as "surplus" labor in the rural sector. Some 900,000 head of cattle were also shipped east, although only 381,000 animals managed to survive the journey to Kazakhstan.[55] They, like the evacuated people, placed an additional burden on a construction industry that had been directed to give first priority to housing heavy industry.

Kazakhstan was the designated arrival point of 142 evacuated factories and their professional staffs. The attraction of Kazakhstan was both the safety of its remoteness and the largely untapped mineral resources of the steppe. By mid-1942, 63 percent of all coal, 68 percent of the iron ore, and 60 percent of the aluminum reserves of the USSR were in German-occupied territories. Consequently, reserves once considered too costly to develop became suddenly viable; among them were the mineral resources, especially the coal, of Kazakhstan. Annual coal production in Kazakhstan rose from the 15,484,000 tons originally projected in the Third Five-Year Plan to 45,722,000 tons in 1945.

The war so strained the Kazakh economy that simply sustaining the prewar economic status quo would have been a feat. However, the regime not only asserted there was but even based its wartime plans on an alleged slack in the prewar economy, which the Soviets believed would permit cultural productivity to increase under wartime conditions. The military economic plan put into effect in early 1942 set fantastic targets for Kazakhstan. The 1942 harvest was to exceed that of 1940 by 10–25 percent, while the herd size was to grow at an even faster rate.[56] However, the 1941 harvest was the last bumper crop in

Kazakhstan for over a decade; whereas in 1941 the state had bought 100,423,900 poods of grain from farms in the Kazakh S.S.R., by 1943 only 43,216,700 poods were available for purchase. The harvest dropped both because of the material difficulties outlined above and because of harsh weather, all compounded by Moscow's unwise agricultural policy.

To punish the kolkhozniki for presumed slacking, official procurement prices were lowered as well as the scale by which the farmer was remunerated for his "work days" in the collective. Many kolkhozniki responded by refusing to store seed for the following year's crop. The 1943 harvest was disastrous; many collective farms sold *no* grain to the state that season. Conditions improved somewhat when the official procurement price was raised for 1944, but the wages for each working day did not rise and "voluntary" purchase of war bonds cost the kolkhozniki most of their limited disposable income for the duration of the war. The harvest increased in 1944 and 1945, but even in 1945 only 65,682,900 poods of grain were harvested, over 10 million fewer poods than in 1940. After 1943 the harvests did increase in average yield per hectare, primarily because the manpower shortage had removed 20 percent of the land from cultivation, although some increased yield came from improved irrigation.

Livestock breeding followed a much steadier course throughout the war; the number of animals increased by nearly 9 percent during 1940–1946. There were more incentives and fewer hardships in this sector, since in an attempt to provision the army and cities Moscow permitted the reintroduction of a limited version of the pre-collectivization *kontraktsiia* (contract) system to purchase animals from privately controlled herds.[57] This caused the slaughter of more animals than was desirable, but was offset by increased attention to the health of the commonly owned herd. The one conspicuous failure of the regime in livestock breeding was among the small, economically nonviable kolkhozy organized at the end of the collectivization drive, many of which were settlements of otkochevniki. The economic straits of the Kazakhs found on these farms grew more severe throughout the war; despite an increase in the total number of livestock in the republic, the number of kolkhoz households owning no private livestock increased from 10.8 percent in 1940 to 21.0 percent in 1945.[58]

Astoundingly, in spite of all these pressures on the agricultural sector, Moscow chose to see the early years of the war as a period in which they had *relaxed* their control over the countryside. Thus, in late 1943, when a Russian victory in World War II first became conceivable, official pronouncements began to grow sterner and reflected the regime's desire to reassert complete control over the economy. The Kazakh party organization was found particularly wanting in supervision of local economic performance. The low level of ideological vigilance shown by many of the regional authorities in Kazakhstan was cited in several Central Committee resolutions and finally attacked directly in the April 23, 1945, resolution, "On the Unstable Leadership of the Kazakh Communist Party."

Official policy toward the rural economy in Kazakhstan was most clearly delineated in two subsequent Central Committee resolutions: the first a September 19, 1946, decree, "On the Elimination of Infringements of the Kolkhoz Charter"; and the second a February 1947 resolution, "On Measures for Raising Agricultural Production in the Postwar Period." The first called for the return to communal cultivation of all land given over to the private control of kolkhozniki during the war. No figures have been published for the amount of such land, but by 1945 about 20 percent of all grain sold to the state was produced on privately held land, that is, both on private plots and on abandoned kolkhoz lands.[59] After the successful conclusion of the war, the state forcibly reasserted its control of this land; between 1946 and 1950 some 600,000 hectares of land were "returned" to the collective farms. At the same time stricter regulation of private livestock ownership was announced, with nearly a quarter of a million animals "transferred" from private herds to direct kolkhoz control. Although the private sector continued to be an important source of both meat and milk, its role in the production of cereal crops disappeared.

Such harsh legislation did little to motivate kolkhozniki to increase productivity, however. It is no surprise that the slight statistical information available for this period suggests that Kazakhstan was economically static. The eminent Soviet economic historian V. P. Danilov suggests this was a general condition; he argues that the tempo of agricultural growth slowed in 1949 after a brief period of partial recovery.[60] Certainly this was the case in Kazakhstan, where the regime lacked the resources either to coerce or induce the Kazakh and Russian peasantry to meet the targeted agricultural quotas. In part the regime was out of touch with life in the countryside, but the sheer ineptitude of reconstruction, combined as it was with the need to sovietize the newly acquired western territories, meant that despite the severity of the food shortages there were simply no spare resources to invest in technology or increased mechanization of agriculture in the eastern regions. Also true was that no matter how haphazard the quality of party rule in areas such as Kazakhstan, Soviet rule was not at stake. Slothful Kazakh kolkhozniki were far less a threat to the security of the Soviet state than were the Ukrainian *Banderovtsy* (members of the West Ukrainian partisan movement). It is therefore no surprise that the inefficient and ineffectual Kazakh leadership during Stalin's lifetime never did succeed in getting the economy to function properly.

In 1946 there were only 61 "millionaire" kolkhozy in all of Kazakhstan, and in that same year the value of production was less than 500,000 rubles annually.[61] The number of weak or nonviable kolkhozy rose to 9.1 percent of the total by the end of the period.

By 1949 the level of agricultural productivity had slumped so low that Moscow was forced to take a more activist stance. The poor performance of agriculture was blamed on poor management, caused by the small size of most existing kolkhozy. Between 1949 and 1953 the number of kolkhozy in the republic declined from 6,737 to 2,966, while the kolkhoz population remained constant. The average number of households per farm therefore doubled (from 92 to 181), the average herd size more than doubled (from 2,329 to 5,326 animals per farm) and the size of the average area under cultivation almost tripled (from 862 to 2,475 hectares).[62] The number of tractors in Kazakhstan nearly doubled in the decade following the war, in 1950 surpassing prewar levels,[63] and the amount of irrigated farmland in Kazakhstan increased by 16 percent. Still, agricultural productivity remained far below official expectations; only in 1950 did the land yield more than 5.6 centners per hectare.[64] The morale in the kolkhozy was so low that in both 1951 and 1952 the republic failed to reach the required minimum number of agricultural work days. The sovkhoz sector of Kazakhstan was worse, if anything, showing a profit only in 1941, 1947, and 1950.[65] While the number of sovkhozy in the republic increased from 190 in 1940 to 255 in 1946, then to 293 in 1953, the contribution of the sovkhoz sector to the meat industry declined and there was only a slender increase in cereal crops.[66]

Livestock breeding performed somewhat better than grain cultivation. The herd size increased slightly each year, although in late 1952 it was still far smaller than the herd of 1928. Moreover, the yield per animal dropped during the period; despite a 32.4 percent increase in the number of the beef herd, the amount of meat produced increased only 10 percent from 1940 to 1950. The performance of the dairy herd declined as well; the number of liters of milk per cow dropped from 705 in 1940 to 629 in 1953, and in some formerly nomadic regions in the Guryev and western Kazakhstan oblasts the 1953 figure was between 300 and 350 liters.[67]

Nevertheless, matters with the annual crops were worse, even approaching catastrophe, especially given that the rural work force increased by several thousand workers (and thus increased the people to feed with already limited supplies) after the demobilization of the wartime army. While the number of ploughed acres increased by nearly 40 percent in 1946–1952, the actual harvest of cereal crops increased by less than 20 percent.[68] This reflects a general decline in the productivity of the land, exacerbated by declining morale and, at least in the winter of 1947–1948, by atypically bad weather. In 1949 the regime managed to purchase as much grain as it had in 1940, but smaller harvests in 1950–1952 once again dropped the amount of grain available to below prewar levels.

The situation in Kazakhstan remained bleak in 1953. Collectivization had failed to result in a new and modernized economy. The nomads had been settled, but to no apparent effect. Most remained in the countryside; the 1939 census reported that only 8 percent of the Kazakh population lived in urban areas. Furthermore, while the Kazakhs made up about one-third of the working class of Kazakhstan, that class contained only 158,000 people—or so reported the 1939 census, the last even vaguely reliable source of occupational data by ethnic group for the Stalin period. One in every three of these workers was employed in the agricultural sector as drivers, mechanics, or supervisory personnel at the MTS and MSS.[69] Most of the rest were employed either in construction or mining-related jobs.

Thus, at the time of Stalin's death in 1953 the primary contribution of Kazakhstan to the all-union economy continued to be food, but agricultural productivity was lower than before collectivization. Although the regime remained convinced that the economic potential of the region was great, they had been able to realize little of it. Because of this, not a year after Stalin's death, Khrushchev attempted yet another agricultural reorganization to better develop the region. These rapid shifts from one mobilization strategy to another—from collectivization to Khrushchev's Virgin Lands Policy—failed to address the shortcomings common to both. Although Moscow could compel economic change by physically (and, if necessary, forcibly) moving animals, men, and machines, the successful functioning of the economy required participation that could not be forced. Participation demanded an active ideological commitment from the population, which the social policy pursued in the final two decades of Stalin's rule failed to produce.

## THE SOCIAL IMPACT OF THE STALINIST SYSTEM IN KAZAKHSTAN

The social impact of Stalin's policies is a topic worthy of its own book, so vast was the scope of the transformation of Kazakh society. Although Soviet scholars have written on the theme, Western scholars generally have not.[70] This is partly because there is little useful data but also, and probably more important, because social change was not actually one of the top priorities in Kazakhstan during these years. Stalin's commitment to economic revolution proved far more costly than he had envisaged and left virtually no surplus resources for nonessential purposes, such as a social policy, which was less pressing than feeding the population. Until the outbreak of World War II, the Russian *muzhik* (peasant) and his Ukrainian counterpart were greater threats to Stalin's goals than the non-European peasantry; one of his top priorities, therefore, was the elimination of the power of the Orthodox church.

In spite of all this, the social policy that was articulated for Kazakhstan aimed at ending the domination of "feudal" (tribal and clan) and religious authorities, who purportedly were actively subverting the development of a progressive socialist order. Funds also had to be found to develop a loyal Kazakh elite of sufficient size to staff the party and state organs. To achieve these goals a three-part strategy was pursued, consisting of mass education, scientific atheism, and an attack on customary practices.

Of the three strategies, the educational policy was most important. It had two goals: to introduce universal primary education and to eradicate adult illiteracy. Estimates of Kazakh adult literacy immediately before collectivization range from 9 to 37 percent of the population; at that time fewer than one-third of all school-age children were enrolled in the state educational system.[71] Education was the keystone of Soviet social control, because universal literacy would open direct communication between the masses and the elite; this would permit the Soviet authorities to reach the Kazakhs without having to depend on intermediaries who could distort their message. The primary education system allowed the state to begin political socialization at an early age and thus to counter the negative influence of the traditional and parental authorities. The successful training of a new elite began in the schools.

Thus, the educational goals of the Soviet state were intended to buttress the collectivization drive. In July 1929 a mass cultural campaign began to eradicate illiteracy in the Kazakh auls, followed in February and May 1930 by further legislation organizing literacy brigades. Once the collectivization drive began to be resisted, however, there were neither resources nor interest in these more utopian pursuits. In 1930, for example, there were only 100 Red Yurts traveling the Kazakh countryside to provide basic adult education; in that same year just a million rubles, 80 percent of the sum allocated, was spent in Kazakhstan on programs designed to eradicate illiteracy. In 1931 and 1932 even smaller percentages of the allocated resources were spent, and these allocations had shrunk when trained cadre were dispatched to other, more pressing tasks.[72]

Stalin's Great Terror also cost the educational program. Trained teachers, especially Kazakhs, were always in short supply, but once the purge began anyone who had had direct or even indirect contact with the Alash Orda–dominated ministry of education became suspect. How many of those arrested in the 1930s were teachers is impossible to know, but it was admitted at the time that the educational system of Kazakhstan was in complete disarray by early 1934. Few teachers were left in the countryside, most rural school buildings had been torn down for use as fuel, and in many communities life was so precarious that—even had schooling been available—children could not have been spared from productive work to attend.[73]

When Moscow began another campaign to eradicate illiteracy in 1934, a special all-union delegation of pedagogues was sent to Kazakhstan to study the situation; their report stressed the weaknesses of the Kazakh education system, especially in the rural areas. They found that while 84.4 percent of the 8–11-year-old group was enrolled in school, fewer than 50 percent of all Kazakh children attended school; the percentage of Kazakh girls remaining at home was much higher than that of Kazakh boys. The rural schools that most Kazakhs attended were primitive, understaffed, in many cases still run by former muhallim, and offered little more than a cursory education. The four-grade primary school was almost a thing of fiction in the Kazakh regions, where nearly 70 percent of the schools offered only one or two years of study.[74] Textbooks and educational materials were in short supply everywhere.

For the remainder of the decade a systematic effort was made to expand and improve the quality of the educational network in Kazakhstan. Over 13,000 new teachers with middle or higher education were employed by the schools, and half of these were Kazakhs. Still, at the end of the decade almost two-thirds of all teachers in the republic had less than a high school education. The establishment of a system of higher education in the republic—Kazakh State University opened in 1934, a Kazakh branch of the Academy of Sciences in 1938, and a number of technical institutes—provided a structure that in time generated an educated elite for the republic. In 1939–1940 there were only 2,672 students enrolled in Kazakhstan's institutions of higher education, of whom 1,025 were Kazakh.[75]

The party educational system was also greatly expanded during this period. Although a branch of the Communist University opened in Kazakhstan in 1930 and a branch of the Institute of Marxist-Leninism in 1931, these were small-scale ventures. Not until 1936 was a Higher Party School organized in the republic; at that time the ten existing Soviet party schools were also organized to provide a structured two-year program to train political propaganda workers.

During the mid-1930s there was also a Moscow-directed effort to draw up a common curriculum, with greater attention paid to the primers and texts to be used in the Kazakh language schools. In 1935 150,000 copies of a new Kazakh primer were printed as well as 500,000 additional copies of another 15 primary school texts. In 1936 the Kazakh publishing industry was reorganized to place both censorship and printing under greater central control, and the number of mass publications, especially newspapers and journals, was increased. By the end of the decade there were 38 different newspapers and bulletins (13 in Kazakh) and 337 magazine titles (193 in Kazakh) published annually, with nearly 2 million copies in circulation each year.

If Moscow was to influence the population, a body of readers had to be created; therefore, in 1936 the literacy drive was renewed and some 12,000 teachers and literacy volunteers were sent to work among the Kazakh population. These volunteers sometimes met physical resistance, often inspired by the Muslim clergy, particularly when their target population was women.[76] The education of women was, in fact, their primary task, since in 1936 almost 75 percent of all Kazakh women were still illiterate.[77] However, by the end of the decade the education drive had made great headway. In 1940–1941, 98 percent of all 8–11-year-old children attended school, and by the end of 1939, 76.3 percent of all men in the republic and 66.3 percent of all women were considered to be literate. Unfortunately, no data by nationality is available.

Despite Moscow's assumption, literacy did not automatically create sympathy or interest in the Soviet cause. Rural correspondents for the Kazakh press were periodically attacked and some even killed while "tracking down" their stories in the countryside.[78] Even the definition of literacy is uncertain, since Kazakh was first printed in Arabic letters, then from 1926 until 1940 in the Latin alphabet, and finally switched to today's modified Cyrillic. Literacy and education also did not create culture, since the point of the educational policy was to create conformity of ideology in these years when the Great Terror raged. A person with any trace of a "nationalist" past was arrested; this included almost a whole generation of Kazakh writers, among them Saken Seifullin (1894–1938), Ilias Dzhansugurov (1894–1937), and Beimbet Mailin (1894–1938), who had made the creation of a Kazakh-Soviet culture their life's work.

Conformity and, even more important, political loyalty were the main goals of the antireligion drives of the late 1920s and 1930s. The religious hierarchy, seen as a rural power base, was attacked by the Soviets along with the bais and "semifeudals" in 1928. A more aggressive antireligious policy was launched with the collectivization drive; mosques, *mekteps*, and madrasahs were closed throughout Central Asia and Kazakhstan. Clergy who resisted were arrested, as were many party members on charges of aiding, abetting, or sympathizing with clergy. However, this policy was vigorously pursued only in the cities, where the clergy were more visible and so more offensive to the party. "Red Detachments" of atheist agitators were sent into the countryside, but most Muslim clerics managed to evade detection and often continued their mosques and schools in an illegal underground. Despite massive antireligious propaganda in the media, popular sympathy remained strongly with Islam and its embattled clerics. According to some sources, Islam became even more deeply entrenched in southern Kazakhstan during these years, because the mullahs served as figures of authority in a period of relative anarchy, often using their power to thwart the efforts of the Soviet regime.[79] One account from 1930 describes a mullah who managed to keep a medical detachment out of an aul in Dzharkent by convincing the population that the doctors had come to sterilize the men, capture the women, and kill the children; this suggests not only the power of the mullah but also the popular distrust of things Soviet.[80]

Since the mullahs were particularly important as arbiters in livestock-breeding disputes, in many communities they were able to stop Soviet efforts to introduce artificial insemination, which had been attempted in the late 1930s to raise the size of the stricken herd. Since human survival depended on animal health, Kazakh religious practice had long centered on livestock. In the kolkhozi ritual slaughters were common, both to commemorate major feasts such as *Kurban Bairam* and as part of funerary or marriage celebrations. *Bakshi* (shaman healers) treated sick animals and humans alike,[81] as they do even today in some communities when modern medical science has failed. During the famine in the 1930s such religious figures were much sought after and influential.

When World War II broke out, Moscow adopted a more conciliatory policy toward religion in general and Islam in particular, at least for those Muslim populations far from enemy-held territory, such as the Kazakhs and Central Asian peoples.[82] In 1943 the Muslims were permitted to establish an official religious organization, the Ecclesiastical Administration of Central Asia and Kazakhstan (*SADUM*), which had the right to publish spiritual materials and train clergy under state direction. This muftiate was not powerful, with very limited rights, but its simple existence was a concession to religion and an important precedent. Nevertheless, from the conclusion of World War II until after Stalin's death there were no further concessions, not even symbolic, to the Kazakhs and other non-European nationalities. This was the period of Moscow's sternest drive to achieve ideological conformity, the *Zhdanovshchina*.

Never had the Kazakh intelligentsia been allowed less latitude. Moscow mandated a curriculum that permitted only approbation for Russia and all things Russian in the history of the Kazakhs, both before and after the revolution; although academic reputations were made and broken in the effort, most Kazakhs were little affected. Much closer to the masses was Moscow's renewed drive against religion, begun in 1946 and pursued throughout the next six years, but even so official a source as the most recent volume of the *History of the Kazakh S.S.R.* admits that this drive had only slight impact on rural Islam.[83] Doctrinal Islam, never widely influential among the Kazakhs, had by the early 1950s almost vanished, but ritual Islam, which blended Muslim ritual with Kazakh customary practices, remained almost universal. Many of the customs, such as payment of the kalym and inheritance practices, became largely symbolic, but this was due to the greater poverty of the Kazakh herdsmen rather than to any success of Soviet social legislation.

The party had doomed its own policy from the beginning, when it permitted the traditional authority patterns to replicate themselves on the kolkhozy. Particularly on the smaller collective farms, the aksakals were often the sole authorities for kolkhoz policy; as the only "Soviet" officials present, they were able to interpret Moscow's policies as they wished. Since the farms had to produce required quantities of food, there was little leeway in following Moscow's economic policy; however, there was considerably more flexibility in the application of social policy. Laws against customary practices were simply not enforced, since the Kazakh officials themselves observed them.

Nowhere were transgressions of policy more flagrant than with regard to women. Kazakh women had never been secluded and had always played a strong economic role in the community. This continued to be true after collectivization, although usually in the traditional female occupations such as shearing sheep, tending animals, working in handicraft industries, or farming in all-female brigades. Only about 5 percent of all women held skilled positions.[84] Even once most Kazakh women began to receive some primary school education, they were not seen as candidates for membership in the Soviet elite.

In truth, few Kazakh males were any more attractive candidates for the higher levels of the party or state apparatus. During the first 35 years of their rule, the Soviets failed to change Kazakh social structures either in the old aul or new kolkhoz. Collectivization did settle the nomads, but the party could not undermine traditional clan and religious authority. All Moscow could ultimately do was prevent the old order from replacing itself while waiting for it to die off; Moscow hoped to create a party and state infrastructure from the new, Soviet-born, and spottily socialized generation that followed.

# 9 The Creation of a Soviet Apparatus in Kazakhstan

## INTRODUCTION

During the 1920s and 1930s the Soviet leadership was confronted with the problem of transforming Kazakhstan, as well as the other national regions of the East, from a colonial possession into a member of a multinational state. Although it is quite clear that Russians and Russian culture were to be predominant, the regime wanted to create the structures necessary to defend the fiction that national minorities were fully integrated members of the Soviet system. How this was attempted in the economic sector is examined above; the following chapter examines the ways in which Kazakh participation was encouraged and strengthened in both the party and government, as well as the terms under which such membership was offered.

## THE DEVELOPMENT OF THE PARTY APPARATUS IN KAZAKHSTAN, 1918–1929

In May 1918 the west-Siberian congress of the RKP(b) was held in Omsk with only one Kazakh among the 22 delegates; it was the first organized and sanctioned party congress held in the former Steppe Region. In June 1918 the first congress of Communists of Turkestan was convened, which included a number of Kazakh delegates from the Turgai, Semirech'e, and Syr Darya oblasts. The total Kazakh membership in the Communist Party at this time was only several dozen people, many of whom were members of the Birlik group and who, like Saken Seifullin, objected to the Alash Orda because it was dominated by the sons of the old aristocracy; they were attracted to the Bolsheviks because of the party's egalitarian platform. Others, like Turar Ryskulov, were from the Syr Darya and Semirech'e oblasts, had become political activists at the time of the 1916 uprising, and so identified with the Bolsheviks as champions of the underdog and enemies of the tsar. Yet because the early Kazakh Bolsheviks had some education, they were atypical of the wider Kazakh community; they found it difficult to gain mass support. In late 1918 there were only 26 aul cells in the Syr Darya and Semirech'e oblasts and a handful of cells in the north; the average cell could only boast about five members, while some consisted solely of a chairman and a secretary.

In mid-1919, when the Alash Orda was all but defeated, the Kirrevkom (Kirgiz Revolutionary Committee) and the Musburo (Muslim Bureau, which had jurisdiction over the Syr Darya and Semirech'e oblasts), set about popularizing the party to the Kazakh masses. Markets and wells throughout Kazakhstan became propaganda posts, while a number of similar extraparty organizations—the Red Carts, Red Yurts, and Red Caravans—were organized to dispense information and recruit party members. In late 1920 three organizing conferences of nonparty peasants were held to attract both Russians and Kazakhs. There was greater success among the former than the latter. Archival sources show that there were few party cells in the Kazakh auls of this period and fewer than 1,000 rural party members.

The Kazakh Communist Party was formally organized on January 5, 1920, under the title of the Kirgiz regional committee (*Kirkraikom*) of the RKP(b).[1] A mass membership drive was launched, and both the Kirkraikom and the Communist Party of Turkestan (which was then headed by a Kazakh, Turar Ryskulov) debated criteria for membership. Ryskulov in particular wanted the widest possible native membership in the party, going so far as to urge the creation of a Turkish Communist Party to parallel the Russian one. M. V. Frunze, who still headed the Turkkomissiia, vetoed the suggestion, which was sustained by Lenin himself, in the spring of 1920. Even so, Ryskulov recruited broadly; by mid-1920, 72.4 percent of the 26,085 party members in the Syr Darya oblast were of non-European origin, as were about a third of the 26,405 members in the *Kirkrai* (Kazakh) party.[2]

However, at the end of the Civil War the regime wanted to consolidate its hold. On August 26, 1920, the Kirrevkom was dissolved and replaced by the Kirgiz (that is, Kazakh) ASSR and the Kirobburo (Kirgiz oblast bureau) RKP(b).[3] Party membership took on new importance, making it less desirable to sign up thousands of politically unsophisticated natives as party members. Participation was to be concentrated in the soviet or state organs, but the role of the party was to control the population and this end was better served by

Russian domination. Large numbers of Kazakhs were expelled from the party during the last half of 1920, when almost two-thirds of the total party members in the KazASSR and in the Syr Darya and Semirech'e oblasts were purged; the Kazakhs were expelled on grounds of being nationalists and the Russians of being chinovniki, the term for bureaucrats now used to connote maximalists and Menshevik internationalists. However, this purge only culled the rank and file; no major figures from the Alash Orda leadership were then excluded from the party.

At the Tenth Party Congress, held in March 1921 in the wake of popular disturbances in many parts of the Soviet Union, including Kazakhstan, the party was charged with achieving the greater legitimacy of a broadened popular base without permitting bourgeois elements to dominate the organization. This congress was followed by the first all-Kazakh party conference, convened on June 11, 1921. The delegates who gathered represented some 26,000 members from 1,755 cells; their task was to reorganize themselves so that the program of the Communist Party would be accessible to the average citizen; this was to be accomplished by increasing the political sophistication of the citizenry through both education and propaganda.

The policies pursued by the Kazakh party in 1921 and 1922 can be explained by the impact of the NEP on party politics more generally. As control of a significant portion of the economy was returned to private hands, the party needed even more to function as a committed vanguard of individuals whose loyalty to the Communist Party was primary. Thus, in mid-1921 the party began systematically to purge those members whose loyalty might be questioned—for example, those without previous Bolshevik affiliations such as former Mensheviks, Socialist Revolutionaries, and, in Kazakhstan, former members of the Alash Orda government. The Kazakh party lost 19.1 percent of its membership; the Syr Darya and Semirech'e oblasts expelled 39.2 percent and 16.2 percent of their members respectively, although some of the decline was also due to the deaths and out-migration caused by famine conditions still acute in the steppe. Yet most of the prominent leaders remained, both because of their popular standing and their training, which let them fill key technical positions in the new autonomous republic. Nevertheless, these leaders of the Alash Orda were separated from their cadre and their influence within the party (although not within the government) was substantially reduced.

Following the purge, the party organized a two-week drive to recruit Kazakhs. Although rural membership did increase and almost half of all cells were located in the countryside, Kazakhs accounted for only 8.9 percent of the total membership.[4]

The overwhelming majority of Kazakh members were illiterate, ignorant of all but the most simplistic slogans of the party. Most had joined for opportunistic reasons, either to advance themselves—which in the economic crisis of the time could mean nothing more than better odds of receiving a job and food—or to protect their community from the new regime. This latter reason was particularly important in the Kazakh areas, where the Bolsheviks were seen as a new variant of Russian marauder to be outwitted at their own game. Mullahs and bais thus sought party membership; since after seven years of war even rich Kazakhs looked shabby to the Russian recruiters, they generally received it. New party cells were formed by these Kazakhs, and the new party secretary then took whatever limited resources the regime offered for propaganda and party recruitment to use as the cell saw fit. One archival document records the horror of a Russian party inspector who accidentally discovered that aul-cell no. 13, in the Chirchik region in the Syr Darya oblast, had resolved to use recruitment funds to rebuild their mosque, which had been damaged in the Civil War.[5] Such incidents illustrate the problems the regime faced in building an ideological party from a population that was largely ignorant of state goals and hostile to those goals it did know. At the same time the regime had to make the Communist Party a mass party, since throughout the former Russian empire most of the traditional elite opposed the new Soviet Union articulately and inflexibly. Despite the middling success of mass recruitment drives, therefore, the regime repeated them throughout the 1920s and 1930s, alternating them with periodic purges.

The first attempt to expand the membership base of the party in Kazakhstan came in April 1922, following the Eleventh Party Congress, when the *Kazburo* (Kazakh bureau) of the Central Committee was formed to direct the party activities of Kazakhstan from Moscow; this effectively meant that mass recruitment could go on only under direct supervision by Moscow. This attempt to regulate the activities of the Kazakh party was made over the objections of the Kazakh leadership, who well understood that the move was designed to limit their own discretion in questions of policy. The Kazburo helped coordinate the policy initiatives between Moscow and Orenburg, but it did little to broaden the base of party membership. Its failure led to a special all-union conference on the national question in June 1923.

Many discussions were held and grave concern was voiced, but little was done to broaden the base of party membership until the Lenin Call of October 1924. This party recruitment drive had special importance in Kazakhstan and in Central Asia more generally, because it came as the new national entities were being created, among them the Kazakh Autonomous Socialist Republic (KazASSR) with its capital in Kzyl-Orda. The former Steppe Region was now permanently returned to the Kazakhs, while Orenburg and the northern-most part of the steppe were removed and joined to the RSFSR; in return the new Kazakh republic received the northern-most parts of the Syr Darya and Semirech'e oblasts and with it a population that, although Kazakh, had long been influenced more by Tashkent than by the north. The new and expanding

Kazakh party was thus charged with assimilating an increasingly diverse and potentially antagonistic steppe population.

The Lenin Call changed the complexion of the party in Kazakhstan, since some 8,000 people were admitted. The party went from 11.5 percent to 29.2 percent Kazakh, but the proportion of members from the peasantry dropped from 60 to 53 percent as the result of an effort to draft Russian workers in the Dzhetuis (the Kazakh translation and new name for Semirech'e, meaning seven rivers) and Syr Darya regions to combat the excessively Kazakh quality of the party in the south.

The changed composition of party membership was soon reflected in the party organs. The fourth all-Kazakh party conference, held in March 1923, was made up of only 24.8 percent Kazakh delegates, whereas by the fifth regional party conference in December 1925, 51.8 percent of the delegates were Kazakhs. The national composition of the provincial party committees went from 20.3 percent Kazakh in February 1923, to 33.3 percent Kazakh in December 1925, when 37.7 percent (1,701,457) of the *ukom* (uezd komitet) and *volkom* (volost komitet), or district party organizations, were also Kazakh.

The impact of this Kazakh membership is difficult to assess because these early Kazakh members were not prime material. About three-fourths of them were illiterate,[6] and the few that were literate were not willing to disrupt their communities with new and controversial social and economic policies, which moreover were usually the opposite of their personal beliefs. G. Togzhanov, a prominent Kazakh Communist of the 1920s and 1930s, described the party cell in a Kazakh aul he visited:

> In all, the attitude of the Communists could not be distinguished from that of the mass of Kazakhs. Furthermore six of them went to mosque and believed in God; some were even members of religious societies. One even kept company with a mullah and collected money for religious organizations.[7]

Consequently, as the proportionate representation of the Kazakhs increased, local party apparatuses were given less, not more, discretion. At that time the party was constantly growing. Inadequacies were much lamented; at each of the five republic party conferences held between June 1921 and December 1925 the local party organizations were criticized for their low level of ideological preparedness and for transforming the class struggle into a continuation of the clanic and tribal rivalries that had dominated the steppe in the prerevolutionary period.

Nonetheless the party persisted in the recruitment of the very elements that were being criticized: the rural Kazakhs. Total party membership increased from 22,757 candidates and members on January 1, 1925, to 41,128 on January 1, 1929; Kazakh members went from 6,647 (29.2 percent) to 16,551

(40.2 percent), while the percentage of Kazakhs in the provincial party organization increased to 47 percent.

The Kazakhs were being enlisted to help sovietize the aul, the traditions of which they cherished, so dooming the attempt; thus, increases in party membership were greatest in the grain-growing areas and smallest in the nomadic and seminomadic regions.[8] This tendency was most pronounced on the eve of collectivization; in 1928 party membership in Kustanai (a predominantly Russian, grain-growing region) increased by 139.5 percent, but in the Adai region (an area populated exclusively by Kazakh nomads) only by 8.5 percent.

Although very little archival material has been made available about the level of education of the party membership in Kazakhstan during this period, the fragments have made quite clear that party members and even the local party leaders were illiterate, able neither to understand nor enforce Moscow's decrees. Despite recurrent drives to purify the party ranks, merchants, bazaar leaseholders, bais, and even mullahs were to be found within the party ranks; some were even party secretaries.[9] The leadership of the Kazakh party was aware of the unreliability of the Kazakh party members in general and the rural cadre in particular. In 1928, just as Stalin was making plans to use these cadre to mobilize the nonparty masses for the collectivization drive, F. I. Goloshchekin, then first secretary of the Kazakh Communist Party, warned that "We have no constituted party cells in the *auls*, nor in general do we have *aul* communists who are minimally literate or minimally able to fulfill party directives, free from the influence of clan and *bai*."[10]

What is even more telling for the subsequent experience of collectivization is that the education level of the membership of the other state structure, the soviets, was even worse.

## THE DEVELOPMENT OF A SOVIET ADMINISTRATIVE APPARATUS, 1918–1929

No comprehensive Soviet history of the development of the administrative apparatus in Kazakhstan has yet been written. Accounts of the period that have appeared are scanty, because most Kazakhs of any position in the government and party during those years were liquidated, and many of them are not yet rehabilitated. As a result, the official histories of the period give the impression that the few Kazakhs who were not purged (such as A. Dzhangil'din), and those who have been partially rehabilitated (such as T. Ryskulov, S. Seifullin, and U. Isaev), were running the government and party virtually singlehandedly.[11] One way in which Soviet scholars avoid this problem is to ignore native participation in the government by focusing on the process of policy formulation at the center, rather than its application in the periphery.[12] Scholars are hampered by a continuing official reluctance to make available any materials published locally in those years, particularly serial publications.[13] Not only have republic archives been closed to Westerners, but even Soviet scholars have found access to be difficult; thus, only limited amounts of archival material have been published.[14]

Although it remains impossible to reconstruct precisely the politics of this period in Kazakhstan, A. P. Kuchkin's study, *Sovietization of the Kazakh Aul*, has at least made it possible to provide a reasonably accurate account of the difficulties encountered in extending Soviet rule to the localities.

The policies of the 1920s fall into two distinct periods, divided by Moscow's decision in late 1925 to begin a campaign to sovietize the Kazakh aul; this was official recognition that previous efforts had failed and that Soviet authority in the Kazakh countryside was in name only. With this campaign the Soviets began a more aggressive strategy in the countryside.

Earlier Soviet efforts had been characterized by a commitment to gradual social transformation, which was to be achieved largely through persuasion.[15] The first major post–Civil War effort to enlist Kazakh involvement in the government came in October 1920, when the founding congress of soviets met to elect the central executive committee of the Kirgiz (Kazakh) Autonomous Oblast, with 102 delegates in attendance. No precise data on the national composition of those who attended is available, but the official photo of delegates shows a fairly equal mix of Russian and Kazakh workers. The meeting was presided over by A. M. Alibekov and S. Seifullin, who had few ties with the masses.

Shortly after this congress, elections were held throughout the steppe to choose soviets to administer the territorial units of aul through guberniia. Each administrative aul was to have its own soviet; as in colonial times several auls that camped in relative proximity were grouped together as one administrative aul, with little regard for ethnic divisions. Consequently the first election campaigns tended to institutionalize clan rivalries, particularly since the election petition specified the clan and aul of the candidate.[16] In many areas the Kazakhs simply refused to participate in the electoral process. Overall only 50 percent of the eligible population voted; in many auls, particularly those in which the restricted franchise barred the traditional leaders, elections were simply never held.

Disenfranchisement proved to be an ineffective weapon. Rather than freeing the "oppressed" classes from feudal clutches, the restrictions acted to convince the Kazakhs that the interests of the Bolsheviks were antithetical to the interests of the Kazakhs; to insult a bai or elder was also to insult his clansmen. Despite the inequalities of wealth that certainly existed in the steppe, there was little antagonism within each aul; instead, such tensions were manifested as rivalries between communities. Naturally, some Kazakhs resented the power and authority of a particular bai, but opposition to traditional institutions as a whole was only common among Kazakh graduates of secular schools, and it was these who took the opportunity to leave the countryside.

Some of these graduates returned to the countryside to serve the party and state in supervisory capacities, but such were rare and had little grass roots support. More often the electoral process gave the auls a forum to elect individuals who were manifestly anti-Soviet; popular election slogans included "Drive the Russians out of Kazakhstan" and "Kazakhstan for the Kazakhs."[17]

Soon the Bolsheviks saw that their strategy of alienating the Kazakhs from the traditional rural leadership could expect no short-term success. Instead, a long-term policy of raising ideological awareness through education and political participation was substituted, accompanied by a policy of selective recruitment of increasing numbers of supportive Kazakhs into the apparat. This policy became formally known as korenizatsiia, or nativization, in 1923, when Kazakh was permitted as the language of government transaction at the uezd level and below. The new Soviet Kazakh elite was to come from a different stratum of Kazakh society than had the old, who had been relatively impoverished sons of small- and medium-sized livestock breeders and farmers; the new elite was to consist of loyal individuals with some education who wished to serve the new state and so achieve their own upward mobility. This policy earned the support of the leading Kazakhs in party and government, former Alash Ordists and early Bolsheviks alike, since all shared the desire for a Soviet government composed of Kazakhs and reflecting Kazakh needs, even as they differed on what those needs were. The representation of Kazakhs in all levels of the administration did increase during this period; between 1923 and 1925 the Kazakh participation in aul and village soviets rose from 53.0 percent to 61.2 percent; in volost ispolkoms (executive committees) from 47.1 percent to 64.0 percent; and in uezd ispolkoms from 57.3 percent to 60.1 percent.[18]

While the number of Kazakhs participating may have grown, however, by Moscow's standards the quality of participation did not improve. Virtually all aul, many volost, and even some uezd soviets remained in the control of traditional leaders, the bais and mullahs, who as ever were interested almost exclusively in parochial matters.

A 1925 report reproduced from the Kazakh party archives illustrates what the early Soviet experiment meant in a typical Kazakh community—aul-soviet no. 3, Ambetov volost, Aktyubinsk guberniia. The chairman of the soviet was almost illiterate, unable even to define the term cooperative, let alone devise a plan to place the local economy on a more communal footing. Nor did he have much desire to, since he was both a landowner and a landlord in a community where almost all the land was privately held. He received written instructions from Moscow and Kzyl-Orda but no direct communication; thus, although a soviet was formally organized, no tasks were ever assigned or meetings held.[19]

This aul was not a special case, but rather typified the structure of authority throughout the steppe. One striking example of the quality of Soviet rule is the volost official who in earnest asked a visiting party dignitary, "What is a Communist?"[20] It is not therefore surprising that by late 1925 Moscow had decided to introduce a more aggressive strategy to raise the quality of Soviet rule in Kazakhstan. The campaign to "sovietize the Kazakh aul" grew out of a long debate both within the Kazakh leadership and between Kzyl-Orda and Moscow about how Soviet control in the aul could be improved. What was called the majority position—or, less euphemistically, the Russian position—was ultimately adopted, and it endorsed the construction of a new Soviet administrative apparatus on the ruins of the old clan structures.

The Kazakh leadership, proponents of the defeated position, argued that Bolshevik authority would be accepted by the Kazakh masses only if Moscow could work with and convert the traditional Kazakh leaders. They proposed the creation of clan soviets, which would be ethnically homogeneous, to demonstrate Bolshevik sympathy to the Kazakhs while still permitting programs of political and social reform. The Kazakhs argued that the influence of the clans would decline gradually; as political and economic changes were felt in the communities, the masses would turn gradually away from their former leaders. They also argued that to create ethnically heterogeneous soviets would only increase, not diminish, the power of the clans and might also endanger the economic program, since interclan conflict would preempt reform in the running of the soviets.

The Russians, both in Kzyl-Orda and in Moscow, saw this Kazakh strategy as a nationalist deviation. Traditional society was a vestige of the past, and clans an anachronism; to include them would threaten the whole Soviet experiment.

The continued strength of the bais became glaringly plain when the 1925–1926 election was held and the results tabulated. It was no simple task even to hold the elections; on the appointed day many auls could not be located because they were migrating, and elections had to be rescheduled until the voters could be found. Other communities, although present, simply did not vote. In all only 45 percent of the eligible aul population participated in the election, and in some communities this figure dropped as low as 10 percent.[21]

Even so, the results obtained could not please the party leadership. Of the 4,159 people elected to membership in the aul soviets, only 6.5 percent were Communist Party members or candidates, with another 1.4 percent members of the *Komsomol* (Communist Youth League). Most of the new officials were male (92.9 percent) and either livestock breeders or farmers (88.3 percent). Over one-third (39.6 percent) were totally illiterate, and another third were barely literate. Probably the statistic most disappointing for the Communists was that only 22 percent were poor (*bedniaki*), while a bare 4 percent of those elected were sufficiently impoverished to be exempt from taxation. This suggests little mass involvement in or even awareness of a class struggle.

Instead, as the Kazakh leaders had predicted, many electoral contests became struggles for clan control, around slogans such as "tribal honor." The archives contain a report from the Bastuchu volost in the Dzharkent uezd, in which the chairman of the aul soviet had urged his clansmen to vote, with the promise that if control of the soviet went to a different clan he would simply lead them out of the uezd. Reports from the Syr Darya electoral commission mention that in many of the localities under their jurisdiction the clan rivalries grew so heated that fighting broke out between the supporters of opposing candidates. Yet whatever the rivalries among the various bais to gain control of their aul soviets, all shared a desire to defeat the candidates from the Communist Party and the Koshchi Union. In general, party members were elected to the soviets only in auls in which all males had joined the party to gain advantage over their traditional clan rivals.

The second plenum of the Kazkraikom, held in late April 1926, overturned the recent election and ordered new elections; it blamed the disastrous results on the weak soviet apparat in the countryside, bad organization among the poor, and the failure of the authorities to understand the nature of nomadism. Apparently no lesson was learned, because the party again debated and voted down (by unclear machinations) the organization of aul soviets along clan lines. This decision became virtually irreversible when an editorial in the November 20, 1926, issue of *Bolshevik* characterized clan soviets as playing into enemy hands.[22]

Moscow's interest was clearly not in understanding the nomads but in finding a way to break the hold of the traditional authorities. Preparations for the 1927 elections again emphasized informal pressures. The Koshchi Union was almost entirely disbanded and reconstituted with purportedly more loyal cadre. A massive agitation campaign was launched, 10,000 brochures and 300,000 slogan sheets were printed up in Kazakh, and, for the first time, active electioneering was conducted among the nomads. The Kazakh party was charged with achieving positive results by an editorial in the October 30, 1926, issue of *Izvestiia TsIK SSSR*, which detailed the shortcomings of the 1926 election in Kazakhstan.

Nonetheless, when the votes were counted the renewed efforts of the propagandists proved to have had no great effect. The proportion of party members elected to aul soviets rose to 7.3 percent (from 6.5 percent) and to the volost ispolkoms to 47.7 percent (from 36.5 percent), but reports from the election commissions made clear that in the Kazakh regions the countryside was still firmly in the control of the traditional leadership.[23]

One report from the Syr Darya guberniia election committee discusses the situation in the Dzhuval volost in the Aulie Ata uezd, where the Kazakh leadership had subverted the soviet electoral process entirely; clan leaders had met in advance of the election to divide the aul and volost offices among themselves, then swore on the Quran that these decisions would be ratified on election day.[24]

The decision to launch the 1928 drive to confiscate the bais' livestock thus appears as much political as economic. The Kazakh party leaders acceded to the decision with some hesitation; they wanted to see economic redistribution but feared antagonizing the bais, who might then incite popular resistance to the Soviet government. The Kazakh leadership knew such resistance would endanger their goal of developing a Kazakh society that could participate as an equal in the Soviet community of peoples. Still, the Kazakh party leaders agreed on the promise that the confiscation drive was a one-time expedient and not evidence of an all-out war against Kazakh society. At the same time, as a positive incentive, the Soviets strengthened their commitment to korenizatsiia, to replace the old order with a new generation of Kazakhs.

Soviet policy on the eve of collectivization thus almost conformed to many of the arguments that Kazakh intellectuals had been making since the early 1900s, but neither the nativization program nor the confiscation drive achieved the desired effects. By the end of 1928 only one official in five was a Kazakh, and the bais retained control of their communities and their livestock. The elections scheduled for the spring of 1928 were cancelled and rescheduled for December 1928 and January 1929. In the summer of 1928 the entire Soviet apparatus in Kazakhstan was reorganized in yet another attempt to loosen the hold of the traditional leaders. From 6 guberniias, 20 okrugs, 32 uezds, and 410 volosts were carved 130 okrugs and 192 *raions* (the modern term for administrative district), of which 113 (59.1 percent) were in predominantly Kazakh areas. A total of 3,888 aul-village soviets were created within the raions, 2,199 (56.7 percent) of them in Kazakh auls. Clan leadership survived even this challenge to their authority; in 1928–1929 only 9.6 percent of those elected to membership in the new aul-village soviets were party members. Probably for that reason, however, before the next soviet election was held, the authorities in Moscow deployed a far more effective weapon to defeat the traditional authorities: the collectivization drive.

## THE KAZAKH ELITE, KAZAKH NATIONALISM, AND PARTY POLITICS IN THE 1920s

The history of the Communist Party of Kazakhstan is of an organization dominated by a succession of rival factions that generally contested the nature and meaning of Kazakh nationalism. Kazakh nationalism was not an abstract issue in the 1920s; at stake was the development and advancement of a Kazakh nation. Yet there was little agreement among the Kazakh elite about the desired end or the road by which to reach it. Even greater were the differences between Kazakh and Russian understanding of the question, particularly after Stalin came to power, when Moscow assigned itself an increasingly activist role; this so changed the debate that by the end of the decade "nationalist" had become a crippling, even lethal label to apply to any national minority leader who happened to fall into disfavor.

In the first years of Soviet rule, the Kazakh leaders struggled to insure their own participation in the development of their own republic and in defining the program of social and economic reform to be applied to the Kazakh population. One problem hampering the Kazakh elite was that they were not only a minority within their party but also a divided one; the antagonisms of the Civil War period remained alive in a party made up of both Alash Ordists and their former opponents. Personal rivalries were intensified by real differences of opinion about the role the old order could play in the new regime. Class and status differences divided the Kazakhs as well; most Alash Ordists were from wealthy and even aristocratic Kazakh families and had generally been educated in either Omsk or Orenburg, whereas those Kazakhs who joined the Bolshevik party at the beginning of the Civil War—such as Saken Seifullin and Abdulla Asylbekov—were generally from poorer homes. Still others, such as Turar Ryskulov and S. Asfendiarov, were from the southern part of the steppe and thus had been educated in Tashkent and subjected to very different influences.

The Communist Party in Kazakhstan was first organized with little direction from Moscow. However, when Ryskulov sought to create separate Russian and native organizations, Moscow intervened. Ryskulov's defeat in 1920 created the first major leadership struggle in Central Asia and Kazakhstan, and it set the pattern of all subsequent struggles, which were always resolved against the native Communists. Lenin forbade the formation of a separate Turkish Communist Party that would be parallel and equal to the Russian Communist Party in both rights and responsibilities; this decision firmly established the territorial principle whereby all national groups were to be united in a single organization, and it made this principle the only legitimate basis for the organization of party and government.[25] Ryskulov's defeat was also a major setback for his career.[26] The *kraikom* (regional committee) of the Communist Party of Turkestan (KPT) was disbanded and all who had supported Ryskulov were excluded from the new committee. The KPT became and remained a Russian-dominated organization. The defeat of Ryskulov's proposed Turkish party guaranteed a circumscribed role for Kazakh Communists by making the party organization in the Kirgiz Autonomous Region, where virtually all Kazakhs lived, a constituent unit of the Russian Communist Party.

Thus, by 1920 the Kazakh Communists had to fall back in order to preserve the autonomy of the local party and government; where organizational power was already preserved, they had to prevent the Russians from usurping it. The first major dispute between Kazakh and Russian Communists occurred over land redistribution. The Kazakhs argued for the seizure of land from Russian peasants for award to impoverished Kazakh families. This position, first debated in 1920 and again in February 1921, went considerably beyond what Moscow was willing to grant, which was to give unused state lands to Kazakh families who had lost property after the 1916 uprising. The Russian leaders in Kazakhstan rejected Kazakh demands for seizure of Russian-held land (particularly since the Russian peasants were also suffering from the famine). At first Lenin backed the Kazakh leaders, but at the Twelfth Party Congress, although the Kazakh position was defended by Georgi Safronov, the policy of awarding the Kazakhs only unused lands was sustained.

This was a bitter defeat for the Kazakh leadership, which learned that economic questions were related to political ones; the Russians as the majority and dominant political force would not pass control to a minority, even if that meant betrayal of the purported aims of the revolution. The Kazakhs came to view the Russian officials in Orenburg (and later Kzyl-Orda) as representatives of Moscow, all of whom shared a world view that could be revolutionary but was always Russo-centric. After this defeat some prominent Kazakh leaders tried to revive the idea of creating a separate Turkish party, but this idea was quickly voted down at the party plenum of February 1922.[27] After the plenum, Ryskulov's supporters were accused of membership in a rival caucus and were stripped of their posts within the party. Several prominent former members of the Alash Orda were removed from state posts at the same time, including Ahmed Baitursunov, who was dismissed as minister of education.[28] In June 1923 the former Alash Ordists were branded "national deviationists."

Moscow wanted Kazakhs in the highest levels of the party, but it wanted only those individuals who would accept the Russians' claim to the leading role in defining and orchestrating the revolutionary process. Many Kazakhs seem to have accepted this principle, since they chose to remain within the party, but the tensions and arguments over land only grew worse. Land, in particular grazing land, was the key element of any plan for the reconstruction of the steppe. The Kazakhs had supported the new Soviet government because they had understood the Bolsheviks' revolution in the countryside to mean redistribution of land to the Kazakhs, but no Kazakh leader seasoned by the political activism of 1916–1920 could voluntarily cede to Moscow sole right to decide the land question in Kazakhstan. By the end of 1922 the Kazakhs in the party leadership were still divided on the issue of participation by the former Alash Orda, which the so-called right wing favored and the so-called left wing opposed, but almost no Kazakhs supported without qualification Moscow's position on the land question.

In 1923 all nonparty cadre who had actively participated in the Alash Orda government were removed from their government posts. Gradually the opprobrium of nationalist deviation expanded to party members who had supported this government, then to nonparticipants who were simply considered sympathetic to the aims of the Alash Orda. Ultimately, by 1926, simple opposition to or even criticism of the land policy was labeled nationalism. This created great difficulties for the Kazakhs because, with the policy of sovietization of the Kazakh aul, the official policy line began to depart drastically from what virtually all Kazakh Communists saw as the proper path of socialist development in the steppe.

Many Kazakhs—especially those of the so-called right wing of the party, which included S. Khodzhanov and S. Sadvakasov, who were prominent Kazakhs never associated with the Alash Orda—argued that sovietization could succeed only if tribal democracy and tribal command were left intact. They maintained that the Kazakh masses were basically sympathetic to the ideas of communism, since the aul itself was a form of primitive communism.[29] To threaten the integrity of the aul was to threaten the basis of Kazakh society and would not only turn the Kazakhs against Soviet rule, but would also transform the soviet elections into bitter clan rivalries, defeating the ends that the aul soviets were to accomplish.

Moscow, however, was no longer willing to tolerate the potential rivals it claimed to see in the clan leaders. At the fifth Kazakh regional conference of the Communist Party in December 1925, it was decided that the sovietization of the aul could be accomplished only if the power base of the bais was destroyed by reducing their livestock holdings. This policy was the personal choice of F. I. Goloshchekin, the new first secretary in Kazakhstan, a Russian who had earlier served on the Turkkomissiia and had been affirmed in the face of stiff expert opposition. Most leading Russian and Kazakh agronomists agreed that the livestock-breeding economy was regulated and controlled by the clanic authorities, and to disrupt this authority was to risk economic instability. Moreover, as experienced steppe observers from the prerevolutionary period were quick to point out, animal husbandry was suited to the topography of the area and grain growing was not.[30]

How to choose strategy for the development of the steppe was no longer simply an economic question. The issue had become more one of political control: who would control the countryside, and who would control the party. In Kazakhstan, as in the other national regions, Russians intended to dominate the natives who had thus far controlled the countryside.

In Kazakhstan, therefore, as everywhere else in the USSR, the land question served as a litmus test for admission to the party leadership. The shakeup in the Kazakh party organization began at the December 1925 conference when the few remaining former Alash Ordists lost their party posts; the first attack on the Kazakh so-called right wing came when S. Khodzhanov and D. A. Ermekov were expelled from the party leadership. The drive to discredit this right wing raged throughout 1926. In April the second party plenum of the Kazkraikom was devoted to cleansing the Kazakh government and soviet apparatus. Both Russians and Kazakhs were attacked as having pro-kulak or pro-bai sympathies. Several Russians with Menshevik or Socialist Revolutionary backgrounds lost their positions on the TsIK, while two prominent members of the Alash Orda government—A. Bukeikhanov and Sultanbekov—were publicly discredited.

When the third plenum of the Kazkraikom convened in November 1926, Kazakh party members were singled out for particular scrutiny. It was resolved to launch a "decisive struggle with the ideological and organizational perversions of the party line of Kazakhstan in general; in particular it is necessary to strengthen the ideological struggle with the ideology of the *Alash Orda*, and the national 'right' and 'left' deviations among the Kazakh communists."[31]

With both the right and left as targets, almost no Kazakh Communist escaped criticism. The two most prominent targets were S. Sadvakasov and S. Khodzhanov, who were already expelled from their executive positions. The attack on Khodzhanov, who had come to prominence in the party organization of Semirech'e in 1920 (then part of Turkestan), widened to include as "Khodzhanovtsy" the *Ak Zhol* (White Road) group, which included former members of the Kazakh-language organ of the Communist Party of Turkestan. However, all Syr Darya and Semirech'e organizations were attacked; Goloshchekin seems to have had a special dislike for the Kazakh Communists from the south.

In 1927–1928 the Kazakh Communists of the right wing fought a losing battle to regain official favor. A small delegation of the right visited Trotsky in early 1927 to urge him to plead their cause in Moscow; at the later purge trials of the delegates, this visit became proof of treason. Trotsky wrote to G. Y. Sokolniki, but the Kazakh grievances were not redressed. Trotsky's letter, dated March 11, 1927, is the only detached but informed picture of the Kazakh party organization we have for the period.

Trotsky described the Kazakh party as consisting of four factions: the Russians; Kazakhs who sympathized with the Russians; the right; and the left. He believed that the biggest division was between the Russians and the Kazakhs: "Between the European and Kazakh communists there is a wall. They live totally apart. They don't even play chess together."[32]

Trotsky accepted his visitors' claim that the Russians were encouraging disagreement within the Kazakh ranks to prevent a unified Kazakh opposition. He argued that the positions of the right and left were not dissimilar; the right faction was more outspoken in criticism of the current economic policy, but the left, although nominally allies of Goloshchekin, was often equally opposed to this position. Most important, both groups shared a sense of their exclusion from power. Their representation at the republic level was small, and their advice was generally discredited on grounds of alleged immaturity. Nowhere was this more galling than on the question of economic policy; the Kazakh right wing accused the Soviets of having a different attitude toward the Kazakh auls than toward the Russian villages:

> Goloshchekin's opinion is that the Russian *kulak* has been weakened and sufficiently put down, but that the *bais* have hardly been touched, for which reason a new October must pass through the *auls*. In other words, Goloshchekin preaches civil peace in the Russian village and civil war in the *aul*.[33]

From late 1927 on, public criticism such as the Kazakh delegation voiced to Trotsky was no longer tolerated. At the sixth regional conference in mid-November, on the eve of the Fifteenth Party Congress, Goloshchekin and his strongest Kazakh supporter, U. Isaev, who was chairman of the *Sovnarkom* (Council of People's Commissars), asked that the members of the right faction be removed from their party posts. The request was not only honored but many left-wing Communists, led by U. K. Dzhandosov, rose to condemn their former friends as nationalists. The right wing made one last attempt to gain sympathy within the party for their position. This took the form of an article written by Sadvakasov and published in *Bolshevik* in the January 1928 issue. The article was a strong attack both on Stalin's nationality policy and its application in Kazakhstan; it criticized the (first) Five-Year Plan for disregarding the needs of the periphery, which thus contravened the nationality plank of the party program adopted at the Twelfth Party Congress.[34]

The (first) Five-Year Plan, which called for increased state control of agriculture, was unacceptable both to the right and to the left Kazakh Communists, who had already been uncomfortable with the drive to sovietize the Kazakh aul. That drive had proved to them that the Russians certainly did not understand the economic basis of Kazakh rural society, and possibly did not even care to, since the whole economic policy was designed to exploit the peripheral states for the sake of Moscow.

Public opposition to the plan certainly hastened the end of the Kazakh left, but as pretext, not cause. Goloshchekin had long sought to promote Kazakh cadre who owed their loyalty solely to him. Once the left wing was attacked, the only Kazakhs still in favor were opportunists who had joined the party for personal advancement and who now clung to Goloshchekin without regard for his programs. This indifference distinguished them from the earlier Kazakh party elite, in which both left and right had shared a desire to develop a modern

Kazakh economy in a reinvigorated Kazakh culture. They had understood communism less as the teachings of Marx and Lenin than as the expression of a socialist and, more important, equalitarian model of development. Both sides believed that the Bolsheviks would give the Kazakhs the means and the inspiration to develop a modern equalitarian society.

However, the Kazakh national Communists were not willing to accept a policy that consisted of more slogan than substance; such a policy would again make the Kazakhs the audience for, rather than actors in, their own development. In the late 1920s the Soviet regime not only curbed initiative and opposition within the party, but also embarked on an economic policy that threatened the very fibre of the Kazakh community, predicated as it was on subordinating Kazakh interests to those of the Russians. Almost by definition, then, the Kazakhs were forced into opposition. For the first time many Kazakh party members came to believe that Kazakh nationalism and communism were in fact inimical, while the disastrous collectivization drive of late 1929 and early 1930 left the regime especially sensitive to criticism. Thus, when the seventh regional conference convened in late May 1930 in the newly established capital of Alma-Ata, the Kazakh left was removed from the buro of the party.

## THE PURGES: CONSOLIDATION AND CONTROL OF THE KAZAKH PARTY AND STATE IN THE 1930s

The 1930s in Kazakhstan brought a change in the deployment of personnel. The collectivization drive ended active participation by nonparty cadre, and then the purges limited the participation even of party members. Yet while criteria for membership in both party and state hierarchies changed throughout the decade, the idea of nativization remained strong; both the proportionate and absolute representation of Kazakhs steadily increased, and Moscow juggled the hunt for "kulaks" and "nationalist elements" with the need to fill a growing number of vacant posts. At its worst, the Great Terror swallowed the Kazakh leaders, but for the most part the Kazakhs remained unaffected by past associations; most of them had not supported either the now-discredited Kazakh Bolsheviks or the traitorous nationalists of the Alash Orda. Kazakh passivity in the 1920s thus permitted untainted membership in the Communist Party of the 1930s.

No comprehensive history of party or state in the 1930s is yet possible, despite the ample evidence of the decade's evils. Few of the actors-who-became-victims of those years have been fully rehabilitated; even recent histories of the party plenums of the 1920s people those conferences largely with the anonymous family of *drugie*, the "others" who still may not be named.[35] Very little archival material has been published, and most of the stenographic accounts of party plenums and meetings are still locked in restricted-access collections. Kazakh newspapers of the 1930s are almost entirely unavailable in the West and largely closed to Western scholars in the Soviet Union. Nevertheless, the broad shape of the decade can be discerned.

The collectivization drive of 1930 met universal and instant resistance. The Kazakh Communist Party, particularly F. I. Goloshchekin and his new second secretary, I. M. Kuramysov, had to actively search for scapegoats on whom to blame the violence and destruction in the countryside. Some they blamed on the inexperience of local officials, who had exceeded their instructions in order to please their superiors, but such excess did not explain the ferocity of the Kazakh response, for which the Alash Orda made a better whipping boy. A. Baitursunov was held particularly responsible for the debacle; in early 1930 the OGPU charged him with trying to organize the overthrow of Soviet rule. All auls where collectivization met stiff opposition were labeled "centers of resistance" and were considered to be organized as part of the plot. The policy of collectivization was itself vindicated, since the violence of the Kazakh resistance could be explained away as politically motivated. The former Alash Ordists were now considered traitors, and those who had ever supported them became adjuncts to treason. The purge of past supporters of the Alash Orda plumbed the lowest levels of the party and hit particularly hard at the guberniia control commissions; 42 percent of all control-commission members, including all six members of the Syr Darya organization, were purged, many for "insufficiencies" dating back to the 1928 drive to confiscate the bais' livestock.[36]

Such dismissals paled against the purge that began in mid-1932. The policy of slowing the tempo of collectivization had generally failed in Kazakhstan; the Kazakhs refused to join the collective farms and slaughtered their livestock instead, until by the summer of 1932 the situation reached crisis proportions. Several hundred thousand former nomads faced famine when there was virtually no harvest to carry the population into 1933. As a consequence, in the fall of 1932 Goloshchekin and Kuramysov were dismissed as party secretaries, and U. Isaev lost his job as chairman of the Sovnarkom. All of them were charged with serious errors in the collectivization drive, especially in the livestock-breeding regions. Moscow seemed determined to use nationalism to stitch together a conspiracy in Kazakhstan as well, and so Goloshchekin was accused of such failures of leadership that "fed" nationalist aims as misunderstanding and misrepresenting the history of the revolutionary period with overly positive evaluation of the bais and clan leaders in the decade following the revolution.[37] Goloshchekin and Kuramysov were further accused of having accepted Ryskulov's "erroneous" argument that the revolution lacked a popular basis in Kazakhstan.

What had been issues only of historiography thus literally became issues of life and death for Goloshchekin's and Kuramysov's supporters, who were fired by the hundreds throughout 1933–1934. The question under debate was whether the Kazakh masses had embraced Bolshevism in 1918–1919 or had chosen to continue to respect the authority of their traditional leadership. Virtually all Kazakh Communists subscribed to the latter stance, holding that the revolution did not actually occur in the countryside until 1929; however, although this argument conformed to historical facts, it could not be sustained in the face of Stalin's decision to arrange history for a maximum of political loyalty.

The official Stalinist version of the revolution in Kazakhstan denied that the bais had exercised any *recognized* or *legitimate* authority during the period 1920–1928. Those communists who had argued in the 1920s that the bais were a potent social force (which virtually all Kazakhs did) or, worse, that the clan authorities were the force that bound the aul together (as did some in the right wing) in the 1930s, were characterized as dupes or counterrevolutionaries. The historiography of the Alash Orda changed as well; the members of the Kazakh autonomous government were accused of having participated in the Soviet government in order to sabotage Bolshevik rule.[38] The writings of prominent Alash Orda leaders were so edited and reprinted as to cast them in the most negative light possible, and any Kazakh who had failed publicly to criticize the Alash Orda in the early 1920s became suspected of collusion.[39]

Such a broad definition of national deviation included all Kazakhs who had participated in the party in the 1920s and certainly all who were active in the Civil War period. The fall of Goloshchekin whipped the old guard of the Kazakh Communists into a self-protecting frenzy of recantation and representation of earlier views.

Kazakh historians quickly rewrote their accounts of the Civil War period; Ryskulov issued a new edition of his history of Kazakhstan and wrote several journal articles to condemn his earlier works and to argue now that the Kazakhs had supported the revolution en masse.[40] The Alash Orda was trickier to recast, even though it had always been a rival to most of the now-endangered Kazakh Communists; the Alash Ordists had nonetheless been legitimate political actors and the record of association between the Alash Orda and the Communist Party could not be erased. For that reason both Ryskulov and Togzhanov had to honor the positions of the Alash Orda in order to make their errors benign ones of degree, not evil ones of kind.[41] What Togzhanov had concluded in an article in *Kzyl Kazakhstan* in 1927 was even more true in 1935 when Ryskulov reprinted it:

In the prerevolutionary period the only political education we received was from the nationalists. We saw and knew only Ali Khan Bukeikhanov, Ahmed

Baitursunov, and Mir Yakub Dulatov. They were the example for us. From them there was one road, nationalism, and by this nationalism we came to the revolution. Nationalism did not come from the head of Ahmed and Ali Khan. Nationalism was the general desire of the Kazakhs. Nationalism was directed against Tsarism and the Russian bourgeoisie.[42]

In other words, the now-vilified Alash Ordists had led so many Kazakhs toward communism that the beleaguered Kazakh Communists had now to defend them as primitive protocommunists. To this end Ahmed Baitursunov's 1926 article on the Kazakh economy was widely reprinted in the early 1930s; he argued that:

The Kazakh people accepted the idea of communism earlier than any others. In their daily routine even now lives the idea of communism, in particular, in the free hospitality offered everyone by the Kazakhs, free help offered by the *bais* for their poor fellow clansmen, in *saun aitmai, sagum*, etc. The Kazakhs have a communal clan interest.[43]

To honor such teachers in the 1930s only hastened the departure of the Kazakh Communists from the political scene. Recantation probably helped to taint some prominent Civil War veterans, such as the Kazakh poets Saken Seifullin and Ilias Dzhansugurov, who by remaining silent in the early 1930s had managed to continue to serve the regime; Dzhansugurov was even chosen to head the Kazakh Writers' Union in 1934. Ultimately, however, these personalities fell into disfavor and were finally killed in 1938.

By this time it was obvious that no nationalist was safe, no matter how tenuous his former association with the nationalist cause. An entire generation of Kazakh Communists was systematically destroyed, first by L. I. Mirzoian, buro first secretary, and S. Nurpeisov, buro second secretary; when S. M. Kirov came to Kazakhstan in September 1934 to personally supervise the harvest, Mirzoian and Nurpeisov used the occasion to rout counterrevolutionaries in an effort to spare themselves blame for the economic failures of Kazakhstan. Kazakh Communists were next destroyed by the "exchange of party documents" following Kirov's death. Everywhere old faces were supplanted by cadre who joined the party in the late 1920s.

The first congress of the Communist Party of Kazakhstan, held in June 1937 soon after Kazakhstan gained full republic status, spoke both to Mirzoian's success and to his ultimate weakness. This congress brought the final political death of the Alash Orda and of both the Kazakh right and left, which completed the campaign of vigilance that had begun at the third plenum in November 1927. Shortly after the 1937 congress, mass arrests began; by the end of the year a whole generation of Kazakh intellectuals, historians, journalists, poets, and writers were found guilty and executed for the crime of dedication to the Kazakh people. The most prominent of them, Turar Ryskulov, was tried in Moscow and executed in February 1939.[44]

The purgers themselves were next; before another year had passed every member of the Kazakh buro of that first congress was arrested and charged with the "defamation and repression of party members." These arrests triggered hundreds of additional arrests, including many members of the Central Committee and most secretaries of the oblast *gorkoms* (city committee) and *raikoms* (district committee). With this group were killed the remaining old Kazakh Communists who had joined the party in 1920, such as U. K. Dzhandosov, A. Rozybakiev, and A. Asylbekov. They were replaced by a whole new group of leaders, most of whom had joined the party in the 1920s and 1930s, headed by N. A. Skvortsev and Zhumabai Shaiakhmetov. These two were appointed first and second secretaries respectively in 1939; Shaiakhmetov held the latter post until 1946, when he became the first Kazakh to serve as first secretary of the Kazakh Republic.

Oddly enough, throughout the Great Terror, Moscow was replacing the dismissed personnel and increasing the proportional representation of the Kazakhs in both party and state to create a simulation of popular participation. In 1930, 20.2 percent of all regional (krai) level administrators were Kazakh, as were 25.2 percent of all those serving at the oblast level and below.[45] In 1936 a good study on the ethnic composition of the labor force in Kazakhstan was commissioned and published; it shows that 30.8 percent of all government administrators in the republic were Kazakh, including 40.0 percent of the TsIK. Only 19.7 percent of the senior administrators were Kazakhs, however, with representation concentrated most heavily in educational, cultural, and agricultural establishments and of course more in oblast governments than city ones.[46] Kazakhs controlled the raion governments as well as the kolkhoz administrations, which had by the late 1930s completely subsumed the former aul administrations. The local soviets were run under the jurisdiction of the raion party structure. Yet party officials could not be omnipresent and had their own problems, so supervision was spasmodic; there was also a limited supply of qualified and sympathetic personnel in time of rapid turnover, and thus traditional leaders were once again able to maintain control of the kolkhoz administrations and aul soviets, especially in the smaller and ethnically homogeneous kolkhozy.[47]

All levels of administration were purged, particularly in late 1932 after F. I. Goloshchekin was removed, and again in late 1937 when Mirzoian and the entire buro of the party was dismissed. Elaborate chains of collaboration and disloyalty were allegedly proven after each fall, sometimes taking more than a year to reach the lowest administration, but reaching it infallibly. The personnel of all local administrative organs changed at least twice in the 1930s, and many several times more; a stable administrative apparatus was not established until the very eve of World War II.

The party, too, changed membership repeatedly throughout the 1930s in a pattern of alternating recruitment and expulsion. Entrance was easier for Kazakhs than Russians, since there were arguably more Russian kulaks to exclude than Kazakh bais. Major membership drives occurred in 1930, 1931, and 1932, and the total party membership nearly doubled between 1930 and 1933; the percentage of Kazakhs in the party rose from 43.0 percent to 53.1 percent.[48] Many of these new members became the cadre who carried out the collectivization drive, with responsibilities far beyond their training; the exchange of party documents that began in January 1933 undoubtedly purged with good reason some of these members in the 18 months it continued. Reorganization of the party was ordered on July 8, 1933, and the number of people dismissed from the party far outstripped the number of new recruits.[49] Total party membership dropped to a low of 48,322 on January 1, 1938; the percentage of Kazakhs declined to 47.6 percent, which was still considerably greater representation than had been enjoyed in the 1920s. While devastating the ranks of the old cadre, the purges also let a new generation rise to prominence, broadening access to the party and raising the heights to which loyal, competent members might aspire; it is the recruits of this era who still supply the top leadership of the Kazakh republic.

## THE KAZAKH PARTY IN THE
## LAST YEARS OF STALIN'S RULE

What little information is available about either the cadre or the leadership of the Kazakh party during the final years of Stalin's rule comes from two collections of documents, which describe the changing party membership without discussion of the party elite.[50]

Between 1938 and 1946 the Kazakh party tripled its membership, which had steadily increased until 1942, decreased throughout the war, and then expanded rapidly at the war's conclusion.[51] The representation of women rose throughout the war to nearly a third of all members in 1944, then dropped again to approximately 20 percent in the postwar period, where it has remained. The representation of Kazakhs rose until 1942, but dropped rapidly when the entire countryside was both mobilized and inundated with evacuated European party members; as Kazakhs returned to their republic their representation rose again, to about 43 percent, and the party became increasingly rural, with 53.3 percent of all primary party cells in 1945 found in the countryside.[52]

These membership drives emphasized increasing the number of people in the party, not raising the level of ideological purity; this was even more true of the membership campaigns during World War II, when increased popular identification with party and state was vital to the war effort. The party thus became younger but less well versed in the principles of Marxism and Leninism; in 1945 over 50 percent of the party had been members for fewer than five years and 41.2 percent for fewer than three.

After the war Moscow addressed the weaknesses of the Kazakh party organization. In 1947 it sent 670 party workers to Kazakhstan to direct demobilization and removed nearly one-third of all kolkhoz chairmen from their posts in 1946 and 1947.[53] Despite this increased attention to the ideological level of its membership, the party ballooned, growing by 82,479 people—or 155 percent—in the years 1946–1953. Growth of such magnitude makes it hard to imagine that the campaign to raise the quality of party members had any real impact in Kazakhstan, especially since the Kazakh rural population remained a significant source of new members.

Kazakh representation remained about 40 percent, but became vertically better distributed as the generation recruited after the purges acquired the seniority necessary to attend party congresses and to serve in the raikom and obkom (oblast committee) organizations. Just over half of the delegates to the fifth (1949), sixth (1951), and seventh (1952) Kazakh party congresses were Kazakh, and just less than half the obkom membership in this period were "native" cadre.

Although Kazakh participation increased, it could not be argued that Kazakhs had a meaningful role in party decisionmaking. World War II was a sort of interregnum in the political control exercised by Moscow, and republic cadre were permitted some discretion, albeit within certain guidelines. One of the great ironies of the period is that although the Kazakh leadership failed to meet the challenge of tasks given them, they lived to tell the tale. Economic productivity declined during the war years, and reconstruction occurred both slowly and unsatisfactorily afterward. However, the party leadership weathered these storms, either because—as some would have us believe—by the late 1940s Stalin was out of touch with conditions in the countryside and his henchmen feared to intervene as bearers of ill-tidings, or simply because loyalty exceeded efficiency as the official criterion for judging performance during these years.

N. A. Skvortsev, first secretary of the Kazakh Communist Party, and Zh. Shaiakhmetov, his Kazakh second secretary, although not able to do wholly as they wished nonetheless had a great deal of latitude in defining the Kazakh version of ideological orthodoxy. One example of this latitude was the dispute between Alma-Ata and Moscow on the portrayal of Kazakh resistance to colonial rule in the official history of Kazakhstan, which had been written by the noted Russian historian A. Pankratova and Kazakh party secretary M. Abdykalikov.[54] After strong initial praise, the Pankratova history was criticized by Skvortsev and Shaiakhmetov for making insufficient distinction between feudal resistance, which was bad, and peasant resistance, which was better.

During World War II, Moscow's concern over such issues was great; patriotism required a strong commitment to a Russian-dominated homeland, making this no time to depict the Russians in any but the most favorable light. After the war no leeway whatsoever was permitted in historical interpretation of Russian colonialism. Stalin was by then strongly pro-Russian, and he permitted no deviation from positive assessment of past connections between Russian and native, as was made abundantly clear in the Shamil controversy in 1950. The Kazakhs had been warned of this nearly three years earlier, however, after the publication in Alma-Ata of E. Bekmakhanov's *Kazakhstan v 20–40 gody XIX veka* (Kazakhstan in the 1820s–1840s).[55] This book received favorable reviews in the Kazakh press, but was attacked in *Pravda* a year later for glorifying a feudal leader and paying insufficient attention to the positive role of the Russian "elder brother."

Bekmakhanov, a professor of history at the Kazakh State University and director of the Institute of History, Ethnography, and Archaeology of the Kazakh Academy of Sciences, was stripped of his titles and degrees in October 1951[56] and was subjected to public attack by his own students. At stake was more than a simple interpretation of the history of Kazakh-Russian relations; the Kazakhs were trying to define a science of history in their republic. Bekmakhanov's study, by far the most sophisticated work yet written by a Kazakh historian, opened up the study of Kazakh state and society in the nineteenth century by revealing the existence of hundreds of books and archival sources from this period.[57] The nineteenth-century Kazakh society that Bekmakhanov depicted was much more complex than earlier histories had presented; he showed that the resistance of Kenisary had been not only more widespread but also more articulate than previously credited. The history was intended to serve as a model for the new generation of Kazakh historians, which in a way it did, although all his students attacked him. Several of these students—including S. Tolybekov, V. Shakhmatov, and T. Shoinbaev—published only inconsequential, formulaic journal articles until the 1960s and 1970s, when in the freer conditions of Kazakh academic life each was able to publish a major theoretical work.

The late 1940s were difficult years for any Kazakh intellectual or party member with a strong sense of initiative, but those more willing to accept ideological conformity were rewarded with increased responsibility and personal privilege. No one better personified the successful Kazakh party member than Zh. Shaiakhmetov, who spanned the gulf between Stalin's purges and Khrushchev's rise to power. Born in a nomadic aul, he used his limited education to become an aul teacher and then served as a secretary of the volost soviet. Although he did not join the CPSU until 1929, by 1938 he was third secretary of

Kazakh Community Party and in 1939 became second secretary, a post he held until 1946, when he was elevated to first secretary. Moreover, Moscow named him chairman of the Council of Nationalities of the Supreme Soviet, a largely honorific post, which was the type of post that suited him best. The servile independence with which Shaiakhmetov led the Kazakh party ill-suited Khrushchev's more interfering style; Shaiakhmetov's faithful but self-sufficient fiefdom, creating few problems but contributing little, did not survive the introduction of the Virgin Lands Policy, when Kazakhstan was forced into the mainstream of Soviet economic decisionmaking. The success of this policy required loyal but dynamic leadership—a criterion that had until then been ignored in promotion. The leadership Moscow sent to Kazakhstan had to sift carefully through the ranks of the Kazakh party for aggressive Kazakhs and Russians.

# 10 The Virgin Lands and the Creation of a Socialist Kazakhstan

## INTRODUCTION

Khrushchev's decision in late 1953 to create a new breadbasket out of the allegedly underutilized lands of southern Siberia and Kazakhstan affected the Kazakhs more than any other Soviet policy decision, with the possible exception of collectivization. These so-called Virgin Lands were underutilized only from the perspective of Moscow, since the Kazakhs had for generations made good use of them as pasturelands. The development of the Virgin Lands became yet another instance when Russian authorities differed with Kazakhs and placed the goals of Moscow over those of the peripheral states. The Kazakh economy was again forced to adapt. Large grain sovkhozy were built and staffed largely by Europeans, while displaced Kazakhs and their livestock were relocated on new livestock-breeding sovkhozy where "scientific" livestock breeding transformed many traditional Kazakh practices.

Equally important, the campaign to use the Virgin Lands brought the Kazakh party apparat to the attention of the Soviet central government; the new goals required a tried leadership, men Moscow trusted, and so the old Kazakh party cadre were replaced by men whose loyalty and experience were considered more in keeping with the magnitude of the task. Still, these new, hand-picked leaders were meant to revive the Kazakh party apparat rather than to purge it; over time, therefore, a new republic hierarchy emerged that was heavily staffed by Kazakhs. This leadership, proven in making the Virgin Lands scheme into a viable economic structure, was rewarded by promotion and increased responsibility in the Moscow apparat.

The economic policies of the Khrushchev-Brezhnev era led to greater integration of the Kazakh economy and the Kazakh party into those of the Soviet administration. Khrushchev's Virgin Lands Policy, combined with Brezhnev's commitment to modernizing agricultural practices, greatly sped up the developmental process that Stalin had introduced upon the ruins of the colonial system. Today, although Kazakhstan has become a mining center and a republic with an industrial base, agriculture still remains the livelihood of more than 75 percent of the working population. The challenges that now confront Gorbachev are to make agriculture more productive and to integrate a greater portion of the population into the industrial sector.

## THE INTRODUCTION OF THE VIRGIN LANDS SCHEME IN KAZAKHSTAN, 1953–1965

In the years immediately following World War II, the rural economy of the Soviet Union failed to rebuild and stagnated so severely that by 1947 much of the country was gripped by famine. The situation began to improve, but slowly, because of the crisis of leadership in Moscow. Stalin seems increasingly to have lost touch with reality, obsessed instead with real and imagined enemies in the party, which left him and his countrymen little time for experimental policies to raise the level of agricultural productivity. So far as anyone can tell, most of the senior Presidium members (as the Politburo was renamed in 1951) spent the early 1950s waiting for the old tyrant to die, worrying more about their own survival than about feeding cities.

This situation changed almost immediately upon Stalin's death in 1953, when his previously passive lieutenants maneuvered aggressively for position. Among them, N. S. Khrushchev took on the food crisis, hoping to use his agricultural expertise to gather the power to emerge as Stalin's successor.

It is difficult to know precisely when Khrushchev hit upon the Virgin Lands scheme as a way to increase the supply of food, since the idea itself was not new.[1] Since the time of Stolypin in the first decade of the twentieth century, a stream of agronomists had advocated the cultivation of cereal crops on the open grazing lands of Kazakhstan and southern Siberia. The introduction of large state-run farms (the sovkhozy) had long been considered as the final goal of the collectivization drive, which had been interrupted by the outbreak of war in 1941.

Khrushchev took these ideas, jumbled them slightly, and formed them into a campaign to mobilize the country for increased agricultural productivity. The economy of the Soviet Union was decaying, nowhere more obviously than in agriculture. New sources of grain had to be found and livestock breeding had to become more productive and efficient, since massive infusions of meat and bread would help insure that the new leader need not fear his people the way Stalin had. The Virgin Lands scheme was only one part of Khrushchev's push to rationalize the economy, but probably the best publicized part; it was designed to create the impression that Khrushchev was a mighty leader who could master hordes of people to get the economy in motion. The huge scale of the operation had the additional advantage of requiring many changes in the party, thus giving Khrushchev the opportunity to reward his supporters and replace those who opposed him.

By September 1953, at the time of the Central Committee plenum, Khrushchev had clearly made some fairly concrete decisions about the course of agricultural development, but he was not sure when or even if his policy could begin.[2] At the September plenum the scheme received tentative support from Khrushchev's colleagues; the Central Committee published a resolution that called for the strengthening of agriculture through the development of parts of the southeast, Kazakhstan, and western Siberia as major sources of winter wheat. The plenum also demanded the improvement of livestock breeding, and Kazakhstan was the first region to be criticized.[3]

The Kazakh party plenum, convened on October 6, 1953, quickly endorsed the resolutions and pledged to make a sustained effort to increase the amount of land cultivated with winter wheat. Yet the Kazakh party leadership remained skeptical as Khrushchev and his followers tried to mobilize support for a major agricultural campaign in the spring of 1954. First Secretary Shaiakhmetov pointed out that any gains from the introduction of cereal cultivation in Northern Kazakhstan would come at the cost of livestock breeding.[4]

Khrushchev found Shaiakhmetov's attitude unacceptable; starting in late 1953 attacks on the party and state leadership of Kazakhstan appeared frequently in the press, charging failure to supervise livestock breeding adequately, and so causing needless animal deaths by not constructing enough stalls or storing adequate supplies of feed.[5] More telling were accusations that high party officials had failed to learn from their mistakes.[6] It was thus no surprise when the plenary session convened on February 11, 1954, in Alma-Ata, that the first and second secretaries of the Communist Party, Shaiakhmetov and I. I. Afanov, were both dismissed from their posts; the next Central Committee plenary session, in February 1954, named P. K. Ponomarenko and L. I. Brezhnev to succeed them. The local Kazakh leadership also came under attack, and within the next three months the first secretaries of the six Virgin Land oblasts were all replaced.[7]

The public announcement of the leadership change stressed the failure of the dismissed officials to ensure the development of the allegedly virgin and idle lands in Kazakhstan.[8] This same plenum made a formal commitment to the Virgin Lands Policy, which was promulgated on March 28, 1954, in the decree

"On Increasing Grain Production in 1954–1955 Through the Development of Virgin and Idle Lands." This called for the cultivation of 13 million hectares of virgin and idle lands in Kazakhstan, Siberia, the Urals, the Volga region, and some areas of North Caucasus.

During the first year of the drive, 300 new state farms were organized in Kazakhstan to plant cereal crops on 3.5 million hectares of former grazing land. At the same time Moscow began to press for the systematic introduction of modern animal-husbandry techniques in Kazakhstan. Khrushchev was concerned about the general weakness of livestock breeding and the shortage of meat; at the Central Committee plenum of January 25–31, 1955, he announced a new practice in animal husbandry. Millions of hectares of pastureland were to be sown with maize, while feedlots were to be widely introduced in the Soviet livestock-breeding regions. Kazakhstan was an area of particular concern, where the blame for archaic and inefficient practices in livestock breeding could conveniently fall on the leadership shown by Kazakh Party First Secretary Ponomarenko, who was also a supporter of Khrushchev's rival, Malenkov. Ponomarenko was removed from his post in July 1955 and replaced by Brezhnev, a Khrushchev protégé.

Brezhnev firmly established Khrushchev's agricultural policy in Kazakhstan, largely by rewarding promising cadre and demoting the recalcitrant. Shaiakhmetov, who had been demoted to secretary of the southern Kazakh oblast party committee, was dismissed from this post in May 1955 and his supporters were demoted. The June 1955 issue of *Kommunist* declared that Kazakh party opposition to the Virgin Lands Policy was a thing of the past.[9] Brezhnev was rewarded with promotion to Moscow in March 1956, and the second secretary, I. D. Iakovlev, was named to replace him.

With the dissenting members of the Kazakh party leadership removed, the party urged the creation of sovkhozy that would combine the growing of fodder with livestock breeding. The party plenum of December 15–19, 1958, which came immediately after the defeat of the "anti-party" group, gave Khrushchev an even stronger commitment to economic development than he had charted out. The Seven-Year Plan (1959–1965) endorsed at this meeting departed from previous planning both in the length and, more important, in the ambition of the goals set forth. Meat and milk production in Kazakhstan were to increase through the sovkhozy. Again the Kazakh leadership was criticized for the slow growth of the livestock-breeding sector, even though Iakovlev had been relieved of his post in late December 1957; he was replaced by N. I. Beliaev, a long-time Khrushchev supporter now rewarded for his successes in the Altai region.

Although Beliaev became a member of the Politburo, he also did not last long at his Kazakh post. When the 1959 harvest in the Virgin Lands proved worse than in 1958 and Khrushchev's agricultural policies were criticized at the December 1959 plenum, Beliaev was dismissed and Dinmukhamed Akhmedovich Kunaev, the chairman of the Council of Ministers, was named first secretary of the Kazakh party.[10]

Kunaev had to raise the productivity of livestock breeding by reorganizing and combining kolkhozy into sovkhozy—which meant transforming traditional economic practices. In 1960–1961 some 317 new sovkhozy were opened and 754 kolkhozy were disbanded.[11] This was accompanied by a campaign in the Moscow press to highlight the failure of the kolkhoz sector in Kazakhstan. Cited were examples of Kazakh herdsmen using collectively owned pasturage and state property to sustain privately owned herds.[12]

The combination of tighter organizational structure and huge new quantities of fodder permitted the Kazakh herd to grow in size and the amount of meat produced to increase, but Kunaev was not immune from criticism. He was severely attacked at the January 1961 plenum for the shortfalls in grain deliveries in the Virgin Land oblasts and accused of "gross violation of agrotechnology, poor cultivation of the soil and contamination of fields, sowing with poor-quality seed, and loss of grain during harvesting."[13] The Virgin Lands Policy continued to flounder. The yield per hectare dropped in 1960 and again in 1961. Poor party organization was cited as a cause; therefore, in late 1960 the six Virgin Lands oblasts were reconstructed as the Virgin Lands Region, a subregion of Kazakhstan, which was to have its own first secretary who would be nominally subordinate to Kunaev but actually under Moscow's direct control.

In March 1961 Khrushchev himself attended an agricultural conference in Alma-Ata to inspire the leading Kazakh rural workers to raise their productivity. He called upon them to increase the amount of grain grown, improve the irrigation networks, increase mechanization in the rural sector, and turn Kazakhstan into the primary sheep-raising area of the USSR.[14] However, neither exhortation nor reorganization could raise agricultural productivity. The optimism of party reorganization soon faded as the output of the Virgin Lands and the whole rural sector continued to fall short of official expectations. Rural investment remained small and misguided; rail as the press did against shortages of machinery and trained technical employees, Moscow still made no systematic efforts to fund the production of greater supplies of either.

Instead, Khrushchev continued to blame the agricultural failures on the weakness of territorial and republic party organizations. Kunaev, again severely attacked at the March 1962 Central Committee plenum, was entirely ignored at the November plenum and was finally removed on December 26, 1962. He was replaced by I. Iu. Iusupov, the former first secretary of the South Kazakhstan oblast (present-day Chimkent oblast) and M. S. Solomentsev (the same Solomentsev who is now a Politburo member and leads the Party Control Commission) replaced N. N. Rodionov as second secretary.[15] Again, however, personnel shifts only temporarily stilled criticism within the party. Khrushchev's policies had so clearly failed to produce rational development in agriculture that by the December 1963 plenum, after another disastrous harvest, he was willing to admit that agricultural practices had to be modernized, for which he called for the development of chemical fertilization. Instead, the Central Committee chose to attack the question directly; at the February 1964 plenum Khrushchev did not give a formal address until he had listened to several days' discussion of the problems of agriculture.

The resolution adopted at this February meeting called for a 200–300 percent increase in the production of grain, meat, and milk; this demonstrates vividly how unsuccessful Khrushchev's agricultural strategy had proven. Furthermore, the plenum shifted the focus from extending the area under cultivation to improving the quality of agriculture and livestock breeding. Introduction of scientific practices became the watchword, meaning the use of fertilizers, the development of irrigated agriculture, and increased mechanization throughout the rural sector. The days of "simple" farming were over; crop rotation and high-yield plant strains became crucial, as did hybridization and the health of the herd.[16] Kazakhstan was a national area for such attention, so Iusupov quickly took up the themes of the February plenum, especially on livestock breeding, and tried to popularize them in Kazakhstan.[17]

Like Khrushchev himself, however, Iusupov had chosen a Kazakh party apparat that could not meet the challenges posed by the plenum. Khrushchev, awed by U.S. agrarian practices, did not understand the complexities of rural transformation; the February 1964 plenum marked the end of Khrushchev's dream of revolutionizing the Soviet countryside, and the little time left him gave no sign that he could realize any other design for agriculture. Finally, the crises of agriculture, of industry, and of Soviet foreign policy passed beyond tolerable limits, and Khrushchev's colleagues in the Politburo staged a palace coup. On October 14, 1964, Khrushchev was excused from all his party and government posts, and another era of economic experimentation in Kazakhstan ended.

## L. I. BREZHNEV AND THE DEVELOPMENT OF THE MODERN KAZAKH ECONOMY

At the November 1964 plenum, the Soviet leadership again discussed the control and redirection of the economy. Because the 1964 harvest had been a large one, which gave the party breathing space, organizational questions were the first to be addressed. The plenary session resolved to reunify the rural and industrial organizations, which not only increased the prospect of efficient management of the economy but also mandated a large change of personnel; this proved important in the subsequent leadership crises because of the power wielded in making appointments.

Past loyalty was quickly rewarded; the December 8, 1964, Kazakh central committee plenum relieved I. Iu. Iusupov of his duties and appointed D. A. Kunaev once more to the post of first secretary of the Kazakh party; at the time of this writing he continues to occupy that position. M. S. Solomentsev was replaced as second secretary by V. N. Titov, followed by further changes in personnel at the January 1965 plenum.[18]

This new Kazakh team received detailed instructions when the Central Committee met in March 1965; the resolution it adopted formed the framework of Brezhnev's agricultural policy, providing the operating principles by which agricultural planning in Kazakhstan is explained if not actually accomplished.[19] The resolutions of the September 1953 plenum, which for over a decade had represented the party's agricultural program, were repudiated and replaced. Principles of scientific management in both agriculture and industry were to replace the economies of giantism, which—as Brezhnev fulminated in his plenum address—violated economic and agronomic laws. Although many of the March 1965 resolutions had also been endorsed a year earlier, there was a new official determination to accomplish them, to devote financial resources to sponsor technological improvements, to fund irrigation schemes, and to better develop the chemical-fertilizer industry. The decrees published at the conclusion of the plenum left little leeway for the rural sector to refuse, speaking as they did of the need to strengthen the sovkhozy and reorganize weak collective farms, the need for local party leaders better to supervise the farms in their area or face removal, and the need to raise the quality of the rural work force through increased technical education and better pay.

These reforms proved to be only partially successful, in part because old ways die hard, but in part because the Soviet economy offered very little slack. Also hindering rural development was the fact that Brezhnev's colleagues did not all share his belief in the primacy of agriculture; some preferred A. N. Kosygin's arguments for restructuring and modernizing the industrial sector as presented at the September 1965 Central Committee plenum. The two plenums of March and September 1965 both stated official goals for the modern Soviet economy, but did so independently, with no formula to resolve the competing claims for resources made by the two sectors. That there were two separate plenums is not merely symbolic but shows that there were (and still are) distinct and oftentimes conflicting economic constituencies within the leadership; this has meant that disputes over resource allocation between agriculture and industry have had to be decided anew with each Five-Year Plan.

Resource allocation has proven to be the uncrackable nut; it has prevented the formation of a truly scientific modern Soviet economy, which is an important reason why there has been no agricultural revolution in the postwar period.

Today Gorbachev is again asking for a new beginning, but to date the physical organization of Kazakh agriculture is little modified since 1965, when there were some 1,500 sovkhozy in the republic, as compared to just over 2,000 in 1982.[20] Then as now, just over one-third of the state farms grew grain, and the overwhelming majority of these farms were in the Virgin Lands Region. Slightly more than one-third raise sheep, while most of the remainder raise cattle in some combination of meat and milk production.

In Kazakhstan as elsewhere in the USSR, the emphasis has been on improving the quality of agriculture—increasing the amounts of grain, meat, and milk produced—which in Kazakhstan required the solution of a number of problems that had plagued Soviet planners since the settlement of the Kazakh nomads in the nineteenth century; this is the legacy of forced sedentarization. The two most serious and long-standing problems were the shortage of animal stalls and the perennial failure of Kazakh herdsmen to store sufficient fodder to winter the herd over; together these killed thousands of head each winter and meant a significant loss in slaughter weights for the rest.

The Eighth Five-Year Plan, announced in February 1966 and formally adopted at the Twenty-third Party Congress the next month, made the party's chief task increasing productivity of farming and livestock breeding.[21] Virtually all the ideas of the March 1965 plenum were built into the plan as concrete goals: increased use of fertilizers; more irrigation and land reclamation; improvement of communal animal-husbandry practices; and introduction of auxiliary industry (that is, food processing) into agricultural regions. In concert these were expected to provide dramatic increases in the annual yield of grain, meat, milk, and wool.

The twelfth congress of the Kazakh Communist Party in its turn criticized former First Secretary Iusupov and affirmed the Kazakh leaders' commitment to meet the targets of the plan. In addition, Kunaev offered specific suggestions to overcome the weaknesses of Kazakh livestock breeding, including improving the variety and yield of fodder crops, building more animal shelters, and increasing the relative as well as the absolute size of the communal herd.

Perhaps of greatest moment to the Kazakhs was the issue that the May 1966 Central Committee plenum raised when it mandated a general ten-year plan for increasing irrigation and land reclamation. On June 16, 1966, a joint resolution of the Central Committee and the USSR Council of Ministers was issued, entitled "On the Development of Reclamation Efforts." It specifically recommended that during the Eighth Five-Year Plan, 51.6 million hectares of desert and semidesert areas be "reclaimed" as productive pastureland, of which 38 million hectares were in Kazakhstan. Well before the end of the plan period, both Moscow and Kunaev grew unhappy with the performance of local party and administrative officials in Kazakhstan. Plan achievement was uneven throughout the republic; the shortage of animal shelters was not remedied, the fertilizer industry and mechanization were developing more slowly than planned, and, most serious of all, fodder and cereal grains rotted in the fields and on the farms because of slow harvest or bad storage. In partial remedy of this, 12,500 combine drivers, 3,000 skilled agricultural workers, and 3,500 self-propelled combines were dispatched to Kazakhstan to aid the 1967 harvest, but the effort was expensive and temporary. Since its greatest effect was to highlight the failure of the local Kazakh authorities, there followed considerable replacement of cadre at the oblast and raion level; at the same time, Kunaev tried to break up local patronage networks and consolidate his position in the republic.

Moscow continued to address agricultural performance with both praise and criticism; the October 1968 Central Committee plenum praised the accomplishments of the Kazakh grain growers, but it also noted with disfavor a declining rate of growth of the value of production in the republic and pointed out that there could be a better variety of fodder grown in the grasslands of Kazakhstan. However, official patience wore thin when 1969 saw the smallest harvest of the Eighth Five-Year Plan and a large deficit in the livestock-breeding sector as well. Several obkom first secretaries from Northern Kazakhstan were publicly attacked for their inadequate supervision of harvested grain, and the December 1969 plenum of the Kazakh Communist Party focused on how the local leadership could better supervise agriculture.[22] Still, the Five-Year Plan ended with a disastrous winter, during which severe shortages of stored fodder were reported in Kazakhstan, Uzbekistan, and Turkmenistan.

The regime responded by trying production incentives, such as raising the purchase price of milk and cream, and at the same time increasing the direct state involvement in livestock breeding by mandating new "scientific" sovkhozy to be concentrated in Kazakhstan.[23] The July 1970 Central Committee plenum went still further, accusing the kolkhoz sector of Central Asia and Kazakhstan of poor performance in livestock breeding caused by excessive reliance on free grazing. To rectify this an additional 8,600,000 hectares of land were to be ploughed under and sown with fodder grasses.

The Ninth Five-Year Plan, endorsed by the Twenty-fourth Party Congress in March 1971, reiterated many of the themes from the March 1965 plenum. The provisions that most affected the Kazakh economy called for more rational use of natural pastures, improved irrigation, advanced agricultural techniques in the cultivation of corn, and a general rise in the standard of agricultural performance, all of which the June 1971 plenum of the Kazakh Communist Party formally endorsed.

Some leaders, including most prominently D. A. Kunaev, now a full member of the Politburo, desired Kazakhstan to perform as a model agricultural region, but neither the rural work force nor the local party leadership was willing on its own initiative to devote the energy to realize such a goal; Moscow therefore had constantly to prod.

In April 1972 the Council of Ministers passed a resolution, "On Several Measures for Increasing the Material-Technical Base of Agriculture in the Kazakh S.S.R." The resolution systematically listed how the productivity of the rural sector was to be raised and, more important, it allocated money for the mechanization of livestock breeding, the production of phosphate fertilizers (to increase fodder fields), and the construction of both silage elevators and meat-processing plants.[24] Although the money allocated was sufficient to modernize only a fraction of the Kazakh stock farms, even this was more than the agencies of the Kazakh party and state bureaucracy could spend successfully. The press in 1972–1976 is filled with accounts of costly failures leading to unnecessary loss of stock, while little attention was paid to the health of the herd or its variety of bloodlines.[25]

It was hoped that agriculture, in particular fodder yields, would improve through the use of phosphate fertilizers combined with land reclamation.[26] However, the close of the Ninth Five-Year Plan brought the leaders in Alma-Ata only small encouragement, perhaps because of the poor quality of the Kazakh republic planning apparatus, wherein only 50 percent of all executives had a higher education and only 40 percent had five or more years of experience.[27] Even so, Brezhnev hailed the Ninth Five-Year Plan as a general victory and Kunaev echoed suitable accolades for rural and industrial workers of Kazakhstan.

In the Tenth Five-Year Plan, adopted at the Twenty-fifth Party Congress in 1976, Brezhnev acknowledged that there were no longer virgin or unexploited sources of arable land in the Soviet Union and that, although more systematic use of fodder-sown lands was possible, even maximum utilization would not meet the needs of the rapidly expanding herd. Thus, for the first time in over 40 years, the party urged increased reliance on natural grazing lands, augmented now through the application of scientific techniques to increase their feed capacity. This brought Kazakhstan once again to official attention, because over two-thirds of the land in the six Virgin Land oblasts was steppe meadow and pasture yielding an average of only three centners of feed per hectare; many meadows were not easily accessible to livestock or in summer burned up almost as fast as the grass grew. Cultivated grassland had nearly doubled in yield because of improved techniques, such as increased salinization and greater exploitation of underground water resources; it was hoped that the same results could be achieved in the open range.[28]

The Tenth Five-Year Plan was to build upon previous accomplishments of Kazakh agriculture. Brezhnev's address to agricultural workers in Alma-Ata in September 1976 made quite clear that these results were mixed, especially in cereal crops, where annual increases in yield per hectare not only fell short of the plan but even began to fall behind those of their Uzbek neighbors. Even more serious was the Kazakh inability to gather the harvest despite legions of skilled and unskilled workers, who struggled with little success to bring the harvest from field to market.[29] Worse still, this inability threatened to become chronic; while the number of tractors, combines, and trucks grew 20, 50, and 100 percent respectively, the number of trained drivers only increased 14 percent.[30]

Throughout the Tenth Five-Year Plan, the press reported the small victories of regions that met their harvest goals and blasted major defeats, such as when harsh climatic conditions were compounded by local mismanagement or when record amounts of food had to be imported to feed the Soviet population. Some raions of Kazakhstan (in Kustanai, Tselinograd, Chimkent, and Kokchetav) became "model regions," meaning that they had eighteen months of fodder on hand; such victories were few, however. The total number of sheep and goats remained below 35 million, whereas 50 million had been the targeted goal for 1975. Nor did Moscow have much success in raising either the yields of ploughed fodder land or the amount of hay per centner obtained from steppe meadowlands.

Official displeasure with the progress of the Tenth Five-Year Plan surfaced at the July 1978 Central Committee plenum, which called livestock breeding a lagging sector and criticized four oblasts in Kazakhstan (Pavlodar, Turgai, Taldy-Kurgan, and Eastern Kazakhstan); these regions were among a dozen in the nation that had failed to meet targeted goals for increases in the production and sale of meat. The plenum also attacked the slow development of the petrochemical and farm-machinery industries in Kazakhstan.

Criticism grew stronger after the November 1979 Central Committee plenum, when four-year totals showed that while grain-growing in Kazakhstan had kept pace with official targets, animal husbandry was lagging; three oblasts failed to meet their milk quotas and severe shortfalls of milk production were reported in at least two others.[31] Semiannual production plans for meat were also often not achieved.[32]

Little attempt was made, however, to change the responsible personnel. No obkom first secretary was disgraced during the late 1970s and, although some first secretaries from oblasts that failed to meet quotas were reassigned to different oblasts, others remained in their posts; what criteria Kunaev used in making such choices is unclear. In fact, the biggest personnel shifts during this period were among the party elite responsible for the coal industry in Karaganda, not among agriculturalists.[33]

This would suggest that, during the Brezhnev years, party leadership conceded that the Soviet economic system adapts with difficulty to the needs and conditions of modern agriculture and that performance cannot be improved simply by finding scapegoats among high-level regional cadre. This was alluded to in speeches made at the Twenty-sixth Party Congress in February 1981 and stated even more openly in Kunaev's address to the April 1981 Kazakh party plenum, which says clearly that Kazakh agriculture has been incompletely modernized. The cultivation of cereal crops today has stabilized and conforms more or less to the expectations of the regime, but livestock breeding, long the traditional strength of the Kazakh economy, has for more than half a decade failed to develop satisfactorily. During the Ninth Five-Year Plan the number of sheep increased by over 2.8 million, but during the tenth by only 706,000. The goal of 50 million sheep has been put off into the 1990s, and even reaching a herd of 41 million by the end of the Eleventh Five-Year Plan in 1985 did not occur.

In his speech to the April 1981 plenum, Kunaev frankly attributed the failure of many farm managers and raion officials to meet quotas to poor economic management and party supervision, but he claimed that the short-comings were all ones of scientific techniques such as spotty use of fertilizers, insufficient crop rotation, and failure to complete local irrigation schemes. Kunaev pointed out that, where initially such sloppy practices were not as harmful, the growing herd size made the maximum production of feed crops critical and thus raised the cost of such carelessness. Sloppy practices also became more common as farm managers and party officials found it increasingly difficult to reach their production goals. With fodder more scarce, the experimental farms began to cut corners as well, and the slaughter of underweight animals became commonplace. Even more dangerous for animal husbandry was the slaughter of breeding stock, which occurred on some cereal sovkhozi in Northern Kazakhstan; when the price of feed increased, entire herds were destroyed to avoid posting a loss from livestock breeding. Another dangerous sign of the recent past is that the percentage of the total herd used for intrafarm needs has grown, just as the overall health of the herd has fallen.

These harmful practices were so widespread that any curbs decreed by Moscow or Alma-Ata seemed doomed. Five oblasts had fewer sheep at the end of the Tenth Five-Year Plan than they had at the beginning, and two others could slaughter the required number of animals only by routinely killing underweight animals.[34] The farm managers and local party officials were not the only ones at fault. They were, to be sure, inefficient and corrupt; yet the regime itself must bear part of the blame for having given the men in executive positions throughout the countryside the unrealizable responsibilities of restructuring traditional agrarian practices with incomplete official support, for using untrained or poorly trained cadre to run generally shoddily made and poorly maintained machines, and for promising small rewards and actually giving even lesser ones. Even without the traditionally low motivation of rural Soviet society, such conditions would be any manager's nightmare.

On balance it is difficult to give Brezhnev's performance in Kazakhstan substantially higher marks than his predecessor's. Brezhnev's policy was more complex and displayed a better understanding of the needs of agriculture in modern society, but both Khrushchev and Brezhnev were ultimately defeated by the same problem that has thwarted Soviet leaders since the time of the revolution—that is, how to harness the peasantry (Russian or native) and make the system work to prescription. Khrushchev could plough under the Virgin Lands and grow cereal crops, but not very efficiently. Brezhnev, through more intensive techniques and better use of water and fertilizer, could increase yields somewhat, but when efficiency became critical to sustaining economic growth, as with an expanding herd, the increase disappeared. The regime was not able to motivate the peasantry to perform satisfactorily through emotional and ideological appeals, nor did the infrastructure of party and state ever wholly penetrate the countryside. The party remained a conveyor belt of instructions and commands, but because locally recruited cadre had to see to the routine enforcement of policy, the ultimate fate of most fiats remains a mystery. Even when properly trained cadre committed to Moscow's goals were imported, such as the many sovkhoz directors and raion officials in the Virgin Lands Region, they foundered on the realities of the Soviet system of management, which judges performance only by the achievement of stated goals, not by any fostering of long-term development. Good intentions and even training cannot help to meet the stated goals when spare parts are unavailable, truck drivers are in short supply, cattle feed is rotting, and grasslands are burning up from lack of water.

During the brief Andropov period, the replacement of cadre was employed as an incentive to achieve agricultural goals; both Andropov and Chernenko found it difficult to halt the decline, a situation that Gorbachev must redress if the Food Program goals for this region are to be met.

## THE TRANSFORMATION
## OF THE KAZAKH ECONOMY
## IN THE POST-STALIN PERIOD

The commitment made to industrialization and increased mineral extraction in Kazakhstan during World War II was intensified in the postwar period. Currently, only slightly more than 10 percent of the coal mined in the USSR comes from Kazakhstan, as does just less than 5 percent of the oil extracted; the republic produces just over 5 percent of the nation's electrical power and significant quantities of copper. Despite the impact of such changes on the republic's balance sheet, increased industrialization has had little effect on the employment patterns of the Kazakh population. The major agent of economic change among the Kazakh population has been the changing agricultural investment that came with the development of the Virgin Lands.

The Virgin Lands Policy transformed the traditional Kazakh livestock-breeding economy into a more scientific and centrally directed type of animal husbandry. Collectivization brought dramatic changes but not the complete destruction of the traditional authorities in the rural sector it had intended. The old generation of bais and aksakals largely died off, but kolkhoz chairmen often came from traditionally powerful families and many found the old ways of arbitrating disputes better than the new.

The livestock-breeding economy was modified in many critical ways. Over half the herd became "communally" owned, that is, it effectively belonged to the state; norms of production had to be met or no income was earned; long migrations were increasingly ancient history. Yet the Kazakhs maintained many strong links to past practices. Many sheep-raising kolkhozy had summer pasturelands that were physically separate from the kolkhoz site, to which part of the community traveled each summer. The verbal distinction—that they traveled, rather than migrated—allowed the Kazakhs to be considered officially settled, but most Kazakh shepherds preferred to depend on natural forage, so little fodder was prepared for winter. Moreover, the kolkhoz chairmen still preserved a great deal of discretion in managing the affairs of the community, and so marketable surplus was often sacrificed to preservation of the status quo. However satisfactory this situation might have been for the Kazakhs living in the countryside, it was very much at odds with the more efficient agricultural machine that Khrushchev envisaged, and the traditional way of life did not survive the changes brought by the Virgin Lands Policy.

The term "Virgin Lands" was itself a misnomer, probably deliberately. The six Kazakh oblasts included in the Virgin Lands territory may have produced little grain but were not unexploited, for they were Kazakh pasturelands.[35] The push to increase the amount of cereal grown in the Soviet Union was only one aspect of Khrushchev's agricultural policy, if the one best publicized, the goal of which was to increase greatly the production of all foodstuffs, including meat and milk. This meant that the Kazakhs had to increase livestock breeding just as more than 16 million hectares of grazing land were being ploughed under to plant grain. The question of how to feed even the existing herd, to say nothing of expanding it, led to the decision to plough under yet more land, over 8 million hectares; these were to be planted for animal feed, which could be stored for use in feedlots where animals would be fattened up more quickly and slaughtered at a higher weight.

The kolkhoz leadership was not expected to be enthusiastic about these changes; largely uneducated, they were seen as undependable cadre and bad risks for realizing the new reforms.[36] Hundreds of thousands of Kazakh households were shifted from kolkhozy to sovkhozy to place them under the direction of better-trained cadre. This transition, which resulted in the disbanding of six out of every seven kolkhozy, was begun in the mid-1950s and not completed for nearly a decade, although it was accomplished with relatively little physical movement of the population. Power shifted from the old elite to a new one, which was chosen on the basis of technical expertise.

Thus, Moscow had finally found an organizational device to reduce the role of the traditional local authorities; even when the sovkhoz movement began to decline in popularity in official circles at the end of the 1960s, there was no attempt to reintroduce the kolkhoz in the livestock-breeding regions of Kazakhstan. The sovkhozy helped make today's Kazakh economy—as well as the agricultural economy of the entire USSR—more diverse and more complex than it was at the time of Stalin's death; yet the magnitude of the changes in Kazakhstan were so great as to have fundamentally restructured the Kazakh economy, which may not be said for much of the rest of the country.

The biggest change was the enormous increase in the amount of worked land in the republic. Over 25 million hectares of land are now planted with cereal crops annually, an increase of 422 percent since 1950, and nearly 10 million hectares are sown with forage crops, an 806 percent increase over 1950. The greatest increases in the production of fodder have come in the Virgin Land oblasts, but several other oblasts have vastly expanded the amount of fodder grown as well.[37] Naturally, the Kazakhs have increasingly depended on mechanization to work the vast areas of land under their control, but neither the amount of machinery nor the trained personnel has expanded rapidly enough to meet local needs.[38]

The shift from free-range grazing to feedlots has allowed the Kazakh herd size to increase by 30 percent for the period 1950–1980, with the most striking changes in the number of sheep; nevertheless, the goal of 50 million Kazakh sheep is as elusive as ever. Growth in the rate of production in livestock breeding has faltered considerably since 1975 and for the first time lags behind agriculture. Moreover, the herd cannot expand much more without a corresponding increase in the amount of feed available, but unused arable land in Kazakhstan has all but disappeared, and new land cannot be developed without extensive irrigation. Many more irrigation schemes have appeared on the drawing board than in the field.

Inefficiency in livestock breeding has also been a growing problem, which with the increased dependence on mechanized equipment, such as shearing and milking machines, has had a high and rapidly accumulating cost. Yet where the new practices have been relatively well integrated into the rural economy, in oblasts such as Aktyubinsk and Alma-Ata, spectacular gains have been made, especially in sheep breeding. The dairy industry has generally prospered, in large part because of the feedlots. Changed practices in livestock breeding have increased the absolute number of cattle in all the Virgin Land oblasts.

The pattern of ownership of livestock has also changed. Today over half of all milk cows, nearly two-thirds of all horned cattle, and over three-fourths of all sheep belong to state farms.[39] Communal livestock breeding on kolkhozy has declined, but the private stock of the kolkhozniki make an important contribution to the economy; although the relative percentage of animals in the private sector has declined, the absolute number of such animals has increased. Without this contribution to the production of food, the economy would certainly founder, especially the dairy industry, since nearly 40 percent of all milk cows in Kazakhstan are privately owned.

The value of production of the private sector has remained almost constant throughout the post-Stalin period, at just under 20 percent, but the share of the sovkhoz sector has nearly doubled, now accounting for about two-thirds of the republic's agricultural output. By 1970 nearly 70 percent of all meat and wool and 80 percent of the milk produced in the republic came from state farms.[40] Investment priorities also changed in favor of the stronger sovkhoz sector; whereas in 1965 only 322 sovkhozy registered a profit and 1,185 a loss, by 1970 1,186 state farms were in the black and only 423 still showed a deficit.[41]

Moscow has continued its policy of disproportionate investment in the sovkhoz sector. Today there are five times more sovkhozy than kolkhozy in the republic (2,059 versus 418) but the total production fund of the state farms is 6.57 times greater, and the total agricultural fund is 6.76 times larger than the fund of the collective farms.[42]

Today over 90 percent of all kolkhoz chairmen have middle or higher education, and brigade leaders, too, have a comparable level of educational achievement. The kolkhozy themselves have also been reorganized and now average nearly 500 households each, with the average worked area nearly doubled to permit better use of mechanization. Average herd size per kolkhoz has increased and now almost equals that of the sovkhozy.[43] More efficient animal husbandry practices have also been introduced.

As the Kazakh economy has been transformed, its contribution to the all-union economy has both increased and diversified. The biggest change, of course, has been Kazakhstan's contribution to the production of cereal crops; in 1953 only about 7 million hectares of cereal crops were sown, in 1955 just over 16 million hectares, and by 1958 over 23 million hectares, a figure that has not increased appreciably since. Although Kazakhstan may have become an important source of grain, it has not been a dependable one; as elsewhere in the USSR, not only the absolute harvest but also yield per hectare has varied greatly from year to year. In some years the regime has been able to purchase as much as 20 million tons of grain from Kazakhstan, in others as little as five million tons.[44] The yield per hectare has varied from a high of 11.1 centners to a low of 2.9 centners; yields of 6–7 centners per hectare have been the most typical.[45] The Kazakh contribution to cultivation of cereal crops is hard to gauge, because the

Virgin Lands campaign imported rural labor from other parts of the Soviet Union—over 800,000 people by the end of Khrushchev's campaign, supplemented annually by thousands of temporary harvest workers.[46] In those areas of agriculture dominated by Kazakhs, technical crop cultivation has shown no real expansion while truck farming has doubled during the period.[47]

Livestock breeding, the mainstay of Kazakh agriculture, has become more important as a source of food in the post-Stalin period. The amount of meat, milk, and eggs produced annually has nearly tripled.[48] The Kazakh share of all meat slaughtered in the USSR rose from 5.03 percent in 1950 to 6.78 percent in 1978, and the relative yield of Kazakh livestock has improved faster than the all-union yield.

However, Kazakh agriculture and industry both contribute less to the all-Union economy than Moscow currently demands. The economic stagnation that the republic experienced during the first years of the Eleventh Five-Year Plan was reversed by the end of that period; the production growth rate increased by 4.5 percent in 1985 as opposed to 2.6 percent in both 1981 and 1982. Yet industrial output has continued to lag. During the most recent five-year plan, industrial output grew by only 19.4 percent as against a projected 23.4 percent increase, and labor productivity grew by 10.7 percent as opposed to the targeted 15.3 percent.[49]

In sum, the regime's goal of developing a modern agrarian economy in Kazakhstan has been neither wholly successful nor a total failure. The problems that the regime faces in Kazakhstan are real, but no more severe than elsewhere, and Kazakhstan's contribution to the all-union economy has been as steady and predictable as nature allows. In the past, Kazakhstan was a great disappointment to Moscow when its potential economic contribution was unrealized because of what, in Moscow's eyes, was cultural backwardness and parochial world view. The Kazakhstan of today is much better integrated into the federation of republics than was the Kazakhstan of 25 years ago; this integration has been achieved with Moscow's insistence but also with the assistance of a new Kazakh elite, who are rewarded for their performance by stable party careers at home and increased responsibilities in Moscow.

## D. A. KUNAEV AND THE COMMUNIST PARTY OF KAZAKHSTAN

The Communist Party of Kazakhstan has gained in prominence over the past 25 years, partly because of the role assigned it in opening the Virgin Lands and other efforts in economic policies, but also because L. I. Brezhnev spent two crucial years of his career in that republic. Brezhnev's direct impact on party organization in Kazakhstan was small, but the continuing, indirect impact has been great, for he continued to cultivate the contacts made during those years and promote cadre who worked well with him. Most prominent among these cadre was D. A. Kunaev, who served as first secretary of the Kazakh Communist Party until December 1986 and is the only Kazakh to have ever served in the Politburo. More important, over time Kunaev developed far beyond being a simple "house Kazakh"; he became the Kazakh party's agent in Moscow and during Brezhnev's lifetime used his increasing power to create a stable organizational base both in Kazakhstan and in Moscow. Kunaev's influence waned under Andropov, however, to such a degree that even the appointment as general secretary of his close friend Chernenko was unable to reverse the situation. Under Gorbachev Kunaev's authority has been further weakened, but a campaign encouraged by Moscow to wrest control of the Kazakh party from Kunaev has yet to succeed.

Even during the height of his power, Kunaev experienced mixed success in his attempt to reinvigorate and expand the Kazakh party. The Kazakh Communist Party has grown apace with the population but remains an elite organization, with less than 5 percent of the total population in its ranks. The current party in Kazakhstan has nearly 800,000 members, of whom about 35 percent are Kazakhs.

Kazakh participation in the lower organs probably remains high, but there is data on the ethnic composition of Kazakh party congresses, obkoms, gorkoms, and raikoms only for the Khrushchev years; after 1966 conclusions must be based on more general accounts, which results in an ambiguous picture. In 1954 and 1956 Kazakh participation in the lower organs was disproportionately high; nearly 45 percent of all convention delegates were Kazakh, while Kazakhs filled 48 percent of the obkom slots. By 1960 the influx of Russian party members for work in the Virgin Lands reduced Kazakhs to just one-third of all congress delegates, and Kazakhs made up about 30 percent of gorkom and raikom posts. Their participation in the obkoms nevertheless remained higher, near 40 percent.

The impact of the Virgin Lands program on the structure of the party at the local level is almost impossible to document.[50] Certainly the leadership structure for the six Virgin Land oblasts was all imported, but each new sovkhoz also had its own party cell, which was almost invariably headed by Russians or Ukrainians. The raikoms, which had authority over these new farms, also replaced the old Kazakh party leaders with more dependable Russian cadre. The logical conclusion of this process came in 1960, when the Virgin Lands territory was essentially seized from the Kazakh party and made answerable directly to Moscow.

These organizational changes were short-lived; Kunaev's return to power also brought back Kazakh–dominated patronage networks, and Kazakh participation in the party increased. In 1966, 43 percent of the delegates to the twelfth congress of the Communist Party of Kazakhstan were Kazakh, and Kazakh participation at the lower level remained high, although there is virtually no information about the attitudes or ideology of the current lower-party cadre in Kazakhstan nor about the functioning of the regional and subregional party organization. Certainly the cadre are better educated today than they were 25 years ago and are more likely to have a better understanding of technological society and its implications for Kazakhstan. By 1971 over 50 percent of all delegates to the thirteenth congress had completed some program of higher education, and even the training of rural cadre had improved; almost 40 percent of the sovkhoz and kolkhoz party first secretaries had completed higher education.[51]

One question of party function that has long interested Western observers is the operation of the *nomenklatura* system—that is, who draws up the list of candidates for each post from sovkhoz director to republic second secretary, and where the decisions are made. The question is even more complex in a national republic, where factors such as race and allegiance also enter in. Because of an excellent dissertation by an Australian, John Cleary, some of the questions may be answered, at least for Kazakhstan.[52] Cleary scrutinized the all-union and republic press from 1955 to 1964. He concludes that, while obkoms in theory controlled the appointment process for state-farm directors and kolkhoz chairmen and prepared the nomenklatura lists for raikom positions, in fact their recommendations were studied by the Kazakh central committee, which is dominated by Russians. Obkom appointments, in turn, are not only approved by Moscow but often originate there, as was certainly the case with the obkom first secretaries of the six Virgin Land oblasts. The republic-level appointments, particularly first and second secretaries, are made in Moscow with little or no consultation of the ranking membership of the Kazakh party; the implication is strong that first and second secretaries represent Moscow's interests and not those of the Kazakhs. The nine-year period Cleary studied showed that only two out of eleven individuals who served in these posts were Kazakhs, and none of the Russians posted to Kazakhstan had any previous contact with the region.[53]

Cleary portrays a republic with almost two distinct party and administrative apparatuses: one Kazakh, the other Russian. The latter was linked directly to Moscow with only minimal, even token, Kazakh participation; the former supervised the functioning of the livestock-breeding economy and controlled the raion-level party and state agencies. Only in a few, largely rural oblasts of southern and western Kazakhstan did the Kazakhs dominate the oblast organizations as well.[54]

The rest of the economy, which included cereal crop production, metallurgy, and industry, was controlled by Russians, who were aided by a few Kazakhs. Whereas the career patterns of the Kazakh cadre showed near exile to the rural sector, the Russians' careers often took them from sector to sector and from party to state; Russians also ran the republican party and state organizations, held all the key ministerial portfolios, and headed almost all the departments of the central committee, even though Kazakhs made up more than 40 percent of this committee. Individuals in leading party and state positions worked in their parallel organizations in close contact with Moscow and were subject to the approval of the Moscow apparat, even though nomenklatura lists were probably drawn up in Kazakhstan. Moscow took much less interest in who occupied traditionally Kazakh positions in the administrative hierarchy, such as heads of social security and communal economy and positions pertaining to cultural activities. For the individuals assigned to them, these positions generally proved to be administrative dead ends.

Cleary sees the relative position of the Kazakhs within their republic as likely to deteriorate further over time, and he concludes that:

> In the light of the long term demographic, linguistic and economic trends looked at here, the only conclusion open to the researcher is that the centralized bureaucratic system and its values must prevail over the forces of Kazakh nationalism. Natives still enjoy a privileged position in the sharing of power (appointment to elite positions), but one may expect to see continued erosion of this position at all levels.[55]

This prediction seemed reasonable in the 1960s, when Cleary was writing; the proportion of Kazakhs serving as obkom first secretaries dropped steadily between 1954 and 1964. By 1965, ten of the fifteen first secretaries were Russians or Ukrainians. Yet the erosion failed to occur, and Kazakh participation in their party and state hierarchies is much wider today than it was in 1964.

Cleary missed three factors, which together reversed the downward trend in the republic balance of power: the fact that the immigration of Slavs was temporary as it was linked to the Virgin Lands program, the demographic shift caused by the high Kazakh birthrate, and the powerful leadership of D. A. Kunaev over more than twenty years as first secretary. Under Kunaev, Kazakhs participated increasingly in the leadership of both party and state, whereas much of the old Russian dominance over native cadre broke down, particularly after 1971, when Kunaev became a full member of the Politburo. Many in the West assumed that Kunaev was a mere puppet for Brezhnev, an assimilated Kazakh with no ties to his people, but facts belie this conclusion. Although unquestionably loyal to Brezhnev, Kunaev used his loyalty to secure his own position and to reward his followers, which, unusually enough for a non-European party leader, included large numbers of Russians as well as Kazakhs. Kunaev had a strikingly varied career. Trained as a metallurgist, he made his reputation as the head of Kazakh industry during World War II and rose through the state apparat until he moved to the top echelons of the Kazakh party. As the party first secretary, Kunaev gained both experience in agriculture and new friends from that side of the economy.

Kunaev worked well with Russians and rewarded them nicely as his own power has increased, but not at the expense of the careers of his co-nationals. Whereas Kazakh membership in the party buro has remained constant at around 45 percent, in 1981 the Kazakhs constituted 51.9 percent of the Central Committee. Kazakhs also headed 47 percent of the Central Committee department, although the key economic departments of heavy industry, agriculture, and construction continued to be run by Russians, as was the department of agitation and propaganda. Although since 1981 over 500 new people assumed nomenklatura posts in Kazakhstan,[56] there is no evidence that this generational transition has been accompanied by a change in the pattern of Kazakh representation in the senior party hierarchy.

Kazakh participation in the government has also increased; whereas in 1964 only 33 percent of the members of the Council of Ministers were Kazakh, by 1981 Kazakhs held 60 percent of the posts, and the Kazakh share of ministerial and state chair positions increased from 39 to 61 percent. Even more important is that Kazakhs today are occupying more of the key posts; Kazakhs have served as ministers of heavy industry, agriculture, and construction. Under Kunaev a Kazakh has even served as head of the KGB.

Because he was a member of the Politburo, Kunaev had more personal discretion than previous first secretaries of Kazakhstan, as is shown in the pattern of appointment for republic second secretaries. In Kazakhstan, as in the other republics, Moscow usually named Russians who had no prior association with the republic in which they were to serve; yet the two most recent individuals named to this post—A. G. Korkin (who served from 1976 to 1979) and O. S. Miroshkin, the current second secretary—both had had long careers within the Kazakh party organization before assuming their posts. Not only was each candidate endorsed by Kunaev, but it appears that it was on Kunaev's own initiative that Miroshkin was named second secretary and Korkin went to Karaganda as obkom first secretary, in an attempt to improve the coal industry in Karaganda.

There have also been important changes in the appointment process for obkom first secretaries, where Kunaev's discretionary power was equally apparent. Greater use was made of Kazakhs than previously; in 1981 there were eleven Kazakh oblast first secretaries in the republic, which was 57.9 percent of the total. Moreover, the career patterns of these eleven are quite different from those of the Kazakh first secretaries two decades ago. They are better educated (five of the eleven have been to higher party school) and their careers show more diversity; six, while working exclusively in the agricultural sector, have moved not only between oblasts but also between state and party posts, and four showed mixed careers of broad experience in both the industrial and the agricultural sector. The backgrounds of the Russian obkom first secretaries are equally interesting, at least for those seven (of eight) for whom information is available. For one thing, Russian cadre are no longer drawn only from outside the republic. Six of the first secretaries have been associated with the Kazakh party apparat for all or most of their careers; only one, the obkom first secretary for Eastern Kazakhstan, was appointed directly from outside the republic, and he has held his present position since 1969. Moreover, even the Russians appointed by Gorbachev in 1985 and 1986 to undercut Kunaev's power have all come from within the republic.

Kunaev clearly dominates the Kazakh party, which no longer shows the rift between Russian and Kazakh cadre that was evident in the 1960s. The Kazakhs have been effectively integrated into the party apparat, in part because a Kazakh controls patronage. National differences undoubtedly remain; many key posts in the central party apparat as well as the obkom first secretaryships in the Virgin Land oblasts still appear definitionally reserved for Russians. While Brezhnev was alive, Kunaev had Moscow's absolute trust because he long ago convinced the Soviet leadership that he shared the late general secretary's vision of a modern Kazakh economy that could make a strong contribution to the economy of the Soviet Union. He has also nurtured and promoted a Kazakh cadre who share his vision and who in turn have devoted themselves to the creation of a modern Kazakhstan, working as a team with their Russian counterparts.

For this significant accomplishment Kunaev was generously rewarded, first promoted to candidate and then to full membership on the Politburo. Since that time, Kunaev has used this position to bring his supporters to Moscow; there were ten Kazakhs on the Central Committee elected at the Twenty-sixth Party Congress, including six obkom first secretaries and two senior Russian officials from the republic apparat. At least five other Russians on the Central Committee had long associations with Kazakhstan and may well owe their subsequent promotions to Kunaev.

Kunaev's fortunes waned after his mentor's death. Kunaev seems to have been punished by both Andropov and Gorbachev for advocating the continuation of the Brezhnev policy lines. During 1983–1984 two longtime obkom first secretaries were removed and replaced with younger men, and in December 1983 the Kazakh Komsomol was singled out for particular criticism as a model of what a republic Komsomol organization should not be.[57] Shortly after, the longtime chairman of the Kazakh Council of Ministers was replaced. However, Andropov and Chernenko's deaths found Kunaev still in place.

What is more surprising is that Kunaev's leadership managed to survive Gorbachev's eighteen-month long attack. In the months preceding the twenty-seventh party congress of the CPSU, three additional obkom first secretaries were removed in disgrace, one of whom was a member of the Central Committee.[58] In addition, the failings of the Kazakh party organization received discussion in *Pravda*.[59] But Kunaev skillfully used the sixteenth party congress of the Kazakh Communist Party to attack his foes within his republic party,[60] and he won re-election as first secretary there. *Pravda*'s account of this event clearly reflected the displeasure of some in Moscow.[61] Shortly after the Kazakh Party Congress three more obkom first secretaries were dismissed, as were the head of Kazakh Gosplan and the president of the Kazakh Academy of Sciences, who was Kunaev's half-brother. A month later, at the conclusion of the CPSU congress, Kunaev was re-elected to the Politburo, but the number of obkom first secretaries from Kazakhstan in the Central Committee fell from six to three, with three others confirmed as candidate members. Kunaev was not retained as head of the Kazakh party, and he also failed to appoint his own successor. He was replaced by Gennadii Kolbin, first secretary of the Ulianovsk obkom and formerly a second secretary of the Georgian S.S.R.

Moscow has printed millions of reams of paper praising proletarian internationalism and the glories of the Soviet multiethnic state, but until G. A. Aliev's promotion to first deputy prime minister of the USSR in December 1983, Kunaev's accomplishments and his place in Moscow's hierarchy remained unique. These accomplishments remain impressive. While ethnic separatism and the racial delegation of responsibility still seem to be the Soviet norms, they were no longer widely practiced in Kazakhstan. Part of the explanation may be that the Kazakhs are only a plurality, not a majority, in their own republic; however, the Kirgiz are in the same position, and there is no similar multiethnic pattern in Kirgizia. National peculiarities of the Kazakhs, such as their long history of bilingualism and the weak hold of Islam, may also explain Kazakhstan's seeming success in "resolving" the national problem in party politics. The political coalitions of Kunaev's Kazakhstan do not appear to have been formed solely, or even predominantly, on ethnic grounds. They appear to be based on loyalties for or against Kunaev or one of his potential successors, and there are both Russians and Kazakhs in each of the major cliques in the Kazakh party.

Kunaev's "retirement" was quietly reported on December 17, 1986. But the news that he had been replaced by a Russian, and one who had no previous ties with the republic, triggered widespread rioting in Alma-Ata. The situation was so severe that news of the disturbances was made public in the Soviet media. Western sources reported two hundred injured and up to a thousand jailed. A special commission headed by M. S. Solomentsev was sent to Kazakhstan to calm the situation, which was considered quite serious by Moscow because the rioters seemed to include Kazakh university students, Komsomol members, and even "volunteer" public order officials. How these riots will affect Gorbachev's long-term plans to restructure Kazakhstan's party organization still remains to be seen.

# 11 Conclusion

The Kazakh people have had in effect two foreign rulers in the past century and a half: the tsarist government and the Communist Party. Although the Bolsheviks asserted their distinctiveness and superiority to their tsarist predecessors, from the Kazakh point of view both regimes had much in common. Both were Russian, both tried to end Kazakh nomadism, and both tried to make the Kazakh a citizen of a Russian–dominated multiethnic state.

The goal of Russian imperial policy in the steppe had been to control Kazakh land by settling several million Russian peasants on it; by their example these settlers were to turn the Kazakhs into farmers. The policy was partially successful, but left the Kazakh pastoral nomads without a viable economic form; since little was done systematically to introduce agriculture among the Kazakhs, the average Kazakh was in worse shape on the eve of revolution than he had been at the beginning of colonial rule. Tsarist rule had also introduced real strains into the Kazakh social community. The clan and religious authorities could not easily serve the Russian state; soon a rival elite developed, the graduates of the secular schools, who though small in number sought to mediate between the Kazakh masses and the Russian state. These people served in the state bureaucracy employed as teachers, translators, and state inspectors, and they filled new modern functions working as journalists, writers, and even revolutionaries, but they did not acquire any real legitimacy within the Kazakh community. The old elite did no better, however; they had the general support of their population but lacked legitimacy in the eyes of the imperial administration. After the violent and widespread uprising of 1916, the Russian authorities did not know to whom to turn to administer the fractious Kazakh population: the ineffectual new elite or the disloyal traditional authorities.

The Russian Revolution ended the dilemma of the colonial administrators. Although the Kazakhs were suspicious of their new Russian rulers, the Bolsheviks, they were more interested in ending wartime conditions and reintroducing some economic stability. The defeat of the Alash Orda, combined with the memory of the extreme economic policies of pre-NEP Bolshevism, left many Kazakhs wary, but as the party recruitment drives of the early 1920s brought many of their kinsmen into the new Soviet government, apparently as full partners, most Kazakhs had little choice but to acquiesce and give the new government a chance.

The Bolsheviks, nevertheless, quickly reaffirmed all Kazakh prejudices against the Russians. Not only did Kazakh participation in their own republic rapidly become symbolic, but by the late 1920s Soviet federalism itself became a sham. Moscow made abundantly clear that its centrally controlled development strategy would favor the needs of the center above those of the periphery, the requirements of industrialization over those of agriculture, and, of course, the interests of Russians over those of Kazakhs. The development strategy chosen—that is, collectivization and nationalization of almost all property in the rural sector—was especially devastating to the Kazakhs; traditional Kazakh culture defined a man through the animals he owned, making private ownership of livestock almost the definition of what it was to be a Kazakh. As might be expected, then, the Kazakhs strongly resisted nationalization and when necessary sacrificed their lives and the lives of their animals to try to prevent its introduction. The Kazakh community that survived confiscation was a broken one, its traditional leadership weakened and stripped of many age-old functions; the survivors were malleable and hence of greater value as Soviet citizens.

For those Kazakhs willing to participate in the new government and possessing technical skills as well as a suitably unblemished past, the postpurge period gave unprecedented opportunity for upward mobility. Party membership virtually assured a young Kazakh a sinecure for life, and the more aggressive and hard-working individuals could rise as high as their ambitions demanded. The children of simple shepherds no longer had to share their fathers' fates if they were willing to pay the cost of participation, which was formal subscription to an official ideology that asserted the primacy of Moscow over all the republics and the superiority of the Russian culture over all national ones.

This formula has not substantially changed over time. The Kazakh aspirant who wants to rise in oblast, republic, or all-union politics must still be Russian-speaking (ideally, fluent) and must look and behave as a Russian does. He need not *be* assimilated but he should *appear* assimilated, so as not to "stick out" in Russian-dominated settings any more than his unusual facial characteristics make necessary. The Kazakh candidate must also work harder than his

Russian competitor and prove himself even more loyal. He must demonstrate a commitment to Moscow's goals and endorse its development strategy as the only way that true Kazakh development could be achieved: on the Russian-paved road to communism.

Even this narrow avenue to advancement appears to have worked, both in the past and today. Kazakhstan is a quiescent part of the Soviet Union, not inconsequentially, since Kazakhstan borders on China. As Moscow's attention to ideological vigilance in the border area has increased in recent years, so too has praise for the success of Kazakh efforts in this area. Even very disruptive policies, such as the Virgin Lands drive and the attempt to transform Kazakh livestock breeding, did not provoke any direct resistance from the Kazakh population.[1] The Kazakh party has been reinvigorated in the past two decades by a much greater and more significant Kazakh participation in both republic-level and all-union administration than at any time since the early 1920s.

This narrow avenue is not, however, a guarantee for the future, particularly since Moscow's strategy has built into it potentially dangerous contradictions, encouraging as it does economic and social development within a framework of ideological conformity. The regime is adamant that Moscow and only Moscow may define a citizen's political belief system. The national minorities have been allowed somewhat greater latitude on ideological questions by Stalin's successors, but the regime remains committed to an assimilationist strategy; Russian language and culture form the matrix in which all the national cultures are to be absorbed.

As Western analysts have long maintained, it appears to be impossible to encourage economic and social change without encouraging political development as well.[2] Soviet analysts also seem sensitive to this, and they share the need to channel and control political aspirations that are raised as modernization proceeds.[3] The Soviet model of political socialization, which saturates all media with propaganda and introduces a strong political component in education from nursery school through higher education, has undoubtedly seriously modified political attitudes in Kazakhstan. However, in this era of nation-states, there is ample evidence that it is impossible to cut a people off entirely from its past or totally to restructure that past to fit the designs of a foreign ruler. The Soviet strategy has certainly succeeded in achieving not only mass literacy but also a relatively well educated and technologically sophisticated population and a new Kazakh Soviet elite to staff the party and state organizations. Nevertheless, this elite, although loyal to their Soviet fatherland, is not as malleable as the Soviet leadership would like, especially in the academic and artistic establishments, which wage constant battles with Moscow over the limits of Kazakh self-expression and the definition of cultural conformity. Examples of this are seen in the efforts of intellectuals to develop their literature to recreate their history, to promote the study and use of the Kazakh language, and to preserve and protect their architectural landmarks.

Moscow faces problems not only from the Kazakh elite but from the Kazakh masses as well. Stalin's strategy of social development still remains in effect. His successors have achieved political socialization, but they concentrated on creating a loyal elite large enough to run the system successfully; although the complete social and political transformation of the masses is desired, only limited resources have been devoted to trying to achieve it. Schools have been built, but rural education has long lagged behind urban education, particularly in the national schools. The only other active social policy is the state's antireligious program, which closed mosques and religious schools in the 1930s and again in the 1960s, and which dramatically limited the number of Muslim clergy. The so-called antisocial influence of the family and traditional culture is criticized but otherwise left alone; the regime apparently prefers to view the Kazakhs (and other Muslims) as second-class citizens who nonetheless have an elemental political loyalty. The regime has made a minimal commitment to this population and has received an equally minimal commitment in return.

This strategy only works when minimal demands are made upon this population; the changing demographic parameters of the Soviet Union may well alter the equation significantly.[4] The Russians and Ukrainians who formed a majority of the population of Kazakhstan throughout the 1940s and 1950s, and a plurality in the 1960s and 1970s, will fall to minority status in the 1980s or 1990s. As the Russian population declines and the Muslim population swells, these "second-class citizens" will have to take a more active role in the technical areas of the economy and in the armed services or else force the Soviet leadership to alter their aspirations for sustained economic growth and military superiority.[5]

This changing demographic balance is quite clearly a problem in Kazakhstan, where Russians have long enjoyed numerical dominance over the Kazakhs. The Kazakhs have a much higher birthrate than the Russians, and although this birthrate has begun to decline, the Kazakh population within the republic is likely to increase at nearly three times the rate of the European population for the foreseeable future.[6] The average Kazakh family size is between five and six members, and a survey of Kazakh women done in the mid-1970s indicated that most Kazakh women both wanted and expected to have five or more children, whereas the Russians anticipated having only two or three. The Kazakhs are now 36 percent of the population of the Kazakh S.S.R; barring an unforeseen immigration of Europeans, their proportional strength can only continue to grow.

As this happens, the traditional attitudes of the Kazakh masses that Moscow has grudgingly accepted in the past may become more threatening, with potential political overtones, in the future. However, traditional values appear less entrenched in Kazakhstan than in Central Asia in general: the education rate is higher,[7] women are better integrated in the economy,[8] there is greater occupational differentiation,[9] and social functions of Islam have been diminished, although religion like the legacy of Kazakh pastoralism is still an element of traditional culture.[10] Still, the Kazakh masses, and especially those in the countryside, are not only culturally distinct from their Russian counterparts but are also farther away from attaining the regime's desired social and political norms. In some regions of western Kazakhstan—particularly on the Mangyshlak Peninsula, which is the territory of the Adaev Kazakhs—many cultural practices remain largely unchanged from the prerevolutionary period. In this desert region livestock are still raised much as they were in the past, even though sheep may now graze on lands adjacent to missile silos. Even in less remote environs traditional practices are still quite strong.

It is still common for three generations to reside together, and this is true of rural party members as well as of kolkhoz officials.[11] The role of the elder is still revered, and in ethnically homogeneous settlements elders may have their status confirmed by being named kolkhoz chairmen or brigade leaders. Parental authority is still strong; marriage must receive parental sanction.[12] Although the kalym is banned, the bride's father still traditionally receives costly gifts, usually in the form of livestock, from the family of the groom; a wedding is almost always celebrated by a religious ceremony. Sharp distinctions continue between male and female social and economic tasks. Women leave school early[13] and marry young, by the age of eighteen or nineteen; marriage at sixteen and seventeen is not uncommon.

What must deeply disturb the Soviet policymakers is that an individual's place in the rural community is determined not by his origins nor by his ideological position. While power and authority are respected, the ordinary Kazakh judges character much as his ancestors did, that is, by whether a man is a good father, a good son, and, most important, a good herdsman, someone with "keen knowledge of folk meteorology . . . phenological observations, signs, herbage peculiarities accumulated by the people during the centuries."[14] Although technical education has increased among the Kazakhs faster than among the Central Asians, a shortage of trained cadre persists, in part because many Kazakhs prefer not to seek higher or specialized secondary education if it means leaving their communities.[15]

Probably most threatening to the regime is the continued pervasiveness of Islam, which is difficult to gauge. If recent materials are accurate, up to 50 percent of the population in some rural areas may be practicing Muslims.[16] Moreover, most people give at least ceremonial importance to religion to commemorate birth, marriage, and death; circumcision, the Muslim mark of manhood, is still universal. The major Muslim holidays remain feast days and may still be commemorated by ritual slaughters. Islam is particularly vital in southern Kazakhstan, where thousands of pilgrims come annually to visit the mausoleum of Hodja Ahmed Sultan in the Chimkent oblast or to pray at one of several shrines in the Dzhambul oblast.[17]

It is quite difficult to estimate the percentage of practicing Muslims among the urban population. Reports of large crowds at the mosques during Ramadan provide some evidence of the presence of religious practitioners in the city, as do the articles from *Muslims of the Soviet East* that recount requests for the opening of new mosques.[18] There is reason to believe that increasing numbers of Kazakh youth are turning to Islam to fill the moral void that many growing up in Soviet society today seem to feel. One Kazakh sociologist, N. S. Sarsenbaev, notes this obliquely when he concludes that if communist ideology does not answer man's need for a well defined moral code, he will seek to find faith in religion.[19]

The continued strength of religion clearly disturbs the Soviet regime. Kunaev emphasized the ideological danger it poses in his address to the sixteenth congress of the Communist Party of Kazakhstan. Most troublesome, he maintained, was the fact that Islam was not only not declining in influence but that many party members accepted and even encouraged the observance of religious customs. Kunaev cited the antireligious official from the Dzhezkazgan oblast who had sent to Alma-Ata to get a mullah to bury a relative.[20] Similar criticisms of the lack of party vigilance in this area have appeared wtih increasing frequency in recent years in both the party and Komsomol press.

Some Soviet scholars argue that religious and customary practices need not threaten Moscow. Sarsenbaev, for example, maintains that the Soviets have eliminated the economic basis of traditional society but not the social influence of traditional society on Kazakh daily life. Removing all traces of traditionalism, which includes Islam, is a slow process and may even be impossible, a conclusion that Sarsenbaev implies but does not state. Nevertheless, he is not unduly alarmed, because he argues that traditional values do not definitionally impede the goals of the regime.[21]

Yet it is quite clear that many in Moscow do not share Sarsenbaev's views and fear the influence of both religious beliefs and religious authorities as sources of ideology and authority that challenge the moral supremacy of the state. One trend that Moscow finds dangerous is the explicit link of Islam and nationalism that is made by some Central Asian and Kazakh clergy. These people emphasize that the cultural distinction of the Kazakhs is based in part on their religious heritage, in an attempt to encourage the nonbeliever to discover the religious teachings that explain and form many cultural practices. The Soviets have taken strong exception to the argument that the Muslim *umma* (community) is a nation; they argue that the Central Asian clergy give their people a false consciousness that reduces their loyalty to their "true" nations (that is, to the Kazakhs, Kirgiz, Uzbeks, and so forth).

This understanding of Islam plagues the regime, because it threatens the premise that religion is an enemy to be combated by party faithful and because it transforms religion into neutral or even into positive cultural forces. In his 1975 work, *Islam and Nation*, N. Ashirov wrote that some intellectual and party elite of Central Asia have tacitly accepted Islam as an important component of their national history and cultural heritage and that it is therefore worth preservation or at least special treatment by the regime.[22] Ashirov's argument is now commonly accepted and readily repeated. In recent years Kazakh ideologists have underscored the error of equating religion and nationalism, criticizing the regional party leadership for tolerance and even practice of Islam and criticizing the writers and historians for an all too sympathetic portrayal of Islam.

A group of Kazakh writers and historians has provided particular trouble for the regime because of their preoccupation with the Kazakh past and with the historical figures who helped shape it.[23] These individuals seek the right to present a Kazakh-centered view of history, one which implicitly rejects Moscow's contention that all history must be told from the Russian point of view. However, these people are often treated as though they have taken the first step toward ideological heresy. A case in point is the book *Az i Ia* (Alma-Ata, 1975), by the poet Olzhas Suleimenov, which seeks to retell the "Igor's tale" from a Turkic perspective. After the publication of the book, Suleimenov faced an officially organized attack at a joint meeting of the sections of history and language and literature of the Academy of Sciences of the USSR.[24] Suleimenov's injustices to history were recounted by the renowned medievalist, Academician Likhachev, and the book was removed from circulation. Suleimenov was driven to make a public recantation, which appeared as a letter to the editor in the March 19, 1977, issue of *Kazakhstanskaia Pravda*. The uproar also provided some sense of the bounds of the permissible. Kazakh scholars may study individuals who opposed Russian conquest, but the conquest itself must still be depicted as voluntary submission by the Kazakhs, since Russian contact with the Kazakhs must always be construed as positive. Because Suleimenov's book reversed this relationship and denied the Russians a central role in the history of the medieval period, Moscow reacted furiously.

Still, Kazakh intellectuals remain preoccupied with preserving the historical legacy of their past, particularly since the economic policies of the 1960s and 1970s obliterated the nomadic way of life in all but the desert regions of the republic. These intellectuals, like many of their Third World counterparts, are glorifying a past that poses them no direct risk. They no longer have to suffer the wrath of the traditional leadership, and so the past may be romanticized. Many prominent contemporary Kazakh poets—such as O. Suleimenov and K. Murzaliev—and novelists—such as S. Sanbaev, A. Alimzhanov, and I. Esenberlin—have made their reputations from works that rely heavily on historical themes in a tradition as old as Kazakh oral literature iteslf. Some of these writers, such as Suleimenov and Sanbaev, talk about the old values and tell tales about nomadic life before the revolution; others write historical novels about important personages in Kazakh history, such as Esenberlin's *Khan Kene* (1971, about Kenisary Kasimov) and *Kochevniki* (1979, a three-volume portrait of Khan Abu'l Khayr).

These books, romantic treatments of times long past, reflect the influence of socialist realism as much as of traditional Kazakh themes; they are in no way meant to incite Kazakhs to resist Russians. The books were published and many were widely distributed and translated as well; they are meant to portray the distinctive heritage of which all Kazakhs should be proud. However, Moscow tends to view any increase in Kazakh national self-awareness as dangerous and so watches the Kazakh authors closely. One literary critic, himself a Kazakh, articulated the official position in *Pravda*:

> through closer acquaintance with the varied literary output in the historical genre one can easily tell that the original idea of integrally examining the past in terms of its causal relations with the present has not been realized. The stress has shifted in the direction of primary attention to the past itself. In other words history has entered literature, but the principles of historicism have not yet been genuinely affirmed in it.[25]

*Literaturnoe obozrenie* in 1974 ran two critiques of a pair of novellas, set in Mangyshlak at the end of the nineteenth century, written by S. Sanbaev. In a short concluding piece, the editors of *Literaturnoe obozrenie* criticized Sanbaev for non-Marxist glorification of the past for its own sake:

> In 'Kop-Azhal' the hero tries to tell us that fidelity to the traditions of the eagle hunter has helped him to become a hero of the Great Patriotic War. Tradition is tradition. But the heroic feats of Soviet man are produced by the force of Soviet patriotism and not by the inertia of tradition.[26]

The Kazakh literary establishment continues to come under attack. At the fourteenth congress of the Kazakh Communist Party, First Secretary D. A. Kunaev criticized the Kazakh literary establishment (including the Kazakh Writers' Union and the editorial board of *Gosizdat KazS.S.R.*) for routinely publishing ideologically weak works.[27] Kunaev returned to this theme in his report to the fifteenth congress, attacking the republic's film establishment for its romantic obsession with the past.

Actual punishment, curiously, has been far less severe than the criticism. Soon after Anuar Alimzhanov was replaced as head of the Kazakh Writers' Union, a major two-volume collection of his works appeared.[28] Similarly, in April 1981 the Kazakh film industry was placed under the supervision of

Olzhas Suleimenov, and in December 1983 he was named first secretary of the Kazakh Writers' Union.

Still, the public rebukes demonstrate that Moscow considers such works potentially dangerous; preoccupation with the past has long been understood as a manifestation of national consciousness. One danger of the current Kazakh literary and historical revival is that it may strengthen the bond between a Kazakh secular identity (which is permitted) and a Kazakh Muslim identity. Such a connection has already been made once, during the revolution, when the Kazakh nationalists tried to unify their people; it might be made again if *Qazaqshylyk* (Kazakhness) takes on a more explicitly Muslim cast.

For now the marriage of intellectual elite and religious elite appears to be one of convenience, particularly for the intellectuals, whose views are mild in comparison to the cultural exclusivity preached by the Muslim clergy. Still, it is difficult to predict which group Moscow will find more threatening, since the Muslim mullahs can always be dismissed as definitionally anti-Marxist and vestiges of the past that will fade with time. The philosophy of the Kazakh intellectuals is far more difficult to categorize and may ultimately be more dangerous.

Apparently harmless demands for greater Kazakh cultural self-determination potentially threaten the status quo, although the search for a modern Kazakhstan has thus far been restricted to cultural issues, which do not seem to worry Moscow. Some of the Kazakh requests—such as better Kazakh-language education and more cultural autonomy (witness Suleimenov's reinstatement)—appear to have been met, and Moscow's attack on erring Kazakhs has been relatively low-key. Were the Kazakhs to demand greater control of their economic and political lives, they would be unlikely to receive a mild response.

The writings and teachings of the current generation of Kazakh intellectuals pose yet another threat, that is, to the ideological control that the leadership in Moscow considers its exclusive domain. Suleimenov and his followers implicitly argue that ideology is dynamic and that the official Russo-centrist view is not definitional to either Marxism or communism. This challenges the regime at its core of power; the party elite regulates doctrinal purity as the logical extension of Marxist-Leninist doctrine. Now, as in the 1920s, some Kazakhs and other Central Asians seem to be asking to interpret ideology and to better integrate it with their own cultural values, including some of the cultural and moral values of Islam. Yet, unlike in the 1920s, the Muslims today are not easily contained. The absolute number and relative proportion of Muslims in the USSR is growing steadily. Within the next generation Muslims will be between one-fourth and one-third of the Soviet populace. Furthermore, courtesy of Soviet education, Central Asian intellectuals are able to reach a far larger audience than ever before. Faced with imminent minority status, the

Russian leadership is thus caught in a bind; whereas in theory the Russians should assert cultural superiority to reinforce their political control, they are instead fighting to keep from losing ground against the national minorities who are challenging them, attempting to reclaim their histories, and reasserting their rights to cultural self-determination.

The impact of the tradition of Kazakh secular nationalism on present political developments in Kazakhstan is difficult to assess, but some points are clear. A minority in their own republic, the Kazakhs have managed to exert strong control not only in their political life but in cultural, social, and religious affairs as well; they have politicized cultural issues in a way that other Central Asian nationalities have not. As a result they have managed to preserve at least part of their history from complete reinterpretation by the Soviets. Their literature is strongly linked to that of the prerevolutionary period, and although heavily ideological hack writers exist whose works receive wide distribution, they do not overshadow the large group of serious Kazakh writers.

The Kazakhs are a national minority in a multiethnic state and as such face certain difficulties. Like all the Muslim minorities who were absorbed into the Russian empire, they have confronted the dilemma of how to weigh their own culture against the dominant culture of the Russians. However, the early Kazakh secular nationalists—in part because Islam has always had an ambiguous status in the steppe—did not choose cultural exclusivity. Instead they chose to modify and adopt their culture, and so they have managed to survive as a culturally distinct people, able even to compete with the Russians for control of their social and, to a lesser extent, political life. This choice was reaffirmed by the nationalists' descendants as well. The present Kazakh intellectual elite seems committed to this same strategy of cultural adaptation, first to attain cultural survival and ultimately to achieve full control. If Moscow completely loses the allegiance of this Kazakh elite, it will face grave problems both within and outside of Kazakhstan. Unless Moscow takes measures to repair the allegiance in post-Kunaev Kazakhstan, the Alma-Ata riots could prove to be the prelude to another long period of Russian-Kazakh antagonism.

# APPENDIXES

## APPENDIX 1
## POPULATION OF THE KAZAKH S.S.R. BY NATIONALITY

|  | 1959 | | 1970 | | 1979 | |
|---|---|---|---|---|---|---|
|  | *Number* | *Percentage* | *Number* | *Percentage* | *Number* | *Percentage* |
| Kazakh | 2,787,309 | 30.0 | 4,234,166 | 32.6 | 5,289,349 | 36.0 |
| Russian | 3,972,042 | 42.7 | 5,521,917 | 42.4 | 5,991,205 | 40.8 |
| German | 658,698 | 7.1 | 858,077 | 6.6 | 900,207 | 6.1 |
| Ukrainian | 761,432 | 8.2 | 933,461 | 7.2 | 897,964 | 6.1 |
| Tatar | 191,680 | 2.1 | 287,712 | 2.2 | 313,460 | 2.1 |
| Uzbek | 135,932 | 1.5 | 216,340 | 1.7 | 263,295 | 1.8 |
| Belorussian | 107,348 | 1.2 | 198,275 | 1.5 | 181,491 | 1.2 |
| Uighur | 59,840 | 0.6 | 120,881 | 0.9 | 147,943 | 1.0 |
| Korean | 74,019 | 0.8 | 81,598 | 0.6 | 91,984 | 0.6 |
| Dungan | 9,980 | 0.1 | 17,284 | 0.1 | 22,491 | 0.2 |
| Other | 536,461 | 5.7 | 539,015 | 4.2 | 584,894 | 4.1 |
| TOTAL | 9,294,741 | 100.0 | 13,008,726 | 100.0 | 14,684,283 | 100.0 |

SOURCES: Tsentral'noe statisticheskoe upravlenie SSSR, *Itogi vsesoiuznoi perepisi naseleniia 1970 goda. Tom IV. Natsional'nyi sostav naseleniia SSSR* (Moscow, 1973), table 2; and Tsentral'noe statisticheskoe upravlenie SSSR, *Chislennost' i sostav naseleniia SSSR* (Moscow, 1984), table 22.

# APPENDIX 2
## ADMINISTRATIVE DIVISIONS OF THE KAZAKH S.S.R.
## (POPULATION STATISTICS FROM 1980)

The Kazakh S.S.R. was originally constituted as the Kirgiz ASSR (a part of the RSFSR) on August 26, 1920. It was renamed the Kazakh ASSR in April 1925. Kazakhstan achieved full republic status on December 5, 1936, when it was reconstituted as the Kazakh S.S.R. It occupies the territory from 55°26′–40°56′N and from 45°27′–87°18′E. The republic thus spans the territory from the lower course of the Volga River in the west to the Altai Mountains in the east, and from the Western-Siberian lowlands in the north to the Tien-Shan Mountains in the south. Kazakhstan borders on the RSFSR to the north, the Kirgiz, Uzbek, and Turkmen S.S.R.s to the south, China to the east, and the Caspian Sea to the west. This is an area of 2,717,300 sq. km., making this republic second only to the RSFSR in size.

*Aktyubinsk Oblast*

population: 641,000 (54% urban)
territory: 298,700 sq. km.
oblast organized: March 1932
administrative center: Aktyubinsk (pop. 197,000)
economic base: ferrous metallurgy, chemical industry, heavy industry, and some
   livestock breeding and farming

*Alma-Ata: Capital of the Republic*

population: 932,000
territory: 200 sq. km.
founded in 1854 as Russian settlement of Vernyi, renamed Alma-Ata (in Kazakh,
   Alma Ati) in 1921 and designated the capital city in May 1929

*Alma-Ata Oblast*

population: 860,000 (excluding the city of Alma-Ata) (19% urban)
territory: 104,700 sq. km.
oblast organized: March 1932 from part of former Semirech'e guberniia
administrative center: Alma-Ata
economic base: heavy industry, metal work, food and woodworking industries

*Chimkent Oblast*

population: 1,592,000 (40% urban)
territory: 116,300 sq. km.
oblast organized: March 1932 from part of former Syr Darya guberniia
administrative center: Chimkent (pop. 327,000)
other large cities: Turkestan (pop. 69,000)

economic base: nonferrous metallurgy, heavy industry, and some light industry. Major cotton growing region of Kazakhstan.

### Dzhambul Oblast

population: 940,000 (45% urban)
territory: 144,600 sq. km.
oblast organized: October 1939 from part of former Syr Darya guberniia
administrative center: Dzhambul (pop. 270,000), formerly known as Aulie Ata
economic base: flood-irrigated agriculture and livestock breeding, with some mixed industry

### Dzhezkazgan Oblast

population: 453,000 (77% urban)
territory: 313,400 sq. km.
oblast organized: March 1973 from part of Karaganda oblast
administrative center: Dzhezkazgan (pop. 92,000)
other large cities: Balkhash (pop. 74,000) and Nikoskii (pop. 51,000)
economic base: nonferrous metallurgy and some ferrous metallurgy

### Eastern Kazakhstan Oblast

population: 884,000 (61% urban)
territory: 97,300 sq. km.
oblast organized: March 1932 from part of former Semipalatinsk guberniia
administrative center: Ust-Kamenogorsk (pop. 280,000)
other large cities: Leninogorsk (pop. 68,000) and Zyryanovsk (pop. 52,000)
economic base: nonferrous metallurgy, heavy industry, and most important, the generation of electrical energy

### Guryev Oblast

population: 373,000 (59% urban)
territory: 112,000 sq. km.
oblast organized: January 1938 from part of former Uralsk guberniia
administrative center: Guryev (pop. 134,000)
economic base: oil extraction and refining, fishing and fish processing, and livestock breeding

### Karaganda Oblast

population: 1,260,000 (85% urban)
territory: 85,400 sq. km.
oblast organized: March 1932 from part of former Akmolinsk guberniia
administrative center: Karaganda (pop. 577,000)
other large cities: Abai (pop. 62,300), Saran (pop. 55,000), Temirtau (pop. 213,000) and Shakhtinsk (pop. 50,000)
economic base: coal industry, ferrous metallurgy, and chemical industries

*Kokchetav Oblast*

population: 620,000 (34% urban)
territory: 78,100 sq. km.
oblast organized: March 1944 from part of Akmolinsk guberniia
administrative center: Kokchetav (pop. 106,000)
economic base: farming, dairy-cattle breeding, beef-cattle breeding, and food
  and leather work industries

*Kustanai Oblast*

population: 950,000 (48% urban)
territory: 114,500 sq. km.
oblast organized: July 1936 from the guberniia of the same name
administrative center: Kustanai (pop. 169,000)
other large cities: Rudny (pop. 111,000)
economic base: some mining, food and light industries, intensive farming, meat
  and dairy livestock breeding

*Kzyl-Orda Oblast*

population: 574,000 (63% urban)
territory: 228,100 sq. km.
oblast organized: January 1938 from part of former Syr Darya guberniia
administrative center: Kzyl-Orda (pop. 159,000), formerly Ak Mechet and
  capital from 1924–1928
economic base: food industries, irrigated agriculture (especially rice cultivation
  and truck farming), and karakul sheep breeding

*Mangyshlak Oblast*

population: 261,000 (87% urban)
territory: 166,600 sq. km.
oblast organized: March 1973 from part of Guryev oblast. This is the
  prerevolutionary territory of the Adaev Kazakhs.
administrative center: Shevchenko (pop. 116,000)
economic base: oil and gas extraction and processing

*Northern Kazakhstan Oblast*

population: 575,000 (44% urban)
territory: 44,300 sq. km.
oblast organized: July 1936 from part of former Akmolinsk guberniia
administrative center: Petropavlovsk (pop. 209,000)
economic base: heavy industry, food and light industry, farming, and meat and
  dairy livestock breeding

*Pavlodar Oblast*

population: 821,000 (57% urban)
territory: 127,500 sq. km.
oblast organized: January 1938 from part of Semipalatinsk guberniia
administrative center: Pavlodar (pop. 281,000)
other large cities: Ekibastuz (pop. 74,000)
economic base: mining, metallurgy, energy production, heavy industry, chemical
    industry, farming, meat and dairy livestock breeding

*Semipalatinsk Oblast*

population: 778,000 (48% urban)
territory: 179,600 sq. km.
oblast organized: October 1939 from the guberniia of the same name
administrative center: Semipalatinsk (pop. 286,000)
economic base: meat (and hide) sheep breeding and farming, combined with
    food and light industries

*Taldy-Kurgan Oblast*

population: 670,000 (47% urban)
territory: 118,500 sq. km.
oblast organized: December 1967 (after a brief existence in 1944) from part of
    Alma-Ata and Semipalatinsk oblasts
administrative center: Taldy-Kurgan (pop. 91,000)
economic base: nonferrous metallurgy, some heavy industry, and food and light
    industries

*Tselinograd Oblast*

population: 810,000 (57% urban)
territory: 124,600 sq. km.
oblast organized: October 1939 as Akmolinsk oblast and renamed Tselinograd
    in 1961
administrative center: Tselinograd (pop. 237,000), formerly known as
    Akmolinsk
economic base: large-scale farming and meat (hide) livestock breeding

*Turgai Oblast*

population: 276,000 (31% urban)
territory: 111,900 sq. km.
oblast organized: November 1970 from part of Kustanai oblast
administrative center: Arkalyk (pop 51,000)
economic base: agro-industry

*Uralsk Oblast*

population: 589,000 (38% urban)

territory: 151,200 sq. km.

oblast organized: March 1932 from the guberniia of the same name (but from 1932 to 1962 was known as Western Kazakhstan oblast)

administrative center: Uralsk (pop. 170,000)

economic base: farming, sheep breeding, and cattle breeding

---

SOURCE: *Kazakhskaia Sovetskaia Entsiklopediia: Entsiklopedicheskii spravochnik* (Alma-Ata, 1981), pp. 638–669.

## APPENDIX 3
## BIRTHRATE, DEATHRATE, AND NATURAL INCREASE
## OF POPULATION IN THE KAZAKH S.S.R.
(per thousand population)

| Year | Number Born | Number Died | Natural Increase |
|------|-------------|-------------|------------------|
| 1940 | 40.8 | 21.4 | 19.4 |
| 1960 | 37.2 | 6.6 | 30.6 |
| 1970 | 23.4 | 6.0 | 17.4 |
| 1981 | 24.3 | 8.0 | 16.3 |

SOURCE: Tsentral'noe statisticheskoe upravlenie SSSR, *Narodnoe khoziaistvo SSSR 1922–1982* (Moscow, 1982), pp. 28–29.

## APPENDIX 4
## THE PERSISTENCE OF NOMADISM
## AMONG THE KAZAKHS

| Province | PERCENTAGE OF POPULATION ENGAGED IN AT LEAST LIMITED MIGRATION | |
|----------|------|------|
| | *1916* | *1928* |
| Aktyubinsk | 40 | 14 |
| Semipalatinsk | 73 | 37 |
| Turgai | 63 | — |
| Uralsk | 64 | 12 |
| Akmolinsk | — | 17 |
| Semirech'e | 72 | less than 40 |
| Syr Darya | 61 | less than 40 |

SOURCES: K. A. Chuvelev, "O reorganizatsii kochevogo i polukochevogo khoziaistva Kazakstana," *Narodnoe khoziaistvo Kazakstana*, no. 2 (1928): 50–51; and A. B. Tursunbaev, "Perekhod k osedlosti kochevnikov i polukochevinkov Srednei Azii i Kazakhstana," *Trudy instituta etnografii* 98 (1973): 232.

## APPENDIX 5
## THE DYNAMICS OF COLLECTIVIZATION

| Date | Percentage of Population Collectivized |
|------|----------------------------------------|
| October 1, 1929 | 7.4 |
| February 1, 1930 | 35.3 |
| March 1, 1930 | 42.1 |
| April 1, 1930 | 52.1 |
| May 1, 1930 | 37.5 |
| July 1, 1930 | 31.6 |
| August 1, 1930 | 29.1 |
| November 1, 1930 | 33.2 |
| January 1, 1931 | 36.7 |
| September 1, 1931 | 60.8 |
| November 1, 1931 | 62.7 |
| January 1, 1932 | 62.3 |
| June 1, 1932 | 73.1 |
| June 1, 1933 | 95.0 |

SOURCES: *Piatiletnyi plan narodno-khoziaistvennogo i sotsial'no-kul'turnogo stroitel'stva Kazakskoi ASSR (1928/29–1932/33)* (Alma-Ata: Gosplanizdat, 1931), p. 18; and A. B. Tursunbaev, *Kollektivizatsiia sel'skogo khoziaistva Kazakhstana, 1926–1941* (Alma-Ata, 1967), 1:371.
Reprinted from Martha Brill Olcott, "The Collectivization Drive in Kazakhstan," *Russian Review* 40, no. 2 (1981): 137.

## APPENDIX 6

## THE DECLINE IN THE NUMBER OF HOUSEHOLDS IN KAZAKHSTAN DURING THE PERIOD OF COLLECTIVIZATION

| Date | Number of Households |
|------|----------------------|
| January 1, 1927 | 1,350,000 |
| January 1, 1928 | 1,194,444 |
| January 1, 1929 | 1,233,962 |
| January 1, 1930 | 1,241,754 |
| January 1, 1931 | 1,269,888 |
| January 1, 1932 | 906,839 |
| July 1, 1932 | 750,857 |
| January 1, 1933 | 630,256 |
| July 1, 1933 | 626,950 |

SOURCE: A. B. Tursunbaev, *Kollektivizatsiia sel'skogo khoziaistva Kazakhstana, 1926–1941* (Alma-Ata, 1967), 2:155.

## APPENDIX 7
## LIVESTOCK BREEDING IN KAZAKHSTAN
(in thousands of animals)

| Year | Cattle[1] | Sheep | Total[2] |
|------|-----------|-------|----------|
| 1886 | | | 15,293 |
| 1895 | | | 17,259 |
| 1905 | | | 18,815 |
| 1912 | | | 22,850 |
| 1913 | 4,954 | 17,204 | 25,698 |
| 1920 | 4,103 | 7,360 | 13,802 |
| 1925 | 5,258 | 11,233 | 19,304 |
| 1926 | 6,444 | 16,020 | 27,176 |
| 1927 | 7,592 | 20,780 | 35,159 |
| 1928 | 7,972 | 20,510 | 35,139 |
| 1929 | 7,442 | 21,943 | 36,317 |
| 1933 | 1,600 | 1,727 | 3,327 |
| 1934 | 1,591 | 2,261 | 3,852 |
| 1935 | 1,835 | 2,618 | 4,453 |
| 1936 | 2,684 | 4,311 | 6,995 |
| 1937 | 2,684 | 4,311 | 6,995 |
| 1938 | 3,095 | 5,288 | 8,383 |
| 1941 | 3,356 | 8,132 | 11,488 |
| 1961 | 5,643 | 28,517 | 34,160 |
| 1971 | 7,285 | 32,596 | 39,881 |
| 1982 | 8,900 | 35,000 | 43,900 |

[1] Large horned cattle over one year old.

[2] For 1913–1929 other small animals were omitted from the total.

SOURCES: *10 let Kazakstana 1920–1930* (Alma-Ata: Gosplanizdat, 1930), p. 209; P. Dunaev, "Sotsialisticheskoe stroitel'stvo Kazakstana za 1934–1938," *Bolshevik Kazakstana*, no. 4 (1939): 93; Tsentral'noe statisticheskoe upravlenie, *Narodnoe khoziaistvo SSSR v 1972 g* (Moscow, 1973), pp. 367–368; and Tsentral'noe statisticheskoe upravlenie SSSR, *Narodnoe khoziaistvo SSSR 1922–1982 gg* (Moscow, 1982), pp. 272–273.

## APPENDIX 8
## HARVEST YIELDS FOR THE KAZAKH S.S.R.
(in centners per hectare)

| | 1913 | 1928 | 1932 | 1937 | 1940 | 1950 | 1955 | 1960 | 1965 | 1970 | 1975 | 1981 | 1982 |
|---|---|---|---|---|---|---|---|---|---|---|---|---|---|
| Total grains | 5.6 | 9.2 | 5.1 | 5.0 | 4.3 | 7.9 | 2.9 | 8.5 | 3.1 | 9.8 | 4.7 | 9.3 | 7.7 |
| winter wheat | 6.2 | 9.3 | 7.0 | 6.8 | 8.4 | 6.8 | 7.7 | 10.0 | 4.2 | 9.9 | 4.8 | 9.2 | 7.5 |
| spring wheat | 5.2 | 9.0 | 4.9 | 5.7 | 4.5 | 8.3 | 3.0 | 8.4 | | | | | |
| winter rye | 4.7 | 7.8 | 6.4 | 5.3 | 4.1 | 6.8 | 2.8 | 6.5 | 3.8 | 8.2 | 1.9 | 6.8 | 3.6 |
| maize | 5.9 | 11.3 | 5.5 | 8.3 | 10.5 | 11.5 | 9.2 | 15.2 | 22.7 | 34.0 | 26.9 | 48.1 | 41.6 |
| winter barley | 5.8 | — | — | 8.0 | 11.7 | 7.0 | 5.4 | 7.8 | 2.7 | 10.2 | 4.4 | 9.3 | 7.2 |
| spring barley | 6.3 | 9.6 | 6.1 | 4.8 | 4.7 | 7.8 | 2.6 | 9.2 | | | | | |
| oats | 6.0 | 10.4 | 5.8 | 4.8 | 3.7 | 8.3 | 2.1 | 10.8 | 3.5 | 11.2 | 4.4 | 9.3 | 9.8 |
| millet | 6.1 | 9.6 | 4.4 | 1.7 | 2.3 | 5.4 | 1.1 | 5.1 | 2.0 | 3.9 | 1.1 | 5.0 | 5.7 |
| buckwheat | 4.4 | 9.1 | — | 2.9 | 2.0 | 4.4 | 0.6 | 4.1 | 0.7 | 5.2 | 2.2 | 2.5 | 3.3 |
| rice | 13.4 | — | — | 20.8 | 19.8 | 17.1 | 13.6 | 18.6 | 22.1 | 33.6 | 26.9 | 45.9 | 46.9 |
| leguminous plants | 4.5 | — | — | 3.6 | 4.1 | 6.9 | 2.1 | 4.9 | 2.8 | 8.5 | 3.8 | 6.4 | 7.0 |
| Cotton | | | | | | | | | | 23.5 | 25.9 | 27.4 | 22.4 |
| Seeds of oil-producing plants | | | | | | | | | | 5.8 | 5.5 | 7.9 | 5.2 |
| Sunflower seeds | | | | | | | | | | 8.4 | 7.6 | 11.2 | 8.0 |

SOURCES: *Narodnoe khoziaistvo Kazakhstana* (Alma-Ata, 1968), p. 138; *Narodnoe khoziaistvo Kazakhstana v 1978 g* (Alma-Ata, 1979), p. 70; and *Narodnoe khoziaistvo Kazakhstana v 1982 g* (Alma-Ata, 1982), p. 72.

## APPENDIX 9
## AMOUNT OF IRRIGATED AGRICULTURAL LAND
## IN THE KAZAKH S.S.R. BY OBLAST
(in thousand hectares)

|  | 1966 | 1970 | 1975 | 1980 | 1982 |
|---|---|---|---|---|---|
| Total | 1,026.1 | 1,450.7 | 1,648.2 | 1,960.7 | 2,046.9 |
| Oblast of |  |  |  |  |  |
| Aktyubinsk | 3.2 | 7.2 | 14.1 | 28.8 | 32.4 |
| Alma-Ata | 356.3 | 239.4 | 256.5 | 292.4 | 299.9 |
| Chimkent | 175.0 | — | — | — | — |
| Dzhambul | 197.8 | 227.3 | 241.3 | 256.0 | 260.6 |
| Dzhezkazgan | — | — | 6.8 | 11.5 | 12.3 |
| Eastern Kazakhstan | 72.0 | 77.5 | 83.1 | 86.7 | 89.5 |
| Guryev | 7.8 | 17.4 | 28.7 | 41.8 | 42.6 |
| Karaganda | 20.5 | 26.5 | 28.1 | 51.5 | 61.7 |
| Kokchetav | 1.2 | 2.6 | 5.5 | 10.9 | 11.3 |
| Kustanai | 4.6 | 7.6 | 11.2 | 16.3 | 17.6 |
| Kzyl-Orda | 89.1 | 140.8 | 179.6 | 246.6 | 246.4 |
| Mangyshlak | — | — | 0.2 | 1.1 | 1.1 |
| Northern Kazakhstan | 1.2 | 2.5 | 5.1 | 6.1 | 7.0 |
| Pavlodar | 6.7 | 10.5 | 21.5 | 48.0 | 62.7 |
| Semipalatinsk | 78.9 | 87.1 | 90.1 | 98.1 | 102.6 |
| Taldy-Kurgan | — | 229.2 | 241.8 | 265.7 | 273.9 |
| Tselinograd | 5.5 | 7.8 | 17.2 | 26.9 | 29.2 |
| Turgai | — | 2.2 | 2.7 | 4.8 | 5.4 |
| Uralsk | 6.3 | 15.2 | 23.7 | 50.2 | 59.7 |

SOURCES: *Narodnoe khoziaistvo Kazakhstana* (Alma-Ata, 1968), p. 162; and *Narodnoe khoziaistvo Kazakhstana v 1982 g* (Alma-Ata, 1982), p. 80.

APPENDIX 10

ANNUAL PRODUCTION OF KEY INDUSTRIAL ITEMS;
AMOUNT PRODUCED PER PERSON IN THE KAZAKH S.S.R.

| Industrial Goods | 1913 | 1940 | 1950 | 1955 | 1960 | 1965 | 1970 | 1975 | 1980 | 1982 |
|---|---|---|---|---|---|---|---|---|---|---|
| Electrical energy (in thousand kilowatt hours) | 0.0 | 0.1 | 0.4 | 0.7 | 1.0 | 1.6 | 2.7 | 3.7 | 4.1 | 4.1 |
| Oil (excluding gas) | 21.2kg | 112.6kg | 159.8kg | 177.2kg | 161.9kg 0.2ton | 0.2ton | 1.0ton | 1.7ton | 1.2ton | 1.3ton |
| Coal (in tons) | 0.02 | 1.1 | 2.6 | 3.5 | 3.2 | 3.8 | 4.7 | 6.5 | 7.7 | 7.7 |
| Rolled metal (in kilograms) | — | — | 16.2 | 29.8 | 30.4 | 32.7 | 185.6 | 272.1 | 275.1 | 259.8 |
| *Food and Consumer Goods* | | | | | | | | | | |
| Cloth (in sq. meters) | 0.02 | 0.07 | 1.1 | 2.6 | 2.7 | 2.6 | 5.4 | 8.4 | 11.1 | 13.2 |
| Leather shoes (in pairs) | — | 0.2 | 0.5 | 0.8 | 1.2 | 1.3 | 2.1 | 2.0 | 2.0 | 2.0 |
| Granulated sugar (kg) | — | 11.5 | 10.8 | 9.4 | 12.3 | 14.4 | 13.4 | 10.4 | 18.2 | 17.6 |
| Animal fat (kg) | 0.4 | 2.0 | 3.3 | 3.3 | 2.9 | 3.8 | 3.2 | 3.2 | 4.0 | 3.8 |
| Meat (kg) | — | 15.7 | 16.5 | 24.9 | 27.8 | 34.5 | 40.1 | 49.1 | 40.6 | 41.0 |
| Milk products (kg) | — | — | — | — | 29.0 | 43.0 | 61.0 | 66.0 | 74.0 | 75.0 |

SOURCES: *Narodnoe khoziaistvo Kazakhstana v 1982g* (Alma-Ata, 1982), p. 41; and *Narodnoe khoziaistvo Kazakhstana* (Alma-Ata, 1968), p. 33.

## APPENDIX 11
## AVERAGE FAMILY SIZE IN THE KAZAKH S.S.R.
## BY NATIONALITY, 1979

|  | Number of Families | Average Family Size |
|---|---|---|
| Total Population | 3,293,878 | 4.1 |
| Families where all members belong to a single nationality | 2,584,569 | 4.2 |
| Families where all members are: |  |  |
|    Kazakh | 860,436 | 5.5 |
|    Russian | 1,261,062 | 3.3 |
|    German | 150,746 | 3.8 |
|    Ukrainian | 105,315 | 3.3 |
|    Tatar | 46,543 | 3.7 |
|    Uzbek | 35,028 | 6.2 |
| Families of mixed nationality | 709,309 | 3.8 |
| Urban Population | 1,923,686 | 3.7 |
| Families where all members belong to a single nationality | 1,463,570 | 3.7 |
| Families where all members are: |  |  |
|    Kazakh | 264,213 | 5.0 |
|    Russian | 968,123 | 3.3 |
|    German | 63,759 | 3.7 |
|    Ukrainian | 58,828 | 3.1 |
|    Tatar | 36,121 | 3.6 |
|    Uzbek | 11,929 | 5.8 |
| Families of mixed nationality | 460,116 | 3.7 |
| Rural Population | 1,370,192 | 4.7 |
| Families where all members belong to a single nationality | 1,120,999 | 4.9 |
| Families where all members are: |  |  |
|    Kazakh | 596,223 | 5.7 |
|    Russian | 292,939 | 3.5 |
|    German | 86,987 | 4.0 |
|    Ukrainian | 46,487 | 3.4 |
|    Tatar | 10,422 | 4.1 |
|    Uzbek | 23,099 | 6.4 |
| Families of mixed nationality | 249,193 | 4.1 |

SOURCE: Tsentral'noe statisticheskoe upravlenie SSSR, *Chislennost' i sostav naseleniia SSSR* (Moscow, 1984), table 52.

## APPENDIX 12
## DISTRIBUTION OF KAZAKH POPULATION
## BY NATIVE LANGUAGE

| | 1959 | | 1970 | | 1979 | |
|---|---|---|---|---|---|---|
| | Percentage Kazakh | Percentage Speaking Kazakh as Native Language | Percentage Kazakh | Percentage Speaking Kazakh as Native Language | Percentage Kazakh | Percentage Speaking Kazakh as Native Language |
| USSR | 1.7 | 98.4 | 2.2 | 98.0 | 2.5 | 97.4 |
| Kazakh S.S.R. | 30.0 | 99.2 | 32.6 | 98.9 | 36.0 | 98.6 |
| Aktyubinsk oblast | 43.2 | 99.4 | 47.5 | 99.1 | 50.7 | 98.9 |
| Alma-Ata city | 8.6 | 93.9 | 12.1 | 93.2 | — | — |
| Alma-Ata oblast | 32.2 | 99.3 | 35.6 | 99.3 | 37.5 | 99.1 |
| Chimkent oblast | 44.1 | 99.6 | 47.1 | 99.5 | 51.0 | 99.5 |
| Dzhambul oblast | 39.2 | 99.6 | 40.7 | 99.5 | 44.1 | 99.4 |
| Dzhezkazgan oblast | — | — | — | — | 41.0 | 98.8 |
| E. Kazakhstan oblast | 18.9 | 99.0 | 23.2 | 98.2 | 25.4 | 98.0 |
| Guryev oblast | 72.3 | 99.8 | 62.5 | 99.7 | 76.1 | 99.6 |
| Karaganda oblast | 19.1 | 98.4 | 18.6 | 97.5 | 14.5 | 94.7 |
| Kokchetav oblast | 18.4 | 99.0 | 22.7 | 98.2 | 26.3 | 98.3 |
| Kustanai oblast | 18.7 | 98.8 | 15.5 | 96.5 | 16.6 | 94.5 |
| Kzyl-Orda oblast | 72.1 | 99.7 | 69.7 | 99.8 | 76.1 | 99.7 |
| Mangyshlak oblast | — | — | — | — | 44.3 | 99.3 |
| N. Kazakhstan oblast | 12.4 | 98.0 | 15.0 | 97.1 | 16.6 | 96.9 |
| Pavlodar oblast | 25.6 | 98.9 | 25.2 | 98.3 | 26.8 | 97.7 |
| Semipalatinsk oblast | 35.7 | 99.2 | 43.6 | 99.3 | 47.9 | 99.2 |
| Taldy-Kurgan oblast | — | — | 41.3 | 99.3 | 46.1 | 99.4 |
| Tselinograd oblast | 18.1 | 98.8 | 18.7 | 98.1 | 20.7 | 97.6 |
| Turgai oblast | — | — | 32.5 | 99.2 | 36.8 | 98.3 |
| Uralsk oblast | 50.0 | 99.4 | 49.3 | 99.3 | 51.5 | 99.0 |
| RSFSR | 0.3 | — | 0.4 | 93.3 | 0.4 | 91.1 |
| Uzbek S.S.R. | 4.2 | — | 4.0 | 96.7 | 4.0 | 94.6 |
| Turkmen S.S.R. | 4.6 | — | 3.2 | 98.1 | 2.9 | 97.9 |
| Kirgiz ASSR | 1.0 | — | 0.8 | 85.7 | 0.8 | 80.3 |
| Karakalpak ASSR | — | — | 26.5 | 97.2 | 26.9 | 94.3 |

SOURCES: Tsentral'noe statisticheskoe upravlenie SSSR, *Chislennost' i sostav naseleniia SSSR* (Moscow, 1984), tables 13, 14, 19, 20, 21, 22, 31, and 34; Tsentral'noe statisticheskoe upravlenie SSSR, *Itogi vsesoiuznoi perepisi naseleniia 1970 goda. Tom IV. Natsional'nyi sostav naseleniia SSSR* (Moscow, 1973), tables 1, 2, 4, 5, 11, 12, 13, 14, 22, and 27; and Tsentral'noe statisticheskoe upravlenie SSSR, *Itogi vsesoiuznoi perepsis naseleniia 1959 goda. Kazakhskaia SSR* (Moscow, 1962), tables 53 and 54.

## LEVEL OF EDUCATIONAL ATTAINMENT IN THE KAZAKH S.S.R.
(per thousand people ten years and older)

| | Higher | | | Incomplete Higher | | | Special Secondary | | | General Secondary | | | Incomplete Secondary | | | Primary | | |
|---|---|---|---|---|---|---|---|---|---|---|---|---|---|---|---|---|---|---|
| | 1959 | 1970 | 1979 | 1959 | 1970 | 1979 | 1959 | 1970 | 1979 | 1959 | 1970 | 1979 | 1959 | 1970 | 1979 | 1959 | 1970 | 1979 |
| Total Population | 17 | 35 | 60 | 9 | 12 | 13 | 44 | 63 | 102 | 56 | 111 | 211 | 221 | 247 | 247 | 290 | 303 | 263 |
| Males | 21 | 41 | 65 | 10 | 13 | 13 | 45 | 59 | 91 | 63 | 117 | 224 | 250 | 272 | 277 | 333 | 327 | 267 |
| Females | 13 | 30 | 54 | 9 | 11 | 13 | 43 | 67 | 112 | 51 | 106 | 199 | 195 | 225 | 220 | 253 | 280 | 261 |
| Urban Population | 27 | 51 | 82 | 14 | 17 | 19 | 57 | 83 | 129 | 77 | 137 | 229 | 247 | 270 | 244 | 289 | 266 | 214 |
| Urban Male | 31 | 57 | 90 | 14 | 18 | 19 | 56 | 77 | 115 | 80 | 138 | 233 | 268 | 295 | 276 | 339 | 292 | 220 |
| Urban Female | 23 | 45 | 76 | 14 | 16 | 19 | 58 | 89 | 141 | 74 | 136 | 224 | 230 | 248 | 216 | 247 | 242 | 208 |
| Rural Population | 9 | 17 | 30 | 6 | 6 | 6 | 33 | 40 | 68 | 39 | 81 | 189 | 198 | 221 | 251 | 290 | 345 | 326 |
| Rural Male | 12 | 23 | 35 | 7 | 6 | 6 | 35 | 39 | 62 | 49 | 92 | 213 | 236 | 245 | 279 | 329 | 368 | 323 |
| Rural Female | 6 | 12 | 27 | 4 | 5 | 5 | 30 | 41 | 73 | 31 | 72 | 167 | 165 | 199 | 224 | 257 | 324 | 329 |

SOURCE: Tsentral'noe statisticheskoe upravlenie SSSR, *Chislennost' i sostav naseleniia SSSR* (Moscow, 1984), table 9.

## APPENDIX 14

### COMPARISON OF KAZAKH AND RUSSIAN EDUCATIONAL ATTAINMENT IN THE KAZAKH S.S.R.

(per thousand people ten years and older)

| | Higher | | Incomplete Higher | | Special Secondary | | General Secondary | | Incomplete Secondary | | Primary | |
|---|---|---|---|---|---|---|---|---|---|---|---|---|
| | 1959 | 1970 | 1959 | 1970 | 1959 | 1970 | 1959 | 1970 | 1959 | 1970 | 1959 | 1970 |
| **Urban and Rural Population** | | | | | | | | | | | | |
| Kazakh | 12 | 31 | 10 | 13 | 21 | 36 | 54 | 121 | 282 | 403 | 221 | 291 |
| Russian | 21 | 42 | 10 | 12 | 63 | 86 | 62 | 111 | 403 | 521 | 312 | 293 |
| Male Kazakh | 20 | 44 | 15 | 16 | 32 | 42 | 76 | 140 | 226 | 222 | 229 | 294 |
| Male Russian | 23 | 44 | 9 | 12 | 58 | 74 | 59 | 107 | 266 | 296 | 383 | 338 |
| Female Kazakh | 5 | 20 | 6 | 10 | 12 | 30 | 35 | 104 | 149 | 183 | 215 | 289 |
| Female Russian | 20 | 40 | 12 | 13 | 67 | 95 | 65 | 115 | 232 | 248 | 254 | 255 |
| **Urban** | | | | | | | | | | | | |
| Kazakh | 26 | 58 | 21 | 30 | 25 | 47 | 93 | 177 | 215 | 210 | 221 | 251 |
| Russian | 28 | 51 | 13 | 15 | 65 | 97 | 76 | 129 | 260 | 280 | 298 | 264 |
| Male Kazakh | 38 | 75 | 27 | 35 | 33 | 49 | 118 | 191 | 248 | 224 | 222 | 252 |
| Male Russian | 30 | 54 | 11 | 15 | 66 | 87 | 71 | 122 | 273 | 306 | 368 | 305 |
| Female Kazakh | 13 | 41 | 16 | 26 | 17 | 45 | 68 | 162 | 184 | 196 | 219 | 249 |
| Female Russian | 26 | 49 | 14 | 15 | 72 | 105 | 80 | 134 | 250 | 258 | 243 | 230 |
| **Rural** | | | | | | | | | | | | |
| Kazakh | 7 | 20 | 7 | 6 | 20 | 31 | 42 | 99 | 175 | 199 | 221 | 307 |
| Russian | 12 | 18 | 6 | 6 | 53 | 59 | 41 | 69 | 228 | 246 | 333 | 364 |
| Male Kazakh | 13 | 31 | 11 | 8 | 31 | 39 | 61 | 118 | 219 | 221 | 231 | 312 |
| Male Russian | 13 | 18 | 5 | 5 | 46 | 44 | 41 | 70 | 255 | 271 | 406 | 417 |
| Female Kazakh | 3 | 11 | 3 | 5 | 10 | 25 | 25 | 82 | 138 | 178 | 213 | 303 |
| Female Russian | 11 | 18 | 7 | 6 | 59 | 71 | 41 | 69 | 205 | 224 | 271 | 318 |

SOURCE: Tsentral'noe statisticheskoe upravlenie SSSR, Itogi vsesoiuznoi perepisi naseleniia 1970 goda. Tom IV. Natsional'nyi sostav naseleniia SSSR (Moscow, 1973), table 43.

## APPENDIX 15
## PUBLISHING STATISTICS FOR THE KAZAKH S.S.R.

|  | 1960 | 1965 | 1970 | 1975 | 1980 | 1982 |
|---|---|---|---|---|---|---|
| Total number of books and brochures (titles) | 1,420 | 1,651 | 2,022 | 2,252 | 2,188 | 2,339 |
| Number of the above printed in Kazakh (titles) | 572 | 569 | 627 | 746 | 757 | 754 |
| Tirazh[1] of books and brochures (in thousands) | 15,859 | 17,630 | 22,309 | 25,988 | 27,106 | 29,252 |
| Tirazh of the above in Kazakh (in thousands) | 7,813 | 8,137 | 12,742 | 14,387 | 13,827 | 12,758 |
| Total number of newspapers and periodicals (titles) | 97 | 76 | 153 | 90 | 105 | 114 |
| Number of the above in Kazakh (titles) | 16 | 17 | 24 | 28 | 28 | 31 |
| Tirazh of newspapers and periodicals (in thousands) | 9,166 | 16,539 | 40,800 | 50,320 | 52,254 | 52,554 |
| Tirazh of the above in Kazakh (in thousands) | 6,158 | 10,077 | 18,531 | 25,411 | 26,969 | 24,574 |
| Total number of magazines (titles) | 366 | 294 | 355 | 400 | 430 | 443 |
| Number of the above in Kazakh (titles) | 140 | 101 | 130 | 151 | 161 | 163 |
| Tirazh per magazine issue (in thousands) | 2,138 | 2,947 | 4,166 | 5,121 | 5,335 | 5,399 |
| Tirazh of the above in Kazakh (in thousands) | 727 | 948 | 1,557 | 1,753 | 1,757 | 1,738 |
| Total tirazh of magazines (in millions) | 385 | 548 | 803 | 1,024 | 1,048 | 1,037 |
| Tirazh of the above in Kazakh (in millions) | 131 | 168 | 276 | 320 | 320 | 312 |

[1] Tirazh is the number of items printed in the press or publication run.

SOURCE: *Narodnoe khoziaistvo Kazakhstana v 1982 g* (Alma-Ata, 1982), p. 236.

## APPENDIX 16
## COMMUNIST PARTY MEMBERSHIP IN KAZAKHSTAN
## BY NATIONALITY

| Date (January 1) | Total Number of Communists | Percentage Kazakh | Date (January 1) | Total Number of Communists | Percentage Kazakh |
|---|---|---|---|---|---|
| 1924 | 14,760 | 11.5 | 1949 | 229,455 | 40.2 |
| 1925 | 22,757 | 29.1 | 1950 | 225,556 | 40.6 |
| 1926 | 31,910 | 36.4 | 1951 | 227,668 | 40.3 |
| 1927 | 33,352 | 35.8 | 1952 | 230,668 | 40.2 |
| 1928 | 33,981 | 37.9 | 1953 | 231,091 | 40.4 |
| 1929 | 41,128 | 40.2 | 1954 | 237,397 | 40.6 |
| 1930 | 44,156 | 43.0 | 1955 | 234,193 | 39.9 |
| 1931 | 28,431 | 45.8 | 1956 | 257,055 | 37.5 |
| 1932 | 88,209 | 50.6 | 1957 | 269,294 | NA |
| 1933 | 93,935 | 53.1 | 1958 | 283,851 | NA |
| 1934 | 69,601 | 53.0 | 1959 | 300,118 | NA |
| 1935 | 60,836 | 52.5 | 1960 | 318,502 | 36.3 |
| 1936 | 47,988 | 52.5 | 1961 | 345,115 | 35.4 |
| 1937 | 51,881 | 48.8 | 1962 | 373,648 | 35.4 |
| 1938 | 48,332 | 47.4 | 1963 | 398,026 | 34.1 |
| 1939 | 65,465 | 48.5 | 1964 | 418,331 | 33.3 |
| 1940 | 108,705 | 51.8 | 1965 | 450,486 | 33.0 |
| 1941 | 125,593 | 51.0 | 1966 | 481,582 | 32.8 |
| 1942 | 120,218 | 46.1 | 1967 | 498,065 | 33.2 |
| 1943 | 109,270 | 31.9 | 1968 | 517,061 | 33.5 |
| 1944 | 114,146 | 35.1 | 1969 | 538,923 | 33.9 |
| 1945 | 114,261 | 43.1 | 1970 | 556,508 | 34.3 |
| 1946 | 148,612 | 42.8 | 1971 | 575,459 | 34.6 |
| 1947 | 203,443 | 41.6 | 1972 | 595,103 | 35.1 |
| 1948 | 229,872 | 40.2 | | | |

SOURCES: *Kommunisticheskaia partiia Kazakhstana v dokumentakh i tsifrakh* (Alma-Ata, 1960); and *Kompartiia Kazakhstana za 50 let* (Alma-Ata, 1972), tables 153 and 177.

# Glossary

*Adat*—the unwritten customary law of the Kazakhs

*Ak Suiuk*—the white bone, or Kazakh aristocracy, during the period of the Kazakh khanate

*Aksakal*—a tribal or clan elder

*Akyn*—Kazakh term for itinerant poet-singer who performed at ceremonial occasions

*Alash Orda*—the Horde of Alash, named after Alash, the mythical ancestor of the Kazakhs; this was the name chosen for the Kazakh nationalist party and autonomous government in 1917

*Amanat*—the custom of keeping a relative as hostage to insure a khan's loyalty

*Aqtaban Shubirindi*—the Great Retreat of 1723, when the Kazakhs fled the invasion of Mongol conquerors from the east

*Artel*—short for *selsko-khoziaistvennyi artel'*, the formal name of the *kolkhoz*

*As*—celebrations marking birth and death

*Aul*—the migratory unit of the Kazakhs, which generally consisted of several extended families drawn from the same clan

*Bai*—a local notable, generally used to denote someone of substantial economic worth

*Baigush*—Kazakh term for hired hands

*Bakshi*—shaman healers or holymen whose services were employed to ward off evil spirits

*Balyshi*—Kazakh term for fishermen

*Barymta*—punitive raids in which livestock was captured, launched against the *auls* of clan rivals

*Batir*—Kazakh term for heroic warrior

*Bedniak*—a Russian term for a poor peasant

*Bii*—an *Adat* judge

*Birlik*—unity, the name of the Kazakh youth group founded in Omsk in 1915 whose members became advocates of Bolshevism

*Chinovniki*—functionaries; in the early years of Soviet rule this was used as a pejorative term for people who had served in the imperial bureaucracy

*Desiatin*—2.7 acres

*Distantsiia*—a frontier military outpost

*Eginshi*—Kazakh term for poor farmers

*Gazavat*—a Turkish term for holy war

*Gorkom*—abbreviation of *gorodskoi komitet*, the city committee of the party

*Guberniia*—a province; this administrative designation fell into disuse in the late 1920s

*Hectare*—2.47 acres

*Imam*—a Muslim senior spiritual leader who leads those assembled in the mosque in prayer

*Ittifak al Muslimin*—the union of Muslims formed in Tashkent in November 1917

*Jadidi*—Muslim reformers of the late nineteenth and early twentieth centuries who were active proponents of the new-method (*Jadid*) Muslim schools

*Jailu*—the summer campsite of Kazakh pastoral nomads

*Jatak*—the Kazakh word for lie-about, used for individuals who lived off the proceeds of grain planted on communal summer land

*Jhety Jharga*—Khan Tauke's law, modeled on the Mongol *yasa*, which combined Kazakh customary practice with Muslim precepts

*Jigit*—Kazakh term for warrior

*Jihad*—the Arabic term for holy war

*Jut*—ice-coated grass, caused when freezing rain fell before a snow cover was established, which often induced famine

*Jyrau*—a man who wrote poems and often served as a scribe for the khan as well

*Kadet*—member of the Constitutional Democratic party, which was active during the years of the State Duma

*Kalym*—the so-called bride price paid by the groom's family to the father of the bride between the time of betrothal and the marriage ceremony

*Kara Suiuk*—the black bone, or Kazakh clan elders, during the period of the Kazakh khanate

*Kazburo*—abbreviation of *Kazakskoe buro*, the executive body of the Kazakh Communist Party

*Kazkraikom*—abbreviation of *Kazakskii Kraevoi Komitet*, the Kazakh regional committee of the Communist Party

*Khalat*—traditional male robe-like outer garment

*Kibitka*—Russian term for cart; in prerevolutionary times each household had a "cart" tax levied on it

*Kirkraikom*—abbreviation of *Kirgizskii Kraevoi Komitet*, the Kirgiz regional committee of the Communist Party

*Kirrevkom*—abbreviation of *Kirgizskii Revoliutsionyi Komitet* (Kirgiz Revolutionary Committee), which administered the steppe region as the Civil War drew to a close

*Kishlak*—a Central Asian village

*Kokteu*—the Kazakhs' spring migration

*Kolkhoz*—*kollektivnoe khoziastvo*, or collective farm, is an agricultural enterprise in which land and equipment are technically the property of the community and whose members (*kolkhozniki*) receive proportional compensation for agricultural surpluses

*Komsomol*—acronym used for the VLKSM (*Vsesoiuzyi Leninskii Kommunisticheskii Soiuz Molodezhi*, the All Union Leninist Communist Union of Youth), also known as the Communist Youth League

*Kontraktsiia*—a contract system that paid the peasantry in advance for delivering crops at fixed prices

*Korenizatsiia*—the policy of encouraging the employment of national minority cadre in official positions

*Kstau*—the winter campsite of the Kazakh pastoral nomads

*Kulak*—a Russian word for fist, this term was used to designate the allegedly exploitative class of farmers

*Kun*—blood price or revenge extracted for murdering a relative

*Kungtaji*—title given to the leader of the Kalmyk people

*Kurban Bairam*—the Muslim holiday that commemorates the sacrifice of Abraham, which is celebrated 70 days after the end of Ramadan

*Kazeu*—the Kazakhs' autumn migration

*Madrasah*—Muslim secondary school

*Mektep*—Muslim primary school

*MTS*—abbreviation of *Mashino-traktornaia stantsiia*, Machine and Tractor Stations, which provided heavy equipment for *kolkhozy*

*Mufti*—term used first by the Russians and then by the Soviets to denote the head of a Muslim Ecclesiastical Administration

*Muallim*—teacher in Muslim religious schools

*Mullah*—a Muslim cleric; this term was sometimes used as an honorific title as well as to denote graduates of a *madrasah*

*Musburo*—abbreviation for the Muslim bureau of the party

*Muzhik*—Russian term for peasant

*Narkomnats*—abbreviation of *Narodnyi kommissariat natsional'nostei*, the People's Commissariat of Nationalities, headed by J. V. Stalin until 1924

*Natsotdel*—abbreviation of *Natsional'nyi otdel*, the Department of Nationalities

*NEP*—abbreviation of *Novaia Ekonomicheskaia Politika*, the New Economic Policy of the 1920s, which introduced limited private ownership

*Nomenklatura*—a system for appointing senior party and state officials, whereby candidates are chosen from lists of approved individuals that are prepared by the party leadership

*Obkom*—abbreviation of *oblastnoi komitet*, the *oblast* committee

*Oblast*—a large administrative territory

*Okrug*—a territorial division, larger than an *oblast*

*Orgburo*—the organizational bureau of the party

*Otkochevniki*—Kazakh nomads who had lost their property and wandered the steppe in search of food and shelter

*Pood*—a traditional Russian weight that is slightly more than 36 pounds avoirdupois

*Qazi (Kadi)*—an individual appointed by the ecclesiastical administration to preside over a Muslim court of law

*Raion*—the currently employed term for administrative district

*Raikom*—abbreviation of *raionyi komitet*, the *raion* committee of the party

*Revkom*—abbreviation of *revoliutsionnyi komitet*, the revolutionary committee of the party

*Revvoensovet*—abbreviation of *Revolutsionnyi voennyi komitet*, the Military Revolutionary Soviet

*RKP(b)*—the Russian Communist Party (Bolshevik)

*RSFSR*—the Russian Soviet Federated Socialist Republic

*SADUM*—abbreviation of *Dukhovnoe Upravlenie Musulman Srednei Azii i Kazakhstan*, the Muslim Ecclesiastical Administration of Central Asia and Kazakhstan

*Shari'a*—Muslim law

*Shoshala*—a dirt mound, which was the first permanent structure erected by the Kazakhs

*Shuro Islam*—the all-Russian Provisional Muslim National Council

*Sovkhoz*—*Sovetskoe khoziaistvo*, or state farm, is an agricultural enterprise in which all land and equipment are owned by the state and whose employees (*sovkhozniki*) are wage-laborers

*SR*—member of the Socialist Revolutionary party, which was active during the years of the State Duma

*Toi*—a Kazakh wedding celebration

*TOZ*—abbreviation of *Tovarichestvo dliia obshchestvennoi obrabotki zemli*, a society for the collective cultivation of land

*TsIK*—abbreviation of *Tsentral'nyi Ispolnitel'nyi Komitet*, the Central Executive Committee

*Tulenguts*—an hereditary slave caste composed of foreign captives and their descendants; these people were often trained as warriors

*Turkkomissiia*—abbreviation for the Turkestan Commission, which administered the southern part of the steppe during the years of the Civil War

*Uezd*—a term for district, the *uezd* was composed of *volost*s; this term fell into disuse in the mid-1920s

*Ukase*—a legal decree of the Russian imperial government

*Ulu*—Mongol and Kazakh word for clan

*Umma*—the community of Muslim believers

*Ushur*—annual taxation payable in grain collected in accordance with Muslim law

*Ush Zhuz*—the Three Horde Party formed by Kazakhs in Tashkent to oppose the *Alash Orda*

*Versta* (or *verst*)—3,500 feet

*Volost*—the designation for a small rural district used in the prerevolutionary period and during the early years of Soviet rule

*Waqf*—land owned by Muslim religious institutions

*Yasa*—the Mongol code of law, which combined customary practice with Muslim precepts

*Yasak*—annual tribute paid to the khan

*Yurt*—a circular, domed, portable tent made of felt that was the residence of the Kazakh nomads

*Za'akat*—annual taxation payable in livestock levied in accordance with Muslim law

*Zemstvo*—an elected district council; this institution was introduced by Tsar Alexander II

*Zhdanovshchina*—term used to describe the reassertion of rigid ideological controls in the late 1940s, which takes its name from Iurii Zhdanov, party secretary for ideology at the onset of the period

*Zhuz*—Kazakh term for horde; the Kazakhs were divided into three hordes during the period of the khanate: the Great Horde (*Ulu Zhuz*), the Middle Horde (*Orta Zhuz*), and the Small Horde (*Kichi Zhuz*)

# Notes

## CHAPTER 1

1. Virtually all contemporary sources from this period are grouped together in the volume *Materialy po istorii kazakhskikh khanstv, XV–XVIII vv* (Alma-Ata, 1969).

2. For lengthy excerpts of these travelers' accounts, see *Kazakhsko-russkie otnosheniia v XV–XVIII vv* (Alma-Ata, 1961); and *Kazakhsko-russkie otnosheniia v XVIII–XIX vv (1771–1867 gg): Sbornik dokumentov i materialov* (Alma-Ata, 1964).

3. N. I. Grodekov, *Kirgizy i Karakirgizy Syr'-darinskoi oblasti*, vol. 1, *Iuridicheskii byt'* (Tashkent, 1889), p. 92; and S. E. Tolybekov, *Kochevoe obshchestvo Kazakhov v XVII–nachale XX v* (Alma-Ata, 1971), p. 184.

4. V. V. Barthol'd, *Four Studies on the History of Central Asia*, vol. 3, trans. V. and T. Minorsky (Leiden: E. J. Brill, 1962), p. 129.

5. Chokan Valikhanov, *Sobranie sochinenii*, 5 vols. (Alma-Ata, 1961–1968), 1:207; and *Istoriia Kazakhskoi SSR*, vol. 1 (Alma-Ata, 1957), p. 143.

6. Grodekov, *Kirgizy i Karakirgizy*, p. 1.

7. *Great Soviet Encyclopedia* (New York: Macmillan, 1976), 11:530.

8. Ibid., 11:507.

9. Tolybekov, *Kochevoe obshchestvo*, p. 187; and *Kazakhskaia Sovetskaia Sotsialisticheskaia Respublika: Entsiklopedicheskii spravochnik* (Alma-Ata, 1981), p. 143.

10. Ibid., p. 147.

11. V. V. Vostrov and M. S. Mukanov, *Rodoplemennoi sostav i rasselenie Kazakhov* (Alma-Ata, 1978), p. 20.

12. *Istoriia Kazakhskoi SSR* (1957), 1:141; and Gavin Hambly, ed., *Central Asia* (New York: Delacorte Press, 1969), p. 142.

13. V. V. Vel'iaminov-Zernov, *Issledovanie o kasimovskikh tsariakh i tsarevichakh*, 3 vols. (St. Petersburg, 1864).

14. Vostrov and Mukanov, *Rodoplemennoi sostav*, p. 10.

15. N. A. Aristov, "Zametki ob etnicheskom sostave turkskikh plemen i narodnostei," *Zhivaia starina*, no. 3–4 (1896): 358.

16. Vostrov and Mukanov, *Rodoplemennoi sostav*, p. 56.

17. G. E. Markov, *Kochevniki Azii* (Moscow, 1976), p. 140.

18. This conclusion fits well with a Marxist analysis of history, but it is predicated on an exaggerated and inaccurate understanding of the role played by the Kazakh khans and lesser aristocracy.

19. Markov, *Kochevniki Azii*, p. 150; and Tolybekov, *Kochevoe obshchestvo*, p. 235. See also G. E. Markov, "Problemy definitsii i terminologii skotovodstva i kochevnichestva," *Sovetskaia etnografiia*, no. 4 (1982): 80–86; and, for the opposite viewpoint, Iu. I. Semenov, "Kochevnichestvo i nekotorye obshchie problemy teorii khoziaistva i obshchestva," *Sovetskaia etnografiia*, no. 3 (1982): 48–59.

20. N. G. Appolonova, *Ekonomicheskie i politcheskie sviazi Kazakhstana s Rossii* (Moscow, 1960), p. 76.

21. *Kazakhsko-russkie otnosheniia v XV–XVIII vv*, p. 62.

22. G. E. Markov, "Kochevniki Azii" (Ph.D. dissertation, Moscow State University, 1967), p. 456.

23. Over time the Kazakhs retold the events and legends of Mongol history as their own, and, given their exclusionary marriage practices and migratory patterns, they came to be a distinct people.

24. Barthol'd, *Four Studies*, 3:159.

25. See *Poety Kazakhstana* (Moscow, 1978).

26. K. B. Beisembiev, *Ocherki istorii obshchestvenno-politicheskoi i filosofskoi mysli Kazakhstana* (Alma-Ata, 1976), p. 12.

27. Tolybekov, *Kochevoe obshchestvo*, p. 193.

28. Ibid., p. 197.

29. Ibid., p. 191.

30. Ibid., pp. 199–201.

31. *Pesni stepi* (Moscow, 1936).

32. For a discussion of Kazakh poetry, see *Poety Kazakhstana*, especially the introductory essay.

33. Ibid., pp. 4, 74.

34. More is known about wedding celebrations than about either funereal or birth rites. The oral epic *Er Sain* provides some information about funerals. The Kazakhs observed a year-long period of mourning. There were rites for the safe passage of the spirit of the dead on the 7th, 40th, and 365th days, marked by lamentations and animal sacrifices.

35. The whole notion of stability in these years was a very precarious one, since in 1537–1538 the Mongols, in the service of the Uzbeks, invaded Semirech'e.

36. The Nogai people who lived on the west bank of the Ural River preferred Kazakh rule to the alternative, domination by the Russians, who had taken control of Kazan in 1552.

37. The Kalmyks are also known as Jungars and Oirats.

38. *Istoriia Kazakhskoi SSR* (1957), 1:234.

39. Some Kalmyks actually collected tribute from the indigenous Siberian peoples.

## CHAPTER 2

1. "Sibirskie letopisi" as quoted by T. Shoinbaev, *Progressivnoe znachenie prisoedineniia Kazakhstana k Rossii* (Alma-Ata, 1973), p. 17. For additional documentary materials for this period, see *Materialy po istorii politicheskogo stroiia Kazakhstana*, vol. 1 (Alma-Ata, 1960).

2. "Kazachie Ordy" is the appellation for the Kazakhs used by the Russians of the sixteenth century. A. I. Maksheev', *Istoricheskii obzor Turkestana: Nastupatel'nago dvizheniia v nego russkikh* (St. Petersburg, 1890), p. 28.

3. Amanat was a form of protective custody to assure the loyalty of the hostage's people, a common practice among eastern tribes.

4. *Istoriia Kazakhskoi SSR* (1957), 1:228.

5. *Materialy po istorii politicheskogo*, 1:9. This letter was written in "Kazakh chancellory language" and is reproduced in translation.

6. V. Ia. Basin, *Rossiia i Kazakhskie khanstva v XVI–XVIII vv* (Alma-Ata, 1971), p. 131.

7. Tolybekov, *Kochevoe obshchestvo*, p. 367.

8. Maksheev', *Istoricheskii obzor Turkestana*, p. 31.

9. Sultan Bukenbai of the Small Horde headed the opposition, joined by Janibek of the Middle Horde.

10. Included in this guberniia were the Ufa and Stavropol regions.

11. H. Howorth, *History of the Mongols*, part II (London: Longmans, Green, 1880), vol. 2, p. 662.

12. Ibid.

13. *Istoriia Kazakhskoi SSR* (1957), 1:255.

14. Tolybekov, *Kochevoe obshchestvo*, p. 377; and Basin, *Rossiia i Kazakhskie*, p. 247.

15. For an account of the Pugachev revolt, see John J. Alexander, *Emperor of the Cossacks* (Lawrence: Coronado Press, 1973).

16. M. P. Viatkin, *Ocherki po istorii Kazakhskoi SSR* (Moscow, 1941), p. 181.

17. Throughout the years of the Pugachev uprising there was fighting in the Small Horde, reputedly stirred up by an "invisible" fighter. See N. E. Bekmakhanova, *Legenda o nevidimke* (Alma-Ata, 1968).

18. See Viatkin, *Ocherki po istorii.*

19. Shoinbaev, *Progressivnoe znachenie*, p. 63.

20. *Kazakhsko-russkie otnosheniia v XVIII–XIX vv*, p. 46.

21. Viatkin, *Ocherki po istorii*, p. 193.

22. A. Levshin, *Descriptions des hordes et des steppes des Kirghiz-kazaks ou Kirghiz-kaïssaks*, trans. F. de Pigny (Paris: Imprimerie royale, 1840). Originally published in Russian in St. Petersburg, 1832.

23. See *Poety Kazakhstana* for poetry of the period.

24. *Istoriia Kazakhskoi SSR* (1957), 1:264.

25. Howorth, *History of the Mongols*, p. 647.

26. *Istoriia Kazakhskoi SSR* (1957), and *Istoriia Kazakhskoi SSR*, vol. 3 (Alma-Ata, 1979).

27. S. D. Asfendiarov, *Istoriia Kazakstana (s drevneishikh vremen)*, vol. 1 (Moscow and Alma-Ata, 1935). This view was accepted by Viatkin in *Ocherki po istorii.*

28. E. Bekmakhanov, *Prisoedinenie Kazakhstana k Rossii* (Moscow, 1957); Shoinbaev, *Progressivnoe znachenie*; and Basin, *Rossiia i Kazakhskie.*

29. A. F. Riazanov, *Vosstanie Isataia Taimanova (1836–1838)* (Tashkent, 1924); M. P. Viatkin, *Batyr Srym* (Moscow, 1947); V. F. Shakhmatov, *Vnutrennaia orda vosstanie Isataia Taimanova* (Alma-Ata, 1946); and T. Shoinbaev, *Vosstanie Syrdarinskikh Kazakhov* (Alma-Ata, 1949).

30. This was the thesis of Viatkin's volume *Batyr Srym*, in which he was trying to answer critics of his 1941 history, *Ocherki po istorii.*

31. One gets a strong sense of this in the court communications referring to the Pugachev uprising that are reproduced in *Kazakhsko-russkie otnosheniia v XVIII–XIX vv.*

32. Tolybekov, *Kochevoe obshchestvo*, p. 345.

33. Ibid., p. 278.

34. A *kibitka* was a cart, and a household was taxed on the basis of the number of carts they owned, but in the Kazakh Steppe over time the number of "carts" became synonymous with the number of households.

35. Viatkin, *Ocherki po istorii*, p. 222.

36. As quoted by Viatkin. Ibid., p. 220.

37. Maksheev', *Istoricheskii obzor Turkestana*, p. 111.

## CHAPTER 3

1. Tolybekov, *Kochevoe obshchestvo*, p. 345, quoting Levshin, *Opisanie Kirgiz-Kaisatskikh*, p. 436.

2. S. Z. Zimanov, *Politicheskii stroi Kazakhstana (kontsa XVIII i pervoi polovine XIX vekov)* (Alma-Ata, 1960), p. 18.

3. This law applied to Kazakhs living in the steppe, who upon conviction were to be incarcerated in Russian towns or settlements. Kazakhs living in Russian towns or settlements had been subject to Russian criminal law since December 12, 1837, as were those Kazakhs *caught* committing criminal offenses in Russian towns or settlements.

4. Several commissions were organized to arbitrate territorial disputes of the Small and Middle hordes, but the Kazakhs of the west Siberian territory were not subject to the law of the Orenburg Kazakhs; plunder and robbery between the two groups remained an almost insolvable dilemma throughout the period.

5. These arrangements were formalized by the statute on schools for Kazakh children of July 3, 1857.

6. Zimanov, *Politicheskii stroi Kazakhstana*, p. 201.

7. Eugene Schuyler, *Turkestan* (New York: Scribner, Armstrong, 1877), 1:32.

8. The distantsii were divided into three classes depending upon their size, and their commanders received per annum 75R, 50R and 30R accordingly.

9. *Materialy po istorii politicheskogo*, pp. 216–225.

10. Maksheev', *Istoricheskii obzor Turkestana*, p. 114.

11. This mission was in preparation for Russia's attempt to expand trade across the steppe. N. A. Khalfin, *Russia's Policy in Central Asia, 1857–1868*, condensed and translated by Hubert Evans (London: Central Asian Research Center, 1964), p. 30.

12. Zimanov, *Politicheskii stroi Kazakhstana*, p. 198.

13. Viatkin, *Ocherki po istorii*, p. 247.

14. Ibid., pp. 255–256.

15. Bekmakhanov, *Prisoedinenie Kazakhstana k Rossii*, p. 86.

16. Wrangali reports in 1847–1848 that it was not uncommon for Russian traders to sell Kazakh grain for 2–2½ times the purchase price. E. Bekmakhanov, *Kazakhstan v 20–40 gody XIX veka* (Alma-Ata, 1947), p. 69.

17. Ibid., p. 225.

18. This is the view expressed by Shoinbaev, *Progressivnoe znachenie*; see also *Istoriia Kazakhskoi SSR* (1979).

19. The study was attacked in the December 26, 1950, issue of *Pravda*; see Chapter Nine for a more lengthy discussion of this issue. For the revised work, see Bekmakhanov, *Prisoedinenie Kazakhstana k Rossii*.

20. Il'ias Esenberlin, *Khan Kene* (Moscow, 1971).

21. Bekmakhanov, *Kazakhstan v 20–40 gody XIX veka*, p. 227.

22. Ibid., p. 307.

23. Ibid., p. 292.

24. *Kazakhsko-russkie otnosheniia v XVIII–XIX vv*, p. 109.

25. Asfendiarov, *Istoriia Kazakhstana*, p. 122.

26. M. K. Rozhkova, *Ekonomicheskie sviazi Rossii so Srednei Aziei* (Moscow, 1963), p. 49.

27. N. A. Khalfin, *Russia's Policy in Central Asia, 1857–1868*, trans. Hubert Evans (London: Central Asian Research Center, 1964), p. 66.

28. Bekmakhanov, *Kazakhstan v 20–40 gody XIX veka*, p. 67.

29. Nonetheless, most of the trade with the Kazakhs was of a local character. An 1866 study reports that of 652 merchants in the steppe, 497 were Tatar or Bashkir and 155 were Russian; 131 were classified as petty bourgeois and 290 as peasant. Rozhkova, *Ekonomicheskie sviazi*, p. 126.

30. Ibid., p. 242.

31. Until 1867 the Kazakhs of the Great Horde were under the administration of the governor general of western Siberia.

32. Dmitrius Boulger, *England and Russia in Central Asia* (London: W. H. Allen, 1879), pp. 318–319.

33. See David MacKenzie, *The Lion of Tashkent* (Athens: University of Georgia Press, 1974), for a complete account of this campaign.

34. Transcaspia, which became the Transcaspian Oblast, was not yet under Russian control. Skobelev led the campaign to acquire this territory from 1881 to 1889.

35. Maksheev', *Istoricheskii obzor Turkestana*, p. 261.

36. Judicial reform was the subject of a "Provisional Statute" in 1865, which limited the jurisdiction of customary courts to cases involving property valued at less than 300R and forbade the biis from levying fines in excess of 30R.

37. Kryzhanovskii argued that two oblasts were being cut off from the steppe solely to justify the creation of a second governor-generalship.

38. Such taxes included the *haraj* (one-tenth of the harvest), the *tanap* (the produce from one-eighth a desiatin of land) and the *za'akat* (one-fortieth of one's property).

39. Thus, three separate ministries had divided control of the territory. The ministry of war controlled two of the oblasts, the ministry of finance had control over taxation, and the ministry of interior had control over everything else. Later, the ministry of agriculture and the resettlement administration also got involved when homesteads in the steppe were made available to Russian settlers.

40. The Muslim clergy lost part of their *waqf* lands, and the payment of religious taxes was made voluntary.

41. Sultan Akhmet Kenisarin, *Sultany Kenisara i Sadyk*, E. T. Smirnov, comp. (Tashkent, 1889), p. 12.

42. Word of the tax increase traveled by the *uyun uzak* (long ear) when horsemen carried the tale from aul to aul.

43. M. S. Tursunova, *Kazakhi Mangyshlaka vo vtoroi polovine XIX veka* (Alma-Ata, 1977), p. 69.

# CHAPTER 4

1. According to *Webster's Ninth New Collegiate Dictionary* (Springfield, Mass.: Merriam-Webster, 1984), the definition of agriculture is "science or art of cultivating

the soil, producing crops, and raising livestock and in varying degrees the preparation of these products for man's use and their disposal (as by marketing)."

2. Tolybekov, *Kochevoe obshchestvo*, p. 414.

3. S. Z. Zimanov, *Obshchestvennyi stroi Kazakhov* (Alma-Ata, 1958), p. 45.

4. Tolybekov, *Kochevoe obshchestvo*, p. 450.

5. Bekmakhanov, *Kazakhstan v 20–40 gody XIX veka*, p. 57.

6. Zimanov, *Obshchestvennyi stroi Kazakhov*, p. 37.

7. Bekmakhanov, *Kazakhstan v 20–40 gody XIX veka*, p. 69.

8. See the English translation of the novel by Mukhtar Auezov, *Abai* (Moscow: Progress, 1968) for a graphic description of just such a feud.

9. Tolybekov, *Kochevoe obshchestvo*, p. 492.

10. *Materialy po istorii politicheskogo*, pp. 352–378.

11. Semirech'e was returned to the Turkestan governor-generalship and the jurisdiction of the ministry of war in 1897.

12. *Materialy po istorii politicheskogo*, pp. 387–399.

13. Donald Treadgold, *The Great Siberian Migration: Government and Peasant in Resettlement from Emancipation to the First World War* (Princeton: Princeton University Press, 1957), pp. 78–79.

14. A. A. Kaufman, *Materialy po voprosu ob organizatsii raboty po obrazovaniiu pereselencheskikh uchastkov v stepnikh oblastiakh* (St. Petersburg, 1896), p. 3.

15. A. A. Kaufman, *K voprosu o russkoi kolonizatsii Turkestanskogo kraia* (St. Petersburg, 1903), p. 49.

16. *Zapiski predsedatelia soveta ministrov o poezdke v Sibir' i Povol'zhe v 1910* (St. Petersburg, 1910), p. 91.

17. Thirty-seven percent in Uralsk, 38 percent in Turgai, 48 percent in Akmolinsk, and 23 percent in Semipalatinsk.

18. In Omsk, Kokchetav, Uralsk, Petropavlovsk and Kustanai. George Demko, *The Russian Colonization of Kazakhstan* (Bloomington, Ind.: Mouton, 1969), p. 211.

19. *Aziatskaia Rossiia* (St. Petersburg, 1914), 1:82.

20. K. K. Palen, *Otchet po revizii Turkestanskago kraia, proizvedennoi po vysochaishemu poveleniiu Senatorom Gofmeisterom Grafom K. K. Palenom*, 18 vols. (St. Petersburg, 1907–1910).

21. Ibid., 2:162.

22. This interpretation is that of Tolybekov in *Kochevoe obshchestvo*, but his work is regarded as controversial. For the earlier view, which holds that the seizure of land alone was responsible for the declining economic fortunes of the Kazakhs, see A. B. Tursunbaev, *Iz istorii krestianskogo pereseleniia v Kazakhstane* (Alma-Ata, 1950).

23. Tolybekov, *Kochevoe obshchestvo*, p. 541.

24. S. A. Sundetov, "Torgovlia v Kazakhstane v nachale XX veka'," in P. G. Galuzo, ed., *Agrarnye otnosheniia na iuge Kazakhstana v 1867–1914 gg* (Alma-Ata, 1965).

25. George Demko, *The Russian Colonization of Kazakhstan, 1896–1916* (Bloomington, Indiana: Mouton, 1969), p. 190.

26. This was also true of Semipalatinsk, much of which was included in the so-called "Cabinet" lands, where settlement was restricted.

27. Tolybekov, *Kochevoe obshchestvo*, p. 440.

28. T. R. Ryskulov, *Kazakstan* (Moscow, 1927), p. 31.

29. *Istoriia Kazakhskoi SSR* (1979), 3:36.

30. F. M. Malikov, *Formirovanie rabochego klassa Kazakhstana v periode imperializma v Rossii* (Alma-Ata, 1973).

31. P. P. Rumiantsev, *Kirgizskii narod v proshlom i nastoiashchem* (St. Petersburg, 1910), p. 16.

32. Ryskulov, *Kazakhstan*, p. 32.

33. Ibid., p. 33.

## CHAPTER 5

1. See Alexandre Bennigsen and Chantal Lemercier-Quelquejay, *Islam in the Soviet Union* (London: Pall Mall Press, 1967), pp. 142–150.

2. Shermukhambetov, "Islam i natsional'naia kultura," in *Chelovek, obshchestvo i religiia* (Moscow, 1968), p. 119.

3. *Kazakhsko-russkie otnosheniia v XVIII–XIX vv*, p. 535.

4. K. B. Beisembiev, *Islam i kritika ego mysliteliami dorevoliutsionnogo Kazakhstana* (Alma-Ata, 1962), p. 8.

5. O. Segizbaev, *Traditsii svobodomysliia i ateizma v dukhovnoi kulture kazakhskogo naroda* (Alma-Ata, 1973), p. 121.

6. A. Bukeikhanov, "Kirgizy," in A. I. Kastelianskii, ed., *Formy natsional'nogo dvizheniia* (St. Petersburg, 1910), p. 587. Bukeikhanov, an organizer of the Alash Orda, undertook the above report for the Kadet party.

7. Beisembiev, *Islam i kritika*, p. 9.

8. Abai Kunanbaev was always known quite simply as "Abai," in the eastern style.

9. See his complete collected works in five volumes. Valikhanov, *Sobranie sochinenii*.

10. I. Altynsaryn, *Sobranie sochinenii v trekh tomakh* (Alma-Ata, 1925–1938).

11. Auezov, *Abai*.

12. These are reprinted in Abai Kunanbaev, *Izbrannye sochinenii* (Alma-Ata, 1980).

13. K. B. Beisembiev, *Ideino-politicheskie techeniia v Kazakhstane kontsa XIX–nachala XX veka* (Alma-Ata, 1961), p. 93.

14. M. S. Tursunova, *Kazakhi Mangyshlaka*.

15. Schuyler, *Turkestan*, 1:225.

16. For numerous accounts of such crimes, see Palen, *Otchet po revizii Turkestanskago kraia.*

17. Bukeikhanov, "Kirgizy," p. 594.

18. See *Revoliutsionnoe dvizhenie v Kazakhstane v 1905–1907 gg: Sbornik dokumentov i materialov* (Alma-Ata, 1955); and B. S. Suleimenov, *Revoliutsionnoe dvizhenie v Kazakhstane v 1905–1907 godakh* (Alma-Ata, 1977).

19. E. Fedorov, "1905 goda i korennoe naselenie Turkestana," in *Ocherki revoliutsionnogo dvizheniia v Srednei Azii, sbornik statei* (Moscow, 1926), p. 30.

20. *Revoliutsionnoe dvizhenie v Kazakhstane v 1905–1907 gg*, p. 597.

21. Suleimenov, *Revoliutsionnoe dvizhenie*, p. 77.

22. S. Brainin and Sh. Shafiro, *Ocherki po istorii Alash-Ordy* (Moscow and Alma-Ata, 1935), p. 78.

23. Fedorov, "1905 goda," p. 30.

24. The four Kazakhs who served were A. Bukeikhanov, A. Beremzhanov, M. Kal'menov, and I. Kulamov.

25. Suleimenov, *Revoliutsionnoe dvizhenie*, pp. 163–164.

26. The Kazakhs in the second Duma were A. Beremzhanov, T. Allabergenov, T. Norokenov, Sh. Koshugulov, and B. Karataev.

27. Tresviatskii, *Materialy po zemel'nomu voprosu v Aziatskii Rossii* (St. Petersburg, 1917), p. 5.

28. Alexandre Bennigsen and Chantal Lemercier-Quelquejay, *La Presse et le Mouvement National chez les Musulmans de Russie avant 1920* (Paris: Mouton, 1964), p. 147.

29. Bukeikhanov, "Kirgizy," p. 585.

30. *Alash* was the organ of the *Ush Zhuz* (Three Horde) party formed in Omsk by opponents of the Alash Orda.

31. Beisembiev, *Ideino-politicheskie*, p. 40.

32. Ibid., pp. 254, 257.

33. S. Z. Zimanov, *V. I. Lenin i sovetskaia natsional'naia gosudarstvennost' v Kazakhstane* (Alma-Ata, 1970), p. 96.

34. Beisembiev, *Ideino-politicheskie*, p. 5. The most conservative Muslim intellectuals never supported these newspapers, and many went along with the Ush Zhuz party, about whose activities very little has been published.

35. Beisembiev, *Ideino-politicheskie*, p. 113.

36. Mir Yakub Dulatov, "Akhmed Baitursunov," *Trudy obshchestva izucheniia Kirgizskogo kraia*, no. 3 (1922): 23.

37. Ibid., p. 35.

38. I. Chekanskii, "Vosstanie Kirgiz-Kazakov v Dzhetyskom (Semiricheskom) krae v iule-sentiabre 1916 goda," *Trudy obshchestva izucheniia Kirgizskogo kraia*, no. 8 (1922): 132.

39. S. D. Asfendiarov, *Natsional'no-osvoboditel'noe vosstanie 1916 goda v Kazakhstane* (Moscow and Alma-Ata, 1936), p. 30.

40. B. S. Suleimenov and Ia. Basin, *Vosstanie 1916 goda v Kazakhstane* (Alma-Ata, 1977), p. 74.

41. Ibid., p. 76.

42. Ibid., p. 94.

43. Ibid., p. 86.

44. Ibid., p. 102.

45. Ibid., p. 79.

46. Ibid., p. 111.

47. *Vosstanie 1916 goda v Srednei Azii i Kazakhstane, sbornik dokumentov* (Moscow, 1960), p. 405.

48. Sarymuldaev, "Moi vospominaniia," *Krasnyi Kazakstan*, no. 2–3 (1926): 70.

49. T. R. Ryskulov, *Vosstanie 1916 v Kirgizstane* (Frunze, 1937), p. 63.

50. *Vosstanie 1916 goda v Srednei Azii*, pp. 352, 499.

51. Suleimenov and Basin, *Vosstanie 1916 goda v Kazakhstane*, p. 81.

52. T. R. Ryskulov, "Vosstanie tuzemtsev Turkestana v 1916 g," in *Ocherki revoliutsionnogo dvizheniia v Srednei Azii, sbornik statei* (Moscow, 1926), p. 154.

53. Dulatov's police dossier from July 8 appears in *Vosstanie 1916 goda v Srednei Azii*, p. 712.

54. Suleimenov and Basin, *Vosstanie 1916 goda v Kazakhstane*, p. 53.

55. Chekanskii, "Vosstanie Kirgiz-Kazakov," pp. 111–115.

56. Ryskulov, *Vosstanie 1916 v Kirgizstane*, p. 73.

57. Edward Sokol, *The Revolt of 1916 in Central Asia* (Baltimore: Johns Hopkins Press, 1953), p. 159.

58. Ryskulov, "Vosstanie tuzemtsev Turkestana v 1916 g," p. 154.

59. The tenth anniversary jubilee literature included G. I. Broido, "O vosstanie kazak-kirgizskogo naroda v 1916 gody," *Qizil Qazaqstan*, nos. 3–5 (1925); and T. R. Ryskulov, "Vosstanie 1916 goda," *Qizil Qazaqstan*, nos. 11–14 (1926).

60. *Ves' Kazakhstan* (Moscow and Alma-Ata, 1931), p. 60.

61. S. Brainin and Sh. Shafiro, *Vosstanie Kazakhov Semirech'ia v 1916 godu* (Moscow and Alma-Ata, 1936).

62. See chapter one of Suleimenov and Basin, *Vosstanie 1916 goda v Kazakhstane* for a good bibliographical essay on works from this and earlier periods.

## CHAPTER 6

1. Joseph Castagné, "La Revolution dans Turkestan," *Revue du Monde Musulmans*, no. 1 (1922): 177.

2. Brainin and Shafiro, *Ocherki po istorii Alash-Ordy*, p. 54.

3. Tresviatskii, *Materialy po zemel'nomy voprosy*, p. 5.

4. Ibid., p. 20.

5. S. Seifullin, *Ternistyi put'* (Moscow, 1975), pp. 91–93.

6. Brainin and Shafiro, *Ocherki po istorii Alash-Ordy*, p. 126.

7. Ibid., p. 126.

8. Ibid., item 12.

9. Ibid., item 13.

10. Zimanov, *V. I. Lenin*, p. 149.

11. Ibid., p. 149. They continued to call for this in *Qazaq* (September 2, 1918).

12. Brainin and Shafiro, *Ocherki po istorii Alash-Ordy*, p. 131, see parts 1 and 2.

13. Ibid., p. 129, item 3.

14. Ibid., items 6, 7, 9, 19.

15. Ibid., item 4; the Provisional Government provided for zemstvo governments in sedentary regions only.

16. The best accessible account of these meetings appears in Seifullin, *Ternistyi put'*.

17. Zimanov, *V. I. Lenin*, p. 150.

18. *1917 goda v Kazakhstane* (Alma-Ata, 1977), p. 47.

19. Zimanov, *V. I. Lenin*, p. 149.

20. S. M. Dimanshtein, ed., *Revoliutsiia i natsional'nyi vopros*, vol. 3 (Moscow, 1930), p. 363.

21. Seifullin, *Ternistyi put'*, p. 122.

22. A. K. Bochagov, *Alash-Orda* (Kzyl-Orda, 1927), pp. 41–49.

23. Seifullin, *Ternistyi put'*, p. 165.

24. Ibid., p. 163.

25. G. Togzhanov, "O Baitsursunove i baitursunovshchine," *Bol'shevik Kazakstana*, no. 2–3 (1932): 32.

26. S. Kenzhebaev, *Sovety v bor'be za postroenie sotsializma* (Alma-Ata, 1963), p. 197.

27. This was the thesis of Ryskulov, "Vosstanie tuzemtsev Turkestana v 1916 g."

28. For some examples of post-1930 accounts see S. Brainin and Sh. Shafiro, *Pervye shagi sovetov v Semirech'e* (Moscow and Alma-Ata, 1934); *Bor'ba s kontrrevoliutsiei* (Omsk, 1959); *Grazhdanskaia voina v Orenburzhoe* (Orenburg, 1958); A. S. Elagin, *Sotsialisticheskoe stroitel'stvo v Kazakhstane v gody grazhdanskoi voiny* (Alma-Ata, 1966); and K. Nurpeisov, *Sovety Kazakhstana v bor'be za uprochenie vlasti rabochikh i krest'ian* (Alma-Ata, 1968).

29. *1917 goda v Kazakhstane*, pp. 200–201.

30. There were three major sources published on the Alash Orda: Brainin and Shafiro, *Ocherki po istorii Alash-Ordy*; Bochagov, *Alash-Orda*; and Martynenko, *Alash-Orda* (Tashkent, 1929). While in Moscow I had access to the first two of these sources.

31. Seifullin, *Ternistyi put'*, p. 127; *Qazaq*, no. 254 (December 18, 1917).

32. Ibid.; *Qazaq*, no. 250.

33. Tynyshpaev's board included seven Kazakhs and four Russians. He was also active in the Turkestan autonomy movement, which included Mustafa Chokaev.

34. Seifullin, *Ternistyi put'*, p. 164.

35. *1917 goda v Kazakhstane*, p. 201.

36. G. Abishev, *Kazakhstan v zashchite sotsialisticheskogo otechestva* (Alma-Ata, 1964), p. 62.

37. S. N. Pokrovskii, *Razgrom interventov i vnutrennei kontrrevoliutsii v Kazakhstane 1918–1920 gg* (Alma-Ata, 1967), p. 126.

38. *Innostrannaia voina i grazhdanskaia voina v Srednei Azii i Kazakhstane* (Alma-Ata, 1963), 1:312.

39. Seifullin, *Ternistyi put'*, p. 186.

40. Brainin and Shafiro, *Ocherki po istorii Alash-Ordy*, p. 63.

41. *Innostrannaia voina*, 1:475; Pokrovskii, *Razgrom interventov*, p. 249.

42. Brainin and Shafiro, *Ocherki p istorii Alash-Ordy*, p. 142.

43. *Innostrannaia voina*, 2:60–61.

44. Bochagov, *Alash-Orda*, p. 49.

45. Alibekov's followers called themselves the *Ak Zhol* (White Road). They accused Dos Muhammadov of seeking the title khan and then fled to join the Bolsheviks. Seifullin, *Ternistyi put'*, pp. 180, 186, 187.

46. *Innostrannaia voina*, 2:90.

47. Ibid., 2:112–113.

48. *Grazhdanskaia voina v Kazakhstane* (Alma-Ata, 1974), p. 132.

49. J. F. N. Bradley, *Civil War in Russia, 1917–1920* (London: B. T. Batsford, 1975), p. 105.

50. *Innostrannaia voina*, 2:92.

51. Pokrovskii, *Razgrom interventov*, p. 311.

52. *Innostrannaia voina*, 2:169.

53. Ibid., 2:166.

54. Bochagov, *Alash-Orda*, p. 51.

55. The Basmachi revolt went only as far north as Osh in Kirgiz territory. A. I. Zevelev, *Basmachestvo: vozniknovenie, sushchnost', krakh* (Moscow, 1981), p. 156. There were several reasons for this, including the long-standing administrative separation between Turkestan and the steppe, centuries-old antagonism between Kazakhs and Uzbeks that impeded cooperation, and the fact that the massive land seizures that had helped spur the Uzbek revolt did not occur in Kazakhstan until 1926–1928. See Martha Brill Olcott, "The Basmachi or Freemen's Revolt in Turkestan, 1918–1924," *Soviet Studies* 33, no. 3 (1981): 352–369.

## CHAPTER 7

1. For a discussion of the relief effort see Ralph Fox, *People of the Steppes* (Boston and New York: Houghton Mifflin, 1925).

2. T. R. Ryskulov, *Revoliutsiia i korennoe naselenie Turkestana 1917–1919 gg* (Tashkent, 1925), p. 70.

3. *Sotsialisticheskoe stroitel'stvo v Kazakhstane v vostanovitel'nom periode* (Alma-Ata, 1962), p. 23.

4. Local fighting was quite severe in early 1921; the so-called Ishim-Petropavlovsk uprising of February 1921 cut off much of northern Kazakhstan and western Siberia for two weeks. Most of the resistance fighters were Russians, but they managed to disrupt the Kazakh grain supply. V. Grigor'ev, "X s"ezd RKP(b) i razgrom melkobur-zhuaznoi kontrrevoliutsii na territorii respubliki," in *Voprosy partiinogo stroitel'stva* (Alma-Ata, 1972), p. 218.

5. G. F. Dakhshlieger, "K voprosu ob ekonomike Kazakhskoi ASSR nakanune perekhoda k NEPu," *Izvestiia AN KazSSR*, no. 5 (1957): 17.

6. The former Russian villages became the foundation of many Kazakh settlements. See *Kul'tura i byt kazakhskogo kolkhoznogo aula* (Alma-Ata, 1967), p. 67.

7. G. Skalov, "O soiuze Koshchi," *Zhizn' natsional'nostei*, no. 5 (1923): 19.

8. Kenzhebaev, *Sovety v bor'be*, p. 197.

9. L. N., "Uspekhi Kirgizii," *Zhizn' natsional'nostei*, no. 5 (1923): 19.

10. See G. F. Dakhshlieger, *Sotsial'no-ekonomicheskoie preobrazovanie v aule i derevne Kazakhstana (1921–1929)* (Alma-Ata, 1965); T. E. Eleuov, *Ustanovlenie i uprochenie sovetskoi vlasti v Kazakhstane* (Alma-Ata, 1961); *Istoriia Kazakhskoi SSR*, vol. 2 (Alma-Ata, 1963); and *Istoriia Kazakhskoi SSR*, vol. 4 (Alma-Ata, 1977).

11. According to the 1926 census, only 10 percent of the Kazakh population was considered "pastoral," that is, migrating year-round. This figure reflects the difficulty of migratory conditions.

12. G. Skalov, "Opyt klassovogo rasseleniia v usloviakh Turkestana," *Zhizn' natsional'nostei*, no. 2 (1923): 39.

13. Although Kazakhstan was technically closed to Russian settlement, many Russians [possibly as many as 50,000] moved there illegally. See Martin McCauley, *Khrushchev and the Development of Soviet Agriculture: The Virgin Land Programme, 1953–1964* (New York: Holmes and Meier, 1976), p. 20.

14. As per the TsIK KazASSR resolution of June 28, 1920, cited in *Sotsialisticheskoe stroitel'stvo*, p. 40.

15. The census of 1926 fully demonstrated to the regime the difficulty of dealing with the Kazakhs. Many Kazakhs simply refused to comply and the census was partial at best. See *Sotsialisticheskoe stroitel'stvo*, p. 213.

16. This was permitted in the land codex of 1923.

17. *Sotsialisticheskoe stroitel'stvo*, p. 307.

18. Ibid., p. 310.

19. For examples see M. M. Davydov, "O blizhaishikh perspektivakh sel'skokhoziaistvennogo razvitiia Syr-Dar'inskogo raiona Kazakstana," *Narodnoe khoziaistvo Kazakstana*, no. 3 (1926): 53–63; N. Kenarskii, "Zemleustroistvo kirgizskogo naseleniia," *Sovetskaia Kirgiziia*, no. 5–6 (1924): 131–146; and M. G.

Sirius, "O normakh zemlepol'zovaniia dlia kochevnikogo naseleniia KSSR," *Sovetskaia Kirgiziia*, no. 5 (1925): 52–65.

20. *Sovetskoe stroitel'stvo v selakh i aulakh Semirech'ia 1921–1925 gg* (Alma-Ata, 1957), p. 184.

21. This position was first argued by V. F. Shakhmatov, "K voprosu o slozhenii i spetsifike patriarkhal'no-feodal'nykh otnoshenii v Kazakhstane," *Vestnik Akademii Nauk Kazakhstana*, no. 7 (1951): 18–36; and Shakhmatov's analysis was accepted by the authors and works cited above in footnote 10 of this chapter.

22. *Sotsialisticheskoe stroitel'stvo*, p. 321.

23. Ibid., p. 388.

24. A. P. Kuchkin, *Sovetizatsiia kazakhskogo aula* (Moscow, 1962), p. 255. In this period the Kazakhs made up almost 60 percent of the population in Kazakhstan.

25. The Koshchi Union was a voluntary organization, purportedly of Kazakh poor who were to encourage popular support for Soviet policies. See A. Bogdanov, "The Koshchi Union in Kazakstan," in Rudolf Schlesinger, ed., *The Nationality Problem and Soviet Administration* (London: Routledge and Kegan Paul, 1953), pp. 90–100.

26. For some of the most controversial arguments, see K. A. Chuvelev, "O reorganizatsii kochevogo i polukochevogo khoziaistva," *Narodnoe khoziaistvo Kazakstana*, no. 1 (1926): 42–51; E. A. Polochanskii, *Za novyi aul-kstau* (Moscow, 1926); and V. A. Sokolovskii, *Kazakskii aul* (Tashkent, 1926).

27. *Sovetskaia step'* (May 23, 1926): 2.

28. *Sovetskaia step'* (May 24, 1926): 1.

29. Alec Nove, *An Economic History of the U.S.S.R.* (Baltimore: Penguin Books, 1972), p. 150.

30. *Sovetskaia step'* (October 13, 1927): 1.

31. A. B. Tursunbaev, *Kollektivizatsiia sel'skogo khoziaistva Kazakhstana, 1926–1941 gg*, 2 vols. (Alma-Ata, 1967), 1:96.

32. Ibid., 1:114.

33. A. B. Tursunbaev, "Torzhestvo kolkhoznogo stroia v Kazakhstane," in *Ocherki istorii kollektivizatsii sel'skogo khoziaistva v soiuznykh respublikakh* (Moscow, 1963), p. 269.

34. Kuchkin, *Sovetizatsiia kazakhskogo aula*, p. 285.

35. Ibid., p. 304.

36. Tursunbaev, *Kollektivizatsiia sel'skogo*, 1:171.

37. *Sotsialisticheskoe stroitel'stvo*, p. 50.

38. A. Mamutov, *Prestupleniia sostavliaiushchie perezhitki patriarkal'no-rodogo byta* (Alma-Ata, 1963), p. 75.

39. *Sovetskaia step'* (September 14, 1926): 3.

40. *Sotsialisticheskoe stroitel'stvo*, p. 498.

41. There was a particularly severe outbreak of cholera in 1926.

42. *Sotsialisticheskoe stroitel'stvo*, p. 92.

43. *Sovetskaia step'* (March 9, 1926): 3.

44. S. I. Rudenko, "Ocherk byta severo-vostochnikh Kazakhov," in *Kazaki* (Leningrad, 1930), p. 72.

45. "V kollegii," *Sel'skoe khoziaistvo RSFSR*, no. 24 (1931): 32.

46. For a brief account of the construction of the Turkestan-Siberian railroad, see *Istoriia Kazakhskoi SSR* (1977); and for a more detailed account, see T. R. Ryskulov, "Piat' let raboty Turksiba," *Narodnoe khoziaistvo Kazakstana*, no. 7–8 (1935): 32–35.

47. Kuchkin, *Sovetizatsiia kazakhskogo aula*, p. 252.

48. M. M. Davydov, "Perspektivy tipy khoziaistv dlia khlopknykh raionov Syr-dar'inskogo gubernii Kazakstana," *Narodnoe khoziaistvo Kazakstana*, no. 1 (1926): 43.

49. *Sovetskaia step'* (May 22, 1926): 2.

50. E. Gromov, "K voprosu o rassloenii krest'ianstva v Kazakhstane," *Revoliutsion-nyi vostok*, no. 3 (1928): 170.

51. F. I. Goloshchekin, "Kazakstan po putim sotsialisticheskogo pereustroistva," in U. Isaev, ed., *Sbornik statei i rechei* (Moscow and Alma-Ata, 1931), p. 28.

## CHAPTER 8

1. For a more detailed account of collectivization in Kazakhstan, see Martha Brill Olcott, "The Collectivization Drive in Kazakhstan," *Russian Review* 40, no. 2 (1981): 122–142.

2. D. J. Male, *Russian Peasant Organization Before Collectivization* (Cambridge: Cambridge University Press, 1971), p. 219.

3. F. I. Kolodin, "TOZy v Kazakhstane v gody pervoi i vtoroi piatiletok," *Trudy instituta istorii, arkheologii i etnografii AN KazSSR*, no. 2 (1956): 146.

4. F. N. Bazanov, "Formirovanie natsional'nogo sostava naseleniia Kazakhstana v gody dovoennykh piatiletok," *Vestnik AN KazSSR*, no. 1 (1981): 56.

5. Kuchkin, *Sovetizatsiia kazakhskogo aula*, p. 364.

6. Tursunbaev, *Kollektivizatsiia sel'skogo*, 1:60.

7. Ibid., 1:175.

8. For more detailed accounts of opposition by these individuals and groups, see Moshe Lewin, *Russian Peasants and Soviet Power* (Chicago: Northwestern University Press, 1968); Stephen Cohen, *Bukharin and the Bol'shevik Revolution* (New York: Knopf, 1973); Chuvelev, "O reorganizatsii"; A. N. Donich, "Narod-naselenie Ka-zakstana," *Narodnoe khoziaistvo Kazakstana*, no. 11–12 (1928): 27–56; S. Sad-vokasov, "O natsional'nostiakh i natsionalakh," *Bolshevik*, no. 1 (1928): 56–64; and K. D. Toktabaev, "Puti razvitiia sel'skogo khoziaistva Kazakstana," *Ekonomicheskoe obozrenie*, no. 11 (1928): 51–56.

9. I. I. Larin, "K voprosu o bolee ratsional'nom napravlenii sel'skogo khoziaistvo severo-vostochnogo Kazakstana," *Narodnoe khoziaistvo Kazakstana*, no. 1 (1928);

and I. I. Maslov, "Analiz dinamiki osnovnykh otraslei narodnogo khoziaistva KASSR," *Narodnoe khoziaistvo Kazakstana*, no. 1 (1928): 24–38.

10. Kuchkin, *Sovetizatsiia kazakhskogo aula*. Dakhshlieger, *Sotsial'no-ekonomicheskoe* was written in an attempt to demonstrate that the Kazakh countryside was, in fact, prepared for collectivization.

11. Tursunbaev, "Torzhestvo kolkhoznogo," p. 274.

12. Ibid., p. 272.

13. E. D. Terletskii et al., "Proizvodstvennaia kharakteristika sel'sko-khoziaistvennikh kollektivov," *Na agrarnom fronte*, no. 2 (1929): 79.

14. A. B. Tursunbaev, *Pobeda kolkhoznogo stroia v Kazakhstane* (Alma-Ata, 1957), p. 133.

15. Ibid., p. 132.

16. Tursunbaev, *Kollektivizatsiia sel'skogo*, 1:371.

17. See Gabit Musrepov, "Etnograficheskii rasskaz," *Belaia arauna* (Moscow, 1976), pp. 95–109.

18. The "25,000ers" were alleged to be skilled workers whose talents could be used in building collective farms, but in reality most were unemployed workers or displaced soldiers. See Patricia Kolb, "The Roots of Revolution from Above," M.A. thesis (University of Chicago, 1973).

19. Tursunbaev, *Pobeda kolkhoznogo*, pp. 141–143.

20. M. L. Bogdenko, "Kolkhoznoe stroitel'stvo vesnoi i letom 1930 g," *Istoricheskie zapiski* 67 (1965): 31.

21. Tursunbaev, "Torzhestvo kolkhoznogo," p. 281.

22. Tursunbaev, *Kollektivizatsiia sel'skogo*, 1:353.

23. In June 1930 there were only 416 agronomists and specialists in the republic, of whom only 4 were Kazakhs. A Bogdanov, "Kolkhoznoe stroitel'stvo v natsional'nykh respublikakh i oblastiakh," *Revoliutsiia i natsional'nosti*, no. 1 (1931): 50.

24. Tursunbaev, *Kollektivizatsiia sel'skogo*, 1:287.

25. Kolodin, "TOZy v Kazakhstane," p. 194.

26. Tursunbaev, *Kollektivizatsiia sel'skogo*, p. 1:371.

27. N. Timofeev and S. Brainin, "Kazakhskaia kraevaia organizatsiia VKP(b) v bor'be za kollektivizatsiiu sel'skogo khoziaistva (1930–1939 gg)," *Bol'shevik Kazakhstana*, no. 1 (1939): 87.

28. Only 30 percent of the nomads were completely settled, that is, they had land to sow, buildings for animals, and tools.

29. T. A. Zveriakov, *Ot kochev'ia k sotsializmu* (Alma-Ata, 1934), p. 53.

30. *Kazakstan k IX s"ezdu sovetov (1931–1934 gg)* (Alma-Ata, 1935), pp. 85–86.

31. I. Kuramysov, *Na putiakh sotsialisticheskogo pereustroistva kazakskogo aula* (Moscow and Alma-Ata, 1932), pp. 3–4.

32. A. Savin, "Bol'shevitskaia programa sotsialisticheskoi pereustroiki kazakskogo aula," *Bol'shevik Kazakhstana*, no. 12 (1932): 13.

33. That is, 139,000 households. B. A. Amantaev, *Sotsializm: Korennoe preobrazovanie sotsial'noi prirody kazakhskogo krest'ianstva* (Alma-Ata, 1969), p. 379.

34. *Sel'skoe khoziaistvo SSSR ezhegodnik 1935* (Moscow, 1936), p. 532.

35. All others could own only twenty-five sheep and goats, three cows, and one horse. Tursunbaev, *Kollektivizatsiia sel'skogo*, 1:306.

36. T. A. Aitiev, *Torzhestvo leninskogo kooperativnogo plana v Kazakhstane* (Alma-Ata, 1969), p. 33.

37. Tursunbaev, *Kollektivizatsiia sel'skogo*, 2:440.

38. Naum Jasny, *The Socialized Agriculture of the U.S.S.R.* (Stanford: Stanford University Press, 1941), p. 323.

39. Iu. A. Poliakov and A. I. Chugunov, *Konets Basmachestva* (Moscow, 1976), p. 154.

40. Amantaev, *Sotsializm: Korennoe*, p. 325.

41. I. Kosakov, "Itogi planovogo osedaniia i prakticheskie zadachi," *Revoliutsiia i natsional'nosti*, no. 5–6 (1933): 68.

42. *Kazakstan k IX s"ezdu sovetov*, pp. 85–86.

43. Tursunbaev, "Torzhestvo kolkhoznogo," p. 279.

44. Amantaev, *Sotsializm: Korennoe*, p. 379.

45. With 1929 as a base year ( = 100), in 1933 the relative number of horses in the USSR was 48.4 and in Kazakhstan 11.4; large cattle in the USSR 56.7 and in Kazakhstan 23.0; and sheep and goats in the USSR 34.4 and in Kazakhstan 10.6. Tursunbaev, *Kollektivizatsiia sel'skogo*, 2:480.

46. "Kazakhskaia Sovetskaia Sotsialisticheskaia Respublika (fakty i tsifry)," *Bol'shevik Kazakstana*, no. 3 (1937): 73.

47. *Kazakhstanskaia pravda* (September 30, 1936): 1–2; and Tursunbaev, *Kollektivizatsiia sel'skogo*, 2:392.

48. Aitiev, *Torzhestvo leninskogo*, p. 36.

49. Tursunbaev, *Kollektivizatsiia sel'skogo*, 2:392.

50. Ibid.

51. S. B. Nurmukhamedov, P. B. Savo'ko, and R. B. Suleimenov, *Ocherki istorii sotsialisticheskogo stroitel'stva v Kazakhstane, 1933–1940 gg* (Alma-Ata, 1966), p. 123.

52. G. Chulanov, *Ocherki istorii narodnogo khoziaistva Kazakhskoi SSR* (Alma-Ata, 1962), 2:285.

53. One exception is Bennigsen and Lemercier-Quelquejay, *Islam in the Soviet Union*.

54. V. K. Savos'ko and I. Sh. Shamshatov, *Kolkhoznoe stroitel'stvo v Kazakhstane (1946–1970 gg)* (Alma-Ata, 1974), p. 17.

55. T. B. Balakaev, *Kolkhoznoe krest'ianstvo Kazakhstana v gody velikoi otechestvennoi voini 1941–1945 gg* (Alma-Ata, 1971), p. 147.

56. *Istoriia Kazakhskoi SSR* (1963), 2:466.

57. M. Kozybaev, *Kazakhstan. Arsenal fronta* (Alma-Ata, 1970), p. 397.

58. Savos'ko and Shamshatov, *Kolkhoznoe stroitel'stvo v Kazakhstane*, p. 17.

59. Aitiev, *Torzhestvo leninskogo*, p. 57.

60. V. P. Danilov, "Problemy istorii sovetskoi derevni v 1946–1970 gg (ocherk istoriografii)," in *Razvitie sel'skogo khoziaistva SSSR v poslevoennye gody (1946–1970 gg)* (Moscow, 1972), pp. 10–40.

61. A. Erzhanov, *Uspekhi natsional'noi politiki KPSS v Kazakhstane (1946–1958 gg)* (Alma-Ata, 1969), p. 92.

62. Savos'ko and Shamshatov, *Kolkhoznoe stroitel'stvo*, p. 17.

63. *Narodnoe khoziaistvo Kazakhstana* (Alma-Ata, 1957), p. 68.

64. That year the yield was 7.7 centners per hectare.

65. Aitiev, *Torzhestvo leninskogo*, p. 57.

66. In 1940, 26.6 percent of all meat slaughtered in the USSR came from Kazakhstan; in 1946, 11.7 percent; and in 1953, 16.5 percent. In 1940, 14.0 percent of all cereal crops grown in the USSR came from Kazakhstan; in 1946, 14.6 percent; and in 1953, 17.3 percent.

67. In 1928 there were (in thousands) 19,169 sheep and goats in Kazakhstan as compared to 17,711.7 in 1952; 2,219.6 cows in 1928 as compared to 1,440.8 in 1952; and 6,534.3 horned cattle in 1928 as compared to 4,454.1 in 1952. Data comes from *Narodnoe khoziaistvo Kazakhstana* (1957).

68. *Narodnoe khoziaistvo Kazakhstana. Statisticheskii sbornik* (Alma-Ata, 1968), p. 105.

69. Nurmukhamedov et al., *Ocherki istorii sotsialisticheskogo*, p. 164.

70. Examples of Soviet scholarship include Nurmukhamedov et al., *Ocherki istorii sotsialisticheskogo* and R. B. Suleimenov and Kh. I. Bisenov, *Sotsialisticheskii put' kul'turnogo progressa otstalnykh narodov* (Alma-Ata, 1967). For a Western account of Stalin's policy toward literature in Kazakhstan, see Martha Brill Olcott, "The Fabrication of a Social Past—The Kazakhs of Central Asia," in Myron Aronoff, ed., *Political Anthropology Handbook I* (Rutgers: Transaction Press, 1980), pp. 193–213.

71. The data regarding literacy is quite confusing since it is never clear whether what is being measured is the ability to read and write Kazakh, or Russian, or either language without distinction. See also R. B. Suleimenov, "Iz istorii bor'by za likvidatsiiu negramotnosti v Kazakhstane (1933–1940 gg)," *Trudy instituta istorii, arkheologii i etnografii AN KazSSR* 9 (1960): 125–126.

72. Ibid., p. 114.

73. Ibid., p. 112.

74. Of schools in Kazakhstan, 21.4 percent offered a one-year program, 48.5 percent a two-year program, 16.5 percent a three-year program, and 13.6 percent a four-year program. Nurmukhamedov et al., *Ocherki istorii sotsialisticheskogo*, p. 240.

75. Ibid., p. 243.

76. Ibid., p. 238.

77. Suleimenov, "Iz istorii," p. 114.

78. Nurmukhamedov et al., *Ocherki istorii sotsialisticheskogo*, p. 234.

79. S. Kuzich, "Vosstanovit' znachenie i rol' anti-religioznoi propagandy," *Bol'shevik Kazakstana*, no. 9–10 (1937): 47.

80. V. M. Shvili, "Rabota brigady vrachei sorvana mullami," *Bezbozhnik*, no. 56 (n.d.): 4.

81. D. K. Kryvelev, "Zadachi anti-religioznoi raboty v zhivotnovodcheskikh sovkhozakh," *Antireligioznik*, no. 2 (1934): 15.

82. The Crimean Tatars and North Caucasian peoples were less fortunate; whole nations were forcibly deported. See Aleksandr Nekrich, *The Punished Peoples* (New York: Norton, 1979).

83. *Istoriia Kazakhskoi SSR*, vol. 5 (Alma-Ata, 1981), p. 317.

84. Nurmukhamedov et al., *Ocherki istorii sotsialisticheskogo*, p. 211.

## CHAPTER 9

1. The so-called *Kirpartburo* (Kirgiz party bureau; the Kazakh people were still being referred to as "Kirgiz") was organized on April 30, 1920.

2. Data gleaned from *Kompartiia Kazakhstana za 50 let (1920–1971)* (Alma-Ata, 1972).

3. The Kazakh ASSR was part of the RSFSR until 1936, when it became the Kazakh S.S.R.

4. Ibid., p. 63.

5. E. Andreev, "Iz istorii stanovleniia sistemy partiinogo-prosveshcheniia," in *Voprosy partiinogo stroitel'stva* (Alma-Ata, 1972), p. 234.

6. *Leninskii prizyv v Kazakhstane* (Alma-Ata, 1969), p. 283.

7. G. Togzhanov, *O kazakskom aule* (Kzyl-Orda, 1928), p. 58.

8. Sh. Kusanov, *Ukreplenie aul'nikh i sel'skikh partiinykh organizatsii v Kazakhstane v periode kollektivizatsii* (Alma-Ata, 1958), p. 5.

9. Kuchkin, *Sovetizatsiia kazakhskogo aula*, p. 207.

10. Kusanov, *Ukreplenie aul'nikh*, p. 5.

11. A. Dzhangel'din is a well publicized "Soviet hero" who was first praised for organizing troops from among his native Adaev tribesmen to serve with the Bolsheviks. His reward was membership in the first Kazakh buro, but his high office seems to have been largely honorific. Although he lived until 1953, there is no evidence that he ever played any sort of decisionmaking role in either the party or state bureaucracies.

12. A good example of this is *Istoriia Kazakhskoi SSR* (1977).

13. I was fortunate enough to have had access to Kazakh republic newspapers for the 1920s and 1930s while in the USSR, but only after engaging in several months of bureaucratic infighting.

14. See *Sotsialisticheskoe stroitel'stvo* and *Sovetskoe stroitel'stvo*.

15. That is, this was the attitude taken after the radical social policies of 1918–1919 in Central Asia had led to the Basmachi revolt.

16. *Voprosy istorii kompartii Kazakhstana* (Alma-Ata, 1964), p. 245.

17. Kuchkin, *Sovetizatsiia kazakhskogo aula*, p. 318.

18. M. A. Binder and G. Sapargaliev, "Iz istorii korenizatsii gosudarstvennogo apparata Kazakhstana," *Izvestiia AN KazSSR*, no. 6 (1959): 18.

19. Zh. Ibraev, *Mestnye sovety Kazakhstana v period stroitel'stva sotsializma* (Alma-Ata, 1973), p. 13.

20. V. Riabokon', "K voprosu o sovetizatsii aula," *Krasnyi Kazakstana*, no. 1 (1926): 54.

21. Kenzhebaev, *Sovety*, p. 200, reports that in 1926 only 2–3 percent of the population of Kazakhstan was eligible to vote, and in 1927 only 3–4 percent. See also Kuchkin, *Sovetizatsiia kazakhskogo aula*, p. 154.

22. Kuchkin, *Sovetizatsiia kazakhskogo aula*, p. 141.

23. Ibid., p. 238.

24. Kenzhebaev, *Sovety v*, p. 201.

25. V. M. Ustinov, *Sluzhenie narodu* (Alma-Ata, 1984), pp. 62–78.

26. Ryskulov was a member of the *Sredazburo* (Central Asian Bureau) and chairman of the *Sovnarkom* (the Council of Commissars) of the Turkestan Republic from 1922–1924, but then was posted abroad to Mongolia. He returned to Kazakhstan in 1926 to do relatively unimportant executive work, although he did hold the post of deputy of the RSFSR Sovnarkom. In honor of Ryskulov's ninetieth birthday, a heavily edited collection of writings (T. R. Ryskulov, *Izbrannye trudy* [Alma-Ata, 1984]) and the Ustinov biography (*Sluzhenie narodu*) were published.

27. Casting votes against the separatist party were such prominent Kazakhs as S. D. Asfendiarov, U. K. Dzhandosov, and S. Khodzhanov. These people did, however, support the expropriation of Russian lands.

28. See Dulatov, "Akhmed Baitursunov."

29. Baitursunov argued this position in his 1926 pamphlet, *The Kazakh Economy*, written in Kazakh and presently unavailable in either the West or the USSR.

30. See Zveriakov, *Ot kochev'ia k sotsializmu*; Sokolovskii, *Kazakskii aul*; and M. G. Sirius, "K voprosu o perspektivakh skotovodstva v Kazakstane," *Narodnoe khoziaistvo Kazakstana*, no. 1 (1926): 26–30, and "Perspektivy razvitiia sel'skogo khoziaistva Kazakstana," *Narodnoe khoziaistvo Kazakstana*, no. 3 (1926): 3–15.

31. R. Melikova, "Internatsional'noe vospitanie trudiashchikhsiia v gody sotsialisticheskogo stroitel'stva (1925–1937 gg)," *Voprosy istorii kompartii Kazakhstana*, no. 11 (1974): 220.

32. Leon Trotsky, *The Challenge of the Left Opposition, 1926–1927*, vol. 2, Naomi Allen, ed. (New York: Monthly Review Press, 1980), p. 211.

33. Ibid.

34. Sadvakosov, "O natsional'nostiakh," p. 59.

35. *I drugie* means "and others" and is commonly used to denote that people who are no longer ideologically acceptable participated in the conference.

36. Kuchkin, *Sovetizatsiia kazakskogo aula*, p. 304.

37. Kenzhebaev, *Sovety v*, p. 195.

38. See Brainin and Shafiro, *Ocherki po istorii Alash-Ordy.*

39. G. Togzhanov, "O Baitursunove," no. 2–3 (1932): 29–38; and no. 5 (1932): 20–27.

40. T. R. Ryskulov, *Kazakstan* (rev. ed., Moscow, 1935) and "Protiv izvrashcheniia istorii kazakhskogo naroda," *Bol'shevik Kazakstana*, no. 1–2 (1936): 110–124.

41. Togzhanov, a former member of the Birlik group, served in leading capacities in the Kazakh party and by 1928 had risen to membership in the buro as a member of the "Kazakh-left" group.

42. Ryskulov, "Protiv izvrashcheniia," p. 124.

43. Kenzhebaev, *Sovety v*, p. 207. *Saun aitmai* and *sagum* are traditional forms of material assistance offered to clansmen in distress.

44. Robert Conquest, *The Great Terror* (New York: Macmillan, 1973), p. 277.

45. Kuchkin, *Sovetizatsiia kazakhskogo aula*, p. 341.

46. *Natsional'nyi sostav kadrov predpriatii v Kazakhstane* (Moscow, 1936), p. 42.

47. T. Soldatov, "Po lepsinskom kolkhozam," *Bol'shevik Kazakstana*, no. 1 (1932): 51.

48. This data has been gleaned from *Kommunisticheskaia partiia Kazakhstana v dokumentakh i tsifrakh* (Alma-Ata, 1960).

49. Over half the party membership had joined after 1928.

50. *Kommunisticheskaia partiia Kazakhstana v dokumentakh*, and *Kompartiia Kazakhstana za 50 let.*

51. From 48,322 members in 1938 to 148,612 members in 1946.

52. *Kompartiia Kazakhstana za 50 let*, p. 161.

53. Aitiev, *Torzhestvo leninskogo*, p. 57.

54. A. Pankratova and M. Abdykalikov, *Istoriia Kazakhskoi SSR s drevneishikh vremen do nashikh dnei* (Alma-Ata, 1943). The need for a new history at this time was particularly acute since Viatkin's 1941 history had been officially attacked, and S. Asfendiarov, the author of the widely distributed 1935 history, had been killed as a national-deviationist in the purges.

55. For a detailed history of this, see Lowell Tillet, *The Great Friendship* (Chapel Hill: University of North Carolina Press, 1969).

56. This statement is rather at odds with Tillet's interpretation of the dispute, but Bekmakhanov's book was not available when Tillet did his research. My analysis is based on a close reading of Bekmakhanov.

57. Bekmakhanov was rehabilitated in 1956 and allowed to publish a "replacement" volume: *Prisoedinenie Kazakhstana k Rossii* (Moscow, 1957).

## CHAPTER 10

1. There is quite an extensive literature in English on the Virgin Lands Policy, including McCauley, *Khrushchev and Soviet Agriculture*; Sidney Ploss, *Conflict and Decision-making in Soviet Russia: A Case Study of Agricultural Policy, 1953–1963* (Princeton: Princeton University Press, 1965); Richard M. Mills, "Policy and Administrative Problems in the Soviet Virgin Lands Program in Kazakhstan, 1954–1964" (Ph.D. dissertation, Harvard University, 1965); and Leonid Brezhnev's own account, *The Virgin Lands* (Moscow: Progress Publishers, 1978).

2. *KPSS v resoliutsiakh i resheniakh ch. III 1930–1954 gg* (Moscow, 1954), p. 633.

3. Ibid., p. 617.

4. Mills, "Policy and Administrative Problems," p. 26.

5. *Pravda* (October 10, 1953), and *Izvestiia* (November 11, 1953).

6. *Izvestiia* (November 11, 1953).

7. These oblasts were Akmolinsk (subsequently renamed Tselinograd), Karaganda, Kokchetav, Kustanai, Pavlodar, and Northern Kazakhstan.

8. *Pravda* (February 22, 1954).

9. B. Gafurov, "V. I. Lenin i pobeda sovetskoi vlasti v Srednei Azii," *Kommunist*, no. 6 (1955): 88, 89.

10. See McCauley, *Khrushchev and Soviet Agriculture*, p. 83, and *Plenum TsIK KPSS 22–25/XII/1959 g Stenograficheskii otchet* (Moscow, 1960), p. 574. Beliaev's second secretary was also dismissed; N. N. Rodionov succeeded him.

11. F. K. Mikhailov, *Sovkhoznoe stroitel'stvo v Kazakhstane (1946–1970 gg)* (Alma-Ata, 1973), p. 59.

12. *Current Digest of the Soviet Press* XIII, no. 9 (1961): 27.

13. *Current Digest of the Soviet Press* XIII, no. 3 (1961): 4.

14. *Pravda* (March 26, 1961).

15. This may have been done to reduce the prestige of Brezhnev. Kunaev returned to his former post of chairman of the council of ministers in the Kazakh S.S.R.; Daulenov, the incumbent, was removed on charges of official misconduct and pronational sentiments. J. W. Cleary, "Politics and Administration in Soviet Kazakhstan, 1955–1964" (Ph.D. dissertation, Australian National University, 1967).

16. Regarding hybridization, see *Pravda* (February 16, 1964): 1–2.

17. *Pravda* (May 22, 1964).

18. Party secretary N. D. Dzhandil'din was replaced by S. N. Imashev (a close associate of Kunaev, Imashev still holds this post), and thirteen new oblast secretaries were appointed within a six-month period.

19. *Istoriia Kazakhskoi SSR* (1981), 5:399.

20. One source of the increase was the creation of experimental farms that combined livestock breeding with the processing of food.

21. However, the section of the resolution on industry (part III) preceded that on agriculture (part IV).

22. The obkom first secretary of Pavlodar was attacked in *Izvestiia* (July 1, 1969) and the first secretary of the Northern Kazakh obkom in *Pravda* (May 22, 1969).

23. Resolutions of March 30, 1970 (effective May 1), and June 10, 1970. *Kommunisticheskaia partiia Sovetskogo Soiuza v rezoliutsiiakh i resheniiakh s"ezdov, konferentsii, i plenumov TsK. Tom 10 1969–1971 gg* (Moscow, 1972).

24. *KPSS i sovetskoe pravitel'stvo o Kazakhstane* (Alma-Ata, 1978), p. 299.

25. See *Kazakhstanskaia Pravda* (April 26, 1972); *Pravda* (January 5, 1973); and *Izvestiia* (January 25, 1973).

26. Eighty percent of all phosphate fertilizer manufactured in the USSR during the 1970s came from Kazakhstan.

27. In the raion soviets only 33 percent had a higher education; the poor quality of the cadre is considered to be a function of the low pay scale for these jobs.

28. *Pravda* (April 2, 1976): 1–3.

29. Some 55,000 army trucks, 12,000 combine operators, 2,000 workers, and 13,000 students had been sent into the area to help with the harvest.

30. *Pravda* (September 4, 1976): 1–3.

31. The Alma-Ata, Akmolinsk, and Tselinograd oblasts failed to meet milk production plans, and shortfalls were reported in the Northern Kazakhstan and Kokchetav oblasts.

32. Meat production plans were not met in the Taldy-Kurgan, Aktyubinsk, and Karaganda oblasts.

33. In the late 1970s the problems of Karaganda were so severe that the party's second secretary was sent there as obkom first secretary.

34. The Pavlodar, Turgai, Dzhezkazgan, Kzyl-Orda, and Dzhambul oblasts had fewer sheep at the end of the plan; in Guryev and Chimkent the slaughter of young animals has been standard practice.

35. Cereal crops had been cultivated in these areas by Russians since the late nineteenth century.

36. Over half the kolkhoz chairmen had only completed primary school.

37. In all the Virgin Land oblasts, except for Northern Kazakhstan, at least 800,000 hectares was sown with fodder annually. In the Akmolinsk, Karaganda, Alma-Ata, and Semipalatinsk oblasts, a minimum of 500,000 hectares of fodder was sown annually.

38. In the period 1960–1968 the number of tractors in the republic increased by 153.4 percent, combines by 119.4 percent, and trucks by 127.0 percent.

39. In 1941, 13.7 percent of the milk cows were in state farms, 30.1 percent were in collective-farm herds, and 56.1 percent were privately owned; in 1979, 53.1 percent were on state farms, 9.74 percent in collective-farm herds, and 37.1 percent were privately owned.

In 1940, 16.6 percent of the horned cattle were on state farms, 43.5 percent were in collective-farm herds, and 39.9 percent were privately owned; in 1979, 65.5 percent were in state farms, 10.8 percent were in collective-farm herds, and 23.7 percent were privately owned.

In 1941, 19.5 percent of the sheep and goats were in state farms, 61.5 percent were in collective-farm flocks,and 18.9 percent were privately owned; in 1979, 75.5 percent were on state farms, 15.3 percent were in collective-farm flocks, and 9.5 percent were privately owned.

40. F. I. Kolodin, *Torzhestvo leninskogo plana sotsialisticheskogo preobrazovaniia sel'skogo khoziaistva v Kazakhstane (1946–1969 gg)* (Alma-Ata, 1971), p. 99.

41. Ibid., p. 99.

42. Investment in working machinery is 7.77 times greater in the state-farm sector than in the collective-farm sector, in heavy machinery 7.19 times greater, and in productive cattle 5.54 times greater.

43. The average herd of cattle per collective farm is 2,173 compared to 2,505 in the state farm; there are 13,144 sheep in the collective farms compared to 12,421 in the state farms. *Narodnoe khoziaistvo Kazakhstana 1978 g* (Alma-Ata, 1979), p. 86.

44. The high was in 1976 and the low in 1975.

45. *Narodnoe khoziaistvo* (1979), p. 54.

46. Mills, "Policy and Administrative Problems," p. 61.

47. In 1940 there were 341,000 hectares cultivated with technical crops; in 1978, 365,000 hectares. In 1940 there were 155,600 hectares of land devoted to truck farming; in 1978, 281,700 hectares.

48. In the period 1950–1979, milk production increased by 264 percent, meat production by 318 percent, and egg production by 536 percent.

49. *Kazakhstanskaia pravda* (February 7, 1986), p. 2.

50. This question is avoided in the documentary volumes on the Virgin Lands: *Kommunisticheskaia partiia Kazakhstana v bor'be za osvoenie tselinnykh i zalezhnykh zemel'* (Alma-Ata, 1958), and *Kompartiia Kazakhstana na vtorom etape osvoeniia tseliny* (Alma-Ata, 1963). However, F. T. Morgun, *Khleb i liudi* (Moscow, 1973), p. 151, addresses it obliquely.

51. A. Fugleva, "Partiinye komitety i sel'skie partorganizatsii," in *Voprosy partinogo stroitel'stva* (Alma-Ata, 1972), p. 98.

52. John Cleary, "Politics and Administration."

53. Ibid., pp. 75–82.

54. These oblasts were Kzyl-Orda, Guryev, Uralsk, and Alma-Ata (although the Alma-Ata oblast did not have jurisdiction over the city of Alma-Ata).

55. Cleary, "Politics and Administration," p. 407.

56. *Kazakhstanskaia pravda* (February 7, 1986), p. 6.

57. In February 1984, A. K. Zhakupov became the new obkom first secretary in Dzhambul, and in December 1984, A. V. Milkin replaced A. K. Protozhanov as first secretary in Eastern Kazakhstan. On December 19, 1984, the central committee of the

Komsomol issued a harshly critical resolution about excesses and insufficiencies in the Kazakh Komsomol organization.

58. A. Askarov (a member of the CPSU Central Committee) of Chimkent, T. Esetov of Kzyl Orda, and A. Koikhumanov of Alma-Ata were all removed in disgrace.

59. See *Pravda* (March 29, 1985), p. 2; (December 15, 1985), p. 2; and (December 18, 1985), p. 2.

60. See *Kazakhstanskaia pravda* (February 7–11, 1986).

61. Pravda (February 9, 1986), p. 2.

## CHAPTER 11

1. At least none that was reported in the West.

2. This is almost a classic tenet of Western political development in the 1960s and 1970s. For some examples, see Lucien Pye, *Aspects of Political Development* (Boston: Little, Brown, 1969); Karl Deutsch, *Nationalism and Social Communication* (Cambridge, Mass.: MIT Press, 1966); and David Apter, *The Politics of Modernization* (Chicago: University of Chicago Press, 1965).

3. For a recent example see E. S. Markarian, *Teoriia kul'tury i sovremennaia nauka* (Moscow, 1983).

4. See Murray Feshbach and Stephen Rapawy, "Soviet Population and Manpower Trends and Policies," in *Soviet Economy in a New Perspective* (Washington, D.C.: GPO, 1977), pp. 113–154.

5. See Martha Brill Olcott and William Fierman, "The Challenge of Integration: Soviet Nationality Policy and the Muslim Conscript" (unpublished manuscript).

6. M. Suzhikov and G. Demako, *Vliianiia podvizhnosti naseleniia na sblizhenie natsii* (Alma-Ata, 1974), p. 67.

7. Gail Warshofsky Lapidus, *Women in Soviet Society* (Berkeley: University of California Press, 1979), p. 143.

8. See Nancy Lubin, "Women in Central Asia," *Soviet Studies* 33, no. 2 (April 1981): 182–203.

9. The pattern of occupation differentiation of Kazakhs comes close to replicating the pattern for Russians. *Naselenie Kazakhstana v 1959–1970 gg* (Alma-Ata, 1975), p. 93.

10. See Martha Brill Olcott, "Pastoralism, Nationalism and Communism in Kazakhstan," *Canadian Slavic Papers* (Spring 1983).

11. *Kul'tura i byt'*, p. 188.

12. See Kh. Argynbaev, "Weddings and Wedding Rites Among the Kazakhs," a paper delivered at the IX International Congress of Ethnography and Anthropology (September 1973, Chicago).

13. Suzhikov and Demako, *Vliianiia podvishnosti*, p. 67.

14. G. F. Dakhshlieger, "Settlement and Traditional Social Institutions of the Former

Nomads (an Example of the Kazakh People)," a paper delivered at the IX International Congress of Ethnography and Anthropology (September 1973, Chicago), p. 3.

15. Suzhikov and Demako, *Vliianiia podvishnosti*, p. 66.

16. T. Saidbaev, *Islam i obshchestvo* (Moscow, 1978), pp. 180–190. A great deal of variation is found in Soviet sources in the percentage of the population considered to be believers, depending on how "believer" is defined. Saidbaev uses a loose definition and includes people who observe Muslim ritual, of whom probably only one in ten have any sort of real understanding of Muslim doctrine.

17. *Nastol'naia kniga ateista* (Moscow, 1981), p. 283.

18. *Muslims of the Soviet East*, no. 2 (1981): 19. One reason why it is difficult to ascertain the relative strength of religion in the cities is that the ethnographic literature has by definition focused on the rural areas.

19. N. S. Sarsenbaev, *Obychai i traditsii i obshchestvennaia zhizn'* (Alma-Ata, 1974), p. 155.

20. *Kazakhstanskaia Pravda* (February 5, 1981): 5.

21. N. Ashirov, *Islam i natsiia* (Moscow, 1975), p. 166.

22. Ibid., p. 48.

23. The group concentrates on rehabilitated writers such as S. Seifullin, I. Dzhansugurov, and B. Mailin.

24. See *Current Digest of the Soviet Press* 36, no. 51 (1977): 15; and "Obsuzhdenie knigi Olzhasa Suleimenova," *Voprosy istorii*, no. 9 (1976): 145–154.

25. *Current Digest of the Soviet Press* 26, no. 26 (1974): 34.

26. *Current Digest of the Soviet Press* 26, no. 41 (1974): 21.

27. Attacks by I. Steklova and Kovsky were published in *Literaturnoe obozrenie*, no. 3 (1974): 36–40.

28. See A. Alimzhanov, *Izbrannoe v dvukh tomakh* (Alma-Ata, 1979).

# Bibliography

## WESTERN LANGUAGE SOURCES

Akiner, Shirin. *Islamic Peoples of the Soviet Union*. London: Kegan Paul International, 1983.

Alexander, John T. *Emperor of the Cossacks*. Lawrence, Kans.: Coronado Press, 1973.

Allworth, E. *Central Asian Publishing and the Rise of Nationalism*. New York: New York Public Library, 1965.

Allworth, Edward. *Central Asia: A Century of Russian Rule*. New York: Columbia University Press, 1967.

Allworth, Edward, ed. *The Nationality Question in Soviet Central Asia*. New York: Praeger, 1973.

Apter, David. *The Politics of Modernization*. Chicago: University of Chicago Press, 1965.

Argynbaev, Kh. "Weddings and Wedding Rites Among the Kazakhs." Paper delivered at the *IX International Congress of Ethnography and Anthropology*. Chicago, September, 1973.

Auezov, Mukhtar. *Abai*. Moscow: Progress Publishers, 1968.

Azrael, Jeremy R., ed. *Soviet Nationality Policies and Practices*. New York: Praeger, 1978.

Bacon, Elizabeth. *Central Asia Under Soviet Rule*. Ithaca: Cornell University Press, 1966.

Bartol'd, V. V. *Four Studies on the History of Central Asia*. Translated by V. and T. Minorsky. Leiden: E. J. Brill, 1956–1963.

———. *Turkestan Down to the Mongol Invasion*. Translated by H. A. R. Gibb. London: Luzac, 1928.

Baskakov, N. A. *The Turkic Languages of Central Asia*. Translated by S. Worm. London: Central Asian Research Center, 1960.

Bates, E. S. *Soviet Asia*. London: Jonathan Cape, 1942.

Bennigsen, Alexandre. "La Famille Musulmane en Union Sovietique." *Revue du Monde Musulman*, no. 1 (1959–1960): 82–108.

Bennigsen, Alexandre, and Lemercier-Quelquejay, Chantal. *Islam in the Soviet Union*. London: Pall Mall Press, 1967.

———. *La Presse et le Mouvement National chez les Musulmans de Russie avant 1920*. Paris: Mouton, 1964.

Bennigsen, Alexandre, and Wimbush, S. Enders. *Muslim National Communism in the Soviet Union. A Revolutionary Strategy for the Colonial World*. Chicago: University of Chicago Press, 1979.

Bogdanov, A. "The Koshchi Union in Kazakstan." in Rudolf Schlesinger, ed., *The Nationality Problem and Soviet Administration*. London: Routledge and Kegan Paul, 1953.

Boulger, Dmitrius. *England and Russia in Central Asia*. London: W. H. Allen, 1879.

Bradley, J. F. N. *Civil War in Russia, 1917–1920*. London: B. T. Batsford, 1975.

Brezhnev, Leonid. *The Virgin Lands*. Moscow: Progress Publishers, 1978.

*Cambridge History of Islam*. Cambridge: Cambridge University Press, 1970.

Caroe, Olaf. *The Soviet Empire*. London: Macmillan, 1953.

Carrère d'Encausse, Hélène. *Decline of an Empire: The Soviet Socialist Republics in Revolt*. New York: Newsweek Books, 1979.

Castagné, Joseph. *Les Basmachis*. Paris: Editions Leroux, 1925.

———. "La Revolution dans Turkestan." *Revue du Monde Musulman*, no. 1 (1922): 171–191.

Chadwick, Nora K., and Zhirmunsky, Victor. *Oral Epics of Central Asia*. Cambridge: Cambridge University Press, 1969.

Cleary, J. W. "Elite Career Patterns in Kazakhstan." *British Journal of Political Science*, no. 4 (1974): 323–344.

———. "Politics and Aministration in Soviet Kazakhstan 1955–1964." Ph.D. dissertation, Australian National University, 1967.

———. "The Virgin Lands." *Survey*, no. 56 (1956): 95–105.

Cohen, Stephen. *Bukharin and the Bolshevik Revolution*. New York: Knopf, 1973.

Conolly, Violet. *Beyond the Urals*. London: Oxford University Press, 1967.

Conquest, Robert. *The Great Terror*. New York: Macmillan, 1973.

———. *Soviet Nationalities Policy in Practice*. New York: Praeger, 1967.

Dakhshlieger, G. F. "Settlement and Traditional Social Institutions of the Former Nomads (an Example of the Kazakh People)." Paper delivered at the IX International Congress of Ethnography and Anthropology. Chicago, September, 1973.

Demko, George. *The Russian Colonization of Kazakhstan, 1896–1916*. Bloomington, Ind.: Mouton, 1969.

Deutsch, Karl. *Nationalism and Social Communication*. Cambridge, Mass.: MIT Press, 1966.

Donnelly, Alton. *The Russian Conquest of Bashkiria*. New Haven: Yale University Press, 1968.

Durgin, Frank. "The Virgin Lands Program." *Soviet Studies*, no. 3 (1962): 255–280.

Fell, E. Nelson. *Russian and Nomad*. New York: Duffield, 1916.

Feshbach, Murray, and Rapawy, Stephen. "Soviet Population and Manpower Trends and Policies." In *Soviet Economy in a New Perspective*. Washington, D.C.: Government Printing Office, 1977.

Fox, Ralph. *People of the Steppes*. Boston and New York: Houghton Mifflin, 1925.

"From the Plenary Session of the Kazakh CP." *Current Digest of the Soviet Press* 17, no. 17 (1972): 22.

Gibb, H. A. R. *The Arab Conquests in Central Asia*. London: Royal Asiatic Society, 1923.

Goldhagen, Erich, ed. *Ethnic Minorities in the Soviet Union*. New York: Praeger, 1968.

*Great Soviet Encyclopedia*. Vol. 11. New York: Macmillan, 1973.

Hallen, Fannina. *Women in the Soviet East*. Translated by Mary Green. New York: E. P. Dutton, 1938.

Hambly, Gavin. *Central Asia*. New York: Delacorte Press, 1969.

Harrison, John A. *Founding of the Russian Empire in Asia and America*. Coral Gables: University of Miami Press, 1971.

Hodnett, Grey. *Leadership in the Soviet National Republics*. Oakville, Ontario: Mosaic Press, 1978.

Hostler, C. *Turkism and the Soviets*. London: Allen and Unwin, 1957.

Howorth, H. *History of the Mongols*. Part II. London: Longmans, Green, 1880.

Hudson, Alfred. *Kazakh Social Structure*. New Haven: Human Relations Area File, 1964.

Hunczak, Taras. *Russian Imperialism from Ivan the Great to the Revolution*. New Brunswick, N.J.: Rutgers University Press, 1974.

Jasny, Naum. *The Socialized Agriculture of the U.S.S.R.* Stanford: Stanford University Press, 1941.

Jenkinson, Anthony. *Early Voyages to Russia and Persia*. Edited by Edward Morgan Delmar. London: The Hakluyt Society, 1886.

Katz, Zev, ed. *Attitudes of Major Soviet Nationalities*. Vol. 4, *Central Asia*. Cambridge, Mass.: MIT Center for International Studies, 1973.

"The Kazakhs and the Pugachev Revolt." *Central Asian Review* 8, no. 3 (1960): 256.

Khalfin, N. A. *Russia's Policy in Central Asia, 1857–1868*. Condensed and translated by Hubert Evans. London: Central Asian Research Center, 1964.

Kolarz, Walter. *Russia and Her Colonies*. London: George Philip and Son, Ltd., 1952.

Kolb, Patricia. "The Roots of Revolution from Above." M.A. thesis, University of Chicago, 1973.

Kraeder, Lawrence. *Peoples of Central Asia*. Uralic and Altaic Series, vol. 26. Bloomington: Indiana University Press, 1971.

Lane, David. "Ethnic and Class Stratification in Soviet Kazakhstan." *Comparative Studies in Society and History*, no. 2 (1975): 165–189.

Lapidus, Gail Warshofsky. *Women in Soviet Society*. Berkeley: University of California Press, 1979.

Levin, Alfred. *The Second Duma*. New Haven: Yale University Press, 1940.

Levshin, A. *Descriptions des hordes et des steppes des Kirghiz-kazaks ou Kirghiz-kaïssaks*. Translated by F. de Pigny. Paris: Imprimerie Royale, 1840.

Lewin, Moshe. *Russian Peasants and Soviet Power*. Chicago: Northwestern University Press, 1968.

"The Living and Working Conditions of Kazakh Craftsmen Before the Revolution." *Central Asian Review*, no. 10 (1962): 343–349.

Lubin, Nancy. "Women in Central Asia." *Soviet Studies* 33, no. 2 (April 1981): 182–203.

Lyashchenko, P. I. *History of the National Economy of Russia*. New York: Macmillan, 1949.

McCauley, Martin. *Khrushchev and the Development of Soviet Agriculture: The Virgin Land Programme, 1953–1964*. New York: Holmes and Meier, 1976.

MacKenzie, David. *The Lion of Tashkent*. Athens: University of Georgia Press, 1974.

Male, D. J. *Russian Peasant Organization Before Collectivization*. Cambridge: Cambridge University Press, 1971.

Meiendorf, Igor Fedorovich. *A Journey from Orenburg to Bokhara in the Year 1820*. Calcutta: Foreign Department Press, 1870.

Mills, Richard M. "Policy and Administrative Problems in the Soviet Virgin Lands Program in Kazakhstan, 1954–1964." Ph.D. Dissertation, Harvard University, December 1965.

———. "The Virgin Lands Since Khrushchev: Choices and Decisions in Soviet Policy Making." In Paul Cooks, ed., *The Dynamics of Soviet Politics*. Cambridge, Mass.: Harvard University Press, 1976.

Nekrich, Aleksandr. *The Punished Peoples*. New York: Norton, 1979.

Nolde, Boris. *La Formation de l'Empire Russe*. 2 vols. Paris: Institutes d'études slaves, 1952–1953.

Nove, Alec. *An Economic History of the U.S.S.R.* Baltimore: Penguin Books, 1972.

Olcott, Martha Brill. "The Basmachi or Freemen's Revolt in Turkestan, 1918–1924." *Soviet Studies* 33, no. 3 (1981): 352–369.

———. "The Collectivization Drive in Kazakhstan." *Russian Review* 40, no. 2 (1981): 122–142.

———. "The Fabrication of a Social Past—The Kazakhs of Central Asia." In Myron Aronoff, ed., *Political Anthropology Handbook I*. Rutgers: Transaction Press, 1980.

———. "Pastoralism, Nationalism and Communism in Kazakhstan." *Canadian Slavic Papers* (Spring 1983).

Olcott, Martha Brill, and Fierman, William. "The Challenge of Integration: Soviet Nationality Policy and the Muslim Conscript." Unpublished manuscript.

Park, Alexander G. *Bolshevism in Turkestan, 1917–1927.* New York: Columbia University Press, 1957.

Pierce, Richard. *Russian Central Asia, 1867–1917: A Study in Colonial Rule.* Berkeley: University of California Press, 1960.

Pipes, Richard. *The Formation of the Soviet Union—Communism and Nationalism, 1917–1923.* Revised edition. Cambridge, Mass.: Harvard University Press, 1964.

Ploss, Sidney. *Conflict and Decision-making in Soviet Russia: A Case Study of Agricultural Policy, 1953–1963.* Princeton: Princeton University Press, 1965.

Pye, Lucien. *Aspects of Political Development.* Boston: Little, Brown, 1969.

Raeff, Marc. *Michael Speransky.* 2d edition. The Hague: Martinus Nijhoff, 1969.

———. *Siberia and the Reforms of 1822.* Seattle: University of Washington Press, 1956.

Riasanovskii, V. A. "Customary Law of the Kirgiz." *Chinese Social and Political Review* 21, no. 2 (1937): 190–220.

Rywkin, Michael. *Moscow's Muslim Challenge.* London: C. Hurst, 1982.

Schuyler, Eugene. *Turkestan.* New York: Scribner, Armstrong, 1877.

Skrine, F. H., and Ross, E. D. *The Heat of Russian Turkestan and the Central Asian Khanates from the Earliest Times.* London: Methuen, 1893.

Sokol, Edward. *The Revolt of 1916 in Central Asia.* Baltimore: Johns Hopkins University Press, 1953.

Strauss, Erich. *Soviet Agriculture in Perspective.* New York: Praeger, 1969.

Tillet, Lowell. *The Great Friendship.* Chapel Hill: University of North Carolina Press, 1969.

Treadgold, Donald. *The Great Siberian Migration: Government and Peasant in Resettlement from Emancipation to the First World War.* Princeton: Princeton University Press, 1957.

Trotsky, Leon. *The Challenge of the Left Opposition, 1926–1927.* Vol. 2. Edited by Naomi Allen. New York: Monthly Review Press, 1980.

*The Voice of the Steppe.* Moscow: Progress Publishers, 1981.

Volin, Lazar. *A Century of Russian Agriculture.* Cambridge, Mass.: Harvard University Press, 1970.

Wheeler, Geoffrey. *The Modern History of Soviet Central Asia.* New York: Praeger, 1964.

Winner, Thomas. *The Oral Art and Literature of the Kazakhs of Russian Central Asia.* Durham, N.C.: Duke University Press, 1955.

Zenkovsky, Serge A. *Pan-Turkism and Islam in Russia.* Cambridge, Mass.: Harvard University Press, 1960.

## RUSSIAN LANGUAGE SOURCES

*1917 goda v Kazakhstane.* Alma-Ata, 1977.

A. A. K. "Kazakhskie kraevye iarmarki v 1925 godu." *Narodnoe khoziaistvo Kazakstana,* no. 1 (1926): 82–94.

A. G. "Puti rekonstruktsii kochevnogo khoziaistva." *Narodnoe khoziaistvo Kazakstana*, no. 11–12 (1930): 37–52.

Abishev, G. *Kazakhstan v zashchite sotsialisticheskogo otechestva*. Alma-Ata, 1964.

Abisheva, B. N. *Pod'em kul'turno-tekhnicheskogo urovnia rabochikh ugol'noi promyshlennosti Kazakhstana (1946–1963 gg)*. Alma-Ata, 1965.

Abramson, S. M. "Vliianie perekhoda k obrazu zhizni na preobrazovanie sotsial'nogo stroia, semeino-bytogo uklada i kultury prezhnikh kochevnikov i polukochevnikov (na primere Kazakhov i Kirgizov)." *Trudy instituta etnografii* 98: 235–248.

Aitiev, T. A. *Torzhestvo leninskogo kooperativnogo plana v Kazakhstane*. Alma-Ata, 1969.

Aldamzharov, Z. A. "Sovremennaia sovetskaia istoriografiia Velikogo Oktiabria v Kazakhstane." *Istoriia SSSR*, no. 4 (1983): 74–81.

Aleksandrov, N. N. *Zemledelie v Syr-Dar'inskom oblasti*. Tashkent, 1916.

Alektorov, A. E. *Materialy dlia izucheniia strany, istorii i byta Kirgizov*. Orenburg, 1892.

Alifbaev, A. "Ob odnom vazhnom momenta." *Krasnyi Kazakstan*, no. 4 (1926): 54–61.

Alimzhanov, A. *Izbrannoe v dvukh tomakh*. Alma-Ata, 1979.

———. *V raznye gody*. Alma-Ata, 1980.

Alkin, Ilias. "Natsional'no-gosudarstvennoe razmezhevanie Srednei Azii i VII s"ezd sovetov SSSR." *Revoliutsionnyi vostok*, no. 6 (1934): 114–137.

Altynsaryn, I. *Izbrannye proizvedeniia*. Alma-Ata, 1957.

———. *Sobranie sochinenii v trekh tomakh*. Alma-Ata, 1925–1938.

Amantaev, B. A. *Sotsializm: Korennoe preobrazovanie sotsial'noi prirody kazakhskogo krest'ianstva*. Alma-Ata, 1969.

Andreev, A. "Zhivotnovodstvo-pervoocherednaia zadacha." *Revoliutsiia i natsional'nosti*, no. 8 (1934): 28–36.

Andreev, E. "Iz istorii stanovleniia sistemy partiinogo-prosveshcheniia." In *Voprosy partiinogo stroitel'stva*. Alma-Ata, 1972.

Anichkov, I. V. *Ocherki narodnoi zhizni severnago Turkestana*. Tashkent, 1899.

*Antologiia Kazakhskoi poezii*. Moscow, 1958.

Appolonova, N. G. *Ekonomicheskie i politicheskie sviazi Kazakhstana s Rossii*. Moscow, 1960.

Aristov, N. A. "Opyt resheniia etnicheskago sostava Kirgiz-Kazakov bolshoi ordy i Karakirgizov." *Zhivaia starina*, no. 3–4 (1894): 391–486.

———. "Zametki ob etnicheskom sostave turkskikh plemen i narodnostei," *Zhivaia starina*, no. 3–4 (1896).

*Arkheologicheskie issledovaniia v Kazakhstane*. Alma-Ata, 1973.

Asfendiarov, S. D. *Istoriia Kazakstana (s drevneishikh vremen)*. Vol. 1. Moscow and Alma-Ata, 1935.

———. *Istoriia natsional'no-revoliutsionnykh dvizhenii na vostoke*. Kzyl-Orda, 1932.

————. *Natsional'no-osvoboditel'noe vosstanie 1916 goda v Kazakhstane.* Moscow and Alma-Ata, 1936.

————, ed. *Proshloe Kazakhstana v istochnikakh-materialakh.* Alma-Ata, 1936.

Ashmarin. "Kochevye puti, zimovye stoibishcha i letovki." *Sovetskaia Kirgizia*, no. 5 (1925): 111–124.

Auezov, M. *Abai.* 2 vols. Alma-Ata, 1980.

*Aziatskaia Rossiia.* 2 vols. St. Petersburg, 1914.

B–n, D. "Sel'skoe khoziaistvo Kazakhstana i perspektivy ego razvitii." *Sotsialisticheskaia rekonstruktsiia sel'skogo khoziaistva*, no. 4–5 (1930): 211–213.

Baibulatov, B. *Ot kochev'ia k sotsializmu.* Frunze, 1969.

Baipakov, K. M. "Tipologiia srednevekovykh gorodishch iuzhnogo Kazakhstana i Semirech'ia (VI-nachala XIII vv)," *Izvestiia Akademiia Nauk Kazakhskoi SSR*, no. 3 (1981): 26–34.

Baishev, S. B. *Sotsial'no-ekonomicheskoe razvitie sovetskogo Kazakhstana.* Alma-Ata, 1979.

Baishin, A. A. "Rabota Kommunisticheskoi Partii Kazakhstana po ukrepleniiu kolkhoznogo stroia v poslevoennom periode." *Voprosy istorii kompartii Kazakhstana* 8 (1971).

Balakaev, T. B. *Kolkhoznoe krest'ianstvo Kazakhstana v gody velikoi otechestvennoi voini 1941–1945 gg.* Alma-Ata, 1971.

Basilov, V. N. "Traditsii zhenskogo shamanstva u Kazakhov." *Polevye issledovaniia instituta etnografii.* Moscow, 1974.

Basin, V. Ia. *Rossiia i Kazakhskie khanstva v XVI–XVIII vv.* Alma-Ata, 1971.

Batalov, M. *Ocherki po kazakhskomu folkloru.* Alma-Ata, 1933.

Bazanov, F. N. "Formirovanie natsional'nogo sostava naseleniia Kazakhstana v gody dovoennykh piatiletok." *Vestnik Akademii Nauk Kazakhskoi SSR*, no. 1 (1981): 49–57.

————. "Formirovanie natsional'nogo sostava naseleniia Kazakhstana v gody grazhdanskoi voiny; vosstanovleniia narodnogo khoziaistva." *Vestnik Akademii Nauk Kazakhskoi SSR*, no. 1 (1979): 55–63.

Beisembiev, K. B. *Ideino-politicheski techeniia v Kazakhstane kontsa XIX–nachala XX veka.* Alma-Ata, 1961.

————. *Islam i kritika ego mysliteliami dorevoliutsionnogo Kazakhstana.* Alma-Ata, 1962.

————. *Iz istorii obshchestvennoi mysli Kazakhstana vtoroi poloviny XIX v.* Alma-Ata, 1957.

————. *Ocherki istorii obshchestvenno-politicheskoi i filosofskoi mysli Kazakhstana.* Alma-Ata, 1976.

————. *Pobeda marksistsko-leninskoi ideologii v Kazakhstane.* Alma-Ata, 1970.

————. *Progressivno-demokraticheskaia i marksistskaia mysl' v Kazakhstane v nachale XX veka.* Alma-Ata, 1965.

Beisembiev, S., and Kul'baev, S. *Turar Ryskulov*. Alma-Ata, 1974.

———. "Turar Ryskulov (K 80 let so dnia rozhdeniia)." *Voprosy istorii kompartii Kazakhstana*, no. 11 (1974): 225–239.

Bekmakhanov, E. *Kazakhstan v 20–40 gody XIX veka*. Alma-Ata, 1947.

———. "Natsional'no-osvoboditel'noe dvizhenie v Kazakhstane v period pervoi Russkoi burzhuazno-demokratichestoi revoliutsii." *Vestnik Akademii Nauk Kazakhskoi SSR*, no. 4 (1950): 60–75.

———. *Prisoedinenie Kazakhstana k Rossii*. Moscow, 1957.

Bekmakhanova, N. E. *Formirovanie mnogonatsional'nogo naseleniia Kazakhstana i Severnoi Kirgizii*. Moscow, 1980.

———. *Legenda o nevidimke*. Alma-Ata, 1968.

Bekmakhanova, N. E., and Kabuzan, B. M. "Russko-Ukrainskaia migratsiia v Kazakhstane v XIX–nachale XX v." *Izvestiia Akademii Nauk Kazakhskoi SSR*, no. 2 (1982): 14–20.

*Belaia arauna*. Moscow, 1976.

Belan, P. S. *Uchastie Kazakhstantsev v zavenshaiushchikh srazheniiakh velikoi otechestvennoi voiny*. Alma-Ata, 1979.

Ben-Arnazi. "V Kirgizkoi Avtonomnoi Respublike." *Zhizn' natsional'nostei*, no. 2 (1923): 46–57.

Bernshtam, A. N. "Problema raspada rodovikh otnoshenii u kochevnikov Srednei Azii." *Sovetskaia etnografiia*, no. 6 (1934): 85–116.

Binder, M. A., and Sapargaliev, G. "Iz istorii korenizatsii gosudarstvennogo apparata Kazakhstana." *Izvestiia Akademii Nauk Kazakhskoi SSR*, no. 6 (1959).

Biografii, G. G. *Chleny Gosudarstvennoi Dumy*. St. Petersburg, 1906.

Bochagov, A. K. *Alash-Orda*. Kzyl-Orda, 1927.

Bogdanov, A. "Kolkhoznoe stroitel'stvo v natsional'nykh respublikakh i oblastiakh." *Revoliutsiia i natsional'nosti*, no. 1 (1931): 50–60.

———. "Reshaiushchie momenty kolkhoznogo stroitel'stva v natsional'nykh raionakh." *Revoliutsiia i natsional'nosti*, no. 7 (1930): 29–39.

Bogdenko, M. L. "Kolkhoznoe stroitel'stvo vesnoi i letom 1930 g." *Istoricheskie zapiski* 67 (1965): 17–41.

Boiovich, M. M. *Chleny gosudarstvennoi dumy vtoroi sozyv, 1907–1912 gg.* Moscow, 1977.

Borsykh, N. P. "Rasprostrannost' mezhnatsional'nykh brakov v respublikakh Srednei Azii i Kazakhstana v 1930–x godakh." *Sovetskaia etnografiia*, no. 4 (1970): 87–96.

Bozhko, F. *Grazhdanskaia voina v Srednei Azii*. Tashkent, 1930.

———. *Oktiabr'skaia Revoliutsiia v Srednei Azii*. Tashkent, 1932.

———. *Vosstanie 1916 g v byvshem Turkestane k 10 letiiu vosstaniia*. Tashkent, 1926.

Bozhko, F., and Galuzo, P. *Vosstanie 1916 g v Srednei Azii*. Moscow and Tashkent, 1932.

Brainin, S. "Iz istorii bor'by za sovetizatsiiu kazakhskogo aula." *Proletarskaia revoliutsiia*, no. 3 (1940): 100–133.

Brainin, S., and Shafiro, Sh. "Ob istokakh alashskogo dvizheniia." *Bol'shevik Kazakstana*, no. 6 (1933): 44–53.

———. *Ocherki po istorii Alash-Ordy*. Moscow and Alma-Ata, 1935.

———. *Pervye shagi sovetov v Semirech'e*. Moscow and Alma-Ata, 1934.

———"Protiv idealizatsii proshlogo alashskogo dvizheniia." *Bol'shevik Kazakstana*, no. 1–2 (1934): 81–92.

———. *Vosstanie Kazakhov Semirech'ia v 1916 godu*. Moscow and Alma-Ata, 1936.

Broido, G. "Materialy k istorii vosstaniia Kirgiz v 1916 godu." *Novyi Vostok*, no. 6 (1924): 407–434.

———. *Natsional'nyi i kolonial'nyi vopros*. Moscow, 1924.

Bukeikhanov, Ali Khan. "Kirgizy." In A. I. Kastelianskii, ed., *Formy natsional'nogo dvizheniia*. St. Petersburg, 1910.

Chekanskii, I. "Vosstanie Kirgiz-Kazakov v Dzhetyskom Semirecheskom krae v iulesentiabre 1916 godu." *Trudy obshchestva izucheniia Kirgizskogo kraia*, no. 8 (1922): 77–136.

Chelintsev, A. N. "Perspektivy razvitiia sel'skogo khoziaistva Kazakstana." *Narodnoe khoziaistvo Kazakstana*, no. 4–5 (1928): 1–39.

*Chelovek, obshchestvo i religiia*. Moscow, 1968.

Cherkasov, K. "Vypolnim reshenie TsK o kollektivizatsii." *Bol'shevik Kazakstana*, no. 1 (1931): 11–15.

Cherneieshev, E. J. "Vostochnaia pechat' v epokhu reaktsii XX veka." *Izvestiia obshchestva arkheologii istorii i etnografii Kazanskogo universiteta* 33, no. 1 (1925): 105–130.

Chernikov, V. S. "Razvitie zemledeliia v severnom Kazakhstane." *Voprosy istorii*, no. 8 (1983): 43–54.

Chulanov, G. *Ocherki istorii narodnogo khoziaistva Kazakhskoi SSR*. Vol. 2. Alma-Ata, 1962.

Chuloshnikov, A. P. "Kazak-Kirgizskie kochevye ordy i Pugachevshchina (1773–1774)." *Novyi Vostok*, no. 25 (1925): 201–210.

———. "K istorii feodalnikh otnoshenii v Kazakhstane v XVII–XVIII vv." *Izvestiia Akademii Nauk SSSR*, no. 3 (1936): 497–523.

Chuvelev, K. A. "O reorganizatsii kochevogo i polukochevogo khoziaistva." *Narodnoe khoziaistvo Kazakstana*, no. 1 (1926): 42–57.

Dakhshlieger, G. F. *Istoriografiia sovetskogo Kazakhstana*. Alma-Ata, 1969.

———. "K voprosu ob ekonomike Kazakhskoi ASSR nakanune perekhoda k NEPu." *Izvestiia Akademii Nauk Kazakhskoi SSR*, no. 5 (1957): 3–20.

———. *Sotsial'no-ekonomicheskoe preobrazovanie v aule i derevne Kazakhstana (1921–1929)*. Alma-Ata, 1965.

———. *V. I. Lenin i problemy Kazakhstanskoi istoriografii*. Alma-Ata, 1973.

Dakhshlieger, G. F., and Nurpeisov, K. *Istoriia krest'ianstva sovetskogo Kazakhstana.* Vol. 1. Alma-Ata, 1985.

Danilov, V. P. "Problemy istorii sovetskoi derevni v 1946–1970 gg (ocherk istoriografii)." In *Razvitie sel'skogo khoziastva SSSR v poslevoennye gody (1946–1970 gg).* Moscow, 1972.

Davydov, D. "Rekonstruktsiia zhivotnovodstva-ocherednaia zadacha." *Na fronte kollektivizatsii,* no. 3 (1929): 14–25.

Davydov, M. M. "O blizhaishikh perspektivakh sel'sko-khoziaistvennogo razvitiia Syr-Dar'inskogo raiona Kazakstana." *Narodnoe khoziaistvo Kazakstana,* no. 3 (1926): 53–63.

———. "Perspektivy tipy khoziaistv dlia khlopnykh raionov Syr-dar'inskogo gubernii Kazakstana." *Narodnoe khoziaistvo Kazakstana,* no. 1 (1926): 42–51.

*Desiat' let' Kazakstana, 1920–1930 gg.* Alma-Ata, 1930.

Dimanshtein, S. M., ed. *Revoliutsiia i natsional'nyi vopros.* Vol. 3, Moscow, 1930.

———. *Voprosy osedaniia kochevnikov.* Moscow, 1932.

Divaev, A. A. *Iz oblasti kirgizskikh verovanii, baksy, kak lekor i kollun.* Kazan, 1899.

Dobromyslov, D. I. *Sud' u Kirgizov Turgaiskoi Oblasti v VIII–XIX vekakh.* Kazan, 1904.

Dokumental'nye istochniki po istorii kommunisticheskoi partii Kazakhstana. Alma-Ata, 1963.

*Dolgosrochnoe prognozirovanie razvitiia otraslei narodnogo khoziaistva.* Alma-Ata, 1976.

Donentaev, S. *Izbrannoe.* Alma-Ata, 1958.

Donich, A. N. "Narodnonaselenie Kazakstana." *Narodnoe khoziaistvo Kazakstana,* no. 11–12 (1928): 27–56.

———. "Prolema novogo kazakhskogo aula." *Narodnoe khoziaistvo Kazakstana,* no. 4–5 (1928): 141–168.

Dulatov, Mir Yakub. "Akhmed Baitursunov." *Trudy obshchestva izucheniia Kirgizskogo kraia,* no. 3 (1922): 1–24.

Dulatova, D. I. *Istoriografiia dorevoliutsionnogo Kazakhstana (1861–1917 gg).* Alma-Ata, 1984.

Dzhandil'din, N. D. *Priroda natsional'noi psikhologii.* Alma-Ata, 1971.

Dzhantleuov. "Otdel'nye momenty vosstaniia v 1916 godu." *Krasnyi Kazakstan,* no. 4 (1926): 92–103.

Dzhumaliev, K. *Ocherki po istorii kazakhskoi dorevoliutsionnoi literatury.* Alma-Ata, 1968.

———. *Zamechatel'nye liudi.* Alma-Ata, 1977.

Dzhunusov, M. *Obshchestvennyi progress i natsional'nye otnosheniia.* Alma-Ata, 1976.

E. Kh. "Blizhaishie zadachi v oblasti zemleustroistva." *Sovetskaia Kirgizia,* no. 2–3 (1923): 51–54.

*Effektivnost' regional'noi ekonomiki Kazakhstana.* Alma-Ata, 1977.

Elagin, A. S. "Formirovanie pervykh chastei Krasnoi Armii v Kazakhstane." *Izvestiia Akademii Nauk Kazakhskoi SSR*, no. 2 (1980): 16–23.

Eleuov, T. E. "Geroicheskaia oborona Ural'ska (1919 g)." *Trudy instituta istoriia, arkheologii i etnografii Akademii Nauk Kazakhskoi SSR*, no. 2 (1956): 5–67.

———. *Ustanovlenie i uprochenie sovetskoi vlasti v Kazakhstane*. Alma-Ata, 1961.

El'konina, F. I. *Kazakhskaia literatura*. Moscow, 1973.

Ermekov, A. A. "Organizatsiia shkol sredi kazakhskogo naseleniia." *Narodnoe khoziaistvo Kazakstana*, no. 1 (1926): 113–124.

Ermolenko, A. "Kazakhstanskaia derevnia." *Na agrarnom fronte*, no. 9 (1925).

Ermolin, A. P. "Iz istorii bor'by za ustanovlenie vlasti sovetov na Iuzhnom Urale." *Istoriia SSSR*, no. 4 (1983): 103–112.

Erzhanov, A. *Kommunisticheskaia partiia Kazakhstana v poslevoennyi period (1946–1958)*. Alma-Ata, 1972.

———. *Uspekhi natsional'noi politiki KPSS v Kazakhstane (1946–1958 gg)*. Alma-Ata, 1969.

Esenberlin, Il'ias. *Khan Kene*. Moscow, 1971.

Fedorov, E. "1905 goda i korennoe naselenie Turkestana." In *Ocherki revoliutsionnogo dvizheniia v Srednei Azii, sbornik statei*. Moscow, 1926.

———. *Kontrevoliutsionnye vrediteli sel'skogo khoziaistva v Kazakstane*. Alma-Ata, 1930.

———. *Ocherk natsional'no-osvoboditel'nogo dvizheniia v Srednei Azii*. Alma-Ata, 1927.

Fetisov, M. I. *Zaprozhdenie kazakhskoi publistiki*. Alma-Ata, 1961.

Fugleva, A. "Partiinye komitety i sel'skie partorganizatsii." In *Voprosy partiinogo stroitel'stva*. Alma-Ata, 1972.

Gafurov, B. "V. I. Lenin i pobeda sovetskoi vlasti v Srednei Azii." *Kommunist*, no. 6 (1955).

Galiev, V. Z. *Ssyl'nye revoliutsionery v Kazakhstane*. Alma-Ata, 1978.

Galuzo, P. G. *Turkestan-koloniia*. Moscow, 1929.

———, ed. *Agrarnye otnosheniia na iuge Kazakhstana v 1867–1914 gg*. Alma-Ata, 1965.

Geins, A. K. "Kirgizy-Kaisaki (v Zaural'skoi Stepi)." In *Sobranie literaturnykh trudov*. Vol. 1. St. Petersburg, 1897.

———. "Motirovannaia vremennaia instruktsiia uezdnym nachal'nikam Turgai'skoe oblasti." In *Sobranie literaturnykh trudov*. Vol. 2. St. Petersburg, 1898.

Glazov, M. "V Kirgizii." *Narodnyi uchitel'*, no. 1 (1924): 89–92.

*God raboty po osvoeniiu tselennykh i zalezhnykh zemel' v Kazakhstane*. Moscow, 1955.

"Golod v Kirgizskoi Respublike." *Zhizni natsional'nostei*, no. 120 (October 17, 1921): 3.

Goloshchekin, F. I. *Desiat' let partiinogo stroitel'stva v Kazakstane*. Alma-Ata, 1930.

———. *Kazakstan na oktiabr'skom smotru*. Kzyl-Orda, 1927.

──────. *Kazakstan no putiakh sotsialisticheskogo pereustroistva*. Moscow, 1931.

──────. *O kollektivizatsii v kazakhkom aule*. Alma-Ata, 1932.

*Grazhdanskaia voina v Kazakhstane*. Alma-Ata, 1974.

Grigor'ev. "X s"ezd RKP(b) i razgrom melkoburzhuaznoi kontrrevoliutsii na territorii respubliki." In *Voprosy partiinogo stroitel'stva*. Alma-Ata, 1972.

Grodekov, N. I. *Kirgizy i Karakirgizy Syr'-dar'inskoi oblasti*. Vol. 1, *Iuridicheskii byt'*. Tashkent, 1889.

Gromov, E. "K voprosu o rassloenii krest'ianstva v Kazakhstane." *Revoliutsionnyi vostok*, no. 3 (1928): 168–187.

Gumen. "Kollektivizatsiia v Tsaian-Aul'skom raione." *Bol'shevik Kazakstana*, no. 2–3 (1931): 41–45.

Iakunin, A. F. "Revoliutsiia 1905–1907 gg v Kazakhstane." *Revoliutsiia 1905–1907 gg v natsional'nykh raionakh Rossii*. Moscow, 1955.

Ibraev, Zh. *Mestnye sovety Kazakhstana v period stroitel'stva sotsializma*. Alma-Ata, 1973.

Il'minskii, N. I. *Vospominaniia ob Altynsaryne*. Kazan, 1895.

*Innostrannaia voina i grazhdanskaia voina v Srednei Azii i Kazakhstane*. Alma-Ata, 1963.

Inoisiani, A. "Ocherk kul'turi Kazakstane." *Kommunisticheskoe prosveshchenie*, no. 5 (1935): 84–99.

Isaev, U. "15 let Kazakstana i nashi zadachi." *Narodnoe khoziaistvo Kazakstana*, no. 7–8 (1935): 1–27.

──────. *Oktiabr'skaia Revoliutsiia i stroitel'stvo sotsializma*. Moscow and Alma-Ata, 1932.

──────, ed. *Sbornik statei i rechei*. Moscow and Alma-Ata, 1931.

"Istoricheskoe razvitie narodnogo obrazovaniia v Kazakstane." *Krasnyi Kazakstan*, no. 4 (1926): 71–91.

*Istoriia industrializatsii Kazakhskoi SSR (1926-iun' 1941 gg)*. 2 vols. Alma-Ata, 1967.

*Istoriia kazakhskoi literatury*. 3 vols. Alma-Ata, 1968–1979.

*Istoriia Kazakhskoi SSR*. 2 vols. Moscow, 1957–1963.

*Istoriia Kazakhskoi SSR*. 5 vols. Alma-Ata, 1975–1981.

*Itogi vsesoiuznoi perepisi naseleniia 1970 g*. Vol. 6. Moscow, 1973.

Ivanov, P. V. "Dzhut 1927/28 v Syr-Darinskoi guvernii." *Trudy obshchestva izucheniia Kazakstana*, no. 10 (1929): 143–182.

I–vich. "K perestroike partiinoi raboty v khlopkovykh raionakh." *Bol'shevik Kazakstana*, no. 2–3 (1931): 36–40.

*Iz istorii partiinogo stroitel'stva v Kazakstane*. Alma-Ata, 1936.

K. G. "25-tysiachiki v bor'be za kollektivizatsiiu (k itogam kraevogo scheta)." *Bol'shevik Kazakstana*, no. 1 (1931): 15–18.

Kaip-Nazarov, A. "Dostizheniia i nedochety kazakhskikh kolkhozov Dzhanibekskogo raiona." *Bol'shevik Kazakstana*, no. 12 (1931): 52–55.

Kalmyrzaev, A. S. *Esteticheskoe v tvorchestva Abaia*. Alma-Ata, 1979.

Kanapin, A., and Iandorov, A. *Rastsvet kul'tury Kazakhskogo naroda*. Alma-Ata, 1977.

Kanimkulov, A. K. "Evakuatsiia predpriiatii i naseleniia v Aktiubinskuiu oblast' v gody velikoi otechestvennoi voiny." *Vestnik Akademii Nauk Kazakhskoi SSR*, no. 3 (1981): 51–56.

Karpych, V. "Sovetskoe kraevedenie v Srednei Azii." *Sovetskoe kraevedenie*, no. 1–2 (1930): 22–27.

Kaufman, A. A. *K voprosu o russkoi kolonizatsii Turkestanskogo kraia*. St. Petersburg, 1903.

———. *Materialy po voprosu ob organizatsii raboty po obrazovaniiu pereselencheskikh uchastkov v stepnikh oblastiakh*. St. Petersburg, 1896.

———. *Otchet po komandirovke v Turgaiskuiu oblast' dlia vyiasneniia voprosa o vozmozhnosti ee kolonizatsii*. St. Petersburg, 1896.

*Kazakhskaia Sovetskaia Sotsialisticheskaia Respublika: Entsiklopedicheskii spravochnik*. Alma-Ata, 1981.

"Kazakhskaia Sovetskaia Sotsialisticheskaia Respublika (fakty i tsifry)." *Bol'shevik Kazakstana*, no. 3 (1937): 72–88.

*Kazakhskie narodnye skazki*. Alma-Ata, 1979.

*Kazakhsko-russkie otnosheniia v XV–XVIII vekakh*. Alma-Ata, 1961.

*Kazakhsko-russkie otnosheniia v XVIII–XIX vekakh (1771–1867 gody): Sbornik dokumentov i materialov*. Alma-Ata, 1964.

*Kazakhstan*. Moscow, 1936.

*Kazakhstan v ogne grazhdanskoi voiny*. Alma-Ata, 1960.

*Kazakhstan v velikoi otechestvennoi voine*. Alma-Ata, 1968.

*Kazakhstan za 40 let*. Alma-Ata, 1960.

*Kazaki*. Leningrad, 1927.

Kazakskii Kraevoi Komitet VKP(b). *Rezoliutsii i postanovleniia VII Vsekazakskoi Partkonferentsii Iun' 1930 goda*. Alma-Ata, 1930.

*Kazakstan k IX s"ezdu sovetov (1931–1934)*. Alma-Ata, 1935.

Kazanskii, B. "Iz opyta kolkhoznogo stroitel'stva v zernovom raione Kazakstane." *Na agrarnom fronte*, no. 6 (1930): 129–139.

Kenarskii, N. "Kolonizatsiia i pereselenie v Kirkrai." *Sovetskaia Kirgizia*, no. 12 (1924): 119–136.

———. "Zemleustroistvo kirgizskogo naseleniia." *Sovetskaia Kirgizia*, no. 5–6 (1924): 131–146.

Kenisarin, Sultan Akhmet. *Sultany Kenisara i Sadyk*. Compiled by E. T. Smirnov. Tashkent, 1889.

Kenzhebaev, M. T. *Kommunisticheskaia partiia Kazakhstana v bor'be za intensifikatsiiu sel'skogo khoziaistva (1956–1966)*. Alma-Ata, 1971.

Kenzhebaev, S. *Sovety v bor'be za postroenie sotsializma*. Alma-Ata, 1963.

Khalfin, N. A. *Prisoedenie Srednei Azii k Rossii*. Moscow, 1965.

———. *Rossiia i khanstva Srednei Azii (pervaia polovina XIX veka)*. Moscow, 1974.

Khudiakov, E. "Kazakstan na putiakh kul'turnogo stroitel'stva." *Kommunisticheskaia revoliutsiia*, no. 16 (1932): 57–60.

Khusainov, K. Sh. *V. V. Radlov i kazakhskii iazyk*. Alma-Ata, 1981.

Kikibaev. *Torzhestvo leninskoi natsional'noi politiki v Kazakhstane*. Alma-Ata, 1969.

Klimovich, L. *Islam v tsarskoi Rossii*. Moscow, 1936.

Kolodin, F. I. "K voprosu o razvitii TOZov v kazakhskom aule v 1930–1940 gg." *Izvestiia Akademii Nauk Kazakhskoi SSR*, no. 2 (1955): 61–78.

———. *Torzhestvo leninskogo plana sotsialisticheskogo preobrazovaniia sel'skogo khoziaistva v Kazakhstane (1946–1969 gg)*. Alma-Ata, 1971.

———. "TOZy v Kazakhstane v gody pervoi i vtoroi piatiletok." *Trudy instituta istorii, arkheologii i etnografii Akademii Nauk Kazakskoi SSR*, no. 2 (1956): 134–147.

Komitet Sibirskoi zheleznoi dorogi. *Kolonizatsiia Sibiri v sviazi s obshchem pereselenchiskim voprosom*. St. Petersburg, 1900.

*Kommunisticheskaia partiia Kazakhstana v bor'be za osvoenie tselinnykh i zalezhnykh zemel'*. Alma-Ata, 1958.

*Kommunisticheskaia partiia Kazakhstana v dokumentakh i tsifrakh*. Alma-Ata, 1960.

*Kommunisticheskaia partiia Kazakhstana v rezoliutsiiakh i resheniiakh s"ezdov, konferentsii i plenumov*. 2 vols. Alma-Ata, 1981.

*Kommunisticheskaia partiia Sovetskogo Soiuza v rezoliutsiiakh i resheniiakh s"ezdov, konferentsii, i plenumov TsK. Tom 10 1969–1971 gg*. Moscow, 1972.

*Kommunisticheskaia partiia Turkestana i Uzbekistana v tsifrakh 1918–1967 gg*. Tashkent, 1968.

*Kompartiia Kazakhstana na vtorom etape osvoeniia tseliny*. Alma-Ata, 1963.

*Kompartiia Kazakhstana za 50 let (1921–1971)*. Alma-Ata, 1972.

"Kontrol'nye tsifry tret'ego goda piatiletki i zadachi Kazakhstana." *Bol'shevik Kazakstana*, no. 1 (1931): 2–7.

Kosakov, I. "Itogi planovogo osedaniia i prakticheskie zadachi." *Revoliutsiia i natsional'nosti*, no. 5–6 (1933).

Koshanov, A. K. *Industrial'nyi progress Kazakhstana v period razvitogo sotsializma*. Alma-Ata, 1979.

Kozybaev, M. *Kazakhstan. Arsenal fronta*. Alma-Ata, 1970.

*KPSS i sovetskoe pravitel'stvo o Kazakhstane*. Alma-Ata, 1978.

*KPSS v resoliutsiakh i resheniakh ch. III 1930–1954 gg*. Moscow, 1954.

Kryvelev. "Zadachi anti-religioznoi raboty v zhivotnovodcheskikh sovkhozakh." *Antireligioznik*, no. 2 (1934): 14–20.

Kuchin, A. P. *Sovetizatsiia kazakhskogo aula*. Moscow, 1962.

*Kul'tura drevnikh skotovodov i zemledel'tsev Kazakhstana*. Alma-Ata, 1969.

*Kul'tura i byt kazakhskogo kolkhoznogo aula*. Alma-Ata, 1967.

*Kul'turnoe stroitel'stvo kazakhskoi SSR.* Alma-Ata, 1960.

Kunaev, D. A. *Izbrannye rechi i stat'i.* Moscow, 1978.

Kunanbaev, Abai. *Izbrannye sochinenii.* Alma-Ata, 1980.

Kuramysov, M. "Kul'turnoe stroitel'stvo na novom etape." *Bol'shevik Kazakstana,* no. 9–10 (1931): 21–30.

———. *Na putiakh sotsialisticheskogo pereustroistva kazakskogo aula.* Moscow and Alma-Ata, 1932.

Kusanov, Sh. *Ukreplenie aul'nikh i sel'skikh partiinykh organizatsii v Kazakhstane v periode kollektivizatsii.* Alma-Ata, 1958.

Kuzich, S. "Vosstanovit' znachenie i rol' anti-religioznoi propagandy." *Bol'shevik Kazakstana,* no. 9–10 (1937).

L. N. "Uspekhi Kirgizii." *Zhizn' natsional'nostei,* no. 5 (1923): 19.

Larin, I. I. "K voprosu o bolee ratsional'nom napravlenii sel'skogo khoziaistvo severovostochnogo Kazakstana." *Narodnoe khoziaistvo Kazakstana,* no. 1 (1928): 24–38.

*Leninskii prizyv v Kazakhstane.* Alma-Ata, 1969.

Madanov, Kh. M. *Deiatel'nost' KPSS po osushchestvleniiu leninskoi agrarnoi politiki v Kazakhstane.* Alma-Ata, 1980.

Maksheev', A. I. *Istoricheskii obzor Turkestana: Nastupatel'nago dvizheniia v nego russkikh.* St. Petersburg, 1890.

Malikov, F. M. *Fevral'skaia burzhuazno-demokraticheskaia revoliutsiia v Kazakhstane.* Alma-Ata, 1972.

———. *Formirovanie rabochego klassa Kazakhstana v periode imperializma v Rossii.* Alma-Ata, 1973.

Mamiev, E. A. *Proniknovenie marksistskikh idei i revoliutsionnoe dvizhenie v iuzhnom Kazakhstane (1894–1914).* Alma-Ata, 1969.

Mamutov, A. *Prestupleniia sostavliaiushchie perezhitki patriarkal'no-rodogo byta.* Alma-Ata, 1963.

Markarian, E. S. *Teoriia kul'tury i sovremennaia nauka.* Moscow, 1983.

Markov, G. E. "Kochevniki Azii." Ph.D. dissertation, Moscow State University, 1967. Published under the same title, Moscow, 1976.

———. "Nekotorye problemi obshchestvennoi organizatsii kochevnikov Azii." *Sovetskaia etnografiia,* no. 6 (1970): 74–89.

———. "Problemy definitsii i terminologii skotovodstva i kochevnichestva." *Sovetskaia etnografiia,* no. 4 (1982): 80–86.

Maslov, I. I. "Analiz dinamiki osnovnykh otraslei narodnogo khoziaistva KASSR." *Narodnoe khoziaistvo Kazakstana,* no. 1 (1928): 24–38.

*Materialy po istorii kazakhskikh khanstv XV–XVIII vv.* Alma-Ata, 1969.

*Materialy po istorii politicheskogo stroiia Kazakhstana.* Vol. 1. Alma-Ata, 1960.

*Materialy po kirgizskomy zemlepol'zovaniiu sobrannye i razrabotannie ekspeditsiei po issledovaniu stepnykh oblastei. Semipalatinsk oblast. Karkaralinsk uezd.* Vol. 6. St. Petersburg, 1905.

*Materialy po obsledovaniiu khoziaistva i zemlepol'zovaniia Kirgiz Semipalatinskoi oblasti.* Pavlodarsk uezd. Vol. 1. St. Petersburg, 1913.

*Materialy po obsledovaniiu tuzemnogo i russkogo starozhilcheskogo khoziaistva i zemlepol'zovanii v Semirecheskoi oblasti.* Vol. 2. St. Petersburg, 1913.

*Materialy po voprosu ob organizatsii rabot po obrazovaniiu pereselencheskikh uchastkov v stepnykh oblastiakh.* St. Petersburg, 1897.

Melikova, R.. "Internatsional'noe vospitanie trudiashchikhsiia v gody sotsialisticheskogo stroitel'stva (1925–1937 gg)." *Voprosy istorii kompartii Kazakhstana,* no. 11 (1974): 216–224.

Mikhailov, F. K. *Sovkhoznoe stroitel'stvo v Kazakhstane (1946–1970 gg).* Alma-Ata, 1973.

Mindlin, Z. "Kirgizy i revoliutsiia." *Novyi Vostok,* no. 5 (1924): 217–229.

Morgun, F. T. *Khleb i liudi.* Moscow, 1973.

Morosanov. "Akmolinskaia derevnia." *Na agrarnom fronte,* no. 7–8 (1925): 179–193.

Mukanov, M. S. *Etnicheskii sostav i rasselenie Kazakhov srednego zhuza.* Alma-Ata, 1974.

Muraveiskii. *Materialy po istorii Oktiabr'skii Revoliutsiia v Turkestane.* Tashkent, 1922.

*Narodnoe khoziaistvo Kazakhskoi SSR. Statisticheskii sbornik.* Alma-Ata, 1957.

*Narodnoe khoziaistvo Kazakhstana.* Alma-Ata, 1957.

*Narodnoe khoziaistvo Kazakhstana 1978 g.* Alma-Ata, 1979.

*Narodnoe khoziaistvo Kazakhstana. Statisticheskii sbornik.* Alma-Ata, 1968.

*Narodnoe khoziaistvo Kazakhstana v 1983 g.* Alma-Ata, 1984.

*Naselenie i trudove resursy Kazakhstana.* Alma-Ata, 1979.

*Naselenie Kazakhstana v 1959–1970 gg.* Alma-Ata, 1975.

*Naselenie SSSR.* Moscow, 1980.

Nasrullin. "Skotovodstvo i kochevanie v Ural'skoi gubernii." *Narodnoe khoziaistvo Kazakstana,* no. 11–12 (1928): 269–274.

*Nastol'naia kniga ateista.* Moscow, 1981.

*Natsional'nyi sostav kadrov predpriatii v Kazakhstane.* Moscow, 1936.

Neishtadt, S. A. *Sotsialisticheskoe preobrazovanie ekonomiki Kazakhskoi SSR 1917–1937 gg.* Alma-Ata, 1957.

Nurmakov, N. *Stroitel'stvo Kazakstana.* Kzyl-Orda, 1929.

Nurmukhamedov, S. B.; Savo'ko, P. B.; and Suleimenov, R. B. *Ocherki istorii sotsialisticheskogo stroitel'stva v Kazakhstane, 1933–1940 gg.* Alma-Ata, 1966.

Nurpeisov, A. N. *Formirovanie i razvitie sovetskogo rabochego klassa v Kazakhstane.* Alma-Ata, 1966.

"Obsuzhdenie knigi Olzhasa Suleimenova." *Voprosy istorii,* no. 9 (1976): 145–154.

"Ocherednye zadachi partorganizatsii Kazakstana v sviazi c obrazovaniem oblastei." *Bol'shevik Kazakstana,* no. 4 (1932): 1–16.

*Ocherki istorii kazakhskoi sovetskoi literatury.* Moscow, 1960.

*Ocherki istorii kommunisticheskoi partii Kazakhstana.* Alma-Ata, 1963.

Onishchenko, K. T. "Khlebnye tseny Kazakhstana." *Narodnoe khoziaistvo Kazakstana,* no. 1 (1929): 83–90.

*O razvertyvanii sotsialicheskogo zhivotnovodstva. Postanovlenie Kazkraikoma VKP(b) v Sovnarkom KASSR.* Alma-Ata, 1931.

Ostroumov, N. *Konstantin Petrovich Fon-Kaufman-uchitel' Turkestanskago Kraia.* Tashkent, 1899.

*Osvoenie tseliny.* Alma-Ata, 1966.

Pakhmurnyi. "Pervaia konferetsiia kommunistov Kazakhstana." *Voprosy partiinogo stroitel'stva.* Alma-Ata, 1972: 183–215.

Palen, K. K. *Otchet po revizii Turkestanskago kraia, proizvedennoi po vysochaishemu poveleniiu Senatorom Gofmeisterom Grafom K. K. Palenom.* 18 volumes. St. Petersburg, 1907–1910.

Pankratova, A., and Abdykalikov, M. *Istoriia Kazakhskoi SSR s drevneishikh vremen do nashikh dnei.* Alma-Ata, 1943.

Pashukanis, E., ed. *15 let sovetskogo sroitel'stva 1917–1932 gg.* Moscow, 1932.

*Piatiletnii plan narodnogo: khoziaistvennogo i sotsial'no-kul'turnogo stroitel'stva Kazakskoi ASSR (1928/29–1932/33).* Alma-Ata, 1931.

Pishchulin, K. A. *Iugo-vostochnyi Kazakhstan v seredine XIV-nachale XVI vekov.* Alma-Ata, 1977.

*Plenum TsIK KPSS 22–25/XII/1959 g. Stenograficheskii otchet.* Moscow, 1960.

Podnek, A. "Kazakstan na putiakh sotsialisticheskoi rekonstruktsii." *Revoliutsiia i natsional'nosti,* no. 6 (1930): 33–40.

Podnek, A., and Pavlov, K. *Kazakstan v sisteme narodnogo khoziaistva SSR.* Alma-Ata, 1930.

*Poety Kazakhstana.* Moscow, 1978.

Pogorel'skii, N. B., and Batrakov, B. *Ekonomika kochevogo aula Kirgizistana.* Moscow, 1930.

Pogudin, S. A. *Put' sovetskogo krest'ianstva k sotsializmu.* Moscow, 1976.

Pokrovskii, S. N. *Razgrom interventov i vnutrennei kontrrevoliutsii v Kazakhstane 1918–1920 gg.* Alma-Ata, 1967.

———. *Vneshnaia torgovlia i vneshnaia torgovaia politika Rossii.* Moscow, 1947.

Poliakov, Iu. A., and Chugunov, A. I. *Konets Basmachestva.* Moscow, 1976.

Poliakov, S. P. *Istoricheskaia etnografiia Srednei Azii i Kazakhstana.* Moscow, 1980.

Polochanskii, E. A. *Za novyi aul-kstau.* Moscow, 1926.

*Polozhenii o zemleustroistve kochevogo, polukochevogo i perekhodiashchego k osedlomu khoziaistvu KASSR.* Kzyl-Orda, 1928.

"Postanovlenie biuro kraevogo komiteta VKP(b) o meropriatiakh po vypolneniiu reshenia dekabr'skogo plenuma TsK i TsIK o skotozatovkakh." *Bol'shevik Kazakstana,* no. 1 (1931): 30–36.

Potatskii, A. P. *Narodnoe khoziaistvo Kazakstana i osnovnye tendentsii ego razvitiia.* Kzyl-Orda, 1927.

*Pravovaia okhrana prirody Kazakhskoi SSR.* Alma-Ata, 1977.

"Raznye otmena 'kuna'." *Zhizn' natsional'nostei,* no. 4 (102) (February 13, 1921): 4.

*Revoliutsiia 1905–1907 gg v Kazakhstane.* Alma-Ata, 1949.

*Revoliutsionnoe dvizhenie v Kazakhstane v 1905–1907 godakh: Sbornik dokumentov i materialov.* Alma-Ata, 1955.

*Rezoliutsii 3-go plenuma Kazakskogo kraevogo komiteta VKP(b).* Kzyl-Orda, 1927.

*Rezoliutsii i postanovleniia VIII Kazakstanskoi konferentsii VKP(b).* Alma-Ata, 1934.

Riabokon', V. "K voprosu o sovetizatsii aula." *Krasnyi Kazakstan,* no. 1 (1926): 34–62.

Riadnin, M. "Za kolkhozy kadry." *Bol'shevik Kazakstana,* no. 1 (1931): 19–32.

Riazanov, A. F. *Vosstanie Isataia Taimanova (1836–1838).* Tashkent, 1924.

Rodnevich, B. *Ot kolonial'nogo vyrozhdeniia k sotsialisticheskomu rastsvetu.* Moscow, 1931.

Romanov, G. P. "Kazakstan na putiakh k sploshnoi gramatnosti." *Prosveshchenie natsional'nostei,* no. 3 (1934): 16–18.

Rozhkova, M. K. *Ekonomicheskie sviazi Rossii so Srednei Aziei.* Moscow, 1963.

Rudenko, S. I. "Ocherk byta severo-vostochnikh Kazakhov." In *Kazaki.* Leningrad, 1930.

Rumiantsev, P. P. *Kirgizskii narod v proshlom i nastoiashchem.* St. Petersburg, 1910.

Rybnikov, A. A. "Perspektivy ratsionalizatsii i rekonstruktsii skotovodstva zasluzhlivogo tsentral'nogo Kazakstana." *Narodnoe khoziaistvo Kazakstana,* no. 1–2 (1930): 3–22.

Rychkov, P. P. *Istoriia Orenburgskaia (1730–1750 gg).* Orenburg, 1896.

Ryskulov, T. R. *Dzhetyuiskie voprosy.* Tashkent, 1923.

———. "Eshche o kharakteristike vosstaniia 1916 g." *Kommunisticheskaia mysl',* no. 4 (1926): 142–152.

———. *Izbrannye trudy.* Alma-Ata, 1984.

———. "Iz istorii bor'by za osvobozhdenie Vostoka." *Novyi Vostok,* no. 6 (1924): 267–270.

———. *Kazakstan.* Moscow, 1927. Revised edition, Moscow, 1935.

———. "O vosstanie Kazakov i Karakirgizov v 1916 godu." *Krasnyi Kazakstan,* no. 5 (1926): 14–34.

———. "Piat' let raboty Turksiba." *Narodnoe khoziaistvo Kazakstana,* no. 7–8 (1935): 32–35.

———. "Piat' let raboty Turksiba." *Revoliutsiia i natsional'nosti,* no. 7 (1935): 5–8.

———. "Protiv izvrashcheniia istorii kazakhskogo naroda." *Bol'shevik Kazakstana,* no. 1–2 (1936): 110–124.

———. *Revoliutsiia i korennoe naselenie Turkestana 1917–1919 gg.* Tashkent, 1925.

———. *Vosstanie 1916 v Kirgizstane.* Frunze, 1937.

———. "Vosstanie tuzemtsev Turkestana v 1916 godu." In *Ocherki revoliutsionnogo dvizheniia v Srednei Azii, sbornik statei.* Moscow, 1926.

———. *Vosstanie tuzemtsev v Srednei Azii v 1916 godu.* Kzyl-Orda, 1927.

S. M. "Osedanie-vazhneishii etap likvidatsii natsional'nogo neraventsva." *Revoliutsia i natsional'nosti,* no. 7 (1932): 32–34.

Sadvakasov, S. "O natsional'nostiakh i natsionalakh." *Bol'shevik,* no. 1 (1928): 56–64.

Safarov, G. *Kolonial'naia revoliutsiia (Opyt Turkestana).* Moscow, 1921.

Saidbaev, T. *Islam i obshchestvo.* Moscow, 1978.

Sapargaliev, G. S., and Baianov, E. B. *Pravovye osnovy razvitiia narodnogo obrazovaniia.* Alma-Ata, 1983.

Sarmurzin, A. G. *Deiatel'nost' KPSS po industrail'nomu razvitiiu Kazakhstana (1959–1975 gg).* Alma-Ata, 1981.

Sarsenbaev, N. S. *Obychai i traditsii i obshchestvennaia zhizn'.* Alma-Ata, 1974.

———. *Obychai i traditsii v razvitii.* Alma-Ata, 1965.

Sarymuldaev. "Moi vospominaniia." *Krasnyi Kazakstan,* no. 2–3 (1926).

Satpaeva, Sh. K. *Kazakhskaia literatura i Vostok.* Alma-Ata, 1982.

———. *Kazakhsko-evropeiskie literaturnye sviazi XIX i pervoi poloviny XX vv.* Alma-Ata, 1972.

Satybekova, G. K. *Zhurnal "Ai-kap" kak istochnik po istorii Kazakhstana.* Alma-Ata, 1966.

Savin, A. "Bol'shevitskaia programma sotsialisticheskoi pereustroiki kazakskogo aula," *Bol'shevik Kazakstana,* no. 12 (1932): 17–26.

Savos'ko, V. K., and Shamshatov, I. Sh. *Kolkhoznoe stroitel'stvo v Kazakhstane (1946–1970 gg).* Alma-Ata, 1974.

*Sbornik zakonov Kazakhskoi SSR i ukazov presidiuma verkhovnogo soveta Kazakhskoi SSR 1938–1981.* 2 vols. Alma-Ata, 1981.

Segizbaev, O. *Traditsii svobodomysliia i ateizma v dukhovnoi kul'ture kazakhskogo naroda.* Alma-Ata, 1973.

Seifullin, S. *Ternistyi put'.* Moscow, 1975.

*Sel'skoe khoziaistvo SSSR ezhegodnik 1935.* Moscow, 1936.

Semenov, Iu. I. "Kochevnichestvo i nekotorye obshchie problemy teorii khoziaistva i obshchestva." *Sovetskaia etnografiia,* no. 3 (1982): 48–59.

Shakhmatov, V. F. "Instituta tulengutsva v patriarkhal'nom feodal'nom Kazakhstane." *Izvestiia Akademii Nauk Kazakhskoi SSR,* no. 2 (1955): 79–106.

———. *Kazakhskaia pastbishchno-kochevaia obshchina: voprosy obrazovania, evolutsii i razrusheniia.* Alma-Ata, 1974.

———. "K voprosu o slozhenii i spetsifike patriarkhal'no-feodal'nykh otnoshenii v Kazakhstane." *Vestnik Akademii Nauk Kazakhstana,* no. 7 (1951): 18–36.

———. *Vnutrennaia orda i vosstanie Isataia Taimanova.* Alma-Ata, 1946.

Shalabaev. *Istoriia kazakhskoi prozy.* Alma-Ata, 1968.

Shamshatov, I. Sh. *Kolkhozy Kazakhstana.* Alma-Ata, 1985.

Shataev, B. *Migratsiia naseleniia i internatsional'noe vospitanie*. Alma-Ata, 1977.

Shauman, M. Kh. *Ot kochev'ia k sotsializmu*. Alma-Ata, 1965.

Shchemist-Polochanskii, E. *K voprosu ob organizatsii sotsialislicheskogo zhivotnovodstva*. Moscow, 1931.

Shlaskii, O. "Pereselentsy i agrarnyi vopros v Semirechenskoi oblasti." *Voprosy kolonizatsii*, no. 1 (1907): 19–22.

Shoinbaev, T. *Progressivnoe znachenie prisoedineniia Kazakhstana k Rossii*. Alma-Ata, 1973.

———. *Vosstanie Syr-darinskikh Kazakhov*. Alma-Ata, 1949.

Shoinbaev, T. Zh. *Dobrovol'noe v khozhdenie kazakhskikh zemel' v sostav Rossii*. Alma-Ata, 1982.

Shulembaev, K. W. *Shagi, bogi i deistvitel'nost'*. Alma-Ata, 1963.

Sirius, M. G. "K voprosu o perspektivakh skotovodstva v Kazakstane." *Narodnoe khoziaistvo Kazakstana*, no. 1 (1926): 26–30.

———. "O normakh zemlepol'zovaniia dlia kochevnikogo naseleniia KSSR." *Sovetskaia Kirgiziia*, no. 5 (1925): 52–65.

———. "Perspektivy razvitiia sel'skogo khoziaistva Kazakstana." *Narodnoe khoziaistvo Kazakstana*, no. 3 (1926): 3–15.

Skalov, G. "Opyt klassovogo rasseleniia v usloviakh Turkestana." *Zhizn' natsional'nostei*, no. 2 (1923): 34–42.

———. "O soiuze Koshchi." *Zhizn' natsional'nostei*, no. 5 (1923): 15–19.

Slashchukin. "Sotsialisticheskoe pereustroistvo kochevogo kazakhskogo aula." *Sovetskaia etnografiia*, no. 1 (1933).

Sokolovskii, V. A. *Kazakskii aul*. Tashkent, 1926.

Soldatov, T. "Po Lepsinskom kolkhozam." *Bol'shevik Kazakstana*, no. 1 (1932): 44–54.

Soskin, S. N. *O preodelenii razlichii mezhdu gorodom i derevnei*. Alma-Ata, 1967.

*Sotsialisticheskoe stroitel'stvo v Kazakhstane v vostanovitel'nom periode*. Alma-Ata, 1962.

*Sotsial'no-ekonomicheskie voprosy razvitiia Kazakastana v period razvitogo sotsializma (60–70 e gody)*. Alma-Ata, 1977.

*Sovetskoe stroitel'stvo v selakh i aulakh Semirech'ia 1921–1925 gg*. Alma-Ata, 1957.

*Spravochnaia knizhka dlia aul'nykh, volostnykh upravitelei i narodnykh sudei*. Omsk, 1909.

Strelkova, I. *Valikhanov*. Moscow, 1983.

Subkhanberdina. *Kazakhskaia dorevoliutsionnaia periodicheskaia pechat'*. Alma-Ata, 1964.

Suiushaliev, Kh. M. *Stanovlenie i razvitie kazakhskoi literatury*. Alma-Ata, 1969.

Suleimenov, B. S. *Agrarnyi vopros v Kazakhstane poslednei treti XIX–nachala XX vv (1867–1907)*. Alma-Ata, 1963.

———. *Revoliutsionnoe dvizhenie v Kazakhstane v 1905–1907 godakh*. Alma-Ata, 1977.

Suleimenov, B. S., and Basin, V. Ia. "Istoricheskaia khronika vazhneishikh sobytii dobrovol'nogo prisoedeniia Kazakhstane k Rossii." *Vestnik Akademiia Nauk Kazakhskoi SSR*, no. 4 (1982): 3–9.

———. *Vosstanie 1916 goda v Kazakhstane.* Alma-Ata, 1977.

Suleimenov, R. B. "Iz istorii bor'by za likvidatsiiu negramotnosti v Kazakhstane (1933–1940 gg)." *Trudy instituta istorii, arkheologii i etnografii Akademii Nauk Kazakhskoi SSR* 9 (1960): 110–126.

———. *Leninskie kul'turnye revoliutsii i ikh obshchestvlenie v Kazakhstane.* Alma-Ata, 1972.

Suleimenov, R. B., and Bisenov, Kh. I. *Sotsialisticheskii put' kul'turnogo progressa otstal'nykh narodov.* Alma-Ata, 1967.

Sundetov, S. A. "Torgovlia v Kazakhstane v nachale XX veka'." In P. G. Galuzo, ed. *Agrarnye otnosheniia na iuge Kazakhstana 1867–1914 gg.* Alma-Ata, 1965.

Suzhikov, M. *Obrazovanie SSSR i sotsial'nyi progress kazakhskogo naroda.* Alma-Ata, 1972.

———. *Sotsial'no-ekonomicheskie problemy natsional'noi konsolidatsii.* Alma-Ata, 1968.

Suzhikov, M., and Demako, G. *Vliianiia podvizhnosti naseleniia na sblizhenie natsii.* Alma-Ata, 1974.

Tastanov, Sh. Iu. *Kazakhskaia sovetskaia intelligentsiia.* Alma-Ata, 1982.

Tatimov, M. B. "XXV s"ezd KPSS i sotsial'nye problemy demografii." *Izvestiia Akademii Nauk Kazakhskoi SSR. Seriia obshchestvennykh nauk*, no. 3 (1977): 15–22.

———. *Razvitie narodnonaseleniia i demograficheskaia politike.* Alma-Ata, 1978.

Tazhibaev, T. T. *Kazakhskaia shkola pri Orenburgskoi: pogranichnoi komissii (1850–1869 gg).* Alma-Ata, 1961.

———. *Razvitie prosveshcheniia i pedagogicheskoi mysli v Kazakhstane vo vtoroi polovine XIX veka.* Alma-Ata, 1958.

Terletskii, E. D., et al. "Proizvodstvennaia kharakteristika sel'sko-khoziaistvennikh kollektivov." *Na agrarnom fronte*, no. 2 (1929).

Timofeev, N., and Brainin, S. "Kazakhskaia kraevaia organizatsiia VKP(b) v bor'be za kollektivizatsiiu sel'skogo khoziaistva (1930–1934 gg)." *Bol'shevik Kazakhstana*, no. 1 (1939): 82–89.

Togzhanov, G. "Eshche raz o burzhuazno-natsionalisticheskoi kontseptsii tov. Ryskulov i dr." *Bol'shevik Kazakstana*, no. 6 (1935): 68–86.

——— *Kazakskyi kolonialnyi aul.* Moscow, 1934.

———. "O Baitursunove i baitursunovshchine." *Bol'shevik Kazakstana*, no. 2–3 (1932): 29–38; and no. 5 (1932): 20–27.

———. *O kazakskom aule.* Kzyl-Orda, 1928.

Toktabaev, K. D.. "Puti razvitiia sel'skogo khoziaistva Kazakstana." *Ekonomicheskoe obozrenie*, no. 11 (1928): 51–56.

Tolstov, S. P. *Narody Srednei Azii i Kazakhstana.* 2 vols. Moscow, 1962–1963.

Tolybekov, S. E. *Kochevoe obshchestvo Kazakhov v XVII–nachale XX veka*. Alma-Ata, 1971.

Tresviatskii. *Materialy po zemel'nomu voprosu v Aziatskii Rossii*. St. Petersburg, 1917.

Tsabel, L. N. "Vliianie kolonizatsii na kirgizskoe khoziaistvo." *Voprosy kolonizatsii*, no. 2 (1907).

Tulebaev, T. *Politotdely MTS Kazakhstana v bor'be za organizatsionno-khoziaistvennoe ukreplenie kolkhozov (1933–1934 gg)*. Alma-Ata, 1965.

Tulepbaev, B. A. "Dobrovol'noe prisoedinenie Kazakhstana k Rossii i ego progressivnoe znachenie." *Naveki vmeste: k 250-letiiu dobrovol'nogo prisoedineniia Kazakhstana k Rossii*. Alma-Ata, 1982: 41–62.

———. *Sotsialisticheskie agrarnye preobrazovaniia v Srednei Azii i Kazakhstane*. Moscow, 1984.

———. *Torzhestvo leninskikh idei sotsialisticheskogo preobrazovaniia sel'skogo khoziaistva v Srednei Azii i Kazakhstane*. Moscow, 1971.

Turiakulov, N. "Turkestanskaia Avtonomnaia Respublika." *Zhizn' natsional'nostei*, no. 1 (1923): 86–95.

Turkestanskii, G. "Natsional'noe osvoboditel'noe dvizhenie Srednei Azii." *Kommunisticheskaia mysl'*, no. 3 (1926): 190–223.

*Turkestano-Sibirskaia magistral*. Moscow, 1929.

*Turkestanskii sbornik*. St. Petersburg, 1878.

Tursunbaev, A. B. *Iz istoriia krest'ianskogo pereseleniia v Kazakhstane*. Alma-Ata, 1950.

———. *Kazakhskaia SSR v soiuze ravnykh*. Alma-Ata, 1972.

———. *Kolkhoz krest'ianstva Kazakhstana*. Alma-Ata, 1960.

———. *Kollektivizatsiia sel'skogo khoziaistva Kazakhstana, 1926–1941 gg*. 2 vols. Alma-Ata, 1967.

———. "Perekhod k osedlosti kochevnikov i polukochevnikov Srednei Azii i Kazakhstana." *Trudy instituta etnografii* 91 (1973): 223–234.

———. *Pobeda kolkhoznogo stroia v Kazakhstane*. Alma-Ata, 1957.

———. "Torzhestvo kolkhoznogo stroia v Kazakhstane." In *Ocherki istorii kollektivizatsii sel'skogo khoziaistva v soiuznykh respublikakh*. Moscow, 1963.

Tursunova, M. S. *Kazakhi Mangyshlaka vo vtoroi polovine XIX veka*. Alma-Ata, 1977.

*U istokov Kommunisticheskoi Partii Kazakhstana, Letopis' vazhneishikh sobytii*. Alma-Ata, 1966.

Undasynov, N. "O sostoianii i zadachakh ravitiia khoziaistva v Kazakhstane." *Narodnoe khoziaistvo Kazakhstana*, no. 1 (1939): 35–44.

Ustinov, V. M. *Sluzhenie narodu*. Alma-Ata, 1984.

Valikhanov, Chokan. *Sobranie sochinenii*. 5 vols. Alma-Ata, 1961–1968.

———. *Sobranie sochinenii v piati tomakh*. 4 vols. Alma-Ata, 1984–1985.

Vasil'ev, N. *Kochevniki Turkestana*. Samarkand, 1890.

Vel'iaminov-Zernov, V. V. *Issledovanie o kasimovskikh tsariakh i tsarevichakh*. 3 vols. St. Petersburg, 1864.

*Velikii Oktiabr' v Kazakhstane*. Alma-Ata, 1977.

*Verkhovnyi sovet soiuznoi respubliki i ego konstitutsionnye polnomochiia (na materialakh Kazakhskoi SSR)*. Alma-Ata, 1979.

Veseletskii, S. N. *Semirech'e oblast' i ee kolonizatsiia*. Petrograd, 1916.

*Ves' Kazakhstan*. Moscow and Alma-Ata, 1931.

Viatkin, M. P. *Ocherki po istorii Kazakhskoi SSR*. Moscow, 1941.

———. *Batyr Srym*. Moscow, 1947.

Vints, Ia. "Prosveshchenie i prosveshchentsy v Kazakstane." *Narodnyi uchitel'*, no. 1 (1929): 57–66.

"V kollegii." *Sel'skoe khoziaistvo RSFSR*, no. 24 (1931): 32.

*Voprosy istorii kompartii Kazakhstana*. Alma-Ata, 1964.

*Voprosy sotsialisticheskogo stroitel'stva v Kazakhstane*. Vol. 4. Alma-Ata, 1977.

*Vosstanie 1916 goda v Srednei Azii i Kazakhstane, sbornik dokumentov*. Moscow, 1960.

Vostrov, V. V. *Material'naia kul'tura kazakhskogo naroda na sovremennom etape*. Alma-Ata, 1972.

Vostrov, V. V., and Mukanov, M. S. *Rodoplemennoi sostav i rasselenie Kazakhov*. Alma-Ata, 1978.

*Zapiski predsedatelia soveta ministrov o poezdke v Sibir' i Povol'zhe v 1910*. St. Petersburg, 1910.

*Zernovoe khoziaistvo v zonakh osvoennoi tseliny*. Alma-Ata, 1979.

Zevelev, A. I. *Basmachestvo: vozniknovenie, sushchnost', krakh*. Moscow, 1981.

Zhdanko, T. A. "Problema poluosedlogo naseleniia v istorii Srednei Azii i Kazakhstane." *Sovetskaia etnografiia*, no. 2 (1961): 53–62.

Zhelezov, V. "Aulnaia iacheika, kak ona est'." *Bol'shevik Kazakstana*, no. 7–8 (1931): 32–35.

Zimanov, S. Z. *Obshchestvennyi stroi Kazakhov*. Alma-Ata, 1958.

——— *Politicheskii stroi Kazakhstana (kontsa XVIII i pervoi polovine XIX vekov)*. Alma-Ata, 1960.

———. *Rossiia i Bukeevskoe Khanstvo*. Alma-Ata, 1982.

———. *V. I. Lenin i sovetskaia natsional'naia gosudarstvennost' v Kazakhstane*. Alma-Ata, 1970.

Zimanov, S.; Sauletova, S.; and Ismagulov, M. *Kazakhskii otdel narodnogo komissariata po delam natsional'nostei RSFSR*. Alma-Ata, 1975.

Zveriakov, T. A. *Ot kochev'ia k sotsializmu*. Alma-Ata, 1934.

## KAZAKH LANGUAGE SOURCES

Abubakyrov, S. "Qazagstannin inzhener—tekhnikaliq kadrarin daiarlau tarikhinan (1946–1960 zh zh)." *Izvestiia Akademii Nauk Kazakhskoi SSR*, no. 5 (1982): 43–49.

Arginbaev, Kh. A. *Qazaq khalgindaghi sem'iia men neke*. Alma-Ata, 1973.

Balaqaev, T. *Sovet Okimeti jolindaghi. Kuresker.* Alma-Ata, 1960.

Derbisalin, A. *Qazaqsting Oktiabr' Aldindaghi demokratiiashil Adebieti.* Alma-Ata, 1966.

Dvoskin, B. Ia.; Daulenov, S. D.; and Aristanbekov, M. A. *Qazaqstanning ondirgish kushterin orna stiru problemlari.* Alma-Ata, 1973.

Ismaghulov, M. Sh. "'Qazaqstan' gazeting shighu tarikhi men oning ideialiq mazmnui." *Trudy instituta filosofii i prava Akademii Nauk Kazakhskoi SSR* 6 (1962): 263–273.

Jumaliev, K. *XVIII–XIX ghasirlardaghi Qazaq adebieti.* Alma-Ata, 1967.

Junisbaev, K. "Qazaqstanning XVII–XVIII gasirlardagi tarikhina baylanisti Qazaq tilindegi keyibir tarikhi derekter turali." *Trudy instituta istorii, arkheologii, etnografii Akademii Nauk Kazakhskoi SSR* 15 (1962): 155–169.

Kenzhebaev, B. *Qazaq adebieti tarikhining maseleri.* Alma-Ata, 1973.

———. *Qazaq khalqining XX ghasir basindaghi demokrat zhasushilari.* Alma-Ata, 1958.

Nurpeisov, K. *Qazaqstannin sharualar sovettery (1917–1929 zhildor).* Alma-Ata, 1972.

———. "SSSR-dying kurilui—Kommunistyk Partiianin lenindyk ult saisatinin saltanati." *Izvestiia Akademii Nauk Kazakhskoi SSR*, no. 5 (1982): 1–8.

Qayirgaliev, M. "Sogisqa deiyngy beszhildigtar dauyryndegi Qazaqstan men Orta Aziia respublikalariningh mal sharuashilighin damytu zholindaghi uzara kumegy (1928–1941 zhildar)." *Izvestiia Akademii Nauk Kazakhskoi SSR*, no. 3 (1980): 62–66.

*Qazaqstaning korkem adebieti (1946–1957).* Alma-Ata, 1958.

Qirabaev, Serik. *Revoluntsiia zhane adibieti.* Vols. 1 and 2. Alma-Ata, 1977.

Sabirkhanov. *Qazaqstan men Rossiianing XVIII gasirdaghy garim-katynosi.* Alma-Ata, 1970.

Shaiakhmetov, Zh. "Ideologiia maydanindaghi gizmetkerlerdin aybindi mindettri." *Izvestiia Akademii Nauk Kazakhskoi SSR. Seriia literaturnaia*, no. 6 (1948): 3–14.

## PERIODICALS

*Agitator Kazakhstana.* Alma-Ata, 1938.

*Antireligioznik.* Moscow, 1926–1941 (Monthly, 1926–1931; 1937–1941. Semimonthly, 1932. Bimonthly, 1933–1936).

*Bol'shevik.* Moscow, 1924–1952 (1952 as *Kommunist*).

*Bol'shevik Kazakstana.* Alma-Ata, 1931– (since 1952, *Partiinaia zhizn' Kazakhstanna*).

*Current Digest of the Soviet Press.* Columbus, Ohio, 1949–.

*Ekonomicheskoe obozrenie.* Moscow, 1923–1930 (since 1930, *Planovoe khoziaistvo*).

*Istoricheskie zapiski.* Moscow, 1937–.

*Istoriia SSSR.* Moscow, 1957–.

*Izvestiia.* Moscow, 1917–.

*Izvestiia Akademii Nauk Kazakhskoi SSR.* Alma-Ata, 1963–.

*Izvestiia Akademiia Nauk SSSR.*

*Izvestiia obshchestva arkheologii istorii i etnografii Kazanskogo Universita.* Kazan, 1878–1929.

*Kazakhstanskaia pravda.* Alma-Ata, 1923–.

*Kommunist.* Moscow, 1924–.

*Kommunisticheskaia mysl'.* Tashkent, 1926–1927.

*Kommunisticheskoe prosveshchenie.* Moscow, 1920–1936.

*Krasnyi Kazakstan.* Kyzyl-Orda, May–August 1926.

*Literaturnoe obozrenie.* Moscow, 1973–.

*Muslims of the Soviet East.* Tashkent, 1974–.

*Na agrarnom fronte.* Moscow, 1925–1935.

*Na fronte kollektivizatsii.* Moscow, 1929–1930.

*Narodnoe khoziaistvo Kazakstana.* Alma-Ata, 1926–.

*Narodnyi uchitel'.* Moscow, 1924–1935.

*Novyi vostok.* Moscow, 1922–1930.

*Orenburgskii listok.* Orenburg, 1901–1906.

*Pravda.* Moscow, 1912–.

*Proletarskaia revoliutsiia.* Moscow, 1921–1941.

*Prosveshchenie natsional'nostei.* Moscow, 1929–1935.

*Qazaq.* Orenburg, 1913–1918.

*Revoliutsiia i natsional'nosti.* Moscow, 1930–1937.

*Revoliutsionnyi vostok.* Moscow, 1927–1937.

*Revue du monde musulman.* Paris, 1906–1926.

*Sotsialisticheskaia rekonstruktsiia i nauka.* Moscow, 1937–(?).

*Sel'skogo khoziaistva.* Moscow, 1959–.

*Sovetskaia etnografiia.* Moscow, 1931–.

*Sovetskaia Kirgiziia.* Orenburg, 1923–1925.

*Sovetskaia step'.* Kzyl-Orda, ceased publication 1926.

*Sovetskoe kraevedenie.* Moscow, 1930–1936.

*Stepnaia gazeta.* Omsk, 1906.

*Trudy instituta etnografii.* Moscow, 1934–1938; 1947–.

*Trudy instituta istorii arkheologii i etnografii Akademii Nauk Kazakhskoi SSR.* Alma-Ata, 1956–.

*Trudy obshchestva izucheniia Kazakstana.* Orenburg and Alma-Ata, 1921–1929.

*Trudy obshchestva izucheniia Kirgizskogo kraia.* Orenburg and Alma-Ata, 1921–1925.

*Vestnik Akademii Nauk Kazakhstana.* Alma-Ata, 1944–.

*Voprosy istorii,* Moscow, 1945–.

*Voprosy istorii Kommunisticheskoi partii Kazakhstana.* Alma-Ata (also known as "Kompartii"), 1963–1964; 1967.

*Voprosy kolonizatsii.* St. Petersburg, 1907–1916.

*Zhivaia starina.* St. Petersburg, 1890–1916.

*Zhizn' natsional'nostei.* Moscow, 1922–1924.

# Index